Infant Pathways
to Language

Infant Pathways to Language

Methods, Models, and Research Directions

Edited by
John Colombo
Peggy McCardle
Lisa Freund

Psychology Press
Taylor & Francis Group

New York   London

Lawrence Erlbaum Associates
Taylor & Francis Group
270 Madison Avenue
New York, NY 10016

Lawrence Erlbaum Associates
Taylor & Francis Group
2 Park Square
Milton Park, Abingdon
Oxon OX14 4RN

© 2009 by Taylor & Francis Group, LLC
Lawrence Erlbaum Associates is an imprint of Taylor & Francis Group, an Informa business

Printed in the United States of America on acid-free paper
10 9 8 7 6 5 4 3 2 1

International Standard Book Number-13: 978-0-8058-6063-4 (Hardcover)

Library of Congress Cataloging-in-Publication Data

Infant pathways to language : methods, models, and research directions / editors, John Colombo, Peggy McCardle, Lisa Freund.
   p. cm.
Includes bibliographical references and index.
ISBN 978-0-8058-6063-4 (hardback : alk. paper)
1. Language acquisition. I. Colombo, John. II. McCardle, Peggy D. III. Freund, Lisa.

P118.I4325 2009
401'.93--dc22
               2008025211

Visit the Taylor & Francis Web site at
http://www.taylorandfrancis.com

and the LEA and Routledge Web site at
http://www.routledge.com

Contents

Foreword

Over the past 25 years, researchers in the area of infant cognitive and language development have become increasingly concerned with individual differences, identification of individuals at risk, and prediction of mature function. As such, the field has begun to explore the feasibility of applying basic science technologies and measurement to clinical issues. Although movement toward this goal was steady, it was also characteristically slow. In addition, most of this work typically focused on more general aspects of cognitive and intellectual function, rather than on other more specific abilities or skills in later development.

Among the topics left relatively unexplored was the relation between infant abilities and later language outcomes, including language impairment. This was surprising, given that work on infant abilities relevant to language acquisition and outcome was available both in good quantity and in high quality. Those who worked in the area knew that, at least theoretically, such work held great promise for direct application to typical and atypical language development, but there had been little, if any, formal consideration of the degree to which infant paradigms and protocols might be useful or translatable for specific applications to language. Most importantly, there was no summative body of work directed specifically toward this topic.

In the context of the expressed national priority for promoting translational research in all sciences, and the desire to further explore and expand this agenda for the health and well-being of the field of developmental science, in late 2003 the editors of this volume began talking with me, as the Director of the Merrill Advanced Studies Center at the University of Kansas, about the need for a small conference to address these issues. The editors bring a powerful blend of programmatic research expertise in infancy and the national priorities for basic-to-translational research. The idea was to bring together a small group of expert researchers with programmatic externally funded investigations in this realm to address these issues, and to produce a volume that would represent the state of the science in this area.

The conference was held September 15–17, 2005 at the Tempe Mission Palms Hotel in Phoenix, Arizona, under joint sponsorship of the Merrill Advanced Study Center at the University of Kansas and the Eunice Kennedy Shriver National Institute of Child Health and Human Development (NICHD). The speakers presented their research programs in infant cognitive development and how they saw those programs interfacing with the understanding and prediction of language acquisition and outcomes including language impairment. In many cases, researchers presented for the first time data on infants who had been tested with their laboratory measures and whose language status had been subsequently assessed. These examples often provided a remarkable—and, in some cases, very provocative—empirical confirmation that the promise of addressing the pathways to language from infancy was indeed attainable.

The relatively small number of outstanding scholar/participants created many opportunities for informal interactions and discussions that furthered the possibility of new insights and collaborative approaches across labs. The chapters in this book represent the amalgamation of the ideas that the presenters brought to the meeting and the ways those ideas were adjusted by the input and reaction from the other participants. The summaries that appear here reflect the care and thought that is characteristic of each of their research programs, as well as the innovative and theoretically well grounded interpretations each brings to the topic of language outcomes.

The Merrill Advanced Studies Center is pleased to help facilitate working conferences with such a timely topic as this one. The ways in which the infancy period sets the stage for language acquisition are vital for us to understand if we are to develop accurate means of assessment and prediction that allow for early and effective intervention and also allow for a better understanding of the causes of language acquisition and impairment. The chapters in this book bring to the reader the contributions of very productive investigators dedicated to studies of infants from a fairly wide range of perspectives. This is a good beginning for pulling together vital areas of relevant inquiry. We hope the content of this volume not only informs the reader but also inspires new insights about the infant pathways to language and how to sort out the antecedents of varying outcomes.

Mabel L. Rice

Preface*

In September 2005, a small group of researchers was invited to a workshop sponsored jointly by the Merrill Advanced Studies Center and the Eunice Shriver National Institute of Child Health and Human Development. The charge to this group was to explore current progress in research in infant cognitive and language development, to explain the different tools they are using, to discuss ways to increase innovation, and to describe and evaluate research needs and current directions. The chapters in this volume are derived from the individual presentations that were given at that workshop, and have been informed and influenced by the discussions that took place there. The organizers felt that it was time to bring together actual users of and believers in different paradigms and approaches to create a group that was diverse not only in backgrounds and disciplines but also in the approaches used to study these topics. The organizers also hoped to encourage participants, through discussion and perhaps, at times, disagreement, to seek a common ground for communication that could result in advances in theory and approaches and that could both describe the next frontiers and begin a push toward them. In fact, this is exactly what happened—the discussions were fruitful for all who participated, and this book is an effort to share the knowledge that was both presented and developed at that workshop.

We offer this volume not only to inform the field about the work of some of the leaders in infant cognitive and language development but also to serve as an example of the types of disciplines that can and should be communicating with one another if we are to continue to progress in ways that integrate multiple disciplines and techniques, that are informed by theories, that test those theories, and that openly accept—even welcome—challenges to those theories that will

---

* The opinions and assertions herein are those of the authors and should not be construed as representing the policies of the NICHD, the National Institutes of Health, or the U.S. Department of Health and Human Services.

provide an empirical basis on which to judge their value. Thus, this book has as its goal—which was also the goal of the meeting but is now stated in a broader context—to both inform and engage multiple disciplines, to engage everyone to think across disciplines and paradigms, and to embrace the integration of creativity and science.

We need new paradigms, and we need to fully explore new ways of using old paradigms. We need new measures and new approaches to measurement. We need to continuously refine and improve our theories and to embrace, with an open mind, opposing theories as an opportunity to creatively engage in the best demonstration of our science. We hope that the book will in some ways contribute to the field's addressing those needs.

This volume seeks to offer a blend of theories and empirical evidence to support, refute, or modify them. Most of the chapters examine the link between theory and methodology, and we hope that their appearance together will serve as a waypoint in the establishment of such a movement as we continue to study, in greater depth and with innovative measures and approaches across disciplines, the infant pathways to language.

Peggy McCardle
John Colombo
Lisa Freund

Acknowledgments

The foundational conference that gave rise to the discussions and papers that became this volume, Infant Pathways to Language: Methods, Models, and Research Directions, was held September 15–17, 2005, in Mission Tempe Palms, Phoenix, AZ. It was supported by the Merrill Advanced Studies Center and the Eunice Kennedy Shriver National Institute of Child Health and Human Development (NICHD). The Merrill Advanced Studies Center, one of 12 centers in the Schiefelbusch Institute for Life Span Studies at the University of Kansas (UK), Lawrence, Kansas, is a catalyst for scholarship on disabilities and policies that shape university research. Their conferences and publications establish new directions and build collaborative projects in both science and policy.

The NICHD, which is one of the 27 Institutes and Centers that compose the National Institutes of Health in Bethesda, Maryland, was initially established in 1962 to investigate the broad aspects of human development as a means of understanding developmental disabilities, including mental retardation and the events that occur during pregnancy. Today, the Institute conducts and supports research on all stages of human development, from preconception to adulthood, to better understand the health of children, adults, families, and communities. The editors and authors wish to acknowledge the generous funding from these two organizations, which made possible this conference and its contributions to the advancement of research on infant language and cognitive development.

In addition, we wish to thank several individuals who helped to make the conference a success: Steve Warren, Richard L. Schiefelbusch (for whom the Institute for Life Span Studies at UK is named), and Robert "Bob" Barnhill served as discussants for this conference, although they did not author chapters for the volume. All three were members of the board of directors of the Merrill Advanced Studies Center at the time of the conference and still serve in valued capacities at UK and/or the Merrill Center. Mabel Rice, Director of the Merrill Center, gave wise counsel both in planning and conducting the conference and beyond. Patsy Woods at UK was patient, conscientious, and very helpful in keeping the conference participants organized. Claire Jones at the NICHD also provided valued assistance. We also wish to offer a special thanks to Cathleen Petree, our acquisitions editor at LEA/Taylor & Francis, who skillfully and cheerfully shepherded us through all the necessary processes of making this book a reality.

Contributors

Christa J. Anderson
  Department of Psychology
  University of Kansas
  Lawrence, Kansas

Richard N. Aslin
  Department of Brain
  and Cognitive Sciences
  University of Rochester
  Rochester, New York

Otilia M. Blaga
  Department of Psychology
  University of Kansas
  Lawrence, Kansas

Rechele Brooks
  Institute for Learning
  and Brain Sciences
  University of Washington
  Seattle, Washington

Jason Brunt
  Department of Psychology
  Infant Cognition Laboratory
  University of Texas at Austin
  Austin, Texas

Leslie B. Cohen
  Department of Psychology
  Infant Cognition Laboratory
  University of Texas at Austin
  Austin, Texas

John Colombo
  Department of Psychology
  and The Schiefelbusch
  Institute for Life Span Studies
  University of Kansas
  Lawrence, Kansas

Judy S. DeLoache
  Department of Psychology
  University of Virginia
  Charlottesville, Virginia

Christopher T. Fennell
  School of Psychology
  University of Ottawa
  Ottawa, Ontario

Lisa Freund
*National Institute
of Child Health and
Human Development
(NICDH)
Bethesda, Maryland*

Patricia A. Ganea
*Department of Psychology
Boston University
Boston, Massachusetts*

LouAnn Gerken
*Department of Psychology
University of Arizona
Tucson, Arizona*

Susan Goldin-Meadow
*Department of Psychology
University of Chicago
Chicago, Illinois 60637*

Vikram K. Jaswal
*Department of Psychology
University of Virginia
Charlottesville, Virginia*

Kathleen N. Kannass
*Department of Psychology
Loyola University of Chicago
Chicago, Ilinois*

Patricia K. Kuhl
*Institute for Learning
and Brain Sciences and
Department of Speech
and Hearing Sciences
University of Washington
Seattle, Washington*

Gary F. Marcus
*Department of Psychology
NYU Center for Child
Language
New York University
New York, New York*

Peggy McCardle
*National Institute
of Child Health and
Human Development (NICDH)
Bethesda, Maryland*

Andrew N. Meltzoff
*Institute for Learning
and Brain Sciences
University of Washington
Seattle, Washington*

Elissa L. Newport
*Department of Brain
and Cognitive Sciences
University of Rochester
Rochester, New York*

Hugh Rabagliati
*Department of Psychology
New York University
New York, New York*

Mabel L. Rice
*Dole Human
Development Center
University of Kansas
Lawrence, Kansas*

W. Allen Richman
*Department of Education
Macon State College
Macon, Georgia*

Jenny R. Saffran
*Department of
Psychology and
Waisman Center
University of
Wisconsin—Madison
Madison, Wisconsin*

D. Jill Shaddy
*The Schiefelbusch
Institute for Life Span Studies*

*University of Kansas
Lawrence, Kansas*

Sandra Waxman
*Department of Psychology
Northwestern University
Evanston, Ilinois*

Janet F. Werker
*Department of Psychology
University of British Columbia
Vancouver, British Columbia*

1

Measuring Language in Infancy[1]

PEGGY MCCARDLE, JOHN COLOMBO, AND LISA FREUND

The behavioral and brain sciences are faced with important new challenges in this first decade of the new millennium. With the completion of the mapping of the human genome, the importance of genetic factors in shaping behavioral functions in early childhood and of the domain of gene–environment interactions has come to the forefront of consideration as well. The field of developmental cognitive neuroscience is growing tremendously, particularly toward an understanding of those neural processes that are implicated in developmental disability and delay. In addition, as a result of more than 50 years of research on the effects of early experience and environment, the fields of education, early childhood, and clinical child psychology have come to understand the primacy of early experience and development on brain development and function. For evidence of this change, one need look no further than the widespread success of recent volumes such as *Critical Thinking about Critical Periods* (Bailey, Bruer, Symons, & Lichtman, 2001) and *From Neurons to Neighborhoods* (Shonkoff & Phillips, 2000).

Much of this progress is taking place within the context of an implicit consensus around developmental systems theory (Gottlieb, 1992, 1997; Edelman, 1987; see also Lickliter & Honeycutt, 2003). While there is still some variance in the minor areas in which this theoretical framework is interpreted, its key focal conceptualization is that brain–behavior relationships are both epigenetic and transactional. That is, brain structure and function can be considered both a cause and an effect of experience; experience can be considered both a cause and an effect of brain structure and function. This simple notion captures the rich dynamic nature of developmental processes. Although it paints a daunting picture for the developmental scientist, it also makes a strong call for an interdisciplinary or multidisciplinary research focus on developmental problems.

This newfound approach has attracted scientists from many fields to the study of early development. One particular example of this is the fact that scientists from many fields have now turned to the study of infancy and early childhood in order to address important issues, and scientists who study language have been among those first in line to conduct the work. Language researchers' interests have taken several forms. Some have been interested in the characteristics of the early environment in which skills or capacities develop (e.g., Hart & Risley, 1995, 1999). The extant data suggest that characteristics of the early social or linguistic environment are related to the early and rapid acquisition of words, and that, in turn, this early acquisition profile paves the way to school success (e.g., Walker, Greenwood, Hart, & Carta, 1994). Over the past three decades, spurred on by this emphasis, major advances have been made in the development of paradigms and techniques designed to assess the emergence and development of early language and cognitive functions. Researchers interested in the cognitive underpinnings of language have turned to the use of these paradigms in order to explain the degree, manner, and processes in which those cognitive functions might elucidate language acquisition and development.

For many years, the field of infant cognition has relied on the variants of the looking–habituation paradigm, which utilizes changes in infant visual regard and looking time to determine whether and what kinds of stimulus change infants are capable of detecting or recognizing. The head-turn conditioning and preference procedures have produced a wealth of data during the last decade on language learning in the first year of life. In recent years, researchers have begun to push the envelope and have stretched the technique to address problems and questions beyond simple discrimination and recognition memory.

Based on the framework provided by the developmental systems model, these infant paradigms—long used to assess lower-order cognitive skills (i.e., attention, discrimination, recognition memory, spatial orientation)—have now been adapted to study higher-order cognitive function. These include the study of infants' early conceptions of the physical laws governing objects (Baillargeon, 1994), statistical learning (Saffran, Aslin, & Newport, 1996), the perception of event structure (Baldwin, Baird, Saylor, & Clark, 2001), the linking of multiple object features in categories and concepts (Booth, Waxman, & Huang, 2005), and various forms of endogenous or volitional attention (Colombo & Cheatham, 2006). Several of these have been proposed to underlie some aspect of language. In addition, other important paradigms have also emerged in the last several decades that are unrelated to the common looking-time methods. These include the use of reaching behavior to determine infants' ability to spatially orient to a target or visual eye-tracking to assess infants' ability to attend to and to anticipate an event. As the technology has become increasingly sophisticated and available, researchers have also begun to use neuroimaging techniques such as evoked response potentials, magnetoencephalography, and near infrared spectroscopy, to study the brain–behavior links in infant language and cognition.

The present work assumes that existing assessment instruments or measurement tools represent meaningful measures of cognitive and language function in infancy and early childhood. A second assumption is that the inferential base afforded by these paradigms is rigorous enough to allow for confident assumptions about higher-order cognitive functions and extensions to word learning or language processing. Ideally, one would look to develop a series of tools for assessment or measurement from infancy through preschool that would accurately reflect specific components that represented a state-of-the-science understanding of cognitive function. Ideally, the disciplines involved would develop innovative approaches to the overall study of early cognitive and language functions such that the findings would have greater generalizability.

Both the extant measures and current paradigms do not easily allow for the study of developmental change over time, and mapping such trajectories is essential to our understanding of the brain–behavior relationship as it evolves over time. A major difficulty for researchers interested in change over time has been the difficulty in maintaining comparability of tasks or paradigms as infant and child abilities change over time. Interpreting behavioral results across ages is fraught with difficulty. Infants, children, and adults may show the same behavioral outcome but through different underlying mechanisms. On the other hand, infants, children, and adults may rely on a constant underlying mechanism yet show different behavioral outcomes. By simplifying tasks to their components and keeping the task demands simple, some of these difficulties can be overcome when assessing behavior across ages. That is, the same task can be used across several ages, and the interpretation of behavioral results can be constrained. However, it will be essential to create paradigms that rely on convergence from multiple assessments of multiple task components using multiple methods (e.g., tapping behavior and brain function patterns) to truly understand developing brain–behavior relations over time. Further, one would want such tools and paradigms to be widely available and relatively easy to administer or implement (in the case of novel paradigms) and to interpret. Finally, in order to extend infant language and cognition studies into brain and neurological systems will require measures that are sensitive to individual differences—that is, measures that can be used with a fairly wide range of performance levels at given ages and in a reliable and valid way.

Using existing measures and paradigms for new purposes can cause several things to happen. Their use carries with it possible concern or resistance from those who developed or have been using these measures in more traditional ways; some may be wedded to certain standards and reluctant to see those breached or changed, as it were. Such concerns may be legitimate, but there may be cases where the use of existing measures and approaches for new purposes serves to highlight the limitations of those measures and approaches, calling some of the existing research into question. Intellectual curiosity may be counterbalanced by caution or, worse, distrust or a sense of competition as newcomers enter the turf of more established researchers. While few will say that innovation is not a good thing, most will also admit that the research science infrastructure is conservative. Innovation is risky, as funders seek to balance risk with solid investment, and more junior researchers often are advised by their mentors and more senior colleagues to follow a more conservative path to "get established." At the same time, we all know that innovation and creativity are crucial to pushing the frontiers of any area of science. This is no less true in the area of infant development than in any other area of science.

In this volume, as in the discussions at the conference from which it derives, the authors are pushing the frontiers of research approaches and methods in infant language and cognition. They are innovatively combining methods, introducing new measures, and demonstrating the use of technologies and measurement approaches that can inform the study of word learning and categorization, gaze, attention, gesture, and physiological functions. The book is laid out in four main sections (with an introduction and final chapter not within those sections). The first section of the book, "Recognizing Patterns," deals with infants' ability to recognize and generalize from patterns for linguistic and nonlinguistic input. Discussion centers around similarities and differences in statistical learning and rule learning, how such learning might be constrained, and the value of current approaches to studying infant language. In discussions of statistical learning, it seems clear that while infants are highly sensitive to some aspects of the input, we still have not completely defined or firmly decided what specific statistics are encoded (e.g., in terms of the types of elements encoded) or what decision rules are operating and what the constraints are.

These issues are laid out in Richard Aslin and Elissa Newport's chapter, which emphasizes both how pervasive and puzzling statistical learning is; operating in both humans and nonhumans, across at least three domains, yet it is not sufficient to entirely explain language acquisition. To grasp the global picture and to approach the level of complexity acknowledged to exist, some reconciliation or integration of research findings from statistical learning and rule learning as well with those of other approaches to infant and early childhood language learning is necessary. Are rule learning and statistical learning really different mechanisms, or can one (statistical learning) actually account for at least some aspects of the other (rule learning)?

Jenny Saffran, in her work on predictive dependencies, begins to address the issue of constraints on statistical learning. She has argued that human learning mechanisms play a role in shaping the structure of human languages (Saffran,

Pollack, Seibel, & Shkolnik, 2007); the chapter here focuses on interspecies and intraspecies investigation of two languages—one more predictable (the "P" language) and one less predictable. Both infants and monkeys were able to learn a simple version of this language, but only the infants were able to learn a scaled-up version, wherein rules pertained to categories rather than individual elements. Saffran argues that human learning mechanisms that are not specifically tailored for language learning may nevertheless be constraints that have at least in part shaped the structure of human language. Further research on rule learning that is not unique to language and on the constraints at work in human learning, both for language and in other domains, should continue to shed additional light on this issue.

LouAnn Gerken, in her chapter, examines whether there are constraints on the dimensions learners consider. She laments the lack of tools to investigate infant generalization, highlighting the dilemma of the novelty–familiarity preference and its poorly understood variability. Gerken suggests—based on her findings of both early familiarity and later novelty preferences—that infants are learning both during familiarization and during testing. She hypothesizes that those infants able to master the structure of input during familiarization may demonstrate a novelty preference while those with lower "strength of learning" may demonstrate a familiarity preference. Gerken concludes by calling for the development of methods that will better enable firm conclusions.

In the final chapter of the first section, Mabel Rice examines patterns of a different kind: those that distinguish atypical language development—specific language impairment (SLI)—from typical language development. After reviewing inclusionary and exclusionary criteria for categorizing children as SLI as well as the distinction between delayed versus disordered language, she presents a model (Rice, 2004) in which some elements are disrupted relative to others, leading to an overall lack of synchrony in the linguistic system. Rice asserts that language growth shows strong similarities across all children, yet growth is not uniform across all dimensions of language, and that perhaps different mechanisms drive different dimensions of language (semantics and syntax). She also uses gender differences to illustrate an asynchrony: Boys appear to start later with their language development but are more likely to be able to overcome the early delay. Fertile areas of research into this puzzle include the possible roots in infancy of such gender differences, as well as how genetic influences might operate, and the role of environmental influences (parenting, home resources) as they interact with other factors such as genetic influences. Rice concludes that disordered language may be less different from typical language development than previously assumed.

In Section 2 of the book, "From Patterns to Meaning," the authors address how infant speech perception, social cognition, early conceptualization, and learning link to meaning and how all of this links to language learning itself. As children develop, language abilities unfold or are triggered in ways that we are still seeking to understand. These authors thus address issues of methodology as well as their chosen content areas in the study of child language development, moving us toward more productive approaches to solving the many remaining puzzles about language development.

Janet Werker and Christoper Fennell, in their chapter, lay out two competing theories of lexical development: (1) representational discontinuity, in which lexical representations must be constructed anew when the infant begins to acquire vocabulary; and (2) resource limitation, which assumes that the representation used in vocabulary acquisition is the same one learned earlier but that success or failure is explained by a processing limitation. Using evidence on Werker's own switch task (Werker, Cohen, Lloyd, Casasola, & Stager, 1998) and a complementary methodology, preferential looking, they invoke the PRIMIR (Processing Rich Information from Multidimensional Interactive Representations) framework (Curtain & Werker, 2007) to provide an account of the development change infants experience as they move from associative learning to being able to use a multidimensional lexical representation in more complex word learning. Citing Hindi-English Dutch-English cross-linguistic work, Werker and Fennell illustrate that, in keeping with the PRIMIR framework, infants at 17 months of age can in fact use native-language phonetic detail to guide their word learning.

Sandra Waxman proposes that infant conceptual and linguistic development have at least rudimentary links even before infants being to produce single words. Through a series of cleverly designed experiment with infants of various ages, using both live interactions and an automated procedure, Waxman presents evidence concerning infant learning of nouns, adjectives, and verbs. Using data from multiple studies and two procedures, she argues that infants share with mature language users the expectation that different word types refer to different aspects of a scene or event, that objects fit into categories and have certain properties, and that events also fit into categories. That is, infants begin with general expectations that link novel words to broad commonalities, and over time these are refined to specifically link grammatical forms (nouns, adjectives, and verbs) to particular meanings (categories, properties, and events). Waxman acknowledges the primarily descriptive nature of these findings and sets out the goal of developing necessary analytic tools to capture the timing and course by which infants map novel words to meanings more formally, thereby defining with greater precision the time course of word learning.

In addressing the links between early language acquisition and learning, Judy DeLoache, Patricia Ganea, and Vikram Jaswal argue that infants and young children are not only learning language but are also learning through language. These authors emphasize the importance of interaction with adults for infants to learn about their world and the role that context plays in facilitating the infant or toddler's ability to use the information provided to alter their mental representation of a label. They also present evidence that interactive picture book experiences provide powerful learning experiences for infants and young children, as this provides a powerful tool for gaining information, one on which they will rely increasingly.

In Section 3, "Predictors of Language Emergence," the authors present detailed data to support their contentions that attention, gaze, and gesture, when deconstructed into measurable or observable components, can predict later language outcomes, rate of growth, or the emergence of new language abilities. John Colombo, Jill Shaddy, Otilia Blaga, Christa Anderson, Kathleen Kannass, and Allen Richman, after tracing a history of the development of measures and approaches to studying infant perception and learning, describe the Kansas Early Cognition Project. Using both longitudinal and cross-sectional samples, they collected behavioral (looking) and physiological (heart rate) measures of infant attention. Segmenting looking behavior into three component parts and constructing profiles, Colombo and colleagues show that better language outcomes were associated with clear and precipitous declines in looking across the first year of life, where the proportion of sustained attention was maintained and the proportion of attention termination declined. Their work on looking time and the components of visual attention underline the importance of measuring attention at multiple levels and of using a developmental approach. The Colombo group's analyses reveal prediction for dynamic aspects of the developmental trajectories of language skills that could not be captured in a cross-sectional study. The patterns seen change over time in ways that could be missed unless one studies the same children as they grow.

Andrew Meltzoff and Rechele Brooks address how gaze following relates to infant language development. These authors deconstruct joint visual attention and focus on one component: gaze following. They then build a case for the very specific role of gaze following and describe the measurement technique they have developed to detect infant understanding of the primitive, referential nature of an adult's gaze (the Gaze Following: Eyes Open/Closed test, Brooks & Meltzoff, 2002, 2005). Using this measure, they examined whether infants looked more often at the target when the adult turned his or her head with eyes open versus eyes closed and whether infants looked longer, vocalized, and pointed at the target in the adult eyes open versus closed conditions. They assert from their data that these behaviors develop in a cascade that can be mapped as a developmental trajectory and used to predict vocabulary growth.

Susan Goldin-Meadow, in the final chapter in this section on predictors, reports how gesture can give us clues to children's linguistic preconceptions and can predict language growth. She presents evidence that gesture allows children to express more than investigators in this large project could if limited to verbal communication and that a child using gesture and word together to communicate two individual parts of a phrase is both signaling readiness for the next step in oral language development and using gesture as part of his or her language learning process (gestural facilitation hypothesis). Her data illustrate a difference between complementary gesture–word combinations (the gesture adds information) and supplementary combinations (where the gesture is redundant with information conveyed through speech). Complementary combinations reliably predict the onset of two-word combinations. Gesture, Goldin-Meadow therefore argues, is not only a useful predictor of when the child is preparing to make the next step in language learning but also plays a role in facilitating that next step.

In Section 4, "Models and Methods to Study Language," Patricia Kuhl presents her own model, the Native Language Model; Leslie Cohen and Jason Brunt address methodological approaches in general; and Gary Marcus and Hugh Rabagliatti bring us up to date on statistical modeling; each chapter uses the work of the authors' own laboratory teams to instantiate the discussion with real data. Finally, Lisa Freund discusses neuroimaging tools that can now or may soon in the future be usable with infants and young children. Her chapter includes details about the National Institutes of Health (NIH) Pediatric MRI Study of Normal Brain Development, how they have established cross-site reliability and standard protocols, and other information that can also serve as a reference point for those just beginning to integrate neurobiological measures with behavioral studies of infant language and for those seeking to collaborate and compare or combine data across sites. The tools discussed are those that can now or soon will enable more researchers to integrate neuroimaging data, both structural and functional, on the important questions that the study of language development raises.

Kuhl's laboratory has for several years been examining the relationship between early speech perception skills and later language learning abilities. In this chapter, she summarizes several years' worth of data indicating that data on early infant responses that was once considered "noise" is actually meaningful information on individual differences that can be used to predict the variance in developmental growth patterns in language, and applies these data to her expanded Native Language Model. Kuhl has argued that language acquisition depends on neural commitment, or the development of neural circuitry dedicated to analyzing the patterns (statistical and prosodic) of native languages, and that the degree to which infants retain their early ability to detect nonnative phonetic contrasts reflects the degree of immaturity or un-committedness to the native language speech patterns. Using a head-turn conditioned response task, and later replicating findings with data from event-related potentials (ERPs), Kuhl shows that in 7-month-old infants, native and nonnative speech discrimination differentially predict later language development; native language discrimination positively correlates with word production and rate of vocabulary growth at 18 months, while nonnative discrimination shows a negative correlation for both word production and rate of vocabulary growth. Kuhl discusses "critical period," suggesting that the beginning of such a period for phonetic learning is possibly a maturation trigger that occurs in the last half of the first year of life and has more to do with experience than time. The closing of a critical period, says Kuhl, may be a statistical process—that neural networks stay flexible, stabilizing only when the number and variability of occurrences of particular phonetic units no longer shift the underlying distribution. Studies in her laboratory to date suggest that the ability to learn phonetically from native language exposure plays a greater role in determining rate of language learning than do auditory or cognitive skills.

Cohen and Brunt address methodological issues in early word learning and categorization, as well as recent empirical evidence presented within the context of this discussion of methodology. They take up four major methodological issues that confront infant language researchers: ecological validity versus experimental control; social referencing; novelty versus familiarity; and prior category knowledge. The trade-off between controlling factors that might influence or provide an alternative explanation for findings as opposed to providing an interactive learning setting like the one the infant would be expected to encounter naturally is one that every researcher must consider. Cohen and Brunt opt for control but use their controlled experiments in ways that seek to resolve or at least that begin to address some of the debates over these issues. They deal with each of these major issues in turn and provide data using their measure of infant past experience with objects—the Baby Label and Object Category Knowledge (BLOCK) inventory (Brunt, Gora, & Cohen, 2005)—to illustrate how they examined the effects of past experience in infant label assignment. Cohen and Brunt conclude that research on word learning and categorization is anything but straightforward and involves both determining how the presence of words affects categorization and how knowledge of categorization affects word learning. Both of these questions require researchers to grapple with the methodological issues raised at the beginning of this chapter, but these authors assert that using new measures such as the BLOCK and comparing findings across both experimental and naturalistic settings can lead us to convergent findings that can move the field forward in our knowledge of infant word learning.

A well-known developmental psychologist trained originally in physics once remarked that all theory begins as fiction. Theories are inherently neither good nor bad. They are hypotheses—wonderful whimsical notions that, once conceived, we can test. Interestingly, those theories that annoy the most may be exactly the ones to test; this is perhaps the link between creativity and the scientific method.

Opposing theories should excite us, intrigue us. We should (and will) argue against them, but data and an open mind (which allows that the truth may lie somewhere between what we believe or theorize and what those annoying other theories hold) are keys to our understanding of behavioral phenomena.

Many of our paradigms are built to narrowly examine individual aspects of our pet theories. As long as they do not become blinders, which make us believe that there is a right way and a wrong way to approach any aspect of development—and in this case infant cognitive and language development—then specific paradigms are helping to advance our understanding, to move the field forward. But when we become slaves to our paradigms, when they make us begin to condemn others who enter into our turf, with different approaches, or who use our paradigm in ways we had not envisioned, the challenge should be to demonstrate empirically whether or not those methods or approaches can successfully be applied to the questions being asked.

In creating bridges across disciplines or across paradigms within disciplines, or across approaches and subfields within a field, we must take into account our scientific goals. We should actively work to achieve replication if not standardization, for example, across laboratories in infant word learning, but in addition our work must inform and be informed by the work in other areas (e.g., work on early bilingualism and cross-linguistic work) that may be using the same or similar methods as researchers who study monolingual word-learning in infants, but perhaps with different underlying theories. More broadly, and possibly more far-reaching, this work must also inform and be informed by statistical learning, neuroimaging, and naturalistic observations of phenomena similar to those being explored experimentally in the laboratory.

Those who work in infant language and cognition must not only be aware of the work that is being done using paradigms and methodologies other than their own; they must also consider with an open mind the possibility that these other theories could play a role in their own work. We must embrace the excitement of intellectual debate and infuse it with data. Thus, in surveying the variety of approaches and paradigms, models and methods, and in light of the advances made in these related but still largely separate areas, we decided that it was an ideal time to bring together eminent scholars and ask them to discuss and air their thoughts, their theories, their findings, and their potential or extant disagreements. In our workshop, debate was welcomed, in a forum with no competing sessions and an open atmosphere of acceptance and intellectual interest. To say that the meeting was a success would understate the outcome, yet clearly the ultimate goal—to share this work and these thoughts with the field at large—was not accomplished with one meeting. Rather, the first meeting marked a beginning, an important step forward. The next step, all agreed, was a volume in which what was presented and discussed could be shared, in the hope that others, reading the chapters, would also begin to think even more transdisciplinarily or interdisciplinarily than they were before they read the volume.

This is a movement that has other proponents. This approach has been the mainstay of the journal *Behavioral and Brain Sciences*, which has long championed the format of presenting a provocative lead article that is followed by a series of commentaries and rejoinders. A similar debate format was initiated by the Society for Research in Child Development at its conferences back in the late 1990s (see papers resulting from one debate: Haith, 1998; Spelke, 1998), and the format was also followed by the International Society on Infant Studies at its conferences later on (e.g., Baillargeon & Smith, 1998). The Boston University Conference on Language Development has initiated an annual lunchtime forum that is a "cross-fire" debate where two leading scholars representing opposing theoretical stances present their cases and then engage in discussion with each other and the audience. By publishing this volume, we hope to encourage such healthy debate and the challenging but crucial interdisciplinary, collaborative science that can and must be conducted for the field to innovatively address the enigma of the pathways to infant language development.

ENDNOTE

1. The opinions and assertions herein are those of the authors and should not be construed as representing the policies of the NICHD, the National Institutes of Health, or the US Department of Health and Human Services.

REFERENCES

Bailey, D. B., Bruer, J. T., Symons F. J., & Lichtman, J. W. (Eds.). (2001). *Critical thinking about critical periods*. Baltimore, MD: Paul H. Brookes Publishing.

Baldwin, D. A., Baird, J. A., Saylor, M. M., & Clark, M. A. (2001). Infants parse dynamic action. *Child Development, 72*, 708–717.

Baillargeon, R. (1994). How do infants learn about the physical world? *Current Directions in Psychological Science, 3*, 133–140.

Baillargeon, R. & Smith, L. B. (1998, April). *Debate: Do infants possess innate knowledge structures?* Paper presented at the International Conference on Infant Studies, Atlanta, GA.

Booth, A. E., Waxman, S. R., & Huang, Y. T. (2005). Conceptual information permeates word learning in infancy. *Developmental Psychology, 41*, 491–505.

Brooks, R. & Meltzoff, A. N. (2002). The importance of eyes: How infants interpret adult looking behavior. *Developmental Psychology, 38*, 958–966.

Brooks, R. & Meltzoff, A. N. (2005). The development of gaze following and its relation to language. *Developmental Psychology, 8*, 535–543.

Brunt, R. J., Gora, K., & Cohen, L.B. (2005). *Building BLOCK for the investigation of early word learning and experience*. Poster presented at the 2005 Biennial Meeting of the Society for Research in Child Development, Atlanta, GA.

Colombo, J. & Cheatham, C. (2006). A model for the emergence of endogenous attention in infancy and early childhood. In R. Kail (Ed.), *Advances in child development and behavior.* London: Elsevier.

Curtain, S. & Werker, J. F. (2007). The perceptual foundation of phonological development. In G. Gaskell (Ed). *The Oxford handbook of psycholinguistics.* New York: Oxford University Press.

Edelman, G. M. (1987). *Neural Darwinism: The theory of neuronal group selection.* New York: Basic Books.

Gottlieb, G. (1992). *Individual development and evolution: The genesis of novel behavior.* New York: Oxford University Press.

Gottlieb, G. (1997). *Synthesizing nature-nurture: Prenatal roots of instinctive behavior.* Mahwah, NJ: Lawrence Erlbaum Associates.

Haith, M. M. (1998). Who put the cog in infant cognition? Is rich interpretation too costly? *Infant Behavior and Development, 21,* 167–179.

Hart, B. & Risley, T. R. (1995). *Meaningful differences in the everyday experiences of young American children.* Baltimore, MD: Paul Brookes.

Hart, B. & Risley, T. R. (1999). *The social world of children learning to talk.* Baltimore, MD: Paul Brookes.

Kahneman, D. (2003). Experiences of collaborative research. *American Psychologist, 58,* 723–730.

Lickliter, R. & Honeycutt, H. (2003). Developmental dynamics: toward a biologically plausible evolutionary psychology. *Psychological Bulletin, 129,* 819–835.

Mellers, B., Hertwig, R., & Kahneman, D. (2001). Do frequency representations eliminate conjunction effects? An exercise in adversarial collaboration. *Psychological Science, 12,* 269–275.

Rice, M. L. (2004). Growth models of developmental language disorders. In M. L. Rice and S. F. Warren (Eds), *Developmental language disorders: From phenotype to etiologies.* (pp. 207–240). Mahwah, NJ: Lawrence Erlbaum.

Saffran, J. R., Aslin, R. N., & Newport, E. L. (1996). Statistical learning by 8-month-old infants. *Science, 274,* 1926–1928.

Saffran, J. R., Pollack, S. D., Seibel, R. L., & Shkolnik, A. (2007). Dog is a god is a god. Infant rule learning is not specific to language. *Cognition, 105,* 669–680.

Shonkoff, J. P. & Phillips, D. A. (2000). *From neurons to neighborhoods: The science of early childhood development.* Washington, DC: National Academy Press.

Spelke, E. S. (1998). Nativism, empiricism, and the origins of knowledge. *Infant Behavior and Development, 21,* 181–200.

Walker, D., Greenwood, C., Hart, B., & Carta, J. (1994). Prediction of school outcomes based on early language production and socioeconomic factors. *Child Development, 65,* 606–621.

Werker, J. F., Cohen, L. B., Lloyd, V. L., Casasola, M., & Stager, C. L. (1998). Acquisition of word–object associations by 14-month old infants. *Developmental Psychology 34,* 1289–1309.

I

RECOGNIZING PATTERNS

2

What Statistical Learning Can and Can't Tell Us about Language Acquisition

RICHARD N. ASLIN AND ELISSA L. NEWPORT

INTRODUCTION

In fall 1992, Jenny Saffran entered graduate school at the University of Rochester after having spent four years at Brown University working with Jim Morgan and an additional year as a research assistant with Sheila Blumstein. She already had an interest in the interaction between prosody and word segmentation (Morgan & Saffran, 1995) but sought a research topic for her first-year project. Ironically, in two independent consultations with each of us the suggestion was made to Jenny to read a chapter by Hayes and Clark (1970) in which adults were presented with sequences of noises that contained embedded subpatterns. Hayes and Clark reported that after listening to a continuous stream of noises, performance on a two-alternative forced-choice post-test was above chance for recognizing noise sequences that began and ended at subpattern breaks over noise sequences that began and ended within subpatterns. Four years later, after a number of fits and starts, two papers were published on adult (Saffran, Newport, & Aslin, 1996) and infant (Saffran, Aslin, & Newport, 1996) word segmentation from streams of synthetic speech. These two papers used the term *statistical learning* (SL)—from Charniak's (1993) description of algorithms in computational linguistics—to describe the psychological process by which the transitional probabilities from one syllable to another in the continuous speech streams could enable word segmentation and its complement, what Hayes and Clark referred to as *clustering*.

It would appear that Saffran, Newport, & Aslin (1996) and Saffran, Aslin, & Newport (1996) struck a chord in the language acquisition literature.[1] There have been dozens of follow-up experiments in the subsequent decade, and the term statistical learning is now used to described a subfield of research on impressive feats of rapid learning in a variety of domains within language and visual processing.

The sustained interest in SL stems in part from a broader shift in the field from formal symbolic models of linguistics to probabilistic models that emphasize the distribution of exemplars and the importance of the richness of the input. Yet, to be historically accurate, we never claimed that SL was the only mechanism for solving the word-segmentation problem or that it was sufficient for solving other problems at higher levels of language structure, despite claims on our behalf (Bates & Elman, 1996). A long tradition of structural linguistics (cf. Harris, 1955) and computational linguistics (Charniak, 1993) preceded the fundamental principles of SL as applied to the word-segmentation problem, and in fact these prior investigations were focused on the syntactic parsing problem, which entails considerably more complexity than word segmentation because linguistic categories are, by definition, beyond the surface structure of the input.

Our goals in this chapter are to address four key questions:

1. What is SL, at least as we define it, and over what ages, domains, and species does it operate?
2. How is SL constrained to enable rapid learning to be tractable given the limits of human information processing and the explosive combinatorics of even the simplest language?
3. What are the limits of SL for explaining language acquisition beyond the word-segmentation problem?
4. How might SL go awry in special populations of children who suffer from language deficits?

WHAT IS STATISTICAL LEARNING?

We propose the following three criteria for defining SL. At the most basic level, SL involves the acquisition of structured information from the auditory or visual environment via sensitivity to frequency or probability distributions. Importantly, SL involves no overt reinforcement or direct feedback but rather operates by mere exposure or observation. Finally, in most cases SL involves rapid presentations of stimulus materials and therefore places substantial demands on both short- and long-term memory.

The foregoing definitions of SL provide a context for why it has captured the interest of many researchers, both in language development and in other domains. Something like SL must be how language is acquired. There is no instructor (parental or otherwise) who provides corrective feedback to the young child's ungrammatical utterances (Brown & Hanlon, 1970; Hirsh-Pasek, Treiman, & Schneiderman, 1984; Wexler & Culicover, 1983). And certainly the word-segmentation problem, as well as other aspects of learning the formal structure of languages, is solved by mere exposure to the native language.

SL also captured the interest of the field because, at first blush, it appears to be so implausible. How does an 8-month-old infant extract from a 2-minute stream of continuous speech, consisting of 540 syllables (> 4 syllables/sec), the higher-order statistics of bisyllable frequency or transitional probability? Even adults, with the aid of paper and pencil, could not keep up with this rapid counting exercise. More importantly, such a tabulation, even if it were possible at slower rates of presentation, would not explain how learners extract the specific statistics that describe the actual underlying structure of the input. There is an infinite number of possible statistics even in this simple example of counting co-occurring syllables (e.g., trisyllables, quadruples, and so forth, and a huge number of nonadjacent statistics).

The problem of infinite statistics is referred to as the combinatorial explosion problem or the curse of dimensionality. As the number of distinct elements in a set increases linearly, the number of *combinations* of elements increases exponentially. For example, consider a 10 × 10 array of pixels in a visual image. If each pixel can take on one of eight possible levels of gray (from black to white), there are 8 to the 100th power unique images. Among this vast number of possible images, only a very small fraction of these are actually attested in the natural visual world. A learner confronted with the set of natural images must ignore (or filter out) the much larger set of possible images that are merely noise. Similarly, consider the number of possible words generated by legal combinations of consonants and vowels. In English there are approximately 9,000 legal consonant-vowel-consonant (CVC) words, yet only 11% are actual words. While this has proven useful for psycholinguists who need a large set of nonwords for their research, it illustrates the fact that, like visual images, a language learner must ignore (or filter out) from the possible combinatorics of English phonemes those that do not form lexical items.

Of course, the foregoing examples presume that the learner "knows" the relevant units over which structure is defined (pixels or phonemes). The problem is even more daunting for the naïve learner, who must determine which visual features or bits of sound define the relevant units over which statistics should be computed and which features or bits are "noise." Given infinite time with paper and pencil, a learner could in principle keep track of all possible statistics. But the reality of language and visual processing is that human learners have a finite information processing system that must access rapid streams of speech (4–5 syllables/sec) and complex scenes that occur at the rate of eye movements (2–3 fixations/sec).

How might human learners accomplish the SL tasks given the foregoing impediments? Neither the efficiency of short-term memory in accessing and retaining rapidly presented inputs nor the capacity of long-term memory for storing or computing complex frequency distributions seems plausible, even in adults and certainly not in infants. Yet we know from the psycholinguistics literature that adults have access to highly detailed representations of the input distribution. For example, Howes and Solomon (1951) showed that adults' word-recognition threshold in noise is a function of word frequency (estimated from written corpora). Levelt and Wheeldon (1994) showed that adults' picture naming latency is a function of syllable frequency. Vitevich and Luce (1998) showed that adults' lexical decision time is a function of phoneme frequency. And literally hundreds of psycholinguistic experiments have found the need to control stimuli for word and phoneme frequency, implicitly suggesting that subjects would be sensitive to these variables. Thus, there is clear behavioral evidence that mature users of a language have access to distributional information at the word, syllable, and phoneme level. And despite the "in principle" arguments for the implausibility of SL, there is demonstrable evidence that human learners overcome these impediments. How adults, and infants, do so will be discussed after reviewing recent findings on SL that extended the original studies by Saffran, Aslin, & Newport (1996) and Saffran, Newton, & Aslin (1996).

Statistical Learning since 1996

In our original studies of SL, we chose to study word segmentation because it is a tractable problem that must be solved by all language learners, and it is illustrative of a distributional learning mechanism that *may* apply more broadly (though we made no claim that it is sufficient). Saffran, Newport, Aslin, Tunick, and Barruecco (1997) showed that overt attention was not necessary for SL in preschoolers or adults, although some general level of attention is required (Toro, Sinnett, & Soto-Faraco, 2005). Saffran, Johnson, Aslin, and Newport (1999) showed that SL operates as well over sequences of nonlinguistic tones—in which the statistical structure mimics that of speech syllables—in infants and adults. Perhaps most importantly, Aslin, Saffran, and Newport (1998) investigated precisely what type of statistic is used in SL on speech streams. They showed that 8-month-olds could solve the word-segmentation problem even in the absence of trisyllable co-occurrence frequency differences. When the frequency of occurrence was equated for the words and part-words that were tested after exposure to speech streams, infants still discriminated words from part-words based on the higher-order statistic of transitional probability.[2] This does not mean that frequency is irrelevant to SL but rather that first-order frequency statistics are not the only class of statistics that infants can compute.

Fiser and Aslin (2002a) extended these results from the auditory domain to the visual domain by showing that simple visual shapes presented in temporal sequences (albeit at a slower rate than speech) enable adults to extract both first-order (frequency-based) and second-order (conditionalized) statistics. Kirkham, Slemmer, and Johnson (2002) showed that 2-, 5-, and 8-month-olds are sensitive to first-order statistics in streams of simple shapes. Hunt and Aslin (2001) showed that SL applies to the visual-motor domain in a serial reaction time task with adults. Finally, Fiser and Aslin (2001, 2002b, 2005) moved the SL literature from the temporal to the spatial domain by showing that very similar mechanisms operate in multielement visual scenes, where both adults and 9-month-olds can bind together elements on the basis of first- or second-order statistics to form coherent perceptual "chunks."

Demonstrations of SL in nonhumans, both tamarin monkeys (Hauser, Newport, & Aslin, 2001; Newport, Hauser, Spaepen, & Aslin, 2004) and rats (Toro & Trobalón, 2005) clearly show that at least the simple aspects of SL are not unique to humans. However, only one study of nonhumans has employed the frequency-balanced design of Aslin et al. (1998), which evaluates whether learners show sensitivity to conditional probabilities rather than co-occurrence frequency. In that study the rats failed (Toro & Trobalón, 2005). It is not known whether monkeys are also limited to co-occurrence frequency computations or whether, like human infants, they can compute conditional probability statistics. This failure in rats, however, could be important for explaining why other species do not acquire complex systems like language.

Conditionalized statistics take into account differences in base rates that render first-order statistics less informative for predicting future events. For example, consider a case in which two elements (X and Y) occur frequently but just as often with each other as with other elements, while two other elements (A and B) occur rarely but always with each other. If one simply counted bigram frequency, the number of XY pairs could exceed the number of AB pairs, yet A is more predictive of B than X is predictive of Y. The conditional probability of Y given X and B given A captures this predictiveness better than the frequency of pairs XY and AB does. Interestingly, research on classical conditioning in the rat provides clear evidence of sensitivity to conditional probabilities (Rescorla & Wagner, 1972), but this paradigm places much less demand on memory and computational resources than typical SL paradigms, which require that learners keep track of the conditional probabilities relating many elements at the same time. Again, it is important to note that sensitivity to conditional probabilities does not imply that N-gram frequency of occurrence is unimportant. Highly frequent elements may, for example, serve as anchor points (or filters) that parse the input so that higher-order statistics can be computed over more limited subsets of the data. Several computational models of word segmentation (Swingley, 2005) and form-class learning (Mintz, 2003; Mintz, Newport, & Bever, 2002) use the strategy of operating over only the 200 or 300 most frequent elements.

Another important issue is what use is made of the statistics that are computed from a corpus of input. That is, what decision mechanism operates on those stored statistical values? It seems highly unlikely that statistics computed from a corpus are retained in memory with sufficient fidelity that microdifferences could be used in making decisions about word boundaries or other properties of the underlying structure (e.g., is a transitional probability difference of 0.43 vs. 0.39 meaningful?). But given a reliable difference in some computed statistic, is the decision rule based on a local minimum or on a hard threshold? Saffran, Newport, & Aslin (1996) referred to "dips" in the transitional probabilities (TPs) at word boundaries and suggested that these dips could serve as a cue to word onsets. However, as noted by Yang (2004), such locally relative dips would not be present for single-syllable words (i.e., there would be low TPs both before and after the single-syllable word). However, a hard threshold (e.g., TPs below some criterion) would serve as a useful segmentation algorithm even for single-syllable words. Given the computational modeling of Swingley (2005), such a hard threshold is a viable mechanism, although to date we have no empirical evidence that such a mechanism actually operates in infants.

A general concern of artificial language (or artificial lexicon) studies is that they may not "scale up" to real corpora. That is, infants (and adults) may successfully use SL mechanisms to solve word segmentation and other problems when the language is extremely small but perhaps not when the problems reflect the size and complexity of real languages. This, of course, is a serious concern, but it may be offset in many cases by the myriad correlated statistical cues to structure that are present in real languages. We certainly recognized this potential problem in Saffran, Aslin, & Newport (1996): "Although experience with speech in the real world is unlikely to be as concentrated as it was in these studies, infants in more natural settings presumably benefit from other types of cues correlated with statistical information (p. 1928)."

How Is Statistical Learning Constrained?

The studies conducted since 1996 strongly suggest the existence of a robust SL mechanism in adults, infants, and at least two nonhuman animal species. Given the computational problem of explosive combinatorics (the curse of dimensionality), what enables a SL mechanism to operate without attempting to compute too many statistics (or just the wrong ones, those that mismatch the underlying structure)? Here we consider a set of constraints, some innate and some potentially learned from the input, that allow a powerful SL mechanism to be tractable in finite time.

Preferred Units

One problem for a SL mechanism concerns which basic units, out of the many available, are the ones on which statistical computations should be performed. Saffran, Aslin, & Newport (1996) presumed that the unit of analysis for initial word segmentation was the syllable. However, recent work with adults (Newport & Aslin,

2004) showed that statistics that reside at the segment (consonant or vowel) level, in the absence of contrastive syllable statistics, are sufficient for word segmentation.[3] Work in progress (Newport, Weiss, Wonnacott, & Aslin, 2004) suggests that adults and infants in fact rely primarily on segment information or on the alignment of segment and syllable information to solve the word-segmentation problem. When the statistics indicating word boundaries were at the syllable level and not the segment level, both adults and infants failed to segment words from streams of speech. By focusing on a subset of the potential types of units for statistical analysis, the learner reduces the combinatorics and simplifies the SL problem.

Gestalt Principles

A related set of constraints relies on Gestalt principles to bias what is learned. Some elements naturally tend to be linked perceptually, even without any learning process, and statistical relations among these may be most easily learned. For example, Baker, Olson, and Behrmann (2004) conducted a variant of the Fiser and Aslin (2001) studies employing multielement scenes; however, in contrast to Fiser and Aslin, in these studies there was no grid to make clear that each element was an isolated unit prior to learning. In this paradigm, adults are more likely to link together by statistical learning the elements in visual scenes that are connected by thin lines. Another example of a Gestalt constraint in the visual domain comes from Fiser, Scholl, and Aslin (2007). They used dynamic displays in which an object moved behind an occluder and then two objects emerged from the occluder. One object was a perceptually consistent continuation of the preoccluded object's trajectory, while the other was not. Subjects showed a preference for learning the temporal order statistics that conformed to the better continuation—that is, learning the sequence of shapes that appeared as connected.

More relevant to the language domain is a study by Creel, Newport, and Aslin (2004). They presented a sequence of tones as in Saffran et al. (1999), but in one condition the tones alternated between two different octave ranges. This induces a percept called auditory streaming (Bregman, 1990) in which attention is bistable between one or the other of the two octave sequences. Creel et al.'s stimuli had strong statistical relations between nonadjacent tones and weaker cues between adjacent tones. When the tones in both streams came from the same octave, adults learned the weaker statistics among temporally adjacent elements; however, when the streams came from different octaves, adults learned the nonadjacent statistics, favoring a grouping of elements within the same pitch range rather than those that were temporally adjacent. In other words, the perceptual bias of auditory streaming constrained SL. Although the foregoing studies show clear evidence for Gestalt constraints on SL, they are not particularly relevant to word segmentation because perceptual similarity among elements is not a reliable cue to words in natural languages.

Social/Attentional Cues

Language typically occurs in a social context in which there are two or more talkers communicating and in which there is some visual information to complement the auditory information. Baldwin (1993) showed that 14-month-olds are more likely to treat a new label as referring to a novel object that is being looked at by the talker. Based on this work, Yu, Ballard, and Aslin (2005) conducted a study of adults' use of gaze information in a word-segmentation and word-learning task. Learners viewed videotapes of an adult describing the contents of a picture book in Mandarin. In one condition the videotape provided images of the picture book and the pages being turned as the Mandarin speaker described its contents. In the other condition the videotapes also contained information about the talker's eye movements to the picture book as the pictures were being described. The results showed a clear advantage on both word segmentation and word learning for the adults in the gaze condition over the no-gaze condition. These results suggest that, at least in adults, nonlinguistic cues such as eye gaze can aid in learning to segment speech and to attach sounds to referents.

What Are the Limits of SL?

Like other examples of implicit (unsupervised) learning, SL was initially thought to involve minimal overt attention. This was based on the Saffran et al. (1997) study of preschoolers (and adults) who were not instructed to listen to the streams of speech but nevertheless learned to segment them. Of course, one can never know if learners are occasionally directing their overt attention to the speech streams even though, on average, they are not attending to them. Perhaps an occasional "monitoring" of a speech stream is sufficient to extract the underlying statistics. Toro et al. (2005) recently showed that a dual task reduced the performance of adults on a SL task. A more direct test of the role of overt attention was conducted in the visual domain by Turk-Browne, Jungé, and Scholl (2005). They had adults watch streams of simple visual shapes as in Fiser and Aslin (2002a), but they required their subjects to attend only to shapes in one color by having them look for a rare shape repetition. The shapes in the unattended color required no monitoring. The results showed that only statistics residing in the attended color stream were learned, even if there were intervening shapes in the unattended color.

Another limitation on SL is temporal adjacency, though (as described already) this interacts with other Gestalt principles. Newport and Aslin (2004) created streams of syllables in which the statistics forming word groupings resided in nonadjacent syllables. In these stimuli, the TP from syllable 1 to syllable 3 was 1.0, whereas the TP from syllable 1 to syllable 2, from syllable 2 to syllable 3, and from syllable 3 to syllable 1 of the next word was 0.5. Across a large series of experiments, adults failed to learn the words in these nonadjacent syllable languages. In contrast to these negative results, Peña, Bonatti, Nespor, and Mehler (2002) reported successful learning of nonadjacent syllables under similar conditions, but using a different speech synthesizer, a different set of phonetic elements, and Italian- rather than English-speaking adults. It remains unclear why this discrepancy exists, but repeated attempts in our lab to observe learning of these nonadjacent syllable languages by 8- to 24-month-olds have failed over the past three years. In contrast, word groupings formed from the statistics among nonadjacent phonemic segments (consonants or vowels) are readily learned by adults. In this case, the perceptual similarity of the nonadjacent elements (being all consonants or all vowels) may overcome the preference for adjacency.

A final impediment to SL is the familiarity of the elements themselves. Many studies have demonstrated that statistical relations among speech sounds and tones are easily learned (at least in streams that contain adjacent statistics). However, Gebhart, Newport, and Aslin (2004) reported that statistical groupings among unfamiliar nonspeech sounds were very difficult to learn. It took adults more than 45 minutes of exposure across three sessions to extract the same simple triplet-based statistical structure among adjacent elements that was learned in our initial studies in 2 minutes with speech stimuli. This result is similar to findings on early word learning (Fennell & Werker, 2003; Stager & Werker, 1997; Swingley & Aslin, 2007) in which unfamiliar auditory word forms are much more difficult to associate with a picture of an object than familiar word forms.

The foregoing limits on SL—attention, adjacency, and familiarity—all concern the extraction of information from surface forms. But is SL limited only to surface forms? One of the important aspects of language that is not captured by the SL mechanism we have described so far is transfer from one set of surface tokens to novel tokens of the same underlying type (or category). This has been termed *rule learning* (RL) by Marcus, Vijayan, Bandi Rao, and Vishton (1999), who showed that 9-month-olds could learn a pattern such as ABB instantiated in 16 different exemplars and then generalize that ABB pattern to novel exemplars. Since SL operates on surface forms, Marcus et al. argued that RL and SL are qualitatively different mechanisms and suggested that RL necessarily involves encoding variables and relations, not the statistical properties of specific elements.

Additional work in the RL paradigm (Gómez & Gerken, 1999; Saffran & Wilson, 2003) provides strong support for the kind of learning with generalization reported by Marcus et al. (1999) and shows that it is not based on perceptual or phonetic similarity of the surface forms. However, evidence of RL does not eliminate SL as a contributor to the extraction and formation of rules. For example, Gómez (2002), Gómez and Maye (2005), and Mintz (2003) have shown that the distributional properties of the surrounding context affect the formation of a rule (or category). And Endress, Scholl, and Mehler (2005) have shown that repetition of a syllable facilitates rule-based generalizations, especially when repetition occurs at the end of phonological phrases.

More relevant to the distinction between SL and RL is the fact that the RL paradigm differs in an important way from the SL paradigm: The RL paradigm involves strings of finite length (typically three CV or CVC words), whereas the typical SL paradigm involves continuous streams of CV syllables. The pauses that surround finite strings enable the encoding of absolute and relative position information (first element, second element, and so forth) that is lost once a continuous stream of syllables exceeds a dozen syllables. Some of the important differences in learning may arise from this rather than from a qualitative difference of mechanisms.

Clearly, RL operates over categories rather than over the surface forms that serve as the input to SL. But does this imply that RL and SL use a different mechanism? The computation of statistics over categories in RL may involve the same SL mechanism as computation over surface forms. Evidence of RL in tamarins (Hauser, Weiss, & Marcus, 2002) suggests that RL is not unique to humans, and recent evidence (Saffran, Pollak, Seibel, & Shkolnik, 2007) suggests that RL can operate on visual materials (photos of dogs and cats). Thus, despite claims that, unlike SL, RL is unique to spoken language (Fernandes, Marcus, & Little, 2005), it may be more accurate to claim that speech syllables are preferred elements over which RL can operate.

How Might SL Go Awry?

Given the prevalence of SL in studies of normally developing infants, it is natural to ask whether SL may be deficient or delayed in a subset of the general population. For example, perhaps children who exhibit patterns of language delay (e.g., SLI or dyslexia) have difficulty with the earliest phases of language learning. Tests administered in infancy might detect these deficiencies at an age when remediation is effective to enhance long-term outcomes.

A number of features of SL could be susceptible to deficiency or delay. There may be atypical weightings of constraints, such that attention is directed to the wrong units or computations are conducted using the wrong statistics. Another possibility is that the units over which SL is conducted are weakly represented in memory, much like unfamiliar noises in Gebhart et al. (2004), thereby delaying successful SL until additional exposure is obtained.

A more provocative hypothesis is that an early commitment to statistical structure could "block" later SL at higher levels. Support for this hypothesis comes from recent work in both the visual and speech domains using successive presentations of different statistical structures.

Catena, Scholl, and Isola (2005) used the simple successive visual shape paradigm of Fiser and Aslin (2002a) and either preceded or followed a structured stream of shapes with a random stream. Only in the condition where the structured stream came first did adults learn the embedded triplet structure; when the random stream came first, the structure in the subsequent stream was not learned. Gebhart, Aslin, and Newport (in preparation) sequentially presented two different structured streams of speech syllables (two different "languages"), each of which was shown in a baseline experiment to be well learned in 5 minutes of exposure. The two 5-minute streams were presented in immediate succession, without a break, and then a post-test was assessed learning of words versus part-words in each language. Only the first language was learned at above-chance levels (indeed, it was learned as well as when it was presented alone); the second language was not learned. These results suggest that initial extraction of statistical structure inhibits subsequent SL. Indeed, even three times the exposure to the second language was insufficient to bring performance up to the levels of the first language. Interestingly, however, in a follow-up experiment when adults were told there were two languages and were given a 30-second pause between them, performance on both languages was well above chance and similar to performance when either of the languages was presented alone.

CONCLUSIONS

The past decade of research on statistical learning has shown it to be ubiquitous and powerful. SL operates in humans of all ages, in nonhuman species, and in at least three domains (Conway & Christiansen, 2004). Despite the explosive combinatorics of the possible statistics embedded in simple artificial languages or visual scenes, SL solves this problem by employing a set of powerful constraints. Further research will reveal whether these constraints are species and domain specific or if they are universal. It is clear that SL is not sufficient to solve all of the problems necessary for language acquisition. However, it is not yet clear whether SL can account for at least some aspects of rule learning, for example, by operating at the level of categories, or rather whether RL involves a qualitatively different mechanism. Finally, it is possible that an understanding of SL can provide insights into language disorders. A variety of subtle deviations in the constraints on SL could lead to language delays or deficits; exploration of how deviations in SL early in infancy could affect later language development holds the prospect for early diagnosis and remediation of language problems.

ACKNOWLEDGMENTS

The content of this chapter is based on a talk presented in Tempe, Arizona, on September 15–17, 2005, at a workshop sponsored by the Merrill Advanced Studies Center and the National Institute of Child Health and Human Development. This research was supported in part by the Packard Foundation and by National Institutes of Health (NIH) grants HD37082 and DC00167.

ENDNOTES

1. At the time of writing this chapter, Saffran, Aslin, et al. (1996) has been cited 377 times (*Web of Science*).
2. Transitional probability (Miller & Selfridge, 1950) is a temporally ordered version of conditional probability. It is similar to other conditional statistics such as conditional entropy and mutual information. We make no claim about its uniqueness in accounting for the results of SL; most of our results are equally compatible with these other related conditional statistics.
3. Bonatti, Peña, Nespor, and Mehler (2005) replicated these SL results for nonadjacent consonants but not for nonadjacent vowels. The reason for this discrepancy is currently under study.

REFERENCES

Aslin, R. N., Saffran, J. R., & Newport, E. L. (1998). Computation of conditional probability statistics by 8-month-old infants. *Psychological Science, 9*, 321–324.

Baker, C., Olson, C., & Behrmann, M. (2004). Role of attention and perceptual grouping in visual statistical learning. *Psychological Science, 15*, 460–466.

Baldwin, D. A. (1993). Early referential understanding: Infants' ability to recognize referential acts for what they are. *Developmental Psychology, 29*, 832–843.

Bates, E. & Elman, J. (1996). Learning rediscovered. *Science, 274*, 1849–1850.

Bonatti, L., Peña, M., Nespor, M., & Mehler, J. (2005). Linguistic constraints on statistical computations. *Psychological Science, 16*, 451–459.

Bregman, A. S. (1990). *Auditory scene analysis: The perceptual organization of sound.* Cambridge, MA: MIT Press.

Brown, R. & Hanlon, C. (1970). Derivational complexity and order of acquisition. In J. R. Hayes (Ed.), *Cognition and the development of language* (pp. 11–53). New York: Wiley.

Charniak, E. (1993). *Statistical language learning.* Cambridge, MA: MIT Press.

Catena, J. A., Scholl, B. J., & Isola, P. J. (2005). The onset and offset of visual statistical learning. Personal communication.

Conway, C. M. & Christiansen, M. H. (2005). Modality-constrained statistical learning of tactile, visual and auditory sequences. *Journal of Experimental Psychology: Learning, Memory & Cognition, 30*, 24–39.

Creel, S. C., Newport, E. L., & Aslin, R. N. (2004). Distant melodies: Statistical learning of non-adjacent dependencies in tone sequences. *Journal of Experimental Psychology: Learning, Memory, and Cognition, 30*, 1119–1130.

Endress, A. D., Scholl, B. J., & Mehler, J. (2005). The role of salience in the extraction of algebraic rules. *Journal of Experimental Psychology: General, 134*, 406–419.

Fennell, C. T. & Werker, J. F. (2003). Early word learners' ability to access phonetic detail in well-known words. *Language and Speech, 46,* 245–264.

Fernandes, K., Marcus, G., & J. Little (2005, November). *On domain-specificity and a possible dissociation between rule acquisition and rule generalization.* Paper presented at the 30th Boston University Conference on Language Development, Boston, MA.

Fiser, J. & Aslin R. N. (2001). Unsupervised statistical learning of higher-order spatial structures from visual scenes. *Psychological Science, 12,* 499–504.

Fiser, J. & Aslin R. N. (2002a). Statistical learning of higher order temporal structure from visual shape-sequences. *Journal of Experimental Psychology: Learning, Memory, and Cognition, 28,* 458–467.

Fiser, J. & Aslin, R. N. (2002b). Statistical learning of new visual feature combinations by infants. *Proceedings of the National Academy of Sciences, 99,* 15822–15826.

Fiser, J. & Aslin, R. N. (2005). Encoding multi-element scenes: Statistical learning of visual feature hierarchies. *Journal of Experimental Psychology: General, 134,* 521–537.

Fiser, J., Scholl, B. J., & Aslin, R. N. (2007). Perceived object trajectories during occlusion constrain visual statistical learning. *Psychological Bulletin and Review, 14,* 173–178.

Gebhart, A., Aslin, R. N., & Newport, E. L. (2008). Changing structures in mid-stream: Learning along the statistical garden path. Manuscript under review.

Gebhart, A. L., Newport, E. L., & Aslin, R. N. (2004, October). *Statistical learning of adjacent and non-adjacent dependencies among sounds in the non-speech domain.* Poster presented at the annual meeting of the Society for Neuroscience, San Diego, CA.

Gómez, R. L. (2002). Variability and detection of invariant structure. *Psychological Science, 13,* 431–436.

Gómez, R. L. & Gerken, L. A. (1999). Artificial grammar learning by one-year-olds leads to specific and abstract knowledge. *Cognition, 70,* 109–135.

Gómez, R. L. & Maye, J. (2005). The developmental trajectory of nonadjacent dependency learning. *Infancy, 7,* 183–206.

Hauser, M. D., Newport, E. L., & Aslin, R. N. (2001). Segmentation of the speech stream in a nonhuman primate: Statistical learning in cotton top tamarins. *Cognition, 78,* B53–B64.

Hauser, M. D., Weiss, D. J., & Marcus, G. (2002). Rule learning by cotton-top tamarins. *Cognition, 86,* B15–B22.

Harris, Z. (1955). From phoneme to morpheme. *Language, 31,* 190–222.

Hayes, J. R. & Clark, H. H. (1970). Experiments on the segmentation of an artificial speech analogue. In J. R. Hayes (Ed.), *Cognition and the development of language* (pp. 221–234). New York: Wiley.

Hirsh-Pasek, K., Treiman, R., & Schneiderman, M. (1984). Brown and Hanlon revisited: Mothers' sensitivity to ungrammatical forms. *Journal of Child Language, 11,* 81–88.

Howes, D. H. & Solomon, R. L. (1951). Visual duration threshold as a function of word-probability. *Journal of Experimental Psychology, 41,* 401–410.

Hunt, R. H. & Aslin, R. N. (2001). Statistical learning in a serial reaction time task: Simultaneous extraction of multiple statistics. *Journal of Experimental Psychology: General, 130,* 658–680.

Kirkham, N. Z., Slemmer, J. A., & Johnson, S. P. (2002). Visual statistical learning in infancy: Evidence for a domain general learning mechanism. *Cognition, 83,* B35–B42.

Levelt, W. J. M. & Wheeldon, L. (1994). Do speakers have access to a mental syllabary? *Cognition, 50,* 239–269.

Marcus, G. F., Vijayan, S., Bandi Rao, S., & Vishton, P. M. (1999). Rule-learning in seven-month-old infants. *Science, 283,* 77–80.

Miller, G. A. & Selfridge, J. A. (1950). Verbal context and the recall of meaningful material. *American Journal of Psychology, 63,* 176–185.

Mintz, T. H. (2003). Frequent frames as a cue for grammatical categories in child directed speech. *Cognition, 90,* 91–117.

Mintz, T. H., Newport, E. L., & Bever, T. G. (2002). The distributional structure of grammatical categories in speech to young children. *Cognitive Science, 26,* 393–424.

Morgan, J. & Saffran, J. (1995). Emerging integration of sequential and suprasegmental information in preverbal speech segmentation. *Child Development, 66,* 911–936.

Newport, E. L. & Aslin, R. N. (2004). Learning at a distance: I. Statistical learning of non-adjacent dependencies. *Cognitive Psychology, 48,* 127–162.

Newport, E. L., Hauser, M. D., Spaepen, G., & Aslin, R. N. (2004). Learning at a distance: II. Statistical learning of non-adjacent dependencies in a non-human primate. *Cognitive Psychology, 49,* 85–117.

Newport, E. L., Weiss, D. J., Wonnacott, E., & Aslin, R. N. (2004, November). *Statistical learning in speech: Syllables or segments?* Paper presented at the Boston University Conference on Language Development, Boston, MA.

Peña, M., Bonatti, L., Nespor, M., & Mehler, J. (2002). Signal-driven computations in speech processing. *Science, 298,* 604–607.

Rescorla, R. A. & Wagner, A. R. (1972). A theory of Pavlovian conditioning: Variations in the effectiveness of reinforcement and nonreinforcement. In A. H. Black & W. F. Prokasy (Eds.), *Classical conditioning II: Current research and theory* (pp. 64–99). New York: Appleton-Century-Crofts.

Saffran, J. R., Aslin, R. N., & Newport, E. L. (1996). Statistical learning by 8-month-old infants. *Science, 274,* 1926–1928.

Saffran, J. R., Johnson, E. K., Aslin, R. N., & Newport, E. L. (1999). Statistical learning of tone sequences by human infants and adults. *Cognition, 70,* 27–52.

Saffran, J. R., Newport, E. L., & Aslin, R. N. (1996). Word segmentation: The role of distributional cues. *Journal of Memory and Language, 35,* 606–621.

Saffran, J. R., Newport, E. L., Aslin, R. N., Tunick, R. A., & Barrueco, S. (1997). Incidental language learning: Listening (and learning) out of the corner of your ear. *Psychological Science, 8,* 101–105.

Saffran, J. R. & Wilson, D. P. (2003). From syllables to syntax: Multi-level statistical learning by 12-month-old infants. *Infancy, 4,* 273–284.

Saffran, J. R., Pollak, S. D., Seibel, R. L. & Shkolnik, A. (2007). Dog is a dog is a dog: Infant rule learning is not specific to language. *Cognition, 105,* 669–680.

Stager, C. L. & Werker, J. F. (1997). Infants listen for more phonetic detail in speech perception than in word-learning tasks. *Nature, 388,* 381–382.

Swingley, D. (2005). Statistical clustering and the contents of the infant vocabulary. *Cognitive Psychology, 50,* 86–132.

Swingley, D. & Aslin, R. N. (2007). Lexical competition in young children's word learning. *Cognitive Psychology, 54,* 99–132.

Toro, J. M., Sinnett, S., & Soto-Faraco, S. (2005). Speech segmentation by statistical learning depends on attention. *Cognition, 97,* B25–B34.

Toro, J. M. & Trobalón, J. B. (2005). Statistical computations over a speech stream in a rodent. *Perception & Psychophysics, 67,* 867–875.

Turk-Browne, N. B., Jungé, J. A., & Scholl, B. J. (2005). The automaticity of visual statistical learning. *Journal of Experimental Psychology: General, 134,* 552–564.

Vitevitch, M. S. & Luce, P. A. (1998). When words compete: Levels of processing in spoken word perception. *Psychological Science, 9,* 325–329.

Wexler, K. & Culicover, P. W. (1983). *Formal principles of language acquisition.* Cambridge, MA: MIT Press.

Yang, C. D. (2004). Universal grammar, statistics or both? *Trends in Cognitive Sciences, 8,* 451–456.

Yu, C., Ballard, D. H., & Aslin, R. N. (2005). The role of embodied intention in early lexical acquisition. *Cognitive Science, 29,* 961–1005.

3

Acquiring Grammatical Patterns
Constraints on Learning

JENNY R. SAFFRAN

INTRODUCTION

The past decade has seen a resurgence of interest in the possible role played by statistical learning—the detection of patterns in the environment—in the acquisition of language. This is, of course, a very old idea, which received a great deal of attention during the first half of the 20th century. However, learning became something of a "bad word" during the emergence of the disciplines of cognitive science and linguistics. In hindsight, this is due at least in part to the impoverished view of both learning and the learner that dominated these earlier investigations.

The goal of this chapter is to begin to consider a richer conceptualization of statistical learning and to apply it to a central problem in the psychology of language: learning grammar. In particular, we can begin to move away from considering word-to-word statistics and instead consider what happens when there are predictive links between categories of words, as in the grammars of natural languages. More generally, we can assess the current status of the study of statistical learning as a model system for investigating the architecture of infant learning.

STATISTICAL LANGUAGE LEARNING

Could the detection of statistics in language input assist learners? In order for this process to work, it must be the case that (1) relevant statistics exist in the input, and (2) young learners can detect them. These conditions are far from simple to assess. And even in cases where it appears that the relevant statistics exist and are detectable by human infants, a leap of faith is still needed when arguing that infants actually *use* the statistics available in natural language input when learning their native language. Analyses of corpora typically suggest many possible levels of structure that learners might detect and use. For example, analyses of child-directed speech suggest that detection of transitional probabilities between adjacent syllables would be a useful computation when attempting to discover the boundaries between words in fluent speech (Swingley, 2005; see Yang, 2004, for a different view). However, the kinds of experiments typically used to assess the presence of infant learning mechanisms rely on miniature languages that lack the complexity of natural languages. To take a well-studied example, numerous experiments with 8-month-old infants suggest that they can detect the transitional probabilities between syllables in word-segmentation tasks (e.g., Aslin, Saffran, & Newport, 1998; Johnson & Jusczyk, 2001; Saffran, Aslin, & Newport, 1996). How can we tell whether or not these infants, who learn statistics in segmentation-like tasks in the lab, are using them for native language learning? This problem only gets worse as we consider more complex aspects of language, for which it is extremely difficult both to assess the availability of relevant statistics in native language input and to discover the relevant learning mechanisms in infants.

Despite these difficulties, we have seen important progress in addressing questions concerning the role played by statistical learning in language acquisition. Since the initial studies demonstrating that infants are sensitive to transitional probabilities in word-segmentation tasks (Aslin et al., 1998; Saffran et al., 1996), researchers have demonstrated that infant language learners are sensitive to multiple levels of statistical regularities during the first year of postnatal life. Infants can use the distributions of phoneme exemplars along an acoustic continuum to discern artificial phoneme categories (Maye, Werker, & Gerken, 2002). This ability is particularly notable given the detailed grain at which infants must represent the individual sounds whose distributions they are tracking. They can track relationships between nonadjacent syllables, at least under some circumstances (Gómez, 2002; Gómez & Maye, 2005) Infants are also able to track statistical information pertaining to the distribution of elements in sequences, such as the distributions of stressed versus unstressed syllables within words (Thiessen & Saffran, 2007). They can also track higher-level relationships in simple grammar-learning tasks, such as noting which words permissibly precede one another or the location of word repetitions in a sequence (e.g., Gómez & Gerken, 1999; Marcus, Vijayan, Bandi Rao, & Vishton, 1999; Saffran & Wilson, 2003).

Each of the aforementioned studies exposed infants to the relevant input for just a few minutes, demonstrating that infants are capable of rapid implicit learning in the absence of any external reinforcement. Presumably, learning itself is reinforcing in the sense that it allows infants to discern the signal amid the noise, affording a dimensionality reduction that eases the burden of processing language. This reinforcement from signal detection is above and beyond the presumed benefits of acquiring a communicative system, which are likely to be minimal in these experiments as the stimuli are delivered by a disembodied voice in the absence of a social context. The benefits of communication are also unlikely to be a primary motivation in these studies because infants show similar learning in parallel nonlinguistic tasks. For example, infants can learn the same kinds of sequential statistics when they are implemented in sequences of sine wave tones (e.g., Saffran & Griepentrog, 2001; Saffran, Johnson, Aslin, & Newport, 1999), visual object arrays (Fiser & Aslin, 2002), and looming geometric shapes (Kirkham, Slemmer, & Johnson, 2002). Similarly, nonhuman animals, including cotton-top tamarin monkeys (Hauser, Newport, & Aslin, 2001) and even rats (Toro & Trobalón, 2005), can learn these sequential statistics.

The burgeoning empirical results suggest that statistical learning is a powerful mechanism, available as early as it has been measured in postnatal life. On the one hand, this is an extremely exciting development. Studies such as these have allowed researchers to go beyond descriptions of *what* infants know at age X and age Y, uncovering potential mechanisms that might explain *how* infants' knowledge changes from age X to age Y. This opens the door to eventual studies examining the brain mechanisms underlying language learning; such studies are already being performed with adults (e.g., Friederici, Bahlmann, Heim, Schubotz, & Anwander, 2006), and new technologies for infant studies may be promising in this regard (e.g., Aslin, 2006).

Statistical learning is also becoming more "mainstream" across theories of language acquisition. It is now relatively uncontroversial to assert that statistical learning plays at least some role in acquiring aspects of language that vary widely cross-linguistically, such as native language phonemes, word boundaries, and other highly variable linguistic structures. For such linguistic structures, some sort of learning account has always been needed. Statistical regularities in the input are likely to be one of several useful sources of information that learners can use when discovering native language structures; critically, we assume that infants are learning to use multiple cues in combination (e.g., Morgan & Saffran, 1995). Other features of the learning situation that appear to facilitate statistical learning are the use of infant-directed intonation contours (Thiessen, Hill, & Saffran, 2005) and face-to-face interactive contexts (Kuhl, Tsao, & Liu, 2003). Studies that attempt to delimit constraints on the operation of statistical learning mechanisms are particularly helpful in this regard, as they illuminate perceptual constraints that determine the kinds of statistics readily computed by learners. These limits on statistical learning may help us to understand why languages contain some structures but not others (e.g., Newport & Aslin, 2004; Newport, Weiss, Wonnacott, & Aslin, 2004; Saffran & Thiessen, 2003).

ISSUES FACING STATISTICAL LANGUAGE LEARNING ACCOUNTS

On the other hand, the power and ubiquity of statistical learning are potentially quite problematic. Learning-based explanations are neither readily available nor easily testable for many important aspects of language. When considering language acquisition theories in which statistical learning plays an explanatory role, there are four major issues that merit consideration and temper enthusiasm for such theories. Note that these are among the issues that initially (and continually) motivated generative linguistics accounts in which an innate universal grammar plays a central explanatory role.

First, *how is abstract linguistic structure acquired?* When we think about statistical learning, the examples that come to mind concern statistics computed over exemplars that are quite concrete: probabilities of syllable co-occurrences, or distributions of acoustic features. However, a hallmark of human language is its abstractness, both in terms of its structure, which is often nontransparent, and its elements, which are also abstract in that they afford generalizations (e.g., nouns, morphemes, phrases). Does sufficient statistical information exist to allow learners to detect abstract structure that is not transparently mirrored by the surface patterns of sentences? If so, can humans detect this information? Can humans detect statistics over abstract patterns, like lexical categories? The answers to these questions are critical in delimiting the appropriate role for statistical learning in language acquisition.

Second, *why are human languages so similar?* The remarkable commonalities shared by the world's languages are among the major discoveries of 20th-century linguistics. These include everything from the structure of the vowel space to the ubiquity of the major grammatical categories to complex aspects of syntax, such as head direction and recursion. When we invoke learning as a driving force in language acquisition, we need to find a way to explain why these similarities have emerged in languages that are historically unrelated. In particular, if statistical learning is so powerful, why isn't there more variability in the structure of human languages?

Third, *why can't nonhumans acquire human language?* Decades of research on animal learning have illustrated the sophisticated learning capacities of nonhuman animals. Classic studies have demonstrated animals' abilities to probability match and maximize (boost high probabilities while damping lower probabilities) across varied circumstances and domains (e.g., Gallistel, 1993). Rats are able to compute conditional probabilities in operant conditioning paradigms (e.g., Rescorla, 1968). Rats and cotton-top tamarins can compute sequential statistics in word-segmentation tasks (Hauser et al., 2001; Toro & Trobólan, 2005), and tamarins can track patterns of word identity in simple grammar learning tasks (Hauser, Weiss, & Marcus, 2002). Quail can track distributions of phoneme exemplars to discover phoneme categories (Kluender, Diehl, & Killeen, 1987), and starlings appear to be able to discover simple recursive structures following extensive training (Gentner, Fenn, Margoliash, & Nusbaum, 2006). Methods unavailable to human researchers have even demonstrated that neurons in nonhuman animals are attuned to probabilities. For example, midbrain dopamine neurons rapidly adapt to the information provided by reward-predicting stimuli (including probability of reward) in macaques (Tobler, Fiorillo, & Schultz, 2005), and cortical neurons in cats are responsive to the probabilities with which particular sounds occur (e.g., Ulanovsky, Las, & Nelken, 2003). If statistical learning plays a central role in language acquisition, then given all this computational sophistication, shouldn't nonhuman animals get further with language acquisition than they do?

Fourth, there is the *richness of the stimulus* problem, which is the flip side of the classic poverty of the stimulus problem (e.g., the lack of relevant information in the input). Given the vastness and complexity of speech heard by infants, how do learners decide which statistics to compute over which primitives? Any given stimulus set admits a myriad of potential analyses; the fact that it is so difficult to control artificial language stimuli foreshadows the magnitude of this problem in natural language corpora (Seidenberg, MacDonald, & Saffran, 2002). An adequate account that includes statistical learning mechanisms must explain how infants home in on the right generalizations without being sidetracked by incorrect ones.

This list can go on; the point is that demonstrating the existence of powerful learning mechanisms in infant learners raises more questions than it answers. More traditional theories have accounts that address—and, indeed, are motivated by—these issues. Can we reconcile learning-based theories with facts about how language works (or at least with our theories about how languages work)? In particular, is there something about how young humans learn that can help us to understand why, for example, some structures appear across the languages of the world while others do not? Similarly, can we find evidence to explain how infants winnow down the rich stimulus to discover the right kinds of patterns for natural language?

This emphasis on discovering constraints on learning has driven much recent research in our lab and elsewhere (e.g., Bonatti, Peña, Nespor, & Mehler, 2005; Christiansen & Dale, 2004; Conway & Christiansen, 2005; Endress, Scholl, & Mehler, 2005; Gerken, 2006; Newport & Aslin, 2004; Saffran, 2003; Saffran, Reeck, Neibuhr, & Wilson, 2005; Saffran & Thiessen, 2003). There may be features of human perceptual or cognitive systems that constrain the generalizations drawn over language input. Structures that are the best fit with infant abilities to perceive and process information are the most likely to recur cross-linguistically. Part of what makes human language special, then, is that language is shaped by human learners. The goal of the research described in the rest of this chapter was to flesh out this idea and, in doing so, to take on the challenges posed by the issues facing learning-based accounts discussed herein.

STATISTICAL LANGUAGE LEARNING OF PHRASE STRUCTURE I: ADULTS AND CHILDREN

In our most comprehensive investigation of constraints on statistical learning to date, we have been investigating the acquisition of one aspect of syntax: *phrase structure*. Whatever one's theory of grammatical structure, it is evident that words are not simply strung together in sequence. Some words and word classes are linked together much more tightly than others. Consider the sentence, "The mouse ate the green cheese." Intuitively, "the" and "mouse" are more tightly linked together than "mouse ate" or "ate the." Similarly, the three-word sequence "the green cheese" is more tightly linked than "the mouse ate" or "mouse ate the," and so forth. These links are not merely due to the fact that some of these word pairs/triads occur more often than others, a point forcefully made by Noam Chomsky's famous sentence, "Colorless green ideas sleep furiously" (Chomsky, 1957). This sentence, of course, was used to argue that humans' knowledge of grammar goes beyond frequency of occurrence of word pairs to subsume knowledge of abstract relationships between word classes. Our research takes this point seriously, as we attempt to examine links that extend beyond individual words to uncover relationships between classes of words.

To begin our investigations of phrase structure learning, we first asked whether there are cues in the input that might help learners to discover rudimentary phrases in strings of words. Prior work had largely focused on potential roles for correlated cues such as prosodic structures (e.g., Morgan, Meier, & Newport, 1987, 1989). Our goal was to consider potential sequential statistical cues that might point learners to phrasal units. In particular, we decided to examine a distributional cue that had been noted decades earlier by linguists in the structuralist tradition—namely, dependencies between elements within phrases. One way to characterize a phrase is that it contains *predictive dependencies* between its parts. For example, consider a noun phrase (NP), which in its simplest form contains an obligatory noun and an optional determiner (words like *a* and *the*). The presence of a determiner provides a strong cue that a noun must be present as well—if not right next door, then somewhere upstream or downstream, depending on other structural characteristics of the language. Thus, the determiner predicts the presence of the noun; the two elements are coupled, providing a cue to the learner that suggests that those elements should be clumped together. Note that this sort of cue does not require the infant to understand the meanings of the determiner or the noun, just the categories as defined by the distributions of the words.

Similar predictive dependencies exist for other phrasal types. For example, noun phrases can occur without transitive verbs, but the presence of a transitive verb provides a strong cue that an object noun phrase must be present—this link suggests the presence of a verb phrase (verb plus object NP). Similarly, noun phrases occur without prepositions (words like *above, in, over*), but the presence of a preposition provides a strong cue that a noun phrase must be present—this link suggests the presence of a prepositional phrase (preposition plus NP). Note that these predictive dependencies are unidirectional; nouns can occur without determiners but not vice versa. Similar patterns can be seen for the other phrase types.

Taking the prior literature on adult artificial grammar learning as our starting point (e.g., Morgan & Newport, 1981; Morgan et al., 1987, 1989), we began by running experiments designed to assess the utility of the predictive dependency cue to phrase units (Saffran, 2001). Adult learners listened to sentences from an artificial grammar in which the only cues to phrasal units were the dependencies between artificial word classes. Each word class contained 2–4 monosyllabic nonsense words, such as *biff* and *dup*. For example, an A-phrase consisted of an A word paired with an optional D word. The A word could occur either alone or with a D word, but whenever a D word occurred, an A word had to also be present—this pattern simulates the kinds of predictive dependencies seen between a noun and a determiner. Similar patterns were present for other word-class pairs within the phrases of this language.

Importantly, there were no meanings attached to the nonsense words in the language; listeners merely listened to sequences of words organized according to the grammar. In addition, the word categories were not marked for learners in any way (e.g., words within a category did not share phonological characteristics). The classes were discoverable via the distributions of words in sentences, as are lexical categories in natural languages (e.g., Cartwright & Brent, 1997; Mintz, Newport, & Bever, 2002; Redington, Chater, & Finch, 1998). To minimize the likelihood that learners would simply impose their knowledge of English phrase structure, this language was designed to be head-final (e.g., the predictive D word follows the nonpredictive A word), unlike English, which is head-initial (e.g., the predictive determiners precede the nonpredictive nouns). Adults and first- and second-grade children successfully learned this grammar; that is, they performed better than chance on a forced-choice test in which novel grammatical and ungrammatical sentences were systematically paired (Saffran, 2001). The presence of the predictive dependencies apparently facilitated the acquisition of an abstract feature of the language–phrase structure.

If it is the case that predictive dependencies enhance learnability, then we would expect learners to perform better when learning a novel language that contains these dependencies as opposed to a language that does not. We followed this logic in subsequent experiments in which we contrasted the acquisition of two artificial grammars by adults and first- and second-grade children (Saffran, 2002) (Figure 3.1). One of the languages, the P-language (for predictive), shown in (1) in Figure 3.1, was a slightly simplified version of the language used by Saffran (2001), which included predictive dependencies as cues to phrasal units. The

(1) **P-Language**	(2) **NP-Language**
S → AP + BP + (CP)	S → AP + BP
AP → A + (D)	AP → {(A) + (D)}
BP → CP + F	BP → CP + F
CP → C + (G)	CP → {(C) + (G)}

Figure 3.1   The artificial grammars used by Saffran (2002).

other language, the N-language (for nonpredictive), shown in (2) in Figure 3.1, did not contain predictive dependencies. For example, in the A-phrase in the N-language, both the A and D words were optional. Thus, the presence of a D word did not predict an A word and vice versa. This language still contained a phrase structure of a sort, in that there was a negative predictive relationship between A words and D words: One element must occur, so if an A word did not occur, a D word must occur, and vice versa. However, this sort of relationship is not characteristic of natural languages, and negative predictions are likely to be quite difficult to learn.

Following exposure, learners were tested on novel grammatical and ungrammatical sentences. In order to use the same test for learners exposed to the P-language and learners exposed to the N-language, the grammatical test items were both novel and legal in both languages, and the ungrammatical test items were illegal. Importantly, we implemented a number of controls to attempt to ensure that P-language learners would not outperform N-language learners for reasons independent of the presence or absence of predictive dependencies. For example, both languages contained similar vocabulary sizes, which generated similar numbers of possible sentences as well as sentences of similar lengths.

Adults and children exposed to the predictive P-language reliably outperformed those exposed to the nonpredictive N-language (Saffran, 2002). Although performance exceeded chance on the N-language, suggesting that at least some aspects of this system are learnable, P-language learners performed best. Learning in this task was facilitated by the presence of predictive dependencies. Despite the many other consistent patterns present in the N-language, the addition of predictive dependencies had a robust effect on learning, supporting the claim that some structures inherent in natural languages may help to make language easier to acquire.

The idea that humans may be constrained to find some patterns easier to learn than others makes contact with another major theoretical debate in cognitive science and neuroscience: Are our learning, processing, and knowledge systems specialized to operate in particular domains, or do we possess learning mechanisms that are sufficiently general that they can operate across stimuli drawn from multiple domains? The modularity question has its roots in philosophical debates over the nature of the mind (e.g., Fodor, 1983), and has received extensive attention in neuroimaging studies attempting to discern whether, for example, the fusiform gyrus is an area dedicated to faces or an area that processes stimuli that the brain is expert at perceiving due to extensive experience (e.g., Gauthier, Skudlarski, Gore, & Anderson, 2000; Kanwisher & Yovel, 2006).

Even if neuroimaging studies should show conclusively that adult systems are modularized and that processing is domain specific, the question of the ontogenesis of those systems remains. Recent investigations in developmental cognitive science have endeavored to ask whether the particular learning mechanisms that subserve the acquisition of domains of knowledge are themselves domain specific (for a review, see McMullen & Saffran, 2004; Saffran & Thiessen, 2007). As discussed already, infants are able to track sequential statistics in nonlinguistic materials (e.g., Kirkham et al., 2002; Saffran et al., 1999; Saffran & Griepentrog, 2001), suggesting that this mechanism is not tailored specifically for language. Infants can also learn simple grammatical structures in both linguistic and nonlinguistic domains (Marcus et al., 1999; Saffran et al., 2007). Similarly, cottontop tamarin monkeys can perform the simple grammar learning task used by Marcus et al. (1999), suggesting that this ability is unlikely to be part of human cognition solely for language learning (Hauser et al., 2002).

Given these considerations, we chose to examine whether the use of predictive dependencies was limited to linguistic phrases. We hypothesized that using predictive relationships between elements would not be limited to linguistic input, because this sort of information should be useful for discovering structures across multiple domains. Adult learners were exposed to "languages" made of computerized nonlinguistic sounds that were highly discriminable: alert sounds from Windows '98 (Saffran, 2002). Each sound was treated as a word and was organized into "sentences" following the P-language and N-Language grammars. Everything about the experiment was otherwise identical to the studies using linguistic stimuli. Despite the use of nonlinguistic stimuli, P-Language learners continued to significantly outperform N-Language learners. This result was replicated with a new set of auditory nonlinguistic stimuli: computerized bells and whistles, which were designed to be hard to label verbally so that the linguistic system wouldn't be used as a crutch to solve the task (ibid.).

To explore whether predictive dependencies play a role in learning nonauditory stimuli, we next developed a visual analogue of this task using computerized nonsense shapes. The timing parameters were the same as those used in the auditory tasks, with shapes appearing sequentially. Interestingly, under these circumstances, both the P-language and N-language were learned at equivalent levels, significantly better than chance (Saffran, 2002). This suggests no particular benefit for predictive dependencies given sequential visual information. There appears to be an interaction between the structure of the materials and the mode of presentation. In a subsequent experiment, we discovered that when the same shapes were presented simultaneously in a spatial array rather than sequentially, P-language learners again outperformed N-language learners (ibid.). Unlike auditory stimuli, structure in visual stimuli is typically spatial, not sequential, suggesting either that extensive experience in each modality has affected how we learn or that the visual and auditory systems may be predisposed to detect different kinds of structures (see Conway & Christiansen, 2005, for a similar argument using a different statistical learning task).

This body of experimental results supports the claim that some kinds of patterns are more learnable than others. In particular, the predictive dependencies that are characteristic of linguistic phrases provide a cue to learners. This cue is not limited to linguistic materials; nonlinguistic materials that are a good fit to this learning mechanism are also more learnable if they contain predictive dependencies. Such results lend credence to an account that suggests that human languages are shaped by constraints on human learning that are not specific to the linguistic domain. This sort of view is consistent with the fact that the natural environment contains many layers of predictable structure, from paths of motion in objects to relationships between colors in different ambient luminance levels. If our brains have become attuned to these naturally occurring predictive structures, then we might speculate that human languages have been molded accordingly.

STATISTICAL LANGUAGE LEARNING OF PHRASE STRUCTURE II: HUMAN INFANTS AND COTTON-TOP TAMARIN MONKEYS

If human learning mechanisms play a role in shaping the structure of human languages, then we would expect to find that even infants should be able to learn best when predictive dependencies are present in the input. However, nonhuman animals may not be able to make use of these dependencies in the same way as humans if this is a constraint specific to human learning (e.g., Newport, Hauser, Spaepen, & Aslin, 2004). To further explore these issues, we are engaged in a comparative study of grammar learning by infants and cotton-top tamarin monkeys (Saffran et al., 2008). The study is designed to address three questions:

1. Can infants learn materials of this complexity in the lab?
2. Does this process look like natural language learning?
3. Do infants and monkeys diverge in what they can and cannot learn?

We took advantage of previously developed methods that have shown comparable results for human infants and tamarin monkeys (e.g., Hauser et al., 2001, 2002).

In our first experiment, we used a scaled-down version of the P- and N-languages; we were concerned that the large languages previously used by Saffran (2002) to test adults would simply be too complex for 12-month-old infants and monkeys. We thus took the grammars from Saffran (2002), but instead of using word classes that contained 2–4 words we used only a single word from each word class (e.g., one A word, one C word). Learners heard a corpus of 8 sentences ("Biff lum dupp. Rud klor dupp..." repeated for either about 5 minutes (infants) or 2 hours (tamarins). Learners were then tested on novel ungrammatical test items versus familiar grammatical test items (which were taken from the corpus of 8 familiarized sentences due to the small size of this language). The dependent variable for the infants was looking time to the test items, as indexed by a head-turn toward a speaker that was playing the sounds. The dependent variable for the tamarins was the number of times they oriented to the different test items. Both species showed a significant novelty preference, as evidenced by greater interest in the ungrammatical stimuli, but only for the P-language. Even though the N-language was equally small, generating only 8 sentences, and the grammatical test items were drawn from the familiarization corpus, neither the infants nor the tamarins showed any evidence of discriminating the grammatical and ungrammatical sentences. These findings suggest that at least in very simple linguistic domains, both infants and tamarins can make use of predictive dependencies.[1]

What happens when the materials are scaled up to be more complex? In a subsequent experiment, we exposed the infants and tamarins to stimuli identical to the P-language and N-language used with adults and school-aged children by Saffran (2002). As with the adults, the stimulus set consisted of 50 sentences drawn from either the P-language or the N-language, repeated several times (23.5 minutes of exposure for infants, 2 hours for tamarins). The grammatical and ungrammatical test items used in this experiment were all novel. As with the smaller languages used in our first experiment, infants continued to show evidence of learning only in the P-language condition; tamarins, however, showed no evidence of learning in either condition (Saffran et al., 2008). Thus, even when the grammars are written over word categories and generate more than 2,000 possible sentences, infants showed successful learning when predictive dependencies were available. When predictive dependencies were not available, infants were unable to discriminate between grammatical and ungrammatical sentences. These results are consistent with the hypothesis that human learning mechanisms may have shaped the structure of natural languages; the kinds of predictive patterns that occur in human languages apparently facilitate learning even in infancy.

Unlike the successful infants, the tamarins were unable to take advantage of the predictive dependencies in these stimuli. They apparently succeeded when learning patterns of *words*, as in the scaled-down language experiment, but not when learning patterns of *categories* in the full language experiment. One can imagine many hypotheses for why this might be the case, including working memory constraints, difficulty categorizing elements into word classes, or an inability to learn a phrase-structure grammar. To begin to tease apart these potential explanations, we ran a third study in which we tested the infants and tamarins on a grammar intermediate in size between our first two experiments; the word classes contained only two words each, and the P-language grammar was simplified to shorten the sentences. Despite these simplifications, the tamarins continued to fail to show evidence of learning, while the infants continued to successfully discriminate grammatical and ungrammatical sentences (Saffran et al., 2008).

IMPLICATIONS, CAVEATS, AND CONCLUSIONS

While infants appear to be facile at discovering statistical patterns that occur across word categories, tamarins are not, at least under the testing circumstances used in these studies. This discovery may have important implications for theories of statistical learning. Infants can track statistics over abstract categories, like word classes. These classes may have no meanings in our artificial languages, but they are certainly more abstract than syllables, phonemes, or even the individual words that are typically thought of as the primitives over which statistical learning operates. Because word classes, or grammatical categories, play such a critical role in natural language structure, an ability to track their statistics is a prerequisite for applying statistical learning theories to syntactic structure. To the extent that tamarins have difficulty either in the categorization process or in detecting the relationships between categories, their ability to learn anything beyond a very simple grammar is likely to be limited.

Results such as these bolster theories that suggest that statistical learning plays a role in human language acquisition and processing. Infants can learn some grammatical patterns more readily than others. These patterns are mirrored in natural language input, and they are not equally learnable across species. Similar arguments are emerging in phonology (e.g., Gerken, 2004; Newport & Aslin, 2004; Saffran & Thiessen, 2003). One reason these new lines of research are exciting is that developmental psycholinguists are beginning to examine descriptions drawn from linguistics through the lens of learning. We can thus attempt to develop explanations for why languages work the way they do by calling on our understanding of learning as well as language production and processing.

Such investigations also reinforce the obvious yet often overlooked point that more than one learning mechanism must be at work (see also Marcus, 2000). Infants can track sequential transitional probabilities of elements, as shown in many studies over the past decade. However, sequential transitional probability detection cannot explain the P-language versus N-language results (Saffran et al., 2008). Overall bigram statistics (of word pairs or word-category pairs) do not predict the observed outcomes. Instead, the predictive dependencies appear to serve as a bracketing cue, pointing out the relevant subunits over which to do the analyses. Critiques that equate "statistical learning" with bigram transitional probabilities are underselling the potential of this approach. The challenge, of course, is to specify which computations human infants can perform and to link them to particular aspects of language; this is a major undertaking that will likely take many investigators and methodologies.

Another remaining issue is the extent to which these laboratory investigations are tapping the mechanisms used for language learning "in the wild." Certainly, the sheer complexity of the full P-language is an important step in this direction. Such systems, which incorporate the kinds of structures that are actually seen in human languages (albeit in miniature), are an important step beyond the artificial grammar learning studies previously done with infants using finite-state grammars (e.g., Gómez & Gerken, 1999; Saffran & Wilson, 2003) or sequences containing identical repeated elements (e.g., Marcus et al., 1999). Ongoing work is beginning to include multiple cues, not just to ask which cues infants weight above others (e.g., Johnson & Jusczyk, 2001; Mattys, Jusczyk, Luce, & Morgan, 1999; Thiessen & Saffran, 2003) but also to find out how infants integrate the multiple sources of information in complex linguistic input (e.g., Morgan & Saffran, 1995). Recent studies tie the output of statistical learning to the kinds of tasks that infants must perform when linking together multiple learning processes, such as using the output of word segmentation as labels for novel objects (e.g., Graf Estes, Evans, Alibali, & Saffran, 2007). We are also beginning to investigate individual differences in statistical learning, both as they might relate to variance among typically developing children and as a possible explanation for some of the language-learning difficulties seen in children with specific language impairment (Evans & Saffran, 2005).

Learning thus may be able to explain aspects of development that are not transparently due to learning. Returning to our list of the four main issues facing learning-oriented studies, we can see that statistical learning research is *beginning* to tackle (1) how abstract linguistic structure is acquired, (2) why human languages are so similar, (3) why nonhumans can't acquire human language, and (4) the richness of the stimulus problem. On this view, appeals to a set of so-called general learning mechanisms do not mean "blank slate"; statistical learning processes are clearly constrained along multiple dimensions. Appeals to learning also do not entail a non-nativist stance. Indeed, some learning mechanisms must be innate, or else the young infant would have no way to discover structure in the environment. Discovering not only what infants *can* learn but also what infants *can't* learn is likely to be extremely informative in developing theories about the ontogenesis of linguistic knowledge. The structure of human languages may be due, at least in part, to the structure of human learning mechanisms that were not themselves tailored for language learning.

ACKNOWLEDGMENTS

Preparation of this manuscript was supported by grants to the author from the National Institute of Child Health and Human Development (NICHD) (R01HD37466) and the National Science Foundation (NSF) (BCS-9983630). Many thanks to Jessica Hay, Erin McMullen, Bruna Pelucchi, Alexa Romberg, and Sarah Sahni for helpful comments.

ENDNOTE

1. While adults performed better than chance on the N-language (though worse than on the P-language), infants failed to discriminate N-language test items from one another. We do not know whether this suggests a meaningful difference in our subject populations or if, more likely, the infant testing method is less sensitive, and assesses fewer test contrasts, than the adult testing method.

REFERENCES

Aslin, R. N. (2006, June). *Near-infrared spectroscopy for functional studies of brain activity in infants: Promise, prospects, and challenges.* Symposium presented at the International Conference on Infant Studies, Kyoto, Japan.

Aslin, R. N., Saffran, J. R., & Newport, E. L. (1998). Computation of conditional probability statistics by 8-month-old infants. *Psychological Science, 9*(4), 321–324.

Bonatti, L. L., Peña, M., Nespor, M., & Mehler, J. (2005). Linguistic constraints on statistical computations. *Psychological Science, 6*(6), 451–459.

Cartwright, T. A. & Brent, M. R. (1997). Syntactic categorization in early language acquisition: Formalizing the role of distributional analysis. *Cognition, 63*, 121–170.

Chomsky, N. (1957). *Syntactic structures.* The Hague: Mouton.

Christiansen, M. H. & Dale, R. (2004). The role of learning and development in language evolution: a connectionist perspective. In K. Oller, D. U. Griebel, & K. Plunkett (Eds.), *The evolution of communication systems: A comparative approach* (pp. 91–109). Cambridge, MA: MIT Press.

Conway, C. & Christiansen, M. H. (2005). Modality constrained statistical learning of tactile, visual, and auditory sequences. *Journal of Experimental Psychology: Learning, Memory & Cognition, 31*, 24–39.

Endress, A. D., Scholl, B. J., & Mehler, J. (2005). The role of salience in the extraction of algebraic rules. *Journal of Experimental Psychology: General, 134*(3), 406–419.

Evans, J. & Saffran, J. R. (2005, November). *Statistical learning in children with specific language impairment.* Paper presented at the Boston University Conference on Language Development, Boston, MA.

Fiser, J. & Aslin, R. N. (2002). Statistical learning of new visual feature combinations by infants. *Proceedings of the National Academy of Sciences, 99*, 15822–15826.

Fodor, J. A. (1983). *The modularity of mind.* Cambridge, MA: MIT Press.

Friederici, A. D., Bahlmann, J., Heim, S., Schubotz, R. I., & Anwander, A. (2006). The brain differentiates human and non-human grammars: Functional localization and structural connectivity. *Proceedings of the National Academy of Sciences, 103,* 2458–2463.

Gallistel, C. R. (1993). *The organization of learning.* Cambridge, MA: MIT Press.

Gauthier, I., Skudlarski, P., Gore, J. C., & Anderson, A. W. (2000). Expertise for cars and birds recruits brain areas involved in face recognition. *Nature Neuroscience, 3,* 191–197.

Gentner, T. Q., Fenn, K. M., Margoliash, D., & Nusbaum, H. C. (2006). Recursive syntactic pattern learning by songbirds. *Nature, 440,* 1204–1207.

Gerken, L. A. (2004). Nine-month-olds extract structural principles required for natural language. *Cognition, 93,* B89–B96.

Gerken, L. A. (2006). Decisions, decisions: infant language learning when multiple generalizations are possible. *Cognition, 98,* B67–B74.

Gómez, R. L. & Gerken, L. (1999). Artificial grammar learning by 1-year-olds leads to specific and abstract knowledge. *Cognition, 70*(2), 109–135.

Gómez, R. L. (2002). Variability and detection of invariant structure. *Psychological Science, 13*(5), 431–436.

Gómez, R. L. & Maye, J. (2005). The developmental trajectory of nonadjacent dependency learning. *Infancy, 7,* 183–206.

Graf Estes, K. M., Evans, J., Alibali, M. W., & Saffran, J. R. (2007). Can infants map meaning to newly segmented words? Statistical segmentation and word learning. *Psychological Science, 18*(3), 254–260.

Hauser, M. D., Newport, E. L., & Aslin, R. N. (2001). Segmentation of the speech stream in a non human primate: Statistical learning in cotton top tamarins. *Cognition, 78*(3), B53–B64.

Hauser, M. D., Weiss, D. J., & Marcus, G. (2002). Rule learning by cotton-top tamarins. *Cognition, 86,* B15–B22.

Johnson, E. K. & Jusczyk, P. W. (2001). Word segmentation by 8-month-olds: When speech cues count more than statistics. *Journal of Memory & Language, 44*(4), 548–567.

Kanwisher, N. & Yovel, G. (2006). The fusiform face area: A cortical region specialized for the perception of faces. *Philosophical Transactions of the Royal Society of London B, 361,* 2109–2128.

Kirkham, N. Z., Slemmer, J. A., & Johnson, S. P. (2002). Visual statistical learning in infancy: Evidence for a domain general learning mechanism. *Cognition, 83,* B35–B42.

Kluender, K. R., Diehl, R. L., & Killeen, P. R. (1987). Japanese quail can form phonetic categories. *Science, 237,* 1195–1197.

Kuhl, P. K., Tsao, F. M, & Liu, H. M. (2003). Foreign-language experience in infancy: Effects of short-term exposure and social interaction on phonetic learning. *Proceedings of the National Academy of Sciences, USA, 100,* 9096–9101.

Marcus, G. F. (2000). Pa bi ku and ga ti ga: Two mechanisms children could use to learn about language and the world. *Current Directions in Psychological Science, 9,* 145–147.

Marcus, G. F., Vijayan, S., Bandi Rao, S., & Vishton, P. (1999). Rule learning by seven-month-old infants. *Science, 283,* 77–80.

Mattys, S. L., Jusczyk, P. W., Luce, P. A., & Morgan, J. L. (1999). Phonotactic and prosodic effects on word segmentation in infants. *Cognitive Psychology, 38,* 465–494.

Maye, J., Werker, J. F., & Gerken, L. (2002). Infant sensitivity to distributional information can affect phonetic discrimination. *Cognition, 82*(3), B101–B111.

McMullen, E. & Saffran, J. R. (2004). Music and language: A developmental comparison. *Music Perception, 21,* 289–311.

Mintz, T. H., Newport, E. L., & Bever, T. G. (2002). The distributional structure of grammatical categories in speech to young children. *Cognitive Science, 26,* 393–424.

Morgan, J. L., Meier, R. P., & Newport, E. L. (1987). Structural packaging in the input to language learning: Contributions of prosodic and morphological marking of phrases to the acquisition of language. *Cognitive Psychology, 19,* 498–550.

Morgan, J. L., Meier, R. P., & Newport, E. L. (1989). Facilitating the acquisition of syntax with cross-sentential cues to phrase structure. *Journal of Memory and Language, 28,* 360–374.

Morgan, J. L. & Newport, E. L. (1981). The role of constituent structure in the induction of an artificial language. *Journal of Verbal Learning and Verbal Behavior, 20,* 67–85.

Morgan, J. L. & Saffran, J. R. (1995). Emerging integration of segmental and suprasegmental information in prelingual speech segmentation. *Child Development, 66,* 911–936.

Newport, E. L. & Aslin, R. N. (2004). Learning at a distance: I. Statistical learning of non-adjacent dependencies. *Cognitive Psychology, 48,* 127–162.

Newport, E. L., Hauser, M. D., Spaepen, G., & Aslin, R. N. (2004). Learning at a distance: II. Statistical learning of non-adjacent dependencies in a non-human primate. *Cognitive Psychology, 49,* 85–117.

Newport, E. L., Weiss, D. J., Wonnacott, E., & Aslin, R. N. (2004, November). *Statistical learning in speech: Syllables or segments?* Paper presented at the 29th Annual Boston University Conference on Language Development, Boston, MA.

Redington, M., Chater, N., & Finch, S. (1998). Distributional information: A powerful cue for acquiring syntactic categories. *Cognitive Science, 22,* 4250–469.

Rescorla, R. A. (1968). Probability of shock in the presence and absence of CS in fear conditioning. *Journal of Comparative and Physiological Psychology, 66,* 1–5.

Saffran, J. R. (2001). The use of predictive dependencies in language learning. *Journal of Memory and Language, 44,* 493–515.

Saffran, J. R. (2002). Constraints on statistical language learning. *Journal of Memory and Language, 47,* 172–196.

Saffran, J. R. (2003). Statistical language learning: Mechanisms and constraints. *Current Directions in Psychological Science, 12,* 110–114.

Saffran, J. R., Aslin, R. N., & Newport, E. L. (1996). Statistical learning by 8-month-old infants. *Science, 274*(5294), 1926–1928.

Saffran, J. R., Johnson, E. K., Aslin, R. N., & Newport, E. L. (1999). Statistical learning of tone sequences by human infants and adults. *Cognition, 70,* 27–52.

Saffran, J. R. & Griepentrog, G. J. (2001). Absolute pitch in infant auditory learning: Evidence for developmental reorganization. *Developmental Psychology, 37,* 74–85.

Saffran, J. R., Hauser, M., Seibel, R., Kapfhamer, J., Tsao, F., & Cushman, F. (2008). Grammatical pattern learning by human infants and cotton-top tamarin monkeys. *Cognition 107,* 479–500.

Saffran, J. R., Pollak, S. D., Seibel, R. L., & Shkolnik, A. (2007). Dog is a dog is a dog: Infant rule learning is not specific to language. *Cognition, 105,* 669–680.

Saffran, J. R., Reeck, K., Niehbur, A., & Wilson, D. P. (2005). Changing the tune: Absolute and relative pitch processing by adults and infants. *Developmental Science, 8,* 1–7.

Saffran, J. R. & Thiessen, E. D. (2003). Pattern induction by infant language learners. *Developmental Psychology, 39,* 484–494.

Saffran, J. R. & Thiessen, E. D. (2007). Domain-general learning capacities. In E. Hoff & M. Shatz (Eds.), *Handbook of language development* (pp. 68–86). Cambridge, MA: Blackwell.

Saffran, J. R. & Wilson, D. P. (2003). From syllables to syntax: Multi-level statistical learning by 12-month-old infants. *Infancy, 4,* 273–284.

Seidenberg, M. S., MacDonald, M. C., & Saffran, J. R. (2002). Does grammar start where statistics stop? *Science, 298,* 553–554.

Swingley, D. (2005). Statistical clustering and the contents of the infant vocabulary. *Cognitive Psychology, 50*(1), 86–132.

Thiessen, E. D., Hill, E. A., & Saffran, J. R. (2005). Infant directed speech facilitates word segmentation. *Infancy, 7,* 49–67.

Thiessen, E. D. & Saffran, J. R. (2003). When cues collide: Use of statistical and stress cues to word boundaries by 7- and 9-month-old infants. *Developmental Psychology, 39,* 706–716.

Thiessen, E. D. & Saffran, J. R. (2007). Learning to learn: Infants' acquisition of stress-based strategies for word segmentation. *Language Learning & Development, 3,* 73–100.

Tobler, P. N., Fiorillo, C., D., & Schultz, W. (2005). Adaptive coding of reward value by dopamine neurons. *Science, 299,* 1898.

Toro, J. M. & Trobalón, J. B. (2005). Statistical computations over a speech stream in a rodent. *Perception & Psychophysics, 307,* 5715, 1642–1645.

Ulanovsky, N., Las, L., & Nelken, I. (2003). Processing of low-probability sounds by cortical neurons. *Nature Neuroscience, 6,* 391–398.

Yang, C. (2004). Universal grammar, statistics, or both. *Trends in Cognitive Sciences, 8,* 451–456.

4

Are Infants Constrained in Their Linguistic Generalizations? Some Theoretical and Methodological Observations

LouAnn Gerken

THE WHAT AND HOW OF LINGUISTIC GENERALIZATION

The ability to generalize from one experience or a set of experiences to new situations that are functionally similar is the hallmark of adaptive behavior. This ability is also the central mystery in the development of language in human infants. The mystery hinges on how learners determine what is functionally similar in a particular domain for their species or social group. For example, how does a learner determine that different talkers of different genders, with different head sizes and vocal tract lengths, speaking in different registers and at different rates, have all uttered the English word *baby*? Or what set of experiential dimensions allows an English learner to determine that *baby, dream, it,* and *deforestation* can each function as a subject or object noun?

Determining which experiences are functionally similar in language can be divided into two related questions:

1. *What* is the set of possible dimensions that language learners consider when attempting to generalize?
2. *How* do learners ultimately select from the set of considered dimensions the appropriate dimensions of generalization for their particular language (e.g., English, Chinese)?

For example, we can imagine a situation in which the first three instances of the word *baby* that a learner encounters are produced by talkers wearing an item of red clothing. The *what* question essentially asks if the learner would consider, even briefly, the possibility that red clothing is a dimension to consider when determining which word he or she is hearing. The *how* question asks how, assuming that learners do consider red clothing as a linguistically relevant dimension, they could determine that this hypothesis is incorrect.

Although these two questions are logically separable, the field of language acquisition has not had much reason to view them as such. In this chapter, I present three recent studies from my laboratory suggesting that (1) it might be profitable for the field to begin to address the two questions separately in our research, and that (2) we will need new infant testing methods in order to do so in a rigorous way. Let me first outline the ways the field of language development has viewed the two questions.

Conflating What and How—The Biologically Constrained Learner

The most influential theory of language development, Chomsky's (1957, 1981) universal grammar, provides a single answer to the *what* and *how* questions. This view begins with the observation that languages of the world are remarkably similar in the dimensions of generalization that they employ. It is safe to say that seeking and understanding cross-language relations has been the central focus of the field of linguistics for the past 40 years (e.g., Baker, 2001; Greenberg, 1963). Further, when languages are created, either by newly constituted communities (e.g., Senghas & Coppola, 2001) or by children deprived of linguistic input (e.g., Goldin-Meadow & Mylander, 1998), the dimensions of generalization appear to be remarkably consistent with those discovered in cross-linguistic research of long-existing languages. The theory of principles and parameters, the language development component of the theory of universal grammar, holds that the dimensions of linguistic generalization of all human languages are innately given to the learner as a language module and that simply encountering an input datum is sufficient, in the limit, for the learner to determine that a particular dimension is relevant in his or her particular language. From this viewpoint, the learner would never consider red clothing as a possible linguistic dimension, and therefore no additional mechanism is needed to explain how the learner rules out the incorrect hypothesis. Indeed, part of the motivation for this theory is the assumption that learners do not possess the computational capacities that would be required to rule out incorrect hypotheses.

Focusing on the *How*—Sensitivity to Input Statistics

More recently, a number of researchers studying infant learning of language-like systems in the laboratory have begun to explore in depth the question of how learners settle on the appropriate dimensions. In particular, it appears that infants have an impressive ability to keep track of a variety of statistical properties of their input and that doing so may allow them to determine the appropriate dimensions of generalization from a set of possible dimensions. The types of statistical information that researchers have successfully manipulated include conditional probabilities for adjacent items (Aslin, Saffran, & Newport, 1998; Saffran, Aslin, & Newport, 1996), conditional probabilities between adjacent vs. nonadjacent elements (Gómez, 2002), and frequency distributions (Maye, Werker, & Gerken, 2002). Learners' sensitivity to input statistics potentially allows them to ultimately discard irrelevant information like red clothing in their linguistic generalizations. Although the first three utterances of *baby* may be correlated with red clothing, it is exceedingly unlikely that every utterance of the word will exhibit that correlation. It is also likely that many other words will be uttered by people wearing red clothing. Thus, in keeping track of the reliability (conditional probability) of red clothing as a cue to the particular word *baby*, the learner can quickly discard this dimension.

Whence *What*? Identifying Potential Dimensions of Generalization

The understandable excitement of the field of language development in discovering and elaborating mechanisms by which infants might converge on the relevant dimensions of their language has led to a temporary discounting of the *what* question. That is, we have some idea about how learners, who entertain a number of dimensions, might come to select one or more that are most appropriate, but we don't yet have much to say about where the initial set comes from to begin with. We are also temporarily silent about the notion of whether there are linguistic universals, and if there are, of whether they have anything to do with how language develops. One way to reintroduce the *what* question into research on language development is to ask if there are any constraints on the dimensions to which learners will apply their statistical computations. The three experiments I present in the next section are a very early attempt to examine constraints on infants' linguistic generalizations.

However, it is important to first acknowledge that thinking about constraints on generalization is unsatisfying given our current experimental tool set. The basic infant generalization paradigm is one in which learners are exposed for a short time (typically about 2 minutes) to some new stimulus set that fits a particular generalization. They are then tested to determine if they discriminate new instances of this stimulus set from very similar stimuli that do not adhere to the intended generalization. One problem with this approach is that sometimes the dominant response exhibited by a group of infants in an experiment is a preference (long listening time) for novel stimuli, while sometimes the dominant preference is for familiarity. The direction of preference is a significant source of variability that is not yet well understood.

In addition to their direction of preference, infants also differ in the amount of time they attend to any stimuli. That is, some infants are generally "long lookers," while others are "short lookers." These two sources of variation play havoc with statistical analyses of infant data, and especially so when we attempt to address the question of constraints. In order to demonstrate that infants are constrained in the generalizations that they make, we need, at the very least, to demonstrate three statistical findings: (1) infants reliably discriminate one type of generalization; (2) they fail to reliably discriminate another type of generalization; and (3) they show a statistically reliable difference (usually a significant interaction) between the two types of generalization. Given the high variability in infant behavioral data, and given practical limits on the number of infants that can be tested in each condition of an experiment, it is typically very difficult indeed to demonstrate the third finding (the difference between two types of generalization).

I point out direction of preference anomalies and statistical difficulties in the three experiments presented herein. The final section also offers some ideas about possible methods we might use to better explore constraints on linguistic generalization and thereby to reintroduce the question of what dimensions infants consider possible bases of generalization.

THREE STUDIES EXPLORING CONSTRAINTS ON
LINGUISTIC GENERALIZATION BY INFANTS

The three studies presented in this section ask the following:

1. How do infants decide which generalization to make when more than one is possible?
2. Are some statistical relations more noticeable than others?
3. Are some dimensions of generalization more noticeable than others?

Study 1: How Do Infants Decide which Generalization to
Make When More than One Is Possible?

Marcus, Vijayan, Rao, and Vishton (1999) familiarized different groups of infants exposed to stimuli exhibiting either an ABA or AAB pattern (as shown in Table 4.1). They found that when infants were tested on new ABA or AAB patterns, the two groups showed opposite listening preferences, suggesting that they were able to generalize the abstract pattern from the familiarization stimuli to the test stimuli.

Now consider two different subsets of four stimuli in Table 4.1: those on the diagonal and those in the first column. The stimuli on the diagonal exhibit the same property as the entire set of 16. They exhibit an AAB pattern. Only noting the AAB pattern would allow learners to generalize to an entirely new set of

Table 4.1   AAB Familiarization Stimuli Used by Marcus et al. (1999)

A	B			
	di	je	li	we
le	leledi	leleje	leleli	lelewe
wi	wiwidi	wiwije	wiwili	wiwiwe
ji	jijidi	jijije	jijili	jijiwe
de	dededi	dedeje	dedeli	dedewe

Note: The first column and diagonal were used as familiarization stimuli in the current experiments.

syllables. In contrast, the stimuli in the first column exhibit an AAB pattern, but they also end in the syllable *di*. It is this subset of the stimuli that is of most interest, because both descriptions (AAB and ends in *di*) would allow learners to generalize beyond the particular syllables to which they had been exposed to a new set. The question addressed by Gerken (2006) is what information infants discern in the stimuli in the first column of Table 4.1. In particular, do they make only the AAB generalization, only the ends in *di* generalization, both, or neither?

In the first study of two, half of the 9-month-olds were presented with AAB stimuli and half with ABA stimuli. Within each of those groups, half received stimuli from the diagonal, for which the best generalization is the abstract AAB or ABA, and half received stimuli from the first column, in which a less abstract generalization is also possible (ends in *di* or has *di* as the middle element for AAB and ABA stimuli, respectively). Infants were exposed for 2 minutes to familiarization stimuli composed of the syllables shown in Table 4.1, and they were tested using the head-turn preference procedure (Kemler Nelson et al., 1995) with new AAB and ABA strings composed of different syllables (*kokoba* and *popoga* AAB test trials and *bakoba* and *gapoga* on ABA trials).

An analysis of variance, with familiarization condition (column vs. diagonal) as the between-subjects variable and test condition (consistent vs. inconsistent with training) as the within-subjects variable, revealed a main effect of consistency and a marginal interaction between condition and consistency. Planned t-tests were done to examine the performance of the column versus diagonal groups separately. Infants in the column group showed no evidence of discriminating the test items, while infants in the diagonal group showed significant discrimination. I soon return to a brief discussion of the statistics.

To better understand the behavior of the infants in the column condition, a second study was done that was identical in familiarization to the column condition of the first study but in which the test items contained *di* as the B element of the AAB and ABA test items (*kokodi* and *popodi* on AAB test trials and *podipo* and *kodiko* on ABA trials). A t-test on mean listening times for test trials consistent versus inconsistent with familiarization was significant (*t* (15) = 2.26, *p* = .04, two-tailed). These data, coupled with infants' failure to discriminate under the same familiarization conditions in Experiment 1, suggest that infants in the column condition made only the generalization involving the position of the syllable *di*.

Taken together, the two studies suggest that when two generalizations are possible, learners make the more conservative one. This finding is consistent with Bayesian approaches to generalization (e.g., Tenenbaum & Griffiths, 2001), in which learners compare the subset of the input they have received to the range of input generated by different formal descriptions. For example, an infant might tacitly compute that it is extremely unlikely, given an AAB grammar, that the only input ends in *di*. It is important to note, however, that we might consider the most conservative approach to simply store the particular strings that one has encountered and treat them as the only possibilities in the language. Clearly this is not the approach that infants take.

Turning to the nuances of the data in this study, there are two. First, the original study by Marcus et al. (1999) revealed a novelty preference. When piloting the studies already presented, I was not able to replicate the original finding when I used 12 test trials, which was the number used in the original study. However, when I examined the looking times by block, I found that infants typically showed a familiarity preference in the first block of four trials and that some infants showed a novelty preference in the last block of four trials. Therefore, the published study used only one block of four test trials and reported a familiarity preference. The second nuance of the data is the marginal (*p* = 0.11) interaction between test condition and familiarization. For us to be entirely confident that infants exposed to the diagonal versus column stimuli of Table 4.1 learned something different, that interaction should be statistically reliable. The fact that it was not indicates that we must be cautious in discussing possible constraints on generalization. More importantly, the lack of a significant interaction, given the rest of the data, suggests that our ability to detect differences between conditions may be hampered by the variability in listening times exhibited by infants.

Study 2: Are Some Linguistic Relations More Noticeable than Others?

Languages are rife with lexical categories (e.g., noun, verb, feminine noun), and these categories occur in different distributional contexts in sentences. For example, count nouns in English frequently occur after the determiners *the* and *a*. Furthermore, words that follow *the* and *a* can also fill a range of thematic roles (e.g., agent, theme), and they can serve as the referents of pronouns like *it*. If learners were sensitive to these overlapping distributional contexts of lexical classes, they would be able to generalize from one context in which a new word appeared to other likely contexts.

The typical approach to determining whether learners (adults, children, or infants) can infer one legal linguistic context from another is to present learners with incomplete linguistic paradigms. For example, learners might be presented with a paradigm with two M words, six N words, two P words, and six Q words (where M, N, P, and Q refer to word classes). The classes are combined such that M words can precede N words and P words can precede Q words, but no other combinations are possible. Some MN and some PQ combinations are withheld from the initial exposure phase (e.g., M1N5 or P2Q6) and are presented along with illegal combinations (e.g., M1Q6) at test. If learners can discriminate the legal from illegal combinations, they are given credit for having the ability to predict from one linguistic context to another.

It is important to note that learners sensitive to overlapping distributional contexts are also at serious risk of overgeneralizing (e.g., Gleitman & Wanner, 1982). For example, the input phrases *can swing, the swing, can brush, the brush, can eat* might suggest to a learner that *the eat* will be a legal phrase of his or her language. Adults at least appear to avoid this sort of overgeneralization in the sense that they respond roughly at chance to both legal and illegal strings in an MNPQ learning task (Braine, 1966, 1987; Smith, 1966).

Braine (1987) demonstrated that if distributional cues were simultaneously supplemented with referential cues on a subset of the stimuli, correct category learning is possible. He further speculated that any simultaneously available pair of cues could lead to category formation and that reference was not necessary. For example, the fact that a learner might hear *the swings* but not *can swings* and *the brushes* but not *can brushes* may be sufficient to prevent them from forming an overly general category that includes both noun and verb versions of *swing* and *brush*. Note that the determiner and plural marker provide two simultaneous cues to the noun version of the category, a situation that I refer to as double marking of the category. A variety of studies with adults provides differing degrees of evidence that double marking leads to correct category generalization by adults (Brooks, Braine, Catalano, Brody, & Sudhalter, 1993; Frigo & McDonald, 1998; Gerken, Wilson, Gómez, & Nurmsoo, 2002; Kempe & Brooks, 2001; Mintz, 2002; Wilson, 2002). The question addressed in the study presented in this section is whether 17-month-old infants also show category learning in the incomplete linguistic paradigm approach and whether they, too, are more likely to make the correct generalizations in situations in which a subset of the stimuli have at least two simultaneously present cues.

To address this question, two groups of 17-month-olds were familiarized with the incomplete Russian gender paradigms shown in Tables 4.2a and 4.2b (Gerken, Wilson, & Lewis, 2005). The first group was exposed to six masculine and six feminine Russian word stems that occurred with two masculine and two feminine case endings, respectively. Half of the masculine and half of the feminine stems had an additional cue to gender: the derivational inflections -*k* on feminine words and -*tel* on masculine words (Table 4.2a). Two feminine stem-ending combinations and two masculine combinations were withheld from familiarization and presented, along with ungrammatical pairings, at test (using the head-turn preference procedure). None of the test items had the second derivational ending.

The second group of infants was tested on the same items as the first group, but they were familiarized with word stems that had no second cue (no derivational marker) to gender (Table 4.2b). Thus, the only marking came from the two feminine and two masculine case inflections. Based on the studies with adults, only infants in the double-marked familiarization condition should discriminate grammatical from ungrammatical test items. If the predicted result is borne out, we would have evidence that infants are constrained to notice co-occurrence relations only if these relations are highlighted by an additional cue.

Table 4.2a   Stimuli Used in the Double-Marking Condition

Feminine Words

polkoj	rubashkoj	ruchkoj	vannoj	knigoj	korovoj
polku	rubashku	ruchku	vannu	knigu	korovu

Masculine Words

uchitel'ya	stroitel'ya	zhitel'ya	medved'ya	korn'ya	pisar'ya
uchitel'yem	stroitel'yem	zhitel'yem	medved'yem	korn'yem	pisar'yem

Note: Bolded words were withheld during familiarization and comprised the grammatical test items. Ungrammatical words were *vannya, korovyem, medevedoj,* and *pisaru.*

Table 4.2b   Stimuli Used in the Single-Marking Condition

Feminine Words

lapoj	malinoj	ruchkoj	vannoj	knigoj	korovoj
lapu	malinu	ruchku	vannu	knigu	korovu

Masculine Words

tramvaya	iul'ya	zhitel'ya	medved'ya	korn'ya	pisar'ya
tramvayem	iul'yem	zhitel'yem	medved'yem	korn'yem	pisar'yem

Note: Bolded words were withheld during familiarization and made up the grammatical test items. Ungrammatical items were identical to those in the double-marking condition: *vannya, korovyem, medevedoj, pisaru.*

A two-group (double marking vs. single marking) × two-grammaticality (grammatical vs. ungrammatical) analysis of variance performed on the looking-time data revealed a marginal interaction between group and grammaticality. Probing the interaction with a nonparametric test (chi-square) comparing the number of positive versus negative grammatical minus ungrammatical differences was highly significant. Planned t-tests showed that only the double-marking group discriminated the grammatical from ungrammatical test items. These data suggest that infants in the second year of life are able to discern the gender category structure embodied in a morpho-phonological paradigm, provided that at least part of the paradigm has two simultaneously present cues to category. Given the highly redundant cuing system found in natural language, it seems reasonable that the constraint observed in this study is also used by infants in real language-learning situations.

As in the first study, there are nuances to the data in the Russian gender learning study that are potentially important. First, when the data were analyzed by blocks of test trials, there was a significant effect of block. Among the several experiments in the published set (Gerken et al., 2005), two experiments revealed significant discrimination of grammatical versus ungrammatical items only in the last block of trials. Thus, as in the follow-up to the studies by Marcus et al. (1999), the Russian gender research also suggests that something important changes in infants' responding over test trials. Also as in the first study reported herein, the Russian gender study yielded only a marginal interaction (again, $p = 0.11$) with generalization condition (single marking vs. double marking). Although the interaction was quite strong using a nonparametric test, it is becoming painfully clear that in order to say that learners are constrained in some way, we need less variable data.

Study 3: Are Some Dimensions of Generalization More Likely to Yield Generalization than Others?

The previous two studies described in this chapter presented infants with input in which a potential dimension of generalization was present (AAB patterns, case marking cues to Russian gender), but infants appeared not to generalize on that dimension in certain contexts. The third and last study in this chapter also explores the contexts required for generalization, but it also asks whether some dimensions are better bases of linguistic generalization than others.

The three experiments reported here are based on a published set of experiments by Gerken (2004). In those experiments, 9-month-olds were exposed to three- to five-syllable words with stress patterns governed by a set of principles used by real languages (i.e., stress heavy syllables, stress the penultimate syllable, stress alternating syllables from left to right, don't stress two adjacent syllables;

see Table 4.3). The principles are ranked with respect to each other, and infants needed to infer the principles and their rankings in order to demonstrate successful discrimination at test. At test, they heard words with different patterns of stressed and unstressed syllables than they had heard during familiarization. Nevertheless, the words obeyed the same principles as the words they had heard during familiarization, and infants were able to discriminate words that did and did not conform to these principles.

In the published study, the principle *stress heavy syllables* (syllables ending with a consonant) was attested by only one heavy syllable, /ton/. The question addressed in the experiments reported here was whether infants exposed to the heavy syllable /ton/ would generalize to other heavy syllables. In the first experiment, infants were familiarized with the same types of stimuli used in the published experiments. However, the syllable that had been /ton/ in the previous familiarization items became /bom/ in the new items. The test items were identical to those in the published studies; that is, they contained the heavy syllable /ton/. A two-familiarization language (L1, L2) × two-test block (first, second) × two-test item type (L1, L2) revealed only a significant effect of block, such that listening times were longer in the first block. Infants showed no evidence of generalizing from /ton/ to /bom/, suggesting that one instance of a heavy syllable wasn't enough to cause infants to treat *heavy syllable* as a dimension of generalization. What information might be enough to cause them to make this generalization? That question was addressed in a second experiment.

Table 4.3   Principles, Rankings, and Sample Stimuli from Lexical Stress Experiments

Language 1	Language 2
Familiarization stimuli	Familiarization stimuli
HEAVY >> PENULT	HEAVY >> PEN-INITIAL
TON do re	*do re TON*
DO re TON	*TON do RE*
DO re TON mi fa	*do re TON mi FA*
PENULT >> ALT-LEFT	PEN-INITIAL >> ALT-RIGHT
DO re mi FA so	*do RE mi fa SO*
*CLASH >> HEAVY	*CLASH >> HEAVY
TON ton do RE mi	*do RE mi ton TON*
Test stimuli	Test stimuli
HEAVY >> ALT-LEFT	HEAVY >> ALT-RIGHT
do TON re MI fa	*do RE mi TON fa*

Note: See text for variants of the familiarization stimuli. Stressed syllables are capitalized.

In the second experiment, infants were familiarized with the same types of words as before, but now, three different heavy syllables were used, /bom/, /kir/, /sul/. A two-familiarization language × two-block × two-test item type ANOVA revealed a significant effect of block, such that listening times were longer in the first block. Importantly, there was a significant familiarization × test item type interaction. Follow-up tests comparing listening times for consistent versus inconsistent trials demonstrated significantly longer listening times for consistent test trials. This study suggests that infants are capable of generalizing based on the dimension *ends in a consonant;* however, as we saw in the previous studies in this section, they are conservative in their generalizations. In this case, they needed more than a single instance of a syllable ending in a consonant in order to generalize. Three instances appear to be sufficient.

The heart of the question addressed here, however, is not whether infants can form abstract principles or rules in brief laboratory exposures; we already have ample evidence that they can (Gerken, 2004, 2006; Gómez, 2002; Gómez & Gerken, 1999; Marcus et al., 1999; Maye et al., 2002). Rather, the question is whether infants can form abstract principles of the sort found in natural languages but fail to form very similar principles not found among languages of the world. To address that question, a final experiment familiarized 9-month-olds with stimuli that exhibited the principle *stress syllables starting with /t./* On the surface, this principle seems very similar in character to *stress syllables that end in a consonant;* however, the initial consonant of a syllable does not appear to play a role in the word stress systems of the world's languages. A two-familiarization language × two-block × two-test item type ANOVA revealed only a significant effect of block, such that listening times were longer in the first block. Thus, infants tested on the identical test items used in the second experiment failed to show any evidence of having formed the principle *stress syllables starting with /t./*

Close examination of the data from the lexical stress study reveal similarities to the other two studies. First, trial block was a significant factor in characterizing infants' responses. Second, while the interaction between the second and third experiments was statistically reliable, the interaction between the first and second experiments was only marginal ($p < .06$). Third, just as in the original study by Marcus et al. (1999) versus the one presented here, the original study by Gerken (2004) yielded a novelty preference, while the current lexical stress study showed a familiarity preference. The switch in preference could be ascribed to the greater demand of the current task, in which infants must generalize from one set of syllables ending in a consonant to a new syllable that has that property. In contrast, the generalization made by the infants in Gerken (2004) was likely a more surface one: *stress /ton/.*

Summary of the Studies

Before moving on to discuss methodological and statistical issues raised by these studies, let us first consider what generalizations we might make about infants' linguistic generalizations from these three studies and whether we have any evidence that infants are in fact constrained in the generalizations they make. In the first study, we asked how infants decide which generalization to make when more than one is possible. The answer appears to be that infants are conservative, only generalizing as far as the data will allow, but without simply resorting to storing individual stimuli that they have heard (or else they wouldn't generalize at all). The first lexical stress experiment also reinforced infants' conservatism. They did not generalize a principle like *stress syllables ending in a consonant* when they encountered only one such syllable. These two studies suggest that infants become less conservative as they encounter multiple utterance types and multiple tokens of each utterance type. The second question we asked was whether some statistical relations are more noticeable than others? In the case of Russian gender, the statistical relations that held between stems and case endings did not become noticeable until a second cue was added. The third question addressed was whether some dimensions of generalization are more noticeable than others? Only the lexical stress study is directed at this question, which is really the main concern of this chapter. The answer from that study appears to be that not all generalizations appear to be equally learnable and that, in particular, the *principle stress syllables beginning in /t/* does not seem to be as easily learned as *stress syllables ending in a consonant*. Much more work needs to be done to determine if some linguistic generalizations are in fact less learnable than others.

THEORETICAL AND METHODOLOGICAL ADVANCES REQUIRED TO EXPLORE CONSTRAINTS ON GENERALIZATION

In the first section of this chapter, I identified two sources of variability among infants in the sorts of preference paradigms employed in the three studies presented herein. I also noted a statistical criterion that needs to be met before we can conclude that one dimension of generalization is more readily available to infants than another. That statistical criterion is for a significant interaction between test condition (consistent with familiarization vs. inconsistent) and dimension of generalization (e.g., diagonal vs. column input; single-marked vs. double-marked categories; ends in a consonant vs. starts in /t/). Only the lexical stress study presented in the second section of the chapter was able to meet this statistical criterion using parametric statistics (ANOVA). However, all the other studies showed "marginal" interactions of the sort required to draw firm conclusions.

If one of the goals in studying language development is to understand what dimensions of generalization are available to the learner and what constraints on generalizations might exist, we will need to gain a better understanding of why infants demonstrate novelty preferences in some studies and familiarity preferences in others. One way to conceptualize novelty versus familiarity effects is show in Figure 4.1. Infants who are able to master much of the structure of the input during familiarization are likely to show a novelty preference during test, whereas infants whose strength of learning during familiarization is weaker will show a familiarity preference. The analyses by block of test trials reported in this chapter appear to be consistent with the view shown in Figure 4.1. Familiarity preferences appear in earlier test blocks and novelty preferences in later blocks. Such data suggest that there is learning during test as well as during familiarization. Perhaps a greater focus by the field on what happens over blocks of test trials might shed light on the direction of preference mystery.

If the view of infant preference shown in Figure 4.1 is to be our working hypothesis, we will also need to develop research methods in which all infants are brought to the same level of learning strength during familiarization. Many researchers currently using preference techniques familiarize all infants for a set period of time. However, if infants differ in what they are able to learn in that time, performance during test will be variable and weaken our ability to draw conclusions. Perhaps combining a habituation-based familiarization phase with several blocks of test trials will allow for less variability in the data.

In summary, the field of infant language research is at a point where we need to consider not only what infants can learn but also what they cannot learn. To do that, we need methods that allow us to feel safer in drawing conclusions from patterns of significant and null results. I am hopeful that the next decade will

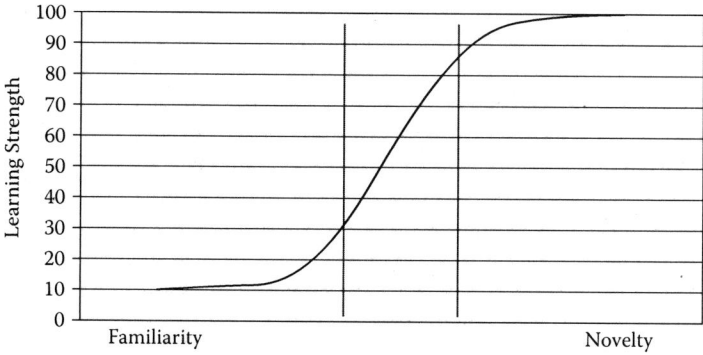

Figure 4.1   One conceptualization of direction of preference effects in infant research.

bring us the research tools that we need so that we can find an answer to the question of whether infants are constrained in their linguistic generalizations.

REFERENCES

Aslin, R. N., Saffran, J. R., & Newport, E. L. (1998). Computation of conditional probability statistics by 8-month-old infants. *Psychological Science, 9*(4), 321–324.

Baker, M. C. (2001). *The atoms of language.* New York: Basic Books.

Braine, M. D. S. (1966). Learning the positions of words relative to a marker element. *Journal of Experimental Psychology, 72*(4), 532–540.

Braine, M. D. S. (1987). What is learned in acquiring word classes—a step toward an acquisition theory. In B. MacWhinney (Ed.), *Mechanisms of language acquisition* (pp. 65–87). Hillsdale, NJ: Lawrence Erlbaum Associates, Inc.

Brooks, P. J., Braine, M. D., Catalano, L., Brody, R., & Sudhalter, V. (1993). Acquisition of Gender-like noun subclasses in an artificial language: The contribution of phonological markers to learning. *Journal of Memory and Language, 32,* 76–95.

Chomsky, N. (1957). *Syntactic structures.* The Hague, The Netherlands: Mouton.

Chomsky, N. (1981). *Lectures on government and binding.* Dordrecht: Foris.

Frigo, L. & McDonald, J. (1998). Properties of phonological markers that affect the acquisition of gender-like subclasses. *Journal of Memory and Language, 39,* 218–245.

Gerken, L. A. (2004). Nine-month-olds extract structural principles required for natural language. *Cognition, 93,* B89–B96.

Gerken, L. A. (2006). Decisions, decisions: Infant language learning when multiple generalizations are possible. *Cognition, 98,* B67–B74.

Gerken, L. A., Wilson, R., Gómez, R. L., & Nurmsoo, E. (2002). *Linguistic category induction without reference: The importance of correlated cues.* Unpublished manuscript, Tucson, AZ.

Gerken, L. A., Wilson, R., & Lewis, W. (2005). 17-month-olds can use distributional cues to form syntactic categories. *Journal of Child Language, 32,* 249–268.

Gleitman, L. & Wanner, E. (1982). The state of the state of the art. In E. Wanner & L. Gleitman (Eds.), *Language acquisition: The state of the art* (pp. 3–48). Cambridge, England: Cambridge University Press.

Goldin-Meadow, S. & Mylander, C. (1998). Spontaneous sign systems created by deaf children in two cultures. *Nature, 391*(6664), 279–281.

Gómez, R. L. (2002). Variability and detection of invariant structure. *Psychological Science, 13*(5), 431–436.

Gómez, R. L. & Gerken, L. A. (1999). Artificial grammar learning by 1-year-olds leads to specific and abstract knowledge. *Cognition, 70*(2), 109–135.

Greenberg, J. H. (1963). Some universals of grammar with particular reference to the order of meaningful elements. In J. H. Greenberg (Ed.), *Universals of language* (pp. 58–90). Cambridge, MA: MIT Press.

Kemler Nelson, D., Jusczyk, P. W., Mandel, D. R., Myers, J., Turk, A. E., & Gerken, L. A. (1995). The headturn preference procedure for testing auditory perception. *Infant Behavior and Development, 18,* 111–116.

Kempe, V. & Brooks, P. J. (2001). The role of diminutives in the acquisition of russian gender: Can elements of child-directed speech aid in learning morphology? *Language Learning, 51*(2), 221–256.

Marcus, G. F., Vijayan, S., Rao, S. B., & Vishton, P. M. (1999). Rule learning by seven-month-old infants. *Science, 283*, 77–80.

Maye, J., Werker, J. F., & Gerken, L. A. (2002). Infant sensitivity to distributional information can affect phonetic discrimination. *Cognition, 82*(3), B101–B111.

Mintz, T. H. (2002). Category induction from distributional cues in an artificial language. *Memory & Cognition, 30*(5), 678–686.

Saffran, J. R., Aslin, R. N., & Newport, E. (1996). Statistical learning by 8-month-old infants. *Science, 274*, 1926–1928.

Senghas, A. & Coppola, M. (2001). Children creating language: How Nicaraguan sign language acquired a spatial grammar. *Psychological Science, 12*, 323–328.

Smith, K. H. (1966). Grammatical intrusions in the recall of structured letter pairs: Mediated transfer or position learning? *Journal of Experimental Psychology, 72*, 580–588.

Tenenbaum, J. B. & Griffiths, T. L. (2001). Generalization, similarity, and Bayesian inference. *Behavioral and Brain Sciences, 24*, 629–640.

Wilson, R. (2002). *Syntactic category learning in a second language.* Unpublished Ph.D. dissertation, University of Arizona, Tucson.

5

How Different Is Disordered Language?

MABEL L. RICE

Studies of infant pathways to language have enlightened our appreciation of the richness of the neurocognitive resources available to babies and how they come prepared to acquire language. In a search for general properties that hold across many infants, the research has focused on healthy, robust babies who are comfortable with the experimental methods and have "normal" language aptitude. The full range of infants, however, includes some who are healthy but do not have strong aptitude for language. This chapter takes up what is known about these youngsters as they grow into the time of language use, the ways their language acquisition parallels or differs from that of other children, and the issues that arise when we try to account for language limitations as well as strengths. The ultimate goal is to arrive at interpretive models that encompass individual variation in language acquisition as well as the broad ways in which children share language acquisition abilities.

The chapter is organized as follows. The first section provides a brief overview of children with specific language impairment (SLI), a condition in which language acquisition does not meet normative expectations, although the children are healthy otherwise. The following sections describe dimensions of language acquisition from infancy onward, with an emphasis on the similarities and differences between affected and unaffected children. The second section begins with language onset, defined as the first use of words at 15–18 months and simple sentences at 24 months and the phenomenon of late language emergence (LLE) as the likely beginning period of SLI. The third section lays out the growth trajectories of children with SLI, from the preschool to the early elementary age range, with evidence of continued delays and disruptions in the grammar, and ways the dimensions of language are synchronous and asynchronous. The fourth section highlights that at the same time there are delays and disruptions there are also striking strengths in the grammar, similar to unaffected children.

The fifth section explores implications of the findings from children with SLI for models of infant pathways to language, and the final section provides brief concluding comments.

CHILDREN WITH SPECIFIC LANGUAGE IMPAIRMENT

Beginning with a clinical case history reported by Gall (1835), the scientific literature has documented the existence of children who are slow to acquire language, although there are no other apparent developmental disabilities and no obvious causal factors. In the modern literature, the commonly accepted research definition of SLI is based on both inclusionary and exclusionary criteria. The inclusionary criteria document that language acquisition does not meet normative expectations by comparing a child's performance with levels expected for the child's age. This is usually done by administering a general test of language acquisition composed of tasks that evaluate multiple dimensions of language in expressive and receptive language formats. The diagnosis of language impairment is defined as performance at the low end of the age level distribution, around the bottom 10th to 15th percentiles. The gold standard for research includes evaluation of speech performance as well to determine if children with poor intelligibility or word pronunciation are unable to demonstrate their vocabulary, morphological, or sentence formulation competencies because of speech limitations. In the full population of children with SLI, speech impairments are orthogonal to language impairments (Shriberg, Tomblin, & McSweeny, 1999), although children enrolled in clinical treatment are more likely to have both speech and language impairments. Children with SLI are likely to be overlooked for clinical services; Tomblin et al. (1997) report that only 29% of the children identified in their epidemiological study of kindergarten children had been identified for treatment.

The exclusionary criteria are intended to select affected children whose developmental impairment is limited to language (see Rice & Warren, 2004; Rice, Warren, & Betz, 2005, for information about language disorders across different clinical groups). Children with hearing loss are excluded. Children diagnosed with Williams syndrome, Down syndrome, and fragile X syndrome, are excluded, as are children with epilepsy and other neurological disorders. Conventionally, children with autism have been excluded, although in the recent shift to the broader clinical category of autism spectrum disorders (ASD) the diagnostic boundary between SLI and autism is somewhat blurred and is currently a matter of active investigation. It is generally accepted that social impairments form the core of ASD whereas language impairments form the core of SLI (see Tager-Flusberg, 2004, 2005, for overviews). Mental retardation is usually ruled out via exclusion of children whose nonverbal intelligence quotient (IQ) performance levels are 85 or below. The range between 70 and 85 nonverbal IQ is sometimes invoked as acceptable for the label of SLI, although it is preferable to label this range as nonspecific language impairment (NLI) (Tomblin & Zhang, 1999) and treat children in this range as a separate clinical group (see Rice, Tomblin, Hoffman, Richman, & Marquis, 2004, for evidence of differences between the SLI and NLI groups in acquisition of past-tense morphology.) Finally, children with dialectal differences or bilingualism are usually excluded from experimental studies of SLI in order to avoid confounds in native language exposure.

A useful distinction in characterizing the nature of language impairment in children with SLI is that of delayed versus disordered language acquisition. It is possible that affected children are like younger typically developing children— that is, that there is a general immaturity in the language acquisition system. Note that this model is inherently conservative in that it assumes that the mechanisms of language acquisition, once activated, are very similar in affected and unaffected children. Experimentally, a delay model is evaluated by means of a control group of younger children at equivalent levels of general language acquisition, most often benchmarked during the preschool years as equivalent levels of mean length of utterance (MLU). This sets up a three-group design in studies of SLI that has proven to be very informative, composed of an affected group, an age-comparison group, and a language-equivalent group. If the SLI group is at lower levels than the age-comparison group but equivalent to the younger language-equivalent group, this is generally viewed as a pattern attributable to the generally lower language competencies of the affected group, more like that of younger children.

The nondelay model of interest here is one of *disruption*—referred to as a *delay within a delay* model in Rice (2003) and updated to a *disruption* notion in Rice (2004). In this model, some elements of language are out of harmony, or disrupted, relative to others, leading to a lack of synchrony in the overall linguistic system. Evidence for this possibility is lower performance of the SLI group compared with either of the control groups on a given linguistic dimension, indicating that affected children's low performance extends beyond that expected for a general immaturity relative to age expectations. Areas of disrupted synchrony are of theoretical interest, because they show how the linguistic dimensions that are tightly intertwined in typically developing children are to some extent independent elements that can be selectively affected and fall behind in acquisition.

This chapter focuses on the comparison of unaffected children and children with SLI. Another perspective on language strengths and weaknesses is apparent when comparing language impairments across different clinical categories (see Rice et al., 2005; Rice & Smolik, 2007). Of interest here are three observations. One is that mental retardation does not fully predict language impairments—that is, children with low nonverbal IQ levels can have language levels commensurate with age expectations. The second is that social impairment does not fully predict language impairment—that is, children with autism can have language levels commensurate with age expectations. Third, language impairment does not necessarily manifest as a global diminution of ability; instead, certain dimensions of language, such as vocabulary development, can be at or near age expectations whereas other dimensions, such as syntax, can lag further behind. Thus, clinical conditions beyond SLI demonstrate the language-specific properties of language impairment and the need for consideration of individual dimensions of language.

DELAYED ONSET AS THE BEGINNING OF SLI: LATE LANGUAGE EMERGENCE (LLE)

As the chapters in this volume attest, language emerges from the infancy period, in the way of early comprehension of spoken language, first words and first combinations of words into simple sentences. Parental report measures of children's first words and word combinations indicate that 10%–20% of 24-month-old children show LLE, defined as using fewer than 50 words or no word combinations (Fenson et al., 1993; Klee et al., 1998; Rescorla, 1989; Rescorla & Achenbach, 2002; Rescorla & Alley, 2001; Rescorla, Hadick-Wiley, & Escarce, 1993). A recent epidemiologically ascertained sample of 1,766 24-month-old children yielded an estimate of 13% LLE, defined according to parental report of children's comprehension as well as production of language (Zubrick, Taylor, Rice, & Slegers, 2007).

The phenomenon of LLE is linked to SLI via the fact that late onset is considered to be a hallmark characteristic of children with language impairments. LLE can be the first diagnostic symptom of a subsequent difficulty with language acquisition. Rice (2004) proposes that a late language start-up may be a unifying feature of language impairment across many different clinical conditions.

In spite of our great progress in investigations of the cognitive and perceptual capacities that infants bring to language onset, the picture does not yet reveal the exact mechanisms that determine when language appears and the interactions among multiple factors that contribute to the timing of language acquisition. An experimental way to approach this question is to investigate variables that could predict which 24-month-old children will show LLE (excluding children with obvious related medical conditions). In the largest study of its kind, Zubrick et al. (under review) examined a large range of possible predictors that describe maternal, home, and child characteristics. It is noteworthy that in this large sample, variables associated with home resources (cf. Entwhistle &

Astone, 1994), including mother's education, family income, socioeconomic status, parental mental health, parenting style, and family functioning, did not predict LLE status. The significant predictors were only a handful out of a large number of variables:

- Gender (2.74 times the risk for boys than girls)
- The family history of speech and language delays (2.11 times the risk for families with a positive history)
- Number of children in the family (double the risk for families with two or more children)
- Perinatal status (1.8 times the risk for children with a low percentage of expected birth weight or gestation age less than 37 weeks)
- The children's early neuromotor skills (more than double the risk for children somewhat late in developing motor skills, although it must be emphasized that the LLE children's motor development is within normative expectations)

One conclusion to be drawn from the outcomes is that across a very wide range of maternal and family differences, including the conventional ways of assessing socioeconomic resources, children can avoid LLE. Put another way, they are likely to share the expected time of language onset regardless of wide variation in family resources. On the other hand, independent of maternal and family factors, children whose relatives were LLE were at greater risk. This suggests that parents or siblings, when they were toddlers, were also likely to be LLE. Shared biological risk, evident at the same developmental period, is implicated, independent of other environmental resources or learning opportunities. Furthermore, neuromotor development at this time is predictive, such that children with LLE are more likely to be less robust in motor development at 24 months. All in all, it appears that individual differences in language onset are linked to individual differences in family members for the same developmental period and that these differences are part of a broader profile of slightly immature neurological development.

To return to the notion of language delay, it is clear that children with LLE are delayed in language onset and, at the same time, that they share many of the factors thought to enhance children's language learning. In turn, this suggests an interaction of child and environment, such that some children cannot benefit from the language learning opportunities to the same extent other children can, and this is evident from onset. Exactly what sets the stage for onset readiness is an important question for studies of infant pathways to language.

PROTRACTED GROWTH OF SLI—DELAYS AND DISRUPTIONS, SYNCHRONIES AND ASYNCHRONIES

Much of the literature on SLI examines language delay versus language difference in the classical three-group cross-sectional design (cf. Leonard, 1998). The evidence of delays versus nondelays is mixed in these cross-sectional comparisons, dependent upon the power to detect group differences (many of the studies have small sample size), the language dimension of interest, the ages of the participants, and other experimental issues. More recently, longitudinal studies provide stronger evidence of similarities and differences over time.

Growth trajectories clearly show that delays are characteristic of some dimensions of language growth whereas disruptions are characteristic of other dimensions. Delays are evident in the growth of MLU and receptive vocabulary in children with SLI. Rice, Redmond, and Hoffman (2006) followed a group of 21 5-year-old children with SLI and 20 MLU equivalent children who were two years younger. The children were assessed at 6-month intervals for MLU, for a total of nine data points over 5 years, encompassing the years 3–9. As depicted in Figure 5.1, the two groups showed remarkable parallels in MLU growth. They were at equivalent levels of MLU at each time of measurement. Growth-curve modeling showed that there were no group differences in the growth trajectories: Each group showed linear and quadratic growth, with negatively accelerating growth; that is, at the later ages there was less of an increase in the MLU between times of measurement. It is as if the mechanisms that guide increased utterance length are working in the same way in the two groups over the observed

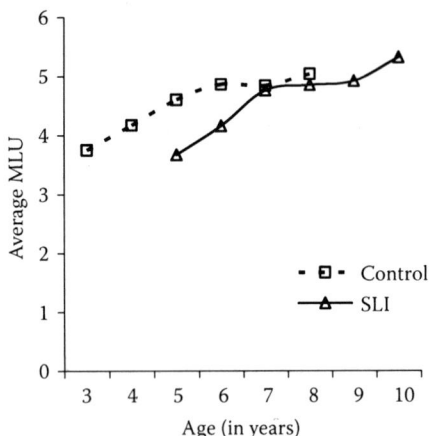

Figure 5.1   Growth in MLU of children with SLI and unaffected younger controls.

time, even though the affected children are two years older than the controls, were enrolled in language intervention at the outset, and were at higher levels of formal education. A further implication is that when the growth trajectories are projected downward to an earlier age, assuming the parallel growth patterns early on, affected children would be likely to have a delayed onset of combining words into phrases and clauses. Thus, the LLE roots of SLI are supported by the pattern of growth during late preschool and beyond.

The growth modeling also evaluated possible predictors of growth in MLU for the two groups. Neither nonverbal intelligence nor mother's education level predicted growth, although for each group nonverbal intelligence predicted initial status (the intercept) in levels of MLU.

Growth in receptive vocabulary was tracked in the two groups as well (Figure 5.2). Receptive vocabulary was measured annually using the Peabody Picture Vocabulary Test-Revised (PPVT-R; Dunn & Dunn, 1981). The groups were not initially selected for equivalency on receptive vocabulary. At the outset, the affected group had a small but statistically significant numerical advantage based on comparisons of PPVT-R raw scores. At the end, the affected group had a small but statistically significant numerical disadvantage. The groups did not differ in the intervening times of measurement. In the growth model, there were significant linear and quadratic growth parameters, with group differences at the intercept (outset) and in linear rates such that the MLU equivalent group overcame the initial lower level of performance with a greater degree of linear change subsequently. It is as if the affected children benefited from the two years' age difference at the outset in the experience needed to acquire new words, but

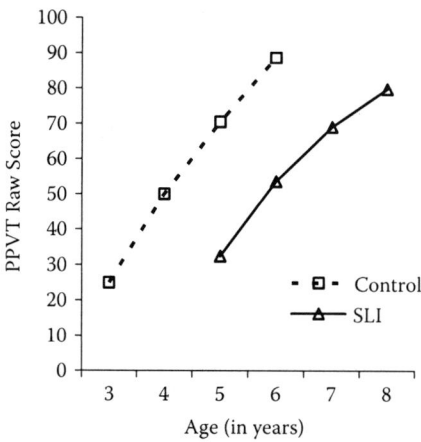

Figure 5.2   Growth in PPVT-R raw score of children with SLI and unaffected younger controls.

this advantage was overcome by a slightly better rate of learning new words in the younger group. The predictor relationships were the same as with the MLU outcomes: Mother's education did not predict growth in vocabulary for either group, and nonverbal intelligence predicted initial status in vocabulary to the same extent in both groups.

Overall, although there are some minor ways in which growth in vocabulary is not exactly parallel across the two groups, the big picture is how strikingly similar growth plays out during this time. It looks as if the dimensions of MLU and vocabulary are tracking in the same way across the groups, once adjusted for a delayed onset for the affected group. It appears that once the system starts, it will move forward with the same momentum for children with SLI as for younger children, and growth in MLU and vocabulary is synchronized, at least at a general level, in the same way for both groups.

The picture is much different with regard to the grammatical function of finiteness marking. At the descriptive level, finiteness is a fundamental structural property of clauses that requires tense and agreement marking (usually in the form of overt morphemes) on the occupant of the main verb position in a clause (cf. Quirk, Greenbaum, Leech, & Svartvik, 1985). Recent theoretical advances in generative grammar (Chomsky, 1995) have linked finiteness (with a morphological requirement) to syntax in rules for movement of elements within a clause. The term *morphosyntax* is used to describe this interaction. Because of its central place in the grammar, there has been great interest in the ways children acquire competency with finiteness across many languages (cf. Guasti, 2002; Schütze, 2004).

The exact ways young children show their understanding of finiteness marking depend on the morphosyntactic properties of their native language. In English, finiteness is marked by the following morphemes:

- Third-person singular present tense -*s*: "Patsy runs home every day."
- Past tense -*ed* or irregular past tense: "Patsy walked/ran home yesterday."
- Copular or auxiliary *be*: "Patsy is happy" or "Patsy is running."
- Auxiliary *do*: "Does Patsy like to run?"

Early on, English-speaking children produce uninflected verbal forms, such as *Patsy go home,[1] or omitted finiteness marking *Be* or *Do*, as in *Patsy happy. Note that the set of morphemes is not limited to verbal affixes but includes irregular stem-internal morphophonologcal variants and free-standing morphemes (forms of *Be* and *Do*).

Wexler (1994, 1996) initially labeled this an *optional infinitive stage*. Later this was amended to an *agreement/tense omission model* (ATOM) (Schütze & Wexler, 1996; Wexler, Schütze, & Rice, 1998) and then to a *unique checking constraint model* (Wexler, 1998). The fundamental notion is that in some languages young children go through a period in which they seem to treat finiteness marking as optional, although it is obligatory in the adult grammar. In English-speaking children this is evident in their tendency to omit finite forms early on. As children develop, the likelihood of finiteness marking in obligatory clausal contexts grows to a level that ultimately reaches the adult levels.

The theory was extended to children with SLI in the prediction that their long delay in the acquisition of verbal morphology is an extension of a phase that is part of younger children's grammatical development (Rice, Wexler, & Cleave, 1995). Early on, it was pointed out that this is, in effect, an enriched *extended development model* (cf. Rice & Wexler, 1996), which recognizes the many ways the language of children with SLI is similar to younger unaffected children but with a greatly protracted period of incomplete acquisition of grammatical tense marking.

Growth-curve data are available for the same children studied for MLU and vocabulary development (cf. Figure 5.1 and Figure 5.2). These data make it clear that, as predicted, affected children do show a delay within a delay in this part of the grammar, leading to a disruption in the expected synchrony across the different dimensions of grammar as growth plays out. Figure 5.3 reports the outcome for affected and unaffected children over the period of 3 to 8 years of age. For unaffected children, the percentage correct in obligatory contexts for a composite estimate of finiteness (collapsing across the different morphemes) starts out around 55% for 3-year-olds at the first time of measurement and quickly moves toward adult usage by age 4. In contrast, the affected children are at much lower levels of use at the first time of measurement at 5 years, and this gap persists for years.

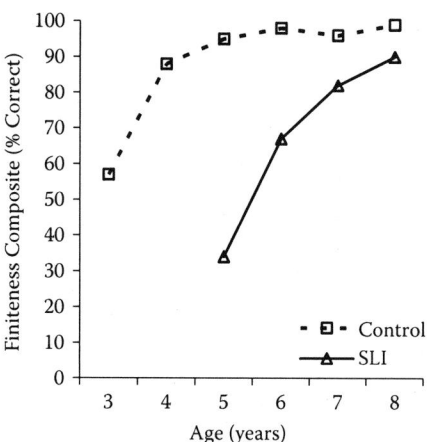

Figure 5.3   Growth in finiteness marking of children with SLI and unaffected control children.

Growth-curve modeling, however, shows that the two groups follow the same models, indicating linear and quadratic components for both groups. The predictor relationships were also the same across groups: Growth was not predicted by a child's nonverbal intelligence, mother's education, or PPVT-R vocabulary scores at the outset, although a child's initial MLU did predict rate of acquisition. The findings replicated for irregular past tense, when irregular accuracy was calculated as finiteness marking by regarding overregularizations as finiteness markers (Rice, Wexler, Marquis, & Hershberger, 2000). Further, the findings also replicate for judgment tasks, indicating that the effects are not restricted to production demands but also are evident in children's likelihood to accept utterances as well formed with the same kinds of omissions that they produce (Rice, Wexler, & Redmond, 1999).

Cross-sectional studies from other labs also find that children with SLI, as a group, are likely to perform less accurately than younger controls on morphemes associated with the finiteness marker (cf. Bedore & Leonard, 1998; Conti-Ramsden, Botting, & Faragher, 2001; Grela & Leonard, 2000; Joseph, Serratrice, & Conti-Ramsden, 2002; Leonard, Eyer, Bedore, & Grela, 1997; Marchman, Wulfeck, & Ellis Weismer, 1999; Oetting & Horohov, 1997). Thus, the empirical phenomenon is well established.

To recapitulate, for MLU and vocabulary acquisition, children with SLI follow a delayed growth trajectory that shows strong similarity to younger unaffected children. For morphosyntax, and more particularly for the property of finiteness, affected children also follow the same growth trajectory as younger unaffected children, but in this dimension the onset is further delayed and the actual levels of performance fall below that of younger children. So whatever is driving growth shows strong similarities across all children, and at the same time growth is not uniform across all dimensions of language, such that semantics and morphosyntax are unlikely to be sharing the same broad mechanisms to drive change.

STRENGTHS IN THE GRAMMAR: AVOIDING OVERT MISTAKES EVEN WITH DELAYS AND DISRUPTIONS

The nature of children's grammatical errors has long been appreciated as a source of information about their acquisition mechanisms. In the domain of morphosyntax, current theories posit conditional relationships between morphology and syntax such that certain errors are predicted not to appear if other elements of clause structure are in place. In particular, the theory of the *optional infinitive stage*, and subsequent modifications to the theory, predict that if finiteness markers appear in obligatory contexts, then certain kinds of other grammatical errors would be very unlikely. This is because the theory carries the related assumption that young children know much of the adult syntactic system, including rules that apply to overt inflected verb forms and the basic configuration of clausal structure that provides the location in a clause where finite forms appear.

Clause-by-clause inspection of children's utterances and responses to elicitation tasks are required to determine if there are errors of morpheme use that would indicate underlying syntactic deficiencies. This is laborious and often not done, especially in studies of children with SLI. More recently, however, data systems have included close examination of possible errors, which include the following:

1. Violation of the requirement that there is only one site for finiteness marking in a clause and no more than one finiteness marker can appear, as shown in the following examples:
   - Runs Patsy home every day?*
   - Does Patsy likes to run?*
   - Patsy is runs home very day.*
   - Does Patsy is happy?*
2. Violation of the requirement that agreement marking on the verb must match the person and number features on the subject, as shown in the following examples:
   - He am happy.*
   - They is mine.*
   - I likes to paint.*
   - She are tired.*
3. Violation of the requirement that nominative-case marking of the subject is required in finite clauses, as shown in the following examples:
   - Him wants a cookie.*
   - Her runs home.*
   - Me am going.*

A general finding is that such errors are rare or very unlikely even during the period when children are likely to use finiteness markers inconsistently or are likely to have nominative-case errors (when accusative case appears it is much more likely to be when finiteness markers are omitted; cf. Wexler et al., 1998). This does not mean that such errors never appear but that when benchmarked to obligatory contexts (opportunities for error) the rate is at best very small. Leonard, Camarata, Brown, and Camarata (2004) report a similar outcome for the observed error patterns in an intensive training study. The empirical generalization is that when finiteness errors are defined as violations of the adult grammar, children's errors (for children with SLI as well as unaffected children) are overwhelmingly omissions of finite forms in obligatory contexts.

The conclusion is that although children with SLI show a laboriously long period of acquisition of finiteness, they nevertheless follow the same growth trajectories as unaffected children and the same relationships with potential predictors of growth and also avoid possible errors in much the same way as unaffected children.

ISSUES FOR WORKING OUT INFANT PATHWAYS TO LANGUAGE

Studies of children with SLI draw our attention to some fundamental issues that don't always show up in the normative literature but that nevertheless are vital components of the general explanation of how babies progress to become such proficient users of language. Beginning with the LLE phenomena described earlier, it raises the question of potential gender effects early on. In contrast to the strong disadvantage for males in the low performance range, there is only a modest advantage for females across the full range of performance (Fenson et al., 1994; Huttenlocher, Haight, Bryk, Seltzer, & Lyons, 1991; Wells, 1985). This suggests that the influences on language abilities in the low performance range may exaggerate influences within the normal range. Furthermore, by kindergarten, in epidemiologically ascertained samples the risk of SLI for boys and girls is nearly the same: 8% for boys and 6% for girls (Tomblin et al., 1997). This is a puzzling picture if indeed boys are likely to start later but are able to overcome the early delay. The roots of these differences appear to be in infancy.

In addition, the idea that babies share with their family members a likelihood of LLE draws our attention to the ways genetic influences might operate. Granted that there are challenges in the measurement systems available to estimate childhood delays from retrospective reports of adults, there are at the same time growing indications of likely genetic contributions to SLI (see Rice & Smolik, 2007, for a review). The recent discovery of genetic causes of risk for prematurity (Wang et al., 2006) alerts us to the need to more systematically investigate biological bases of individual differences in infants.

Related to this point is the fact that, in the evidence reviewed here, the role of environmental influences related to parenting and home resources points away from these variables as causal agents for LLE and SLI. At least in the way such influences have conventionally been indexed, the evidence is meager at best for the intuitive notion that such delays and differences in language are attributable to a lack of appropriate parenting or environmental resources. This is not to say that neglect in extreme cases cannot play a causal role; obviously, it does, and it probably works in multiple ways to increase risk for language acquisition. The point here is that within the broad range of acceptable parenting practices, with presumably a basic level of language input, some children are LLE, and some are not; some children have SLI, and some do not. It also must be said that this conclusion does not rule out environmental intervention as an important element in treating LLE and SLI. It does indicate that additional enrichment is needed and cautions that accelerated growth will be a challenge to achieve. Just as infants' constitutional factors are considered in models of infant attention, cognition, and perception, so they need to be considered in language acquisition.

The picture of growth similarities and differences between SLI and unaffected children poses some very challenging interpretive issues. As noted earlier, there is a parsimony advantage in assuming that children with SLI share the same underlying mechanisms as unaffected children, in tandem with a corollary that language is a specific cognitive domain with internal dimensionality. Contrary to the position of advocates for a global model of language and intelligence, a g factor (cf. Plomin, 1999), evidence from language impairments across clinical conditions strongly indicate that language has specific properties; it can be dissociated from nonverbal intelligence and the growth of certain dimensions, such as morphosyntax, is independent of nonverbal intelligence. Further, growth does not play out the same across language dimensions. To ignore these findings is to invite heterogeneity in empirical assessments that introduce unknown sources of error.

Given this, further examination of the interpretive challenges is warranted. A focus on the differences (i.e., the language impairments relative to unaffected children benchmarked to age levels) invites the hypothesis that children with SLI have fundamental, perhaps language-specific, differences in underlying perceptual or cognitive mechanisms. There have been many versions of this general category of hypotheses, but for this discussion it is not necessary to critique particular ones. The general challenge for such perspectives is to account for the many ways affected and unaffected children are similar. If they have faulty perception, memory, or cognitive mechanisms, what constrains their errors and matches their growth trajectories to those of unaffected children? The similarity in growth trajectories suggests that the gains over time, and possible points of change in the acceleration of growth, are similar for affected and unaffected children. How can this be achieved with systems fundamentally different from unaffected children? If affected youngsters accomplish what they do with defective mechanisms, how do they overcome the putative consequences of such limitations? These questions pose strong challenges for interpretive models.

On the other hand, a focus on the similarities by assuming that the underlying language acquisition mechanisms are fundamentally similar for affected and unaffected children brings other questions: What accounts for the delayed onset? What accounts for selective weaknesses in particular dimensions of language? The *extended optional infinitive* (EOI) hypothesis (Rice et al., 1995) provides an explicit model for a well-defined element of morphosyntax that accounts for selective weakness and parallels to younger children and captures well many empirical predictions pertaining to clause structure and long-term risk for morphosyntax.

This model brings many advantages, including an explicit link to models of adult grammar as the end-state grammar, and explication of some of the constraints that may be operative in avoiding errors. It has inspired many follow-up studies that push the boundaries of morphosyntactic phenomena accounted for, within English and across other languages, and it challenges the technical points of the interpretation.

These advantages notwithstanding, an important phenomenon outside the scope of the EOI model is LLE. Maturational mechanisms are invoked as causal factors that unify the growth patterns of affected and unaffected children (cf. Rice, 2007; Wexler, 2003), but ultimately this is an intermediate abstraction to describe unknown mechanisms for driving time-referenced change during the early period of language acquisition and perhaps as a sustaining time-locked mechanism that plays out in a broader developmental trajectory. Fisher (2005) describes advances in neurogenetics that carry promise for clarifying time-locked phases of cortical development that have relevance for language acquisition and other areas of cognitive development. Although "maturational mechanisms" are not well specified at the moment, a path into this black box may not be too far in the future.

CONCLUSIONS

To reprise the title of this chapter, "How Different Is Disordered Language?" the answer may be, "Not as different as assumed earlier, and surprisingly similar in many important ways." The full picture requires recognition of the dimensions of language, of the difference between language delay and language disruption, of separate contributions of a delayed start-up versus the slope and trajectories of growth once the acquisition system is under way, and of a healthy skepticism toward intuitive models of poor parenting as a causal agent. The least explored parts of the picture are the nature of the language-acquisition path from infancy through the toddler period and beyond, the nature of individual differences that infants bring to the journey, and the ways the two elements interact to create risk for language impairment or to ensure that a child will follow the expected trajectory. The experimental and empirical challenges are considerable, but the potential benefits of more information are substantive, for adding not only to our scientific knowledge about basic human abilities but also to our ability to ensure that each child is maximally prepared to benefit from language ability.

ACKNOWLEDGMENTS

The content of this chapter is based on a talk presented in Tempe, Arizona, on September 15–17, 2005, at a workshop sponsored by the Merrill Advanced Studies Center and the National Institute of Child Health and Human Development. Preparation of this chapter was supported by the Merrill Advanced Studies

Center at the University of Kansas and grants from the National Institutes of Health (NIH) to the University of Kansas through the Mental Retardation and Developmental Disabilities Research Center (P30HD002528), the Center for Biobehavioral Neurosciences in Communication Disorders (P30DC005803), R01DC001803, and R01DC005226.

ENDNOTE

1. Asterisk denotes ungrammatical sentence.

REFERENCES

Bedore, L. M. & Leonard, L.B. (1998). Specific language impairment and grammatical morphology: A discriminant function analysis. *Journal of Speech, Language, and Hearing Research, 41,* 1185–1192.

Chomsky, N. (1995). *The minimalist program.* Cambridge, MA: MIT Press.

Conti-Ramsden, G., Botting, N., & Faragher, B. (2001). Psycholinguistic markers for specific language impairment. *Journal of Child Psychology and Psychiatry, 42,* 741–748.

Dunn, L. M. & Dunn, L. M. (1981). *Peabody Picture Vocabulary Test-Revised.* Circle Pines, MN: American Guidance Service.

Entwhistle, D. R. & Astone, N. M. (1994). Some practical guidelines for measuring youths' race/ethnicity and socioeconomic status. *Child Development, 65,* 1521–1540.

Fenson, L., Dale, P. S., Reznick, S., Thal, D., Bates, E., Hartung, J., et al. (1993). *MacArthur Communicative Development Inventories: Users guide and technical manual.* San Diego: Singular.

Fenson, L., Dale, P. S., Reznick, J. S., Bates, E., Thal, D., & Pethick, S. J. (1994). Variability in early communicative development. *Monographs of the Society for Research in Child Development, 59*(5, Serial No. 242), 1–173.

Fisher, S. E. (2005). Dissection of molecular mechanisms underlying speech and language disorders. *Applied Psycholinguistics 26,* 111–128.

Gall, F. (1835). *The function of the brain and each of its parts. 5, Organology.* Boston: Marsh, Capen, & Lyon.

Grela, B. & Leonard, L. B. (2000). The influence of argument structure complexity on the use of auxiliary verbs by children with SLI. *Journal of Speech, Language, and Hearing Research, 43,* 1115–1125.

Guasti, M. T. (2002). *Language acquisition: The growth of grammar.* Cambridge, MA: MIT Press.

Huttenlocher, J., Haight, W., Bryk, A., Seltzer, M., & Lyons, T. (1991). Early vocabulary growth: Relation to language input and gender. *Developmental Psychology, 27*(2), 236–248.

Joseph, K. L., Serratrice, L., & Conti-Ramsden, G. (2002). Development of copula and auxiliary BE in children with specific language impairment and younger unaffected controls. *First Language, 22,*137–172.

Klee, T., Carson, D., Gavin, W., Hall, L., Kent, A., & Reece, S. (1998). Concurrent and predictive validity of an early language screening program. *Journal of Speech and Hearing Research, 41,* 627–641.

Leonard, L. B. (1998). *Children with specific language impairment.* Cambridge, MA: MIT Press.

Leonard, L. B., Camarata, S. M., Brown, B., & Camarata, M. N. (2004). Tense and agreement in the speech of children with specific language impairment: Patterns of generalization through intervention. *Journal of Speech, Language, and Hearing Research, 47,* 1363–1379.

Leonard, L. B., Eyer, J., Bedore, L., & Grela, B. (1997). Three accounts of the grammatical morpheme difficulties of English-speaking children with specific language impairment. *Journal of Speech, Language, and Hearing Research, 40,* 741–753.

Marchman, V. A., Wulfeck, B., & Ellis Weismer, S. (1999). Morphological productivity in children with normal language and SLI: A study of the English past tense. *Journal of Speech, Language, and Hearing Research, 42,* 206–219.

Oetting, J. B. & Horohov, J. E. (1997). Past-tense marking by children with and without specific language impairment. *Journal of Speech, Language, and Hearing Research, 40,* 62–74.

Plomin, R. (1999). Genetics and general cognitive ability. Nature, 402, C25–C29.

Quirk, R., Greenbaum, S., Leech, G., & Svartvik, J. (1985). *A comprehensive grammar of the English language.* New York: Longman, Inc.

Rescorla, L. (1989). The Language Development Survey: A screening tool for delayed language in toddlers. *Journal of Speech and Hearing Disorders, 54,* 587–599.

Rescorla, L. & Achenbach, T. M. (2002). Use of the Language Development Survey (LDS) in a national probability sample of children 18 to 35 months old. *Journal of Speech and Hearing Research, 45*(4), 733–743.

Rescorla, L. & Alley, A. (2001). Validation of the language development survey (LDS): A parent report tool for identifying language delay in toddlers. *Journal of Speech, Language and Hearing Research, 44,* 434–445.

Rescorla, L., Hadick-Wiley, M., & Escarce, E. (1993). Epidemiological investigation of expressive language delay at age two. *First Language, 13,* 5–22.

Rice, M. L. (2003). A unified model of specific and general language delay: Grammatical tense as a clinical marker of unexpected variation. In Y. Levy & J. Schaeffer (Eds.), *Language competence across populations: Toward a definition of specific language impairment* (pp. 63–95). Mahwah, NJ: Lawrence Erlbaum Associates.

Rice, M. L. (2004). Growth models of developmental language disorders. In M. L. Rice & S. F. Warren (Eds.), *Developmental language disorders: From phenotypes to etiologies* (pp. 207–240). Mahwah, NJ: Lawrence Erlbaum.

Rice, M. L. (2007). Children with specific language impairment: Bridging the genetic and developmental perspectives. In E. Hoff & M. Shatz (Eds.), *Blackwell handbook of language development* (pp. 411–431). Boston: Wiley-Blackwell.

Rice, M. L., Redmond, S. M., & Hoffman, L. (2006). MLU in children with SLI and younger control children shows concurrent validity, stable and parallel growth trajectories. *Journal of Speech, Language, and Hearing Research, 49,* 793–808.

Rice, M. L. & Smolik, F. (2007). Genetics of language disorders: Clinical conditions, phenotypes, and genes. In G. Gaskell (Ed.), *Oxford Handbook of Psycholinguistics* (pp. 685–702). Oxford: Oxford University Press.

Rice, M. L., Tomblin, J. B., Hoffman, L. M., Richman, W. A.., & Marquis, J. (2004). Grammatical tense deficits in children with SLI and nonspecific language impairment: Relationships with nonverbal IQ over time. *Journal of Speech, Language, and Hearing Research, 47,* 816–834.

Rice, M. L. & Warren, S. F. (2004). *Developmental language disorders: From phenotypes to etiologies.* Mahwah, NJ: Lawrence Erlbaum.

Rice, M. L., Warren, S. F., & Betz, S. K. (2005). Language symptoms of developmental language disorders: An overview of autism, Dawn syndrome, fragile X, specific language impairment, and Williams syndrome. *Applied Psycholinguistics, 26,* 7–28.

Rice, M. L. & Wexler, K. (1996). Toward tense as a clinical marker of specific language impairment in English-speaking children. *Journal of Speech and Hearing Research, 39,* 850–863.

Rice, M. L., Wexler, K., & Cleave, P. L. (1995). Specific language impairment as a period of extended optional infinitive. *Journal of Speech, Language, and Hearing Research, 38,* 850–863.

Rice, M. L., Wexler, K., Marquis, J., & Hershberger, S. (2000). Acquisition of irregular past tense by children with SLI. *Journal of Speech, Language, and Hearing Research, 43,* 1126–1145.

Rice, M. L., Wexler, K., & Redmond, S. M. (1999). Grammaticality judgments of an extended optional infinitive grammar: Evidence from English-speaking children with specific language impairment. *Journal of Speech, Language, and Hearing Research, 42,* 943–961.

Schütze, C. T. (2004). Morphosyntax and syntax. In R. D. Kent (Ed.), *The MIT encyclopedia of communication disorders* (pp. 354–358). Cambridge, MA: MIT Press.

Schütze, C. T. & Wexler, K. (1996). Subject case licensing and English root infinitives. In A. Stringfellow, D. Cahana-Amitay, E. Hughes, & A. Zukowski (Eds.), *Proceedings of the 20th Annual Boston University Conference on Language Development* (pp. 670–681). Somerville, MA: Cascadilla Press.

Shriberg, L. D., Tomblin, J. B., & McSweeny, J. L. (1999). Prevalence of speech delay in 6-year-old children and comorbidity with language impairment. *Journal of Speech, Language, and Hearing Research, 42,* 1461–1481.

Tager-Flusberg, H. (2004). Do autism and specific language impairment represent overlapping language disorders? In M. L. Rice & S. F. Warren (Eds.), *Developmental language disorders: From phenotypes to etiologies* (pp. 31–52). Mahwah, NJ: Lawrence Erlbaum.

Tager-Flusberg, H. (2005). Designing studies to investigate the relationships between genes, environments, and developmental language disorders. *Applied Psycholinguistics, 26,* 29–40.

Tomblin, J. B. & Zhang, X. (1999). Language patterns and etiology in children with specific language impairment. In H. Tager-Flusberg (Ed.), *Neurodevelopmental disorders* (pp. 361–382). Cambridge, MA: MIT Press.

Tomblin, J. B., Records, N. L., Buckwalter, P., Zhang, X., Smith, E., & O'Brien, M. (1997). The prevalence of specific language impairment in kindergarten children. *Journal of Speech and Hearing Research, 40,* 1245–1260.

Wang, H., Parry, S., Macones, G., Sammel, M. D., Kuivaniemi, H., Tromp, G., et al. (2006). A functional SNP in the promoter of the *SERPINH1* gene increases risk of preterm premature rupture of membranes in African Americans. *Proceedings of the National Academy of Sciences of the United States of America, 103*(36), 13463–13467.

Wells, G. (1985). *Language development in the pre-school years.* Cambridge, England: Cambridge University Press.

Wexler, K. (1994). Optional infinitives, head movement and the economy of derivations. In D. Lightfoot & N. Hornstein (Eds.), *Verb movement* (pp. 305–350). Cambridge, England: Cambridge University Press.

Wexler, K. (1996). The development of inflection in a biologically based theory of language acquisition. In M. L. Rice (Ed.), *Toward a genetics of language* (pp. 113–144). Mahwah, NJ: Lawrence Erlbaum Associates.

Wexler, K. (1998). Very early parameter setting and the unique checking constraint: A new explanation of the optional infinitive stage. *Lingua, 106,* 23–79.

Wexler, K. (2003). Lenneberg's dream: Learning, normal language development and specific language impairment. In Y. Levy & J. Schaeffer (Eds.), *Language competence across populations: Towards a definition of specific language impairment* (pp. 11–61). Mahwah, NJ: Lawrence Erlbaum.

Wexler, K., Schütze, C. T., & Rice, M. L. (1998). Subject case in children with SLI and unaffected controls: Evidence for the Agr/Tns Omission model. *Language Acquisition, 7,* 317–344.

Zubrick, S., Taylor, C., Rice, M. L. & Slegers, D. (2007). Late language emergence at 24 months: An epidemiological study of prevalence and covariates. *Journal of Speech, Language, & Hearing Research 50*:1562–1592.

II

FROM PATTERNS TO MEANING

6

Infant Speech Perception and Later Language Acquisition
Methodological Underpinnings

JANET F. WERKER AND CHRISTOPHER T. FENNELL

In this chapter we discuss the link between speech perception and later word learning, with a focus on methodology. We begin with a review of the infant speech perception literature, followed closely by a detailed examination of studies showing that at the earliest stages of word learning, infants appear to be unable to use discriminable phonetic detail to distinguish newly learned words. Two explanations for this temporary difficulty have been offered. One suggests a representational discontinuity (RD) between speech perception and word learning, wherein representations have to be constructed anew at the onset of vocabulary acquisition. A second suggests that the representation remains constant in terms of its contents but that processing limitations interfere with the infants' ability to preferentially access the distinguishing phonetic detail. This resource limitation (RL) hypothesis thus contrasts with the RD explanation. We describe how the systematic application of variations in a single methodology, together with the theoretically guided use of complementary methodologies, reveals that the perceptual categories established in infancy do indeed guide word learning, providing support for an initial RL explanation. We argue that without careful attention to, and application of, methodology, the link between speech perception and word learning could be overlooked.

During the first year of life, infants rapidly tune their phonetic perception to match the functional requirements of the language they are learning. Very young infants show broad-based phonetic sensitivities: They discriminate many of the distinctions used across the world's languages—including nonnative phonetic distinctions unlikely to have been heard before (for a review, see Saffran, Werker, & Werner, 2006). But, as they develop across the first year, infants become less sensitive to phonetic distinctions that are not used in the native language, be they segmental (consonants and vowels; see Anderson, Morgan, & White, 2003; Best, McRoberts, LaFleur, & Silver-Isenstadt, 1995; Bosch & Sebastián-Gallés, 2003; Kuhl, Williams, Lacerda, Stevens, & Lindblom, 1992; Werker & Tees, 1984), tonal (Mattock & Burnham, 2006), or visual (sign language; see Baker, Michnick-Golinkoff, & Petitto, 2006). During the same period, infants become increasingly sensitive to phonetic distinctions that are used in the native language (Kuhl et al., 2006; see also Polka, Colontonio, & Sundara, 2001). These two patterns have been characterized as maintenance (listening experience is required to maintain discrimination) and facilitation (listening experience sharpens discrimination), respectively (Aslin & Pisoni, 1980; see Kuhl, 2004, or Werker & Tees, 2005, for a discussion of the effects of experience).

In the two decades following the demonstration of language-specific tuning in the first year of life, a number of different models were proposed to account for the change. Initial models assumed that it was when infants began to map sound onto meaning (i.e., word learning) that they would reorganize their categories in line with the functional requirements of the native language (e.g., Werker & Pegg, 1992). Had these expectations been supported, the link between infant speech perception and word learning would be unambiguous. There is as yet, however, no evidence to support the notion that infants' phonetic categories change in response to knowledge of meaningful contrasts (but see Yeung & Werker, 2006). Instead, there is now strong evidence that simple perceptual learning can account for the changes. Hence, more recent models have focused on perceptual or perceptual-motor based explanations that do not require reference to meaningful words. Two of the most influential have been the Perceptual Assimilation Model (PAM; Best, 1994; Best & McRoberts, 2003) and the Native Language Magnet Model (NLM; Kuhl, 1993, 2004). Both of these are similarity-based models, with PAM rooted in articulation, specifically articulatory phonology, and NLM explained by frequency-based emergent prototypes that serve as attractors in multidimensional acoustic space (e.g., Iverson et al., 2003).

In a recent paper, Maye, Werker, and Gerken (2002) demonstrated that perceptually based distributional learning is a possible mechanism that could account for the changes in phonetic perception without reference to meaning (see also Maye, Weiss, & Aslin, 2008). Building on the statistical learning literature that shows that infants are able to track different types of regularities in the input (e.g., Saffran, Aslin, & Newport, 1996), Maye and colleagues (2002) asked whether infants might change their phonetic categories by tracking distributional frequency characteristics in the language input. They reasoned that infants who grow up in a language that uses a particular distinction (e.g., /r/ vs. /l/) will hear two distributions, one centered on each consonant, whereas infants who grow up in a language without such a distinction will have a distribution with a center point somewhere between the two categories—a unimodal distribution.

Maye and colleagues tested this hypothesis by creating an eight-step continuum within the English [d] phonetic category. One group of infants heard a bimodal distribution (more instances of stimuli 2 and 7), and a second group heard a unimodal distribution (more instances of stimuli 4 and 5). Following 2.4 minutes of familiarization to these [d] stimuli played in random order, infants in the bimodal but not the unimodal condition were able to discriminate the endpoints, stimuli 1 versus 8. Thus, on the basis of distributional learning, infants modified their phonetic categories in just over 2 minutes of familiarization. This effect has now been replicated in two additional studies (Maye et al., 2008; Yoshida, Pons, & Werker, 2006).

The demonstration of statistical learning as a mechanism by which phonetic categories can be changed is of interest, but the fact that categories are induced by perceptual learning rather than linguistic contrast raises the suspicion that perhaps infant speech perception is *not* related to later linguistic use. Hence, we began to explore the question of whether there is a link between perception and word learning by asking whether infants use their native language phonetic categories to guide word learning. Rather than asking whether the acquisition of meaningful words guides phonetic category learning, we have been asking whether the phonetic categories established via perceptual learning guide vocabulary acquisition.

After a number of false starts with insufficiently reliable procedures (see Stager & Werker, 1998), we developed the switch task, in collaboration with Les Cohen, to test infants' ability to associate words with objects (Werker, Cohen, Lloyd, Casasola, & Stager, 1998). In the switch task, the infant is habituated to two moving objects, presented one at a time, each accompanied by a different word (Object A–Word A; Object B–Word B). Following habituation, the infant is tested by comparing his or her looking time in two trials. The *same trial* is a repetition of one of the habituation trials (Object A–Word A). In the *switch trial,* the infant is shown one of the familiar objects and hears one of the familiar words, but the pairing has been changed (Object A–Word B). If the infant has learned not only the words and the objects but also the link between them, the switch should be novel and should garner a longer looking time than the same trial. If the infant has only learned the words and the objects but not the link, both trial types should be equally familiar. In this manner, the switch procedure provides a test of word–object associative learning, a critical step toward full referential word learning.

In the switch task, infants can reliably learn the link between dissimilar sounding words and different objects by, but not before, 14 months of age (Werker et al., 1998). Surprisingly, infants of 14 months fail in this procedure when the auditory labels of the objects are similar sounding—differing only in one consonantal phonetic feature. For example, whereas 14-month-old infants succeed when nonsense words such as *lif* and *neem* are used as object names, they fail when the nonsense labels *bih* and *dih* are used (Stager & Werker, 1997). This failure is seen even though infants this age can discriminate the relevant phonetic difference, [b] versus [d], in a simple syllable discrimination task. This finding that infants have difficulty associating similar-sounding labels to different objects extends to the better-formed novel words *bin* and *din* and to other contrasts such as *pin* and *din* (Pater, Stager, & Werker, 2004) or bisyllabic words such as *dawgoo* and *tawgoo* (Thiessen, 2007). Indeed, infants of 14 months even fail when only a single object–label pairing is required: If habituated to one object called *dih* and then tested with a minimal change in the object's label (e.g., *bih*), infants of 14 months continue to fail. This is particularly surprising because, in this more minimal task, younger infants of 8 months succeed (Stager & Werker, 1997). Stager and Werker (1997) argued that this is because 8-month-old infants treat the task as a simple discrimination task, only attending to the sounds and not the object, whereas at 14 months infants treat it as one of word learning. It is reasoned that the presence of a nameable object coupled with a candidate word invokes word learning at 14 months of age but not at 8 months (for similar arguments, see Hallé & de Boysson-Bardies, 1996; Nazzi & Bertoncini, 2003). It is not until 17 months of age and older that infants, as a group, succeed at learning minimally different novel words in the switch task (Werker, Fennell, Corcoran, & Stager, 2002). This developmental pattern is supported by neurophysiological data. Evidence for confusion of similar-sounding words at 14, but not 20, months of age has been shown using an event related potential (ERP) index of word recognition (Mills et al., 2004).

Why don't infants use discriminable phonetic detail to guide word learning at 14 months? As mentioned earlier, two types of explanations have been offered. According to the RD hypothesis, perceptual phonetic detail is simply not present in the early lexical representation. As maintained by this class of explanation, there is a discontinuity between speech perception and lexical learning—between the phonetic categories formed in the first year and the phonological categories used in word learning (e.g., Barton, 1980; Brown & Matthews, 1997; Ferguson & Farwell, 1979; Fikkert, 2005; Garnica, 1973; Jakobson, 1941/1968; Kay-Raining Bird & Chapman, 1998; Keating, 1984; Pierrehumbert, 1990; Pollock, 1987; Rice & Avery, 1995; Shvachkin, 1948/1973). As infants learn words, they begin forming categories anew based on the phonological contrasts found in their lexicon. Hence, according to RD explanations, there is no necessary link between infant-based speech perception and later word learning. An RD hypothesis could, in some sense, most easily account for the data previously reviewed showing that infants do not use phonetic detail in the initial stages of word learning. We, however, have argued against this class of explanations and have suggested instead an RL hypothesis. According to the RL hypothesis, phonetic detail is detected and represented in words, but it is not used. This explanation posits a continuity between speech perception and word learning but suggests that the processing demands of learning new words interfere with access and use of the phonetic detail (see Fennell & Werker, 2003; Stager & Werker, 1997; Werker & Fennell, 2004), particularly for a novice word learner who is not yet accomplished at associating arbitrary words and objects. More recently, as will be elaborated at the end of this chapter, we have expanded this hypothesis and have suggested that a key reason the computational demands are so high is that initially infants give equal weight to every feature in their lexical representations and do not yet have the mature lexical knowledge that phonetic detail should be given more weight in contrasting word meanings than should features such as the gender or emotional tone of the speaker (Werker & Curtin, 2005).

The experimental evidence to date has been interpreted by some as favoring an RD hypothesis and by others as supporting an RL hypothesis. Some of the results can legitimately be interpreted either way. For example, when infants first begin to treat word as meaningful entities (at 11 to 14 months), they are more likely to treat mispronunciations of known words as familiar (Hallé & de Boysson-Bardies, 1996), particularly if the phonetic difference is on an unstressed syllable (Vihman, Nakai, DePaolis, & Hallé, 2004). The experimental methodology used here is a head-turn preference procedure, wherein infants in some experiments show "false" recognition of mispronunciations. These results have been interpreted as supporting an RD hypothesis (Hallé & de Boysson-Bardies, 1996; Nazzi & Bertoncini, 2003), but the possibility also exists—as argued previously with our own work using the switch task—that the processing demands of the task mask underlying representational detail.

The support for the RL hypothesis is, we believe, more convincing. In a series of studies, Swingley and Aslin (2000, 2002; see also Swingley, 2005) showed infants as young as 14 months two images side by side (e.g., a car and a baby) while simultaneously presenting a spoken word that matched one of the pictures. Infants looked longer at the matching picture when the word is pronounced correctly (e.g., *baby*) than when it is mispronounced (e.g., *vaby*). Thus, by noticing mispronunciations of familiar words, infants appear to access and use full phonetic detail at 14 months of age. The RL hypothesis accounts for the success in the preferential looking versus the switch task by noting that the preferential looking task has measured *recognition* of familiar words rather than word *learning* (see Fennell & Werker, 2003). Word *recognition*, particularly when the image of the referent is also available, is not as computationally demanding as word *learning*. For these reasons, a word recognition task with pictures of the named objects present is likely better able to reveal the phonetic detail in the lexical representation.

More generally, the RL hypothesis argues that if the computational demands are reduced, there should be evidence of phonetic detail in the lexical representation, even at the earliest stages of word learning. To further test this hypothesis, Fennell designed a series of experiments with 14-month-olds using the switch task or a variation of it. Each of the experiments presented here reduced the computational demands in the word learning situation in a different way, and each revealed evidence of phonetic detail in the lexical representation. Four studies are briefly described.

In the first study, infants aged 14 months were tested on *known* words that differed in precisely the same features as the *novel* words they had failed at in the original work. Hence, rather than testing infants on their ability to associate the nonce words *bih* and *dih* with two different objects, infants were tested with the known word–object pairings *ball* and *doll* (these words form a minimal pair in Western Canadian English, as they share a common vowel). In this case, the computational demands were lightened by removing the requirement that the infant actually learn a new word–object pairing in the task. When tested with these previously known words, infants of 14 months succeeded (Fennell & Werker, 2003). According to many proponents of the RD hypothesis (e.g., Jakobson, 1941/1968; Rice & Avery, 1995), contrastive features are added to phonological representations in a stepwise fashion. Once established in the phonology, those features should be available for any lexical item—new or old. Fennell and Werker's (2003) results thus provide two kinds of evidence against an RD hypothesis:

1. These results show that infants of 14 months can access phonetic detail if computational demands are reduced.
2. They are able to access precisely the same detail ([b] versus [d]) that infants this age failed to use in a word-learning version of the task.

One argument that could be offered against the aforementioned experiment is that perhaps particularly well-known words like *ball* or *doll* can stand alone as recognizable items (exemplars). Here, the individual sound segments /b/ and /d/ do not need to be fully phonetically specified in the overall phonology—they are simply available in these highly familiar words. To test this possibility, Fennell (2004) designed a second study wherein the computational requirements were reduced in the switch task by presenting infants not with familiar words but instead with a familiar, but heretofore unlabeled, object. Here, it was reasoned that if infants already know the object, the demands of the task are reduced because infants do not need to learn object details during the habituation phase. This in turn would increase the cognitive resources available and allow the infant to access and use the phonetic detail in the label. To familiarize infants with the object, parents of 12-month-old infants were given a unique, hard-to-label toy to take home. The parents were instructed to show the toy to the infant on a regular basis but not to label it in any way. The infants were brought back into the lab 6–8 weeks later, during their 14th month. At this time, they were tested in the switch task, during which the object was, of course, paired with a novel word, *din*. Following habituation, infants were tested on a mispronunciation of the newly learned word: *gin* (with a hard [g]). The 14-month-old infants who had been familiarized with the toy at home were able to perform successfully: They looked longer to the switch trial . A control group of same-aged infants who had never seen the target object prior to the habituation phase were tested with the exact same object–label stimuli. This group of infants failed to notice the switch in labels. Thus, as predicted by the RL hypothesis, when the computational demands were reduced by using a familiar object, the infants were able not only to successfully link the word and object but also to access and use the phonetic detail.

The computational demands placed on the novice word learner could also be reduced by presenting the target words in a richer referential context—in sentential frames that highlight that the novel word is a noun. In the standard switch procedure, the novel objects are paired with novel labels that are presented repeatedly but in isolation (e.g., "Bin. Bin. Bin."). Within the realm of word learning, presenting words in isolation may complicate infants' task. Arguably, words are not typically presented in isolation in natural speech (Aslin, Woodward, LaMendola, & Bever, 1996; but see Brendt & Siskind, 2001 for evidence that words presented alone are the easiest to learn). When they do occur alone, words are most likely to be commands or exclamations ("Stop!" "Wow!") and are unlikely to be referential or names for things. Even older infants of 17 months are better able to correctly extend a novel word to new members of the relevant object category when it is learned in a sentential frame than when it is learned in isolation (Namy & Waxman, 2000). Following this line of reasoning, Fennell and Waxman (in preparation) and Fennell (2006) proposed that if the novel words are presented within naming phrases, their referential status would become clearer, and that this clarity should alleviate the otherwise difficult task of linking words to objects. This hypothesis was supported in that infants of 14 months were able to notice a minimal change in object label from habituation to test (i.e., *bin* to *din*) in the switch task when the novel label was placed in naming phrases (Fennell, 2006). The infants' success in using phonetic detail is an especially powerful result considering that the novel words were presented in a far more crowded speech space than when presented in isolation, with the infants having to parse the relevant words from the ongoing speech signal before comparing their phonetic detail.

The three studies presented thus far all reduced the computational demands in the habituation phase. However, it has been suggested that the test phase of the switch task might be particularly demanding because it requires infants to *recall* a stored match and to compare that stored memory with the currently presented object stimulus (Ballem & Plunkett, 2005; Fennell & Werker, 2003; Swingley & Aslin, 2002; Swingley & Fernald, 2002). The preferential looking test used in the Swingley and Aslin (2000, 2002) studies is argued to be potentially less demanding because infants see both objects and are only required to *recognize* the object matching the label. Furthermore, whereas the switch task relies on infants' surprise to a novel object–label pairing (necessitating a sufficiently strong "mismatch" signal), preferential visual fixation tasks tap the degree to which the object is a match for the presented sound. Hence, in a final test of the RL hypothesis, we tested access and use of phonetic detail when the resource requirements were reduced in the test phase of the switch task rather than the habituation phase.

To test our hypothesis that a reduction in test demands would also reveal infants' underlying ability to use phonetic detail, we combined the standard habituation phase of the switch procedure with the preferential looking visual fixation testing procedure used by Swingley and Aslin (2000, 2002), among others. We habituated infants of 14 months to two novel words, *bin* and *din*, paired with two novel objects, as in the standard switch task. At test, however, they saw both objects simultaneously and heard the label for one of the two objects. Looking time to the correctly matching object was the dependent variable. When tested in this word recognition design, infants of 14 months succeeded, looking significantly longer to the correct than to the incorrect object (Yoshida, Fennell, Swingley, & Werker, in press; see also Ballem & Plunkett, 2005, for a similar study). These data also answer a question arising from previous work with similar-sounding words in the standard switch task. In those studies, infants' apparent failure to use phonetic detail in novel words could have arisen from an inability to encode the relevant information during learning or an inability to sufficiently retrieve the relevant detail at test. Since the learning (i.e., habituation) phase of this final study did not differ from previous work using the switch task, infants' success in using phonetic detail in the less demanding test phase demonstrates that novice word learners are able to encode relevant phonetic detail when learning novel words.

The previous studies provide strong support for the RL hypothesis. When tested in systematic variations of the switch task that reduce computational demands in the habituation phase, infants of 14 months can use fine phonetic detail to distinguish words. Further, the use of a complementary methodology, the preferential looking procedure, demonstrated that infants encode relevant phonetic detail in the standard habituation phase of the switch and that a reduction in demands in the test phase will reveal that detailed phonetic encoding in novel words. This series of studies, we believe, reveals how careful use of methodology can unpack and clarify an otherwise irresolvable theoretical controversy.

Several unanswered questions remain, however. First and foremost, although a case has been made that the RL hypothesis can account for why infants of 14 months might fail at learning minimally different words in the standard switch task, an explanation has not been offered as to what changes after 14 months that allows infants of 17 months and older to succeed in the standard switch task. We have suggested in previous writings that by 17 months infants are more accomplished word learners and hence can handle the resource requirements (see Werker & Fennell, 2004; Werker et al., 2002). But what does being a more accomplished word learner entail?

Recently, Werker and Curtin (2005; see also Curtin & Werker, 2007) proposed a framework to provide a fuller account of this developmental change. According to this framework, called Processing Rich Information from Multidimensional Interactive Representations (PRIMIR), infants encode rich information from speech both in perception and when learning words. Importantly, however, this rich information includes not only the phonetic detail distinguishing one form from another but also indexical detail such as speaker gender and affect (for evidence, see Singh, Morgan, & White, 2004). At the earliest stages of word learning, particularly when word learning is merely an associative act, infants do not know which information in the rich, multidimensional representation is most important. This makes the resource requirements particularly demanding. And if they hear a new word that is similar in most of the details of the representation (same syllable form, same voice, same intonational contour, same affect, and all segments and phonetic features identical save one), the infant may simply treat the similarities as more important than the differences unless something about the training or testing situation either reduces the representational load or highlights the criterial information. In PRIMIR, it is argued that once the infant establishes a sufficient number of associative word–object lexical entries, phonetic feature values that contrast one word meaning from another emerge as a more consistent regularity than the indexical features. Thus, in learning rudimentary word meanings, a representation with the power and productivity of a commutable "phoneme" emerges. The phoneme, in turn, enables the infant to direct attention in a privileged fashion to phonetic over indexical detail when a new word is being learned. By its very nature, the privileged attentional focus that emergent phonemes afford makes the phonetic detail front and center and, hence, more accessible for use. The emergence of phoneme like units thus has the added advantage of reducing the computational requirements and of facilitating more efficient word learning.

We return now to the initial question that motivated the development of the switch task: Do the language-specific phonetic categories established in the first year via perceptual learning help direct word learning? And finally, we can say "yes." When infants reach 17–20 months (the age at which they can succeed at learning minimally different words in the switch task), they use their native language phonetic categories to guide them. The most exciting demonstration of this is provided in a study of vowel length. Vowel length is used to contrast meaning in Dutch but not in English. At 17 months of age, Dutch- but not English-learning infants use the Dutch vowel-length distinction to guide word learning (Dietrich, Swingley, & Werker, 2004, 2007). By 17 months of age, then, infants can appropriately use native-language phonetic detail to guide word learning. Hence, it can be seen that although there may be difficulties in accessing phonetic detail in the earliest stages of word learning, ultimately the perceptual learning that occurs during the first year of life does indeed *bootstrap* lexical acquisition (Werker & Yeung, 2005).

In summary, this chapter has reviewed the literature investigating the link between infant speech perception and the first steps in word learning. We have shown how the language-specific phonetic categories established in infancy, via perceptual learning, link to later word learning. Although infants may have difficulty accessing and using phonetic detail in the first stages of word learning, we have argued that the detail is available—along with considerable other detail—in the earliest lexical representations. Our ability to reveal the presence of that detail varies as a function of task conditions. As such, we have suggested that the careful and appropriate use of methodology not only can further empirical understanding but also can help resolve theoretical controversies.

REFERENCES

Anderson, J., Morgan, J., & White, K. (2003). A statistical basis for speech sound discrimination. *Language & Speech, 46,* 155–182.

Aslin, R. N. & Pisoni, D. B. (1980). Some developmental processes in speech perception. In G. H. Yeni-Komshian, J. Kavanagh, & C. A. Ferguson (Eds.), *Child phonology: Perception* (Vol. 2. pp. 67–96). New York: Academic Press.

Aslin, R. N., Saffran, J. R., & Newport, E. L. (1998). Computation of conditional probability statistics by 8-month-old infants. *Psychological Science, 9*(4), 321–324.

Aslin, R. N., Woodward, J. Z., LaMendola, N. P., & Bever, T. G. (1996). Models of word segmentation in fluent maternal speech to infants. In J. L. Morgan & K. Demuth (Eds.), *Signal to syntax: Bootstrapping from speech to grammar in early acquisition* (pp. 117–134). Mahwah, NJ: Lawrence Erlbaum.

Baker, S. A., Michnick-Golinkoff, R. M., & Petitto, L. A. (2006). New insights into old puzzles from infants' perception of soundless phonetic units. *Language Learning and Development, 2*(3), 147–162.

Ballem, K. & Plunkett, K. (2005). Phonological specificity in children at 1;2. *Journal of Child Language, 32,* 159–173.

Barton, D. (1980). Phonemic perception in children. In G. H. Yeni-Komshian, J. F. Kavanagh & C. A. Ferguson (Eds.), *Child phonology: Perception* (Vol. 2). New York: Academic Press.

Best, C. T. (1994). The emergence of native-language phonological influences in infants: A perceptual assimilation model. In J. C. Goodman & H. C. Nusbaum (Eds.), *The development of speech perception: The transition from speech sounds to spoken words* (pp. 167–224). Cambridge, MA: MIT Press.

Best, C. T. & McRoberts, G. W. (2003). Infant perception of non-native consonant contrasts that adults assimilate in different ways. *Language & Speech, 46,* 183–216.

Best, C. T., McRoberts, G. W., LaFleur, R., & Silver-Isenstadt, J. (1995). Divergent developmental patterns for infants' perception of two nonnative consonant contrasts. *Infant Behavior and Development, 18*(3), 339–350.

Bosch, L. & Sebastián-Gallés, N. (2003). Simultaneous bilingualism and the perception of a language-specific vowel contrast in the first year of life. *Language and Speech, 46,* 217–243.

Brent, M. R. & Siskind, J. M. (2001). The role of exposure to isolated words in early vocabulary development. *Cognition, 81*(2), B33–B44.

Brown, C. & Matthews, J. (1997). The role of feature geometry in the development of phonemic contrasts. In S. J. Hannahs & M. Young-Scholten (Eds.), *Focus on phonological acquisition* (pp. 67–112). Amsterdam: John Benjamins.

Curtin, S. & Werker, J. F. (2007). The perceptual foundation of phonological development. In G. Gaskell (Ed.), *The Oxford handbook of psycholinguistics.* New York: Oxford University Press.

Dietrich, C., Swingley, D., & Werker, J. F. (2004). Native language governs interpretation of salient speech sound differences at 18 months. *Proceedings of the National Academy of Sciences of the USA.* Vol. 4, 16027–16031.

Fennell, C. T. (2004). *Infant attention to phonetic detail in word forms: Knowledge and familiarity effects.* Unpublished doctoral dissertation, University of British Columbia, Vancouver.

Fennell, C. T. (2006). Infants of 14 months use phonetic detail in novel words embedded in naming phrases. In *Proceedings of the 30th Annual Boston University Conference on Language Development* (pp. 178–189). Somerville, MA: Cascadilla Press.

Fennell, C. T. & Waxman, S. R. Infants' use of phonetic detail in novel words: The case for referential clarity. Manuscript in preparation.

Fennell, C. T. & Werker, J. F. (2003). Early word learners' ability to access phonetic detail in well-known words. *Language & Speech, 46*(2), 245–264.

Ferguson, C. A. & Farwell, C. B. (1979). Words and sounds in early language acquisition. *Language, 51,* 419–439.

Fikkert, P. (2005). Getting sounds structures in mind. Acquisition bridging linguistics and psychology? In A. E. Cutler (Ed.), *Twenty-first* century psycholinguistics: *Four* cornerstones *(pp. 43–56).* Hillsdale, NJ: Lawrence Erlbaum Associates.

Garnica, O. K. (1973). The development of phonemic speech perception. In T. E. Moore (Ed.), *Cognitive development and the acquisition of language* (pp. 215–222). New York: Academic Press.

Hallé, P. & de Boysson-Bardies, B. (1996). The format of representation of recognized words in infants' early receptive lexicon. *Infant Behavior and Development, 19,* 463–481.

Iverson, P., Kuhl, P. K., Akahane-Yamada, R., Diesch, E., Tohkura, Y., Kettermann, A., et al. (2003). A perceptual interference account of acquisition difficulties for non-native phonemes. *Cognition, 87,* B47–B57.

Jakobson, R. (1968). *Child language, aphasia, and phonological universals.* The Hague: Mouton. (Original work published 1941)

Kay-Raining Bird, E. & Chapman, R. S. (1998). Partial representations and phonological selectivity in the comprehension of 13- to 16-month-olds. *First Language, 18,* 105–127.

Keating, P. A. (1984). Phonetic and phonological representation of stop consonant voicing. *Language, 60,* 286–319.

Kuhl, P. K. (1993). Innate predispositions and the effects of experience in speech perception: The native language magnet theory. In B. de Boysson-Bardies, S. de Schonen, P. Jusczyk, P. McNeilage, & J. Morton (Eds.), *Developmental neurocognition: Speech and face processing in the first year of life* (pp. 259–274). Dordrecht: Kluwer Academic Publishers.

Kuhl, P. K. (2004). Early language acquisition: Cracking the speech code. *Nature Reviews Neuroscience, 5,* 831–843.

Kuhl, P. K., Stevens, E., Hayashi, A., Deguchi, T., Kiritani, S., & Iverson, P. (2006). Infants show a facilitation effect for native language perception between 6 and 12 months. *Developmental Science, 9*(2), F1–F9.

Kuhl, P. K., Williams, K. A., Lacerda, F., Stevens, K. N., & Lindblom, B. (1992). Language experience alters phonetic perception in infants by 6 months of age. *Science, 255,* 606–608.

Mattock, K. & Burnham, D. (2006). Chinese and English infants' tone perception: Evidence for perceptual reorganization. *Developmental Science, 10*(3), 241–265.

Maye, J., Weiss, D., & Aslin, R. N. (2008). Statistical phonetic learning in infants: Facilitation and feature generalization. *Developmental Science, 11,* 122–134.

Maye, J., Werker, J. F., & Gerken, L. (2002). Infant sensitivity to distributional information can affect phonetic discrimination. *Cognition, 82,* 101–111.

Mills, D. L., Prat, C., Zangl, R., Stager, C. L., Neville, H. J., & Werker, J. F. (2004). Language experience and the organization of brain activity to phonetically similar words: ERP evidence from 14- and 20-month-olds. *Journal of Cognitive Neuroscience, 16*(8), 1–13.

Namy, L. L. & Waxman, S R. (2000). Naming and exclaiming: Infants' sensitivity to naming contexts. *Journal of Cognition and Development, 1*(4), 405–428.

Nazzi, T. & Bertoncini, J. (2003). Before and after the vocabulary spurt: Two modes of word acquisition? *Developmental Science, 6,* 136–142.

Pater, J., Stager, C. L., & Werker, J. F. (2004). The perceptual acquisition of phonological contrast. *Language, 80,* 384–402.

Pierrehumbert, J. (1990). Phonological and phonetic representation. *Journal of Phonetics, 18*(3), 375–394.

Polka, L., Colontonio, C., & Sundara, M. (2001). A cross-language comparison of /d/ -/ð/ perception: Evidence for a new developmental pattern. Journal of Acoustical Society of America, *109,* 190–220.

Pollock, K. E. (1987). Phonological perception of early words in young children using a visual search paradigm. *Dissertation Abstracts International, 48*(2-B), 405.

Rice, K. & Avery, P. (1995). Variability in a deterministic model of language acquisition: A theory of segmental elaboration. In J. Archibald (Ed.), *Phonological acquisition and phonological theory* (pp. 23–42). Hillsdale, NJ: Lawrence Erlbaum.

Saffran, J. R., Aslin, R. N., & Newport, E. L. (1996). Statistical learning by 8-month-old infants. *Science, 274,* 1926–1928.

Saffran, J. R., Werker, J. F., & Werner, L. A. (2006). The infant's auditory world: Hearing, speech, and the beginnings of language. In R. Siegler & D. Kuhn (Eds.), *Handbook of child development* (6th ed., pp. 58–108). New York: Wiley.

Shvachkin, N. K. (1973). The development of phonemic speech perception in early childhood. In C. Ferguson & D. Slobin (Eds.), *Studies of child language development* (pp. 91–127). New York: Holt, Rinehart & Winston. (Original work published 1948)

Singh, L., Morgan, J., & White, K. (2004). Preference and processing: The role of speech affect in early speech spoken word recognition. *Journal of Memory and Language 51*, 173–189.

Stager, C. L. & Werker, J. F. (1997). Infants listen for more phonetic detail in speech perception than in word-learning tasks. *Nature, 388*, 381–382.

Stager, C. L. & Werker, J. F. (1998). Methodological issues in studying the link between speech perception and word learning. In C. Rovee-Collier, L. P. Lipsitt, & H. Hayne (Eds.), *Advances in infancy research* (pp. 237–256). Stamford, CT: Ablex Publishing Company.

Swingley, D. (2005). 11-month-olds' knowledge of how familiar words sound. *Developmental Science, 8*, 432–443.

Swingley, D. & Aslin, R. N. (2000). Spoken word recognition and lexical representation in very young children. *Cognition, 76*, 147–166.

Swingley, D. & Aslin, R. N. (2002). Lexical neighbourhoods and the word-form representations of 14-month-olds. *Psychological Science, 13*, 480–484.

Swingley, D. & Fernald, A. (2002). Recognition of words referring to present and absent objects by 24-month-olds. *Journal of Memory and Language, 46*, 39–56.

Thiessen, E. D. (2007). The effect of distributional information on children's use of phonemic contrasts. *Journal of Memory and Language, 56*(1), 16–34.

Vihman, M., Nakai, S., DePaolis, R. A., & Hallé, P. (2004). The role of accentual pattern in early lexical representation. *Journal of Memory and Language, 50*(3), 336–353.

Werker, J. F., Cohen, L. B., Lloyd, V. L., Casasola, M., & Stager, C. L. (1998). Acquisition of word-object associations by 14-month old infants. *Developmental Psychology, 34*, 1289–1309.

Werker, J. F. & Curtin, S. (2005). PRIMIR: A developmental model of speech processing. *Language Learning and Development, 1*(2), 197–234.

Werker, J. F. & Fennell, C. T. (2004). Listening to sounds versus listening to words: Early steps in word learning. In D. G. Hall & S. Waxman (Eds.), *Weaving a lexicon* (pp. 79–109). Cambridge, MA: MIT Press.

Werker, J. F., Fennell, C. T., Corcoran, K. M., & Stager, C. L. (2002). Infants' ability to learn phonetically similar words: Effects of age and vocabulary. *Infancy, 3*, 1–30.

Werker, J. F. & Pegg, J. E. (1992). Infant speech perception and phonological acquisition. In C. A. Ferguson, L. Menn, & C. Stoel-Gammon (Eds.), *Phonological acquisition* (pp. 285–311). Parkton, MD: York Press.

Werker, J. F. & Tees, R. C. (1984). Cross-language speech perception: Evidence for perceptual reorganization during the first year of life. *Infant Behavior and Development, 7*, 49–63.

Werker, J. F. & Tees, R. C. (2005). Speech perception as a window for understanding plasticity and commitment in language systems of the brain. *Developmental Psychobiology, 46*(3), 233–251.

Werker, J. F. & Yeung, H. H. (2005). Infant speech perception bootstraps word learning. *Trends in Cognitive Science. 9*(11), 519-527.

Yeung, H. H. & Werker, J. F. (2006, June). *Object-based phonetic categorization of speech: A mechanism of functional reorganization.* Paper presented at the International Conference of Infant Studies, Kyoto, Japan.

Yoshida, K., Fennell, C. T., Swingley, D., & Werker, J. F. (in press). Fourteen-month-old infants learn similar sounding words. *Developmental Science.*

Yoshida, K., Pons, F. G., & Werker, J. F. (2006, June). *Does distributional learning effect perception after native categories are established?* Poster presented at the International Conference of Infant Studies, Kyoto, Japan.

7

How Infants Discover Distinct Word Types and Map Them to Distinct Meanings

SANDRA WAXMAN

More than any other developmental achievement, word learning occupies the crossroad between human conceptual and linguistic development. Facing the conceptual domain, we know that infants form core concepts that capture various relations among the objects and events that they encounter. Facing the linguistic domain, we know that they cull words and phrases from the melody of the human language in which they are immersed. In my research program, our overarching goal has been to discover when and how human language and conceptual organization become linked. It is now apparent that even before infants begin to produce words on their own, they make important advances in each of these domains. Even more remarkably, their early conceptual and linguistic advances are powerfully linked. My goal in this chapter is to outline recent theoretical and empirical approaches to studying these links in infancy and to highlight the methods that permit us to examine it in detail.

OVERVIEW AND THEORETICAL APPROACH

Infants live in an enormously rich environment. Each day, they encounter new objects and witness new events. An essential developmental task is to form concepts that capture commonalities and relations among the objects and events they encounter and to learn words to express them.

I have proposed that even before infants begin to produce words on their own (at roughly 12 months), their conceptual development and linguistic development are linked, in at least a rudimentary way (Waxman, 1998; Waxman & Booth, 2003). As infants begin the process of lexical acquisition, they harbor a broad, universal expectation linking novel content words to a broad range of commonalities among objects and events. This broad link sets the stage for the evolution of more specific expectations, linking particular *kinds* of words (e.g., noun, adjective, verb) to particular *kinds* of relations (e.g., object categories, object properties, relations among objects). These more specific expectations, which are shaped by the structure of the native language under acquisition, do not emerge all of a piece. Instead, infants first tease apart the nouns (from among the other grammatical forms) and map them specifically to object categories. With this noun–category link in place, the precise links between other grammatical forms and their associated meanings will follow.

This is a dynamic proposal that underscores the vital interaction between infants' expectations and the shaping role of the environment. Ultimately, both developmental and cross-linguistic evidence will be essential in discovering the origin of infants' early expectations if we are to identify which expectations (if any) are universal and how these are shaped by infants' experience with the native language under acquisition.

We have employed two kinds of tasks to trace the relation between word learning and conceptual organization in infancy. In the *live interactive tasks*, infants interact directly with a trained experimenter in a structured play session in which she offers them three-dimensional objects to explore while she comments on them. In the *automated tasks,* infants view two-dimensional video images presented on a screen, accompanied by auditory input consisting of prerecorded comments of an individual talking about them. Each of these tasks brings with it strong advantages and disadvantages. Together, they converge to provide a window through to view infants' advances in word learning over the first few years of life.

FOUNDATIONAL ISSUES AND EVIDENCE

Recent years have witnessed a decisive renewal of scientific interest in the relation between conceptual and linguistic development. A central focus has been to discover whether and how the categorization of objects—a conceptual task—is influenced by novel words (Bloom, 2000; Gelman, Coley, Rosengren, Hartman, & Pappas, 1998; Hollich et al., 2000; Smith, 1999; Waxman, 2002; Woodward & Markman, 1998). To illustrate, consider a typical word-learning scenario. A mature speaker (e.g., a parent) points to an ongoing stream of activity (e.g., a flamingo disappearing behind a dune) and utters a novel word (e.g., "Did you see the flamingo?"). To learn a word from this (indeed from any) context, the infant must (1) parse the relevant word (*flamingo*) from running speech, (2) identify the relevant entity from the ongoing stream of activity (e.g., the flamingo, not the dune or the act of disappearing), and (3) establish a word-to-world mapping between them. By the end of their first year, infants are well on their way to solving each of these three elements.

Specifically, in the first year infants become increasingly sensitive to perceptual cues (morphologic, phonetic, prosodic) and distributional regularities that mark word and phrase boundaries in their native language (Fernald, 1992; Jusczyk & Aslin, 1995; Kemler Nelson, Hirsh-Pasek, Jusczyk, & Cassidy, 1989; Marcus, Vijayan, Rao, & Vishton, 1999; Saffran, Aslin, & Newport, 1996). By 9–12 months, with the ability to successfully parse individual words from the speech stream established, infants spontaneously begin to build a lexicon consisting primarily of *open-class* words (or *content* words, including nouns, adjectives, and verbs) (Jusczyk & Kemler Nelson, 1996; Morgan & Demuth, 1996; Shi & Werker, 2003; Shi, Werker & Morgan, 1999; Werker, Lloyd, Pegg, & Polka, 1996).

During their first year, infants also acquire an impressive repertoire of core conceptual knowledge (Baillargeon, 2000; Spelke, 2000). Some of their prelinguistic concepts are focused around richly structured category-based relations (e.g., flamingo, animal); others are focused primarily on property-based relations (e.g., red, soft) (see Quinn & Eimas, 2000); still others concern physical relations among objects (e.g., support; containment). This rich conceptual repertoire sets the stage for what has been described as the *induction problem* problem: In principle, the very richness of infants' conceptual abilities should complicate their efforts to map words to meaning (Quine, 1960; Waxman & Lidz, 2006). How do they so rapidly discover that a given word applied to a particular whole object (e.g., *flamingo*) can be extended to other members of that object category (e.g., other flamingos) but not to salient parts or properties of the object (e.g., its long neck or unusual color) or to salient actions in which it is engaged (e.g., feeding its young) or to salient thematic relations (e.g., a flamingo and palm trees)?

The evidence indicates that infants are guided by constraints, or expectations, that help them home in on the relevant meaning (see Waxman & Lidz, 2006; Woodward & Markman, 1998 for thorough reviews of recent evidence in word learning). For instance, infants are guided by social, pragmatic, and intentional contexts in which novel words are introduced (Baldwin & Baird, 1999; Guajardo & Woodward, 2000; Hollich et al., 2000; Tomasello & Olguin, 1993; Woodward, 2000). In addition, they consistently use the grammatical form of a novel word as a clue to its meaning. For example, by 2 years of age, English-speaking children can extend a count noun ("That is a *blicket*") to the named object and extend it spontaneously to other members of the same category (e.g., flamingo, animal); they map proper nouns ("That is *Blicket*") to the named individual but do not extend them further to other category members; they extend adjectives (and other modifiers) ("That is a *blickish one*") to object properties (e.g., color, textures, size) (see Hall & Lavin, 2004; Waxman, 1998; Woodward & Markman, 1998 for reviews of recent evidence).

Linking Word Learning and Conceptual Organization in Infancy

Clearly, then, by 2 years of age, children have made significant headway into discovering the relevant linguistic units (words), the relevant conceptual units, and the links between them. But how do infants break into this system? To answer this question, my colleagues and I have conducted a series of parallel experiments using *live* and *automated* procedures. These experiments share several fundamental design features. Under either procedure, each experiment is essentially a categorization task used to observe infants' ability to detect commonalities among a series of familiarization events. To examine the influence of novel words on categorization, performance in "neutral" conditions (involving no novel words) to performance when novel words are present is compared. To ensure that the words themselves carry no a priori meaning, novel (e.g., *fauna*) rather than familiar (e.g., *animal*) words are introduced. To examine the influence of grammatical form, the frame in which the novel words are embedded is varied. Short utterances that are typical of those found in infant-directed speech are presented; these utterances are specifically designed to provide clear evidence of the grammatical category assignment of each word (see Gerken & McIntosh, 1993; Shi, Werker & Morgan, 1999; Waxman & Markow, 1995, 1998 for evidence that infants are sensitive to the frames used). Performance in the "no-word" control condition is used to assess how readily infants notice the commonalities among the familiarization events; performance in the conditions involving novel words is used to measure (1) the contribution of words in this conceptual endeavor and (2) the specificity of this contribution.

The First Step: Evidence from Live Tasks

In an early series of experiments, Waxman and Markow (1995) used an interactive novelty-preference task to reveal that at 12 to 13 months of age infants are sensitive to a broad initial link between word learning and conceptual development. Infants were familiarized to members of an object category (e.g., four different animals; Figure 7.1). At test, they saw (1) a new member of the now-familiar category (e.g., another animal) and (2) an object from a contrasting category (e.g., a fruit). Infants manipulated the toys freely, and we used their total accumulated manipulation time as our dependent measure. To examine the influence of words on categorization, infants participated in one of three conditions, which differed only in the experimenter's comments during familiarization (see Figure 7.1 for instructions in each condition). Notice that at test, all infants heard precisely the same phrase ("See what I have?").

The results revealed that by 12 months of age, naming supports the formation of object categories. Infants hearing novel words (either nouns or adjectives) during familiarization successfully formed object categories, as witnessed by their

Familiarization Phase		Test Phase
 Pink duck Purple raccoon	 Blue dog Orange lion	 Yellow cat Red apple
Noun: See the *blicket*?	See the *blicket*?	See what I have?
Adjective: See the *blickish* one?	See the *blickish* one?.	See what I have?
No word: See here?	See here?	See what I have?

Figure 7.1   A representative set of stimuli. (From Waxman, S. R. & Markow, D. B., 1995, *Cognitive Psychology, 29*(3), 265. With permission.)

preference for the novel test objects; those in the no-word control condition failed to do so. This means that the novel words (presented only during familiarization) influenced infants' attention to the new—and as yet unnamed—objects that were presented at test.

We interpreted this as evidence that words serve as *invitations* to form categories and proposed that this simple invitation has dramatic consequences. Naming highlights commonalities among objects that might otherwise have gone undetected. Further evidence suggests that naming points infants toward deeper, sometimes nonperceptible commonalities as well (Booth & Waxman, 2002; Gelman & Markman, 1987; Welder & Graham, 2001). Moreover, the conceptual consequences of naming are evident specifically when the referential status of a novel word is made clear (Fennell, 2004; Fennell & Waxman, 2006; Fennell, Waxman, & Weisleder, 2006). Finally, this link between naming and categorization may be in place, in a rudimentary form, by 6 months of age (Fulkerson & Waxman, 2006; Fulkerson, Waxman, & Seymour, 2006) and is certainly available early enough to support infants as they build their initial lexicon (Waxman & Lidz, 2006).

In a subsequent series involving the live task, Waxman and Booth (2001) and Booth and Waxman (2003) sought to specify the scope of infants' early expectations. We noted that in the natural course of word learning, infants encounter objects that share more than a single kind of commonality (e.g., furry dogs and orange pumpkins). We therefore asked whether infants link novel words specifically to commonalities underlying object categories (e.g., dog, animal) or whether they initially link words to a wider range of groupings including, for example, property-based commonalities (e.g., furry things, orange things)?[1]

In this series, we maintained the logic of our paradigm but shifted the focus to include objects sharing *category-based* as well *property-based* commonalities (Figure 7.2). This design permitted us to ask (1) whether infants could flexibly construe the very *same* set of objects (e.g., four purple animals) *either* as members of an object category (animal) *or* as embodying an object property (purple) and (2) whether their construals were systematically influenced by novel words. This task involved three phases. In the *familiarization phase*, the experimenter introduced infants in all conditions to four distinct objects, all drawn from the same object category (e.g., four animals) and all embodying the same object property (e.g., purple). These were presented in pairs, and infants manipulated them freely. In the *contrast phase*, the experimenter introduced an object from

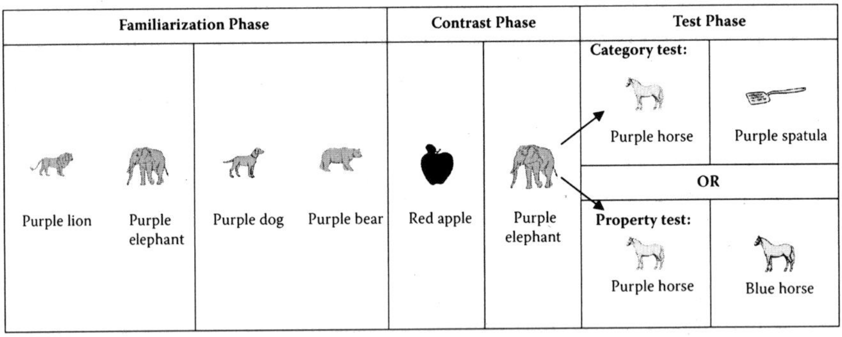

Familiarization Phase				Contrast Phase		Test Phase	
						Category test:	
						Purple horse	Purple spatula
						OR	
Purple lion	Purple elephant	Purple dog	Purple bear	Red apple	Purple elephant	**Property test:**	
						Purple horse	Blue horse

Noun: These are *blickets*.	These are *blickets*.	Uh-oh! This one is not a *blicket*!	Yay! This one is a *blicket*!	Look at these. Can you give me the *blicket*?
Adjective: These are *blickish*.	These are *blickish*.	Uh-oh! This one is not *blickish*!	Yay! This one is *blickish*!	Look at these. Can you give me the *blickish* one?
No word: Look at these.	Look at these.	Uh-oh! Look at this one!	Yay! Look at this one!	Look at these. Can you give me one?

Figure 7.2   A representative set of stimuli. Note the test phase: Infants see either category tests or property tests. (From Waxman, S. R. & Booth, A. E., 2001, *Cognitive Psychology, 43,* 238. With permission.)

a different object category (e.g., not an animal) and embodied a different object property (e.g., not a purple thing). In the *test phase*, infants in all conditions saw a familiar object (e.g., a purple horse) and a novel object. For half of the infants (those assigned to the category-test condition) the novel object was a member of a novel object category but embodied the now-familiar property (e.g., a purple spatula). For the remaining infants (those assigned to the property-test condition) the novel object was a member of the now-familiar object category but embodied a novel object property (e.g., a blue horse). At test, the experimenter presented a target object, drawn from the set of familiarization objects (e.g., a purple elephant), and drew attention to it by pointing and saying, "This one is a *blicket*" (noun condition). She then presented the two test objects, placing them easily within the infant's reach, saying, "Can you give me the *blicket*?" Figure 7.2 presents the instructions in all conditions.

We included infants at both 11 and 14 months of age, reasoning as follows. If infants harbor an initially general expectation linking novel content words (in general) to commonalities among objects (in general), then both nouns and adjectives should highlight both category-based (e.g., animal) and property-based (e.g., purple things) commonalities. That is, infants hearing novel words (either nouns or adjectives) should be more likely to notice commonalities (either category or property based) than would infants in the no-word control condition. Moreover, if infants use this broad initial expectation as a basis upon which to discover the more precise links between particular grammatical forms and their associated meaning, then for older infants more specific patterns should emerge.

The results were consistent with these predictions. At 11 months, infants treated nouns and adjectives similarly. They extended novel words (both nouns and adjectives) systematically to the familiar test object (e.g., the purple horse) on both category- and property-test trials. Infants in the no-word condition performed differently, revealing no systematic preference for either test object on either type of trial. This suggests that by 11 months, novel words (both nouns and adjectives) direct infants' attention quite broadly to either category- or property-based commonalities.

We suspected that at 14 months (once word learning was well under way and infants had established a modest lexicon), a more specific set of expectations would emerge. As predicted, 14-month-olds extended novel nouns *specifically* to category-based (and not property-based) commonalities. In contrast, their expectation for novel adjectives was still quite general, directing attention broadly to both kinds of commonalities.

We next designed a more challenging task. The familiarization and contrast phases were identical to those previously described, but at test we pitted the novel objects from the category- and property-test trials directly against each other (Booth & Waxman, 2003) (Figure 7.3).

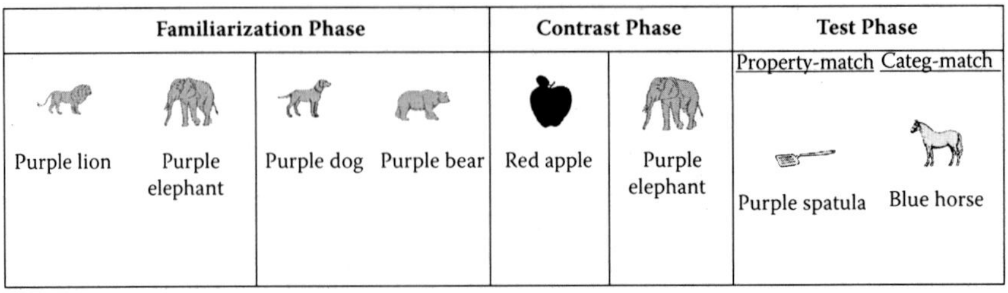

Familiarization Phase				Contrast Phase		Test Phase	
						Property-match	Categ-match
Purple lion	Purple elephant	Purple dog	Purple bear	Red apple	Purple elephant	Purple spatula	Blue horse

Figure 7.3   A representative set of stimuli. Note the test phase. (From Booth, A. E. & Waxman, S. R., 2003, *Journal of Cognition & Development, 6,* 128–135. With permission.)

We reasoned as follows: If infants focus specifically on the category-based commonalities among the familiarization objects, they should extend the novel word to the category match, despite the fact that it now embodied a novel property. If they attend specifically to the property-based commonalities, they should extend the novel word to the property match, despite the fact that it is from a novel category.

Even in this more stringent task, the results held up, suggesting that by 14 months infants expect that nouns refer specifically to category-based, rather than to property-based, commonalities but that their expectations for adjectives is still rather fluid (see Booth & Waxman, 2003 for details).

In sum, evidence from these live tasks reveals that (1) infants begin the task of word learning (at 11 months) with a broad initial expectation that links novel words (independent of their grammatical form) to commonalities among named objects, that (2) this initially broad expectation gives way (at around 14 months) to a more specific set of expectations, linking particular grammatical forms to particular types of meaning (Booth & Waxman, 2003; Waxman, 1999; Waxman & Booth, 2001, 2003; Waxman & Markow, 1995), and (3) that as infants begin to refine their expectations, they first tease apart the form *noun* from among the others and map it specifically to category-based (and not property-based) commonalities. At this same point, infants' expectation for the grammatical form *adjective* remains general, highlighting both category- and property-based commonalities.

The Next Step: Moving to an Automated Task

We went on to develop a task in which we could present the stimuli (both visual and auditory) entirely by computer rather than with a live, interactive experimenter (Booth & Waxman, in press). Booth and I were motivated by (at least) three factors. First, we sought greater control over relevant features, including the duration of auditory and visual stimuli and acoustic features (e.g., rate of speech, pause length, stress, and other prosodic contours). In the live task it was difficult to control for such features, any of which (singly or in combination) could influence infants' ability to pick out novel words in fluent speech and to map them to meaning. By automating the task, we were able to modulate the stimuli to control for several of these factors. We were also able to time the onset of the linguistic stimuli precisely to take advantage of advances in time-course analyses (Allopenna, Magnuson, & Tanenhaus, 1998; Swingley, Pinto, & Fernald, 1999) and to develop analytic tools for tracing the timed interplay between the introduction of a novel word and its consequence for infants' attention as they strive to map the word to meaning.

A second motivation for developing the automated method was to facilitate cross-linguistic investigation (Waxman et al., under review). Cross-linguistic evidence is essential if we are to discover how infants' expectations in word learning are shaped by the ambient language. At the same time, however, we know that across cultures and communities, there are significant differences in the ways adults interact with infants (Schieffelin, 1990). Because the live procedure, by definition, depends on adult–infant interaction, it introduces potential confounds for cross-linguistic investigations. An automated task would offer clear advantages.

Third, the automated method opens the door for extending the paradigm to include a new grammatical form class, *verb*, and new candidate meanings, including actions and relations among objects. With an automated task, we can present objects in motion while controlling the rate and salience of the motions.

Of course, this move to an automated task raised questions of its own. On the one hand, infants might perform better on automated than interactive tasks, particularly because the automated tasks introduce many fewer distractions. However, it was also possible that infants would perform less well in the automated procedure, either because their attention wanders when they are not actively engaged by an experimenter or because their representations of two-dimensional video images are not as rich as their representations of three-dimensional toy objects (DeLoache, Pierroutsakos, Uttal, Rosengren, & Gottlieb, 1998).

Faced with these questions, we first developed an automated procedure that was closely analogous to the live tasks to provide a point of comparison (Booth & Waxman, in press). We began with the more challenging version of the live task in which two novel test objects are pitted directly against each other (Figure 7.3). Our goals were to ascertain whether infants' expectations for novel words were comparable in the live and automated versions and to examine the ways infants deployed their visual attention over the time course of an experimental trial. We created visual stimuli by making digital images of all of the objects used in Waxman and Booth (2001) and auditory stimuli by recording a female voice producing the instructions in each of the conditions. The visual and auditory stimuli were then coordinated using a commercially available package that permitted precise control over their timing. For the experiment itself, the visual stimuli were presented on a large 61-inch screen, with sound emanating from a speaker at the center. Infants were seated in a highchair, 80 inches from the screen. Parents remained in the room during testing but wore a visor to prevent them from seeing the images. Each session was videotaped for later off-line coding by a trained observer who identified for each frame (33 frames per sec) whether the infant looked to the left screen, the right screen, or neither.

We used this frame-by-frame coding to create two types of measures (Booth & Waxman, in press; Waxman et al., under review). First, we created a high-resolution record of the time course of infants' looking behavior throughout the test phase. We calculated for each infant on each frame, the proportion of looks directed toward the familiar test scene (total number of looks devoted to the familiar test scene divided by the total number of looks to the familiar and to the novel test scene) across trials. We then computed an average, across infants for each frame in each condition, to produce a high-resolution record of the time course of infants' looking behavior in each condition. Second, for the purposes of statistical analysis, we identified *response windows* within the test phase. Within each window and for each condition, we calculated the mean proportion of attention devoted to the familiar test scene.

Figure 7.4 displays the continuous time course of infants' looking behavior in each condition throughout the test phase. A glance at this timeline offers several impressions. Before the onset of the test question, infants in both conditions devoted their attention equally to the two test screens, but after the onset of the novel word, infants in the two conditions pulled apart. Those in the noun condition begin to look toward the category match, while those in the adjective condition continue to reveal no preference for either the category or property match (Booth & Waxman, in press).

To provide a point of contact with the live procedure, we compared mean performance during the selected response window. Infants in the noun condition revealed a reliable preference for the category match; those in the no-word and adjective conditions did not.

Infants' performance in the automated task provides several insights. First, the result converges beautifully with the interactive task to suggest (1) that at 14 months infants have a more precise expectation for nouns than for adjectives, and (2) that these effects are robust enough to hold up even under more rigorous experimental control and even in the absence of direct interaction with engaging experimenter. Moreover, the frame-by-frame analysis of infant looking times in the automated procedure offers insights into the ways infants deploy their attention over the course of the test trials and permits us to examine how their interest is modulated by the linguistic input. Finally, the success of the automated method lays the foundation for moving beyond nouns and adjectives to examine infants' expectations for verbs.

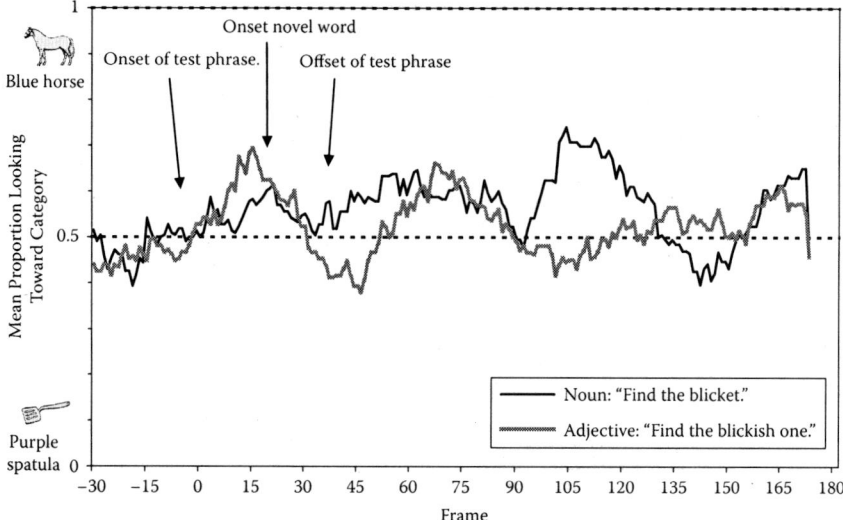

Figure 7.4   Time course of looking behavior. (From Waxman & Braun, in preparation. With permission.)

Our motivation for studying verbs stems not only from their pivotal role in theories of language but also because evidence regarding infants' expectations for this grammatical form will help pinpoint the scope of infants' initial "cut." In other words, we can ask whether infants first tease out the nouns from among all predicate forms (including adjectives and verbs) or whether they tease out both nouns and verbs in advance of adjectives and the remaining predicates.

There are several reasons to favor the former alternative. Most current language-acquisition theories agree that the grammatical category *noun* may be established earlier than other grammatical categories (Dixon, 1982; Gleitman, 1990; Grimshaw, 1994; Maratsos, 1998; Snedeker & Gleitman, 1999; Talmy, 1985; Waxman, 1999). Indeed, the acquisition of the other grammatical forms likely depends on the prior acquisition of nouns. The empirical evidence falls in line with this view, with verbs typically appearing later than nouns in the infant lexicon (Fisher, Hall, Rakowitz, & Gleitman, 1994; Gentner, 1982; Hollich et al., 2000; Huttenlocher & Smiley, 1987; Tomasello & Olguin, 1993; Valian, 1986; but see Choi & Bowerman, 1991; Choi & Gopnik, 1995; Tardif, Shatz, & Naigles, 1997). However, it is difficult to compare the acquisition of nouns, adjectives, and verbs directly. This is because (1) there is comparatively little research on verbs (as compared with nouns) in the very earliest stages of lexical acquisition, and (2) what evidence there is comes from various experimental tasks, each of which presents infants with different kinds of task demands. Because we can now include verbs in our paradigm, we are in a good position to use a comparable task to tap into infants' expectations for these three major grammatical categories. The logic and coding of our automated noun–verb task parallels the noun–adjective tasks described earlier. This time, however, infants observed a series of dynamic scenes (e.g., a man waving a balloon) during familiarization. We constructed the test trials to ask (1) whether infants could construe these scenes flexibly, noticing the consistent action (e.g., waving) as well as the consistent object (e.g., the balloon) and (2) whether their construals would vary with the grammatical form of the novel word used to describe the scene (Figure 7.5; Waxman et al., under review). We made several design decisions in selecting stimuli. First, to clarify the semantic roles of the event participants, all scenes involved animate agents acting upon inanimate patients. Second, to ensure that the actions would be present consistently throughout the entire trial, as were the objects, all actions were continuous (e.g., pet, wave) rather than fleeting (e.g., drop, slap). Third, to reduce the number of potential referents of each novel word, the same

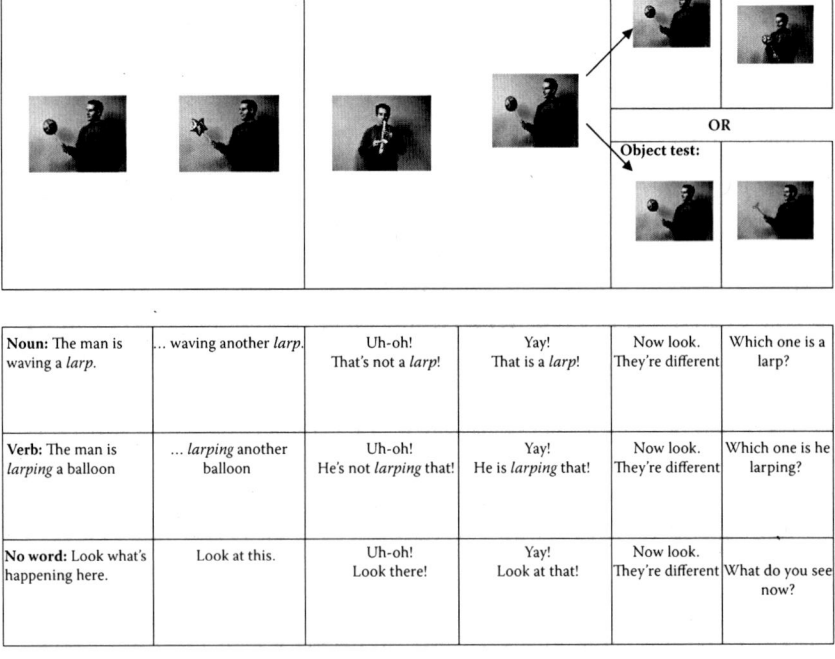

Figure 7.5   A representative stimulus set. Note that infants see either action tests or object tests. (From Waxman et al., under review. With permission.)

agent (e.g., the man) appeared in every scene within a given trial. Fourth, we presented infants with the less challenging test pairings. This meant that infants saw one of two kinds of test trials, and both the action and object tests included a now-familiar scene (e.g. the man waving a balloon). In the action test, the novel scene depicted a novel action (e.g., the man *tapping* a balloon); in the object test, the novel scene depicted a novel object (e.g., the man waving a *rake*). Finally, to examine the influence of language on infants' construals, infants were randomly assigned to a verb, noun, or no-word (control) condition. We reasoned that if infants have specific expectations for both verbs and nouns, then they should map words from these grammatical categories differently, mapping verbs specifically to event categories and nouns specifically to object categories.

The continuous time course of infants' looking behavior for the action-test and object-test trials are depicted in Figure 7.6a and Figure 7.6b, respectively.[2] Consider first infants' performance in the action test. Before the onset of the test question, infants in both conditions were captivated by the novel test scene, suggesting that they detected the novel action. But with the onset of the test question, performance began to diverge. Infants in the noun condition maintained their focus on the novel test scene. This suggests that they interpreted the novel noun as referring to an object and not the action in which it was involved. Because

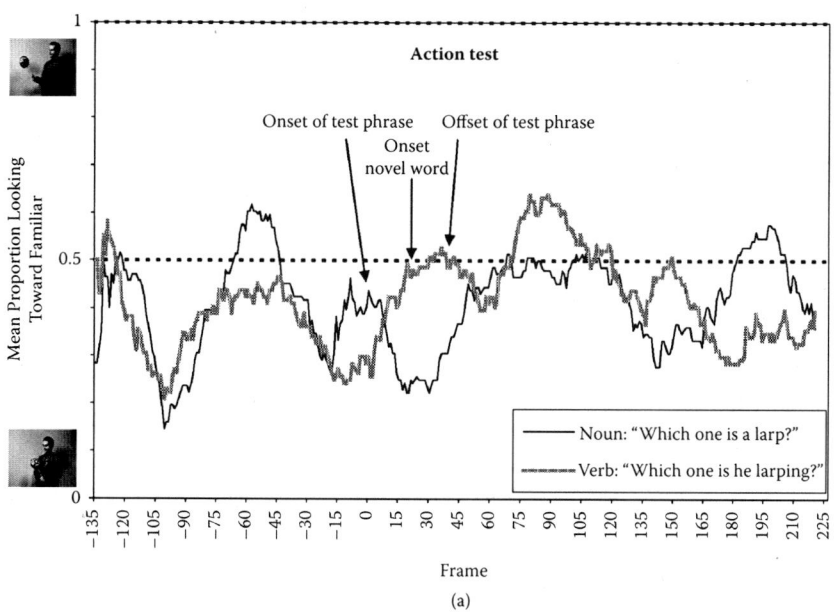

Figure 7.6a   Time course of looking behavior. (From Waxman et al., under review. With permission.)

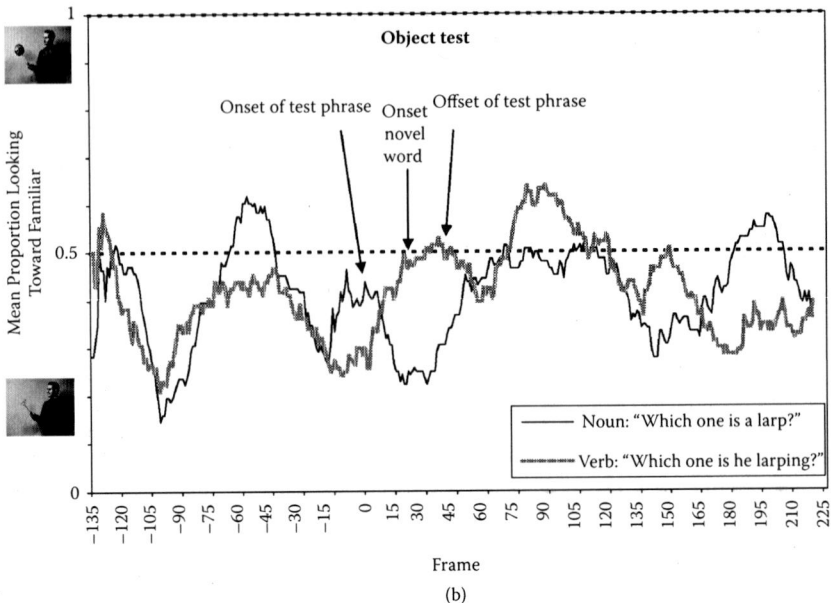

Figure 7.6b   Time course of looking behavior. (From Waxman et al., under review. With permission.)

both scenes on action-test trials involved the now-familiar object, infants hearing nouns had no motivation to redirect their attention from the novel test scene. Infants in the verb condition deployed their attention differently. With the presentation of the test question, these infants moved away from the novel scene, increasingly directing their attention toward the familiar test scene—the only scene that depicted the now-familiar action.

An analysis of mean performance in the response windows echoed this impression. Infants in the verb condition exhibited a reliable change in attention, devoting more attention to the familiar test scene after the test question than before it. This suggests that infants did in fact map novel verbs specifically to categories of events. Infants in the noun condition maintained their preference for the novel scene. This is consistent with the prediction that infants do not consider event categories as possible meanings for nouns and therefore have no motivation to direct their attention away from the novel test scene.

Consider next infants' attention in the object test. A glance at Figure 7.6b reveals that before the onset of the test question, infants in both conditions prefer the novel test scene, suggesting that they detected the novel object. In response to the test question, performance between conditions began to diverge. Infants in the verb condition maintained their focus on the novel test scene.

This suggests that they interpreted the novel verb as referring to the action and not the objects involved in that action. After all, in the category test both test scenes involved the now-familiar action; therefore, infants hearing verbs had no motivation to direct their attention away from the novel test scene. In contrast, infants in the noun condition began to move away from the novel scene, directing increasingly more attention toward the familiar test scene—the only scene that depicted the now-familiar object.

An analysis of mean performance revealed that in the verb condition, infants performed comparably both before and after the test question. This is consistent with the prediction that infants' representation of verb meaning is uncoupled from the objects involved in the event and that as a result infants accept events involving new objects as candidates for verb meaning. In contrast, infants in the noun condition devoted significantly more attention to the familiar test scene after the onset of the test question than before it. This suggests that infants in the noun condition did indeed map novel nouns specifically to categories of object and not to the actions in which they are engaged.

Of course, we have only begun our explorations of infants' expectations for novel verbs and have yet to examine younger infants. We speculate that infants' expectations for the grammatical form *verb* will emerge after the acquisition of the noun-category link.

CONCLUSIONS AND FURTHER DIRECTIONS

In these experiments, we have examined infants' expectations for *nouns, adjectives,* and *verbs* in parallel procedures. Thus far, the results reveal that infants' construals of scenes they observe are influenced by the introduction of novel words. Moreover, their representations of word meaning are sufficiently abstract to permit them to extend novel words of each grammatical form appropriately beyond the precise scenes on which they had been taught.

Taken together, then, these results indicate that although infants' expectations may not be as refined as those of adults, they do share with mature language users an expectation that different kinds of words (e.g., nouns, adjectives, verbs) refer to different aspects of a scene (e.g., object categories, object properties, action categories). I have proposed that infants begin the task of word learning equipped with a broad, universally shared expectation that links novel words (independent of their grammatical form) to a broad range of commonalities and that this initially general expectation gives way to a more specific set of expectations, linking *particular* grammatical forms (e.g., nouns, adjectives, verbs) to *particular* types of meaning (object categories, object properties, actions). These more specific links are shaped by the structure of the native language under acquisition and do not all emerge concurrently. Instead, infants appear to first tease apart the grammatical form *noun* and map this form specifically to category-based commonalities.

With this noun-category link in place, other specific links follow, and these will be sensitive to the correlations between the particular grammatical forms represented in the native language and their associated meanings.

The results described herein are intriguing, and they cry out for further investigation. Perhaps most pressingly, we are now poised to move to new populations, including younger infants and infants acquiring languages other than English. Cross-linguistic research is essential if we are to ascertain which links (if any) are universal and how these are shaped by the structure of the native language. It provides a fascinating opportunity to observe the rich interplay between expectations held by the infant and the shaping role of language input.

The work summarized in this chapter also sets the stage for more detailed developmental analysis. One interesting possibility will be to consider how the time course changes with development. It is likely that as infants become more adept at identifying words in fluent speech, their responses to the introduction of novel words will become more streamlined (Fernald, Perfors, & Marchman, 2006). Furthermore, while the timelines presented here are exciting, they are at this point primarily descriptive. A major goal is to develop the analytic tools necessary to more formally capture the timing and course of infants' performance in the context of mapping a novel word to meaning (e.g., Swingley, Pinto, & Fernald 1999; Suzuki & Grabowecky, 2003; Suzuki & Goolsby, 2003). In doing so, we as a field can look forward to making more precise the time course of children's word learning within the course of a task and over the course of development.

ENDNOTES

1. See Waxman (1999) for a discussion of the psychological distinction between category- and property-based commonalities.
2. In this task, infants' performance became more systematic over the course of the experiment. Therefore, in the interest of clarity, we present the results from infants' last three (out of six) trials.

REFERENCES

Allopenna, P. D., Magnuson, J. S., & Tanenhaus, M. K. (1998). Tracking the time course of spoken word recognition using eye movements: Evidence for continuous mapping models. *Journal of Memory & Language, 38*(4), 419–439.

Baillargeon, R. (2000). How do infants learn about the physical world? In D. Muir & A. Slater (Eds.), *Infant development: The essential readings. Essential readings in development psychology* (pp. 195–212). Malden, MA: Blackwell Publishers, Inc.

Baldwin, D. A. & Baird, J. A. (1999). Action analysis: A gateway to intentional inference. In P. Rochat (Ed.), *Early social cognition: Understanding others in the first months of life* (pp. 215–240). Mahwah, NJ: Lawrence Erlbaum Associates, Inc.

Bloom, P. (2000). *How children learn the meanings of words.* Cambridge, MA: MIT Press.

Booth, A. E. & Waxman, S. R. (in press). A horse of a different color: Specifying with precision infants' mappings of novel nouns and adjectives. *Child Development.*

Booth, A. E. & Waxman, S. R. (2002). Object functions and object names: Effects on categorization in 14-month-old infants. *Developmental Psychology, 38*(6), 948–957.

Booth, A. E. & Waxman, S. R. (2003). Mapping words to the world in infancy: On the evolution of expectations for count nouns and adjectives. *Journal of Cognition & Development, 6,* 128–135.

Choi, S. & Bowerman, M. (1991). Learning to express motion events in English and Korean: The influence of language-specific lexicalization patterns. *Cognition, 41*(1–3), 83–121.

Choi, S. & Gopnik, A. (1995). Early acquisition of verbs in Korean: A cross-linguistic study. *Journal of Child Language, 22*(3), 497–529.

DeLoache, J. S., Pierroutsakos, S. L., Uttal, D. H., Rosengren, K. S., & Gottlieb, A. (1998). Grasping the nature of pictures. *Psychological Science, 9,* 205–210.

Dixon, R. M. W. (1982). *Where have all the adjectives gone?* Berlin: Mouton Publishers.

Fennell, C. T. (2004). Infant attention to phonetic detail in word forms: knowledge and familiarity effects. Unpublished doctoral dissertation, University of British Columbia, Canada.

Fennell, C. T. & Waxman, S. R. (2006). Infants of 14 months use phonetic detail in novel words embedded in naming phrases. In D. Bamman, T. Magnitskaia, and C. Zaller (Eds.), *Proceedings of the 30th Annual Boston University Conference on Language Development* (pp. 178–189). Cambridge, MA: Cascadilla Press.

Fennell, C.T, Waxman, S.R., & Weisleder, A. (2007). With referential cues, infants successfully use phonetic detail in word learning. *Proceedings of the 31st Boston University Conference on Language Development.* Somerville, MA: Cascadilla Press.

Fernald, A. (1992). Human maternal vocalizations to infants as biologically relevant signals: An evolutionary perspective. In J. H. Barkow, L. Cosmides, & J. Tooby (Eds.), *The adapted mind: Evolutionary psychology and the generation of culture* (pp. 391–428). New York: Oxford University Press.

Fernald, A., Perfors, A., & Marchman, V. A. (2006). Picking up speed in understanding: Speech processing efficiency and vocabulary growth across the second year. *Developmental Psychology, 42,* 98–116.

Fisher, C., Hall, G., Rakowitz, S., & Gleitman, L. (1994). When it is better to receive than to give: Syntactic and conceptual constraints on vocabulary growth. *Lingua, 92,* 333–376.

Fulkerson, A. L. & Waxman, S. R. (2006). *Words (but not tones) facilitate object categorization: Evidence from 6- and 12-month-Olds.* Manuscript submitted for publication.

Fulkerson, A. L., Waxman, S. R., & Seymour, J. M. (2006). Linking object names and object categories: Words (but not tones) facilitate object categorization in 6- and 12-month-olds. In D. Bamman, T. Magnitskaia, and C. Zaller (Eds.), *Proceedings of the 30th Annual Boston University Conference on Language Development.* Cambridge, MA: Cascadilla Press.

Gelman, S. A., Coley, J. D., Rosengren, K. S., Hartman, E., & Pappas, A. (1998). Beyond labeling: The role of maternal input in the acquisition of richly structured categories. *Monographs of the Society for Research in Child Development, 63*(1), 1–148.

Gelman, S. A. & Markman, E. M. (1987). Young children's inductions from natural kinds: The role of categories and appearances. *Child Development, 58*(6), 1532–1541.

Gentner, D. (1982). Why nouns are learned before verbs: Linguistic relativity versus natural partitioning. In S. Kuczaj (Ed.), *Language development: Language, thought, and culture* (Vol. 2, pp. 301–334). Hillsdale, NJ: Erlbaum.

Gerken, L. & McIntosh, B. J. (1993). Interplay of function morphemes and prosody in early language. *Developmental Psychology, 29*(3), 448–457.

Gleitman, L. (1990). The structural sources of verb meanings. *Language Acquisition: A Journal of Developmental Linguistics, 1*(1), 3–55.

Grimshaw, J. (1994). Minimal Projection and clause structure. In B. Lust & M. Suner (Eds.), *Syntactic theory and first language acquisition: Cross-linguistic perspectives* (Vol. 1, pp. 75–83). Hillsdale, NJ: Lawrence Erlbaum Associates, Inc.

Guajardo, J. J. & Woodward, A. L. (2000). *Using habituation to index infants' understanding of pointing.* Biennial Meeting of the International Society for Infant Studies, Brighton, UK.

Hall, D. G. & Lavin, T. A. (2004). The use and misuse of part-of-speech information in word learning: Implications for lexical development. In D. G. Hall & S. R. Waxman (Eds.), *Weaving a lexicon.* Cambridge: MIT Press.

Hollich, G. J., Hirsh-Pasek, K., Golinkoff, R. M., Brand, R. J., Brown, E., Chung, H. L., et al. (2000). Breaking the language barrier: An emergentist coalition model for the origins of word learning. *Monographs of the Society for Research in Child Development, 65*(3), 1–123.

Huttenlocher, J. & Smiley, P. (1987). Early word meanings: The case of object names. *Cognitive Psychology, 19*(1), 63–89.

Jusczyk, P. & Aslin, R. N. (1995). Infants' detection of the sound patterns of words in fluent speech. *Cognitive Psychology, 29*(1), 1–23.

Jusczyk, P. W. & Kemler Nelson, D. G. (1996). Syntactic units, prosody, and psychological reality during infancy. In J. L. Morgan & K. Demuth (Eds.), *Signal to syntax: Bootstrapping from speech to grammar in early acquisition* (pp. 389–408). Mahwah, NJ: Lawrence Erlbaum Associates, Inc.

Kemler Nelson, D. G., Hirsh-Pasek, K., Jusczyk, P. W., & Cassidy, K. W. (1989). How the prosodic cues in motherese might assist language learning. *Journal of Child Language, 16*(1), 55–68.

Maratsos, M. (1998). The acquisition of grammar. In D. Kuhn & R. S. Siegler (Eds.), *Cognition, perception, and language* (5th ed., Vol. 2). New York: Wiley.

Marcus, G. F., Vijayan, S., Rao, S. B., & Vishton, P. M. (1999). Rule learning by seven-month-old infants. *Science, 283*(5398), 77–80.

Morgan, J. L. & Demuth, K. (Eds.). (1996). *Signal to syntax: Bootstrapping from speech to grammar in early acquisition.* Mahwah, NJ: Lawrence Erlbaum Associates, Inc.

Quine, W. V. O. (1960). *Word and object: An inquiry into the linguistic mechanisms of objective reference.* New York: John Wiley.

Quinn, P. C. & Eimas, P. D. (2000). The emergence of category representations during infancy: Are separate perceptual and conceptual processes required? *Journal of Cognition and Development, 1,* 55–62.

Saffran, J. R., Aslin, R. N., & Newport, E. L. (1996). Statistical learning by 8-month-old infants. *Science, 274*(5294), 1926–1928.

Schieffelin, B. (1990). *The give and take of everyday life: Language socialization of the Kaluli children.* New York: Cambridge University Press.

Shi, R. & Werker, J. F. (2003). The basis of perference for lexical words in six-month-old infants. *Developmental Science, 6*(5), 484–488.

Shi, R., Werker, J. F., & Morgan, J. L. (1999). Newborn infants' sensitivity to perceptual cues to lexical and grammatical words. *Cognition, 72*(2), B11–B21.

Smith, L. B. (1999). Children's noun learning: How general learning processes make specialized learning mechanisms. In B. MacWhinney (Ed.), *The emergence of language* (pp. 277–303). Mahwah, NJ: Lawrence Erlbaum Associates, Inc.

Snedeker, J. & Gleitman, L. (1999). *Knowing what you know: Metacognitive monitoring and the origin of the object category bias.* Boston University Conference on Language Development, October, Somerville, MA.

Spelke, E. S. (2000). Nativism, empiricism, and the origins of knowledge. In D. Muir & A. Slater (Eds.), *Infant development: The essential readings. Essential readings in development psychology* (pp. 36–51). Malden, MA: Blackwell Publishers, Inc.

Suzuki, S. & Goolsby, B. A. (2003). Sequential priming is not constrained by the shape of long-term learning curves. *Perception & Psychophysics, 65,* 632–648.

Suzuki, S. & Grabowecky, M. (2003). Selective attention during adaptation weakens negative afterimages. *Journal of Experimental Psychology: Human Perception and Performance, 29,* 793–807.

Swingley, D., Pinto, J. P., & Fernald, A. (1999). Continuous processing in word recognition at 24 months. *Cognition, 71*(2), 73–108.

Talmy, L. (1985). Lexicalization patterns: Semantic structure in lexical forms. In T. Shopen (Ed.), *Language typology and syntactic description* (Vol. 3, pp. 249–291). San Diego: Academic Press.

Tardif, T., Shatz, M., & Naigles, L. (1997). Caregiver speech and children's use of nouns versus verbs: A comparison of English, Italian, and Mandarin. *Journal of Child Language, 24*(3), 535–565.

Tomasello, M. & Olguin, R. (1993). Twenty-three-month-old children have a grammatical category of noun. *Cognitive Development, 8*(4), 451–464.

Valian, V. (1986). Syntactic categories in the speech of young children. *Developmental Psychology, 22*(4), 562–579.

Waxman, S. R. (1998). Linking object categorization and naming: Early expectations and the shaping role of language. In D. L. Medin (Ed.), *The psychology of learning and motivation* (Vol. 38, pp. 249–291). San Diego: Academic Press.

Waxman, S. R. (1999). Specifying the scope of 13-month-olds' expectations for novel words. *Cognition, 70*(3), B35–B50.

Waxman, S. R. (2002). Early word learning and conceptual development: Everything had a name, and each name gave birth to a new thought. In U. Goswami (Ed.), *Blackwell handbook of childhood cognitive development* (pp. 102–126). Oxford: Blackwell Publishers.

Waxman, S. R. & Booth, A. E. (2001). Seeing pink elephants: Fourteen-month-olds' interpretations of novel nouns and adjectives. *Cognitive Psychology, 43,* 217–242.

Waxman, S. R. & Booth, A. E. (2003). The origins and evolution of links between word learning and conceptual organization: New evidence from 11-month-olds. *Developmental Science, 6*(2), 130–137.

Waxman, S. R. & Lidz, J. (2006). Early word learning. In D. Kuhn & R. Siegler (Eds.), *Handbook of Child Psychology,* 6th Edition, Vol. 2 (pp. 299–335). Hoboken, NJ: Wiley.

Waxman, S. R., Lidz, J. L., Braun, I., & Lavin, T. (2006). *Twenty-four-month-old infants' interpretations of novel verbs and nouns in dynamic scenes.* Under review.

Waxman, S. R. & Markow, D. B. (1995). Words as invitations to form categories: Evidence from 12- to 13-month-old infants. *Cognitive Psychology, 29*(3), 257–302.

Waxman, S. R. & Markow, D. B. (1998). Object properties and object kind: Twenty-one-month-old infants' extension of novel adjectives. *Child Development, 69*(5), 1313–1329.

Welder, A. N. & Graham, S. A. (2001). The influences of shape similarity and shared labels on infants' inductive inferences about nonobvious object properties. *Child Development, 72*(6), 1653–1673.

Werker, J. F., Lloyd, V. L., Pegg, J. E., & Polka, L. (1996). Putting the baby in the bootstraps: Toward a more complete understanding of the role of the input in infant speech processing. In J. L. Morgan & K. Demuth (Eds.), *Signal to syntax: Bootstrapping from speech to grammar in early acquisition* (pp. 427–447). Mahwah, NJ: Lawrence Erlbaum Associates, Inc.

Woodward, A. L. (2000). Constraining the problem space in early word learning. In R. M. Golinkoff, K. Hirsh-Pasek, L. Bloom, L. B. Smith, A. L. Woodward, M. Tomasello, et al. (Eds.), *Becoming a word learner: A debate on lexical acquisition*. Oxford: Oxford University Press.

Woodward, A. L. & Markman, E. M. (1998). Early word learning. In W. Damon, D. Kuhn, & R. Siegler (Eds.), *Handbook of child psychology, Volume 2: Cognition, perception and language* (pp. 371–420). New York: John Wiley and Sons.

8

Early Learning through Language

JUDY S. DELOACHE, PATRICIA A. GANEA,
AND VIKRAM K. JASWAL

Two hallmarks of what it means to be human are language and culture. Nothing more distinguishes us from other creatures than our extraordinarily creative and flexible use of language. Hence, nothing is more important in the development of a young human than the acquisition and use of language. It is what enables one person to communicate with another and hence to benefit from the knowledge of others. Through language, information can be transferred from one generation to another, thereby making cultural knowledge possible. Related symbol systems based on language, such as writing, vastly facilitate the preservation and accumulation of knowledge—the "wisdom of the ages." Given the centrality of language in cognition and communication, it is not surprising that one of the largest domains of inquiry in developmental science has been language acquisition, from speech perception very early in infancy to the production of complex grammatical structures many years later.

In this chapter, we focus on language as a mechanism for the acquisition of information about the world. Infants' knowledge about the world is initially limited to what they learn from direct experience, and they do, of course, learn an enormous amount that way. For example, babies come to recognize familiar people and objects and to associate certain outcomes with particular people and objects. They learn, for example, which person in their environment is more likely to feed them and which is more likely to play with them.

Infants also form experience-based categories, learning, for example, that entities that move on their own have properties crucially different from those that do not and that self-propelling entities are of very special significance in their lives. They form these and other categories based simply on observing perceptual similarity among objects or from watching others use objects in some particular way.

Language takes infants beyond the necessity for personal observation as the basis for knowledge acquisition. From infancy onward, children learn the names of people, animals, and objects from hearing others refer to them. As this chapter discusses, infants use labels provided by others to form new categories of objects or animals that may share relatively little perceptual similarity. As toddlers, they begin to acquire factual information from what other people tell them about the world. Much of this learning occurs informally in mundane interactions in which a conversational partner talks about objects or events, although some involves didactic intent on the part of the partner. In modern societies, this early learning often occurs in the context of joint picture book interactions in which an infant and an older, more knowledgeable person share an attentional and conversational focus on pictures. Eventually, children become increasingly privy to the wisdom of the ages by learning to read on their own.

The acquisition of information about the world, of cultural knowledge in general, thus depends to a large extent on the development and use of both spoken and written language. Accordingly, it is important to study the processes involved in infants' and young children's exploitation of information communicated to them by other people. In this chapter, we examine some of the growing literature on symbol-based learning in the first years of life, both by language alone and by language in the context of joint picture book interactions. The work we review belongs to the developmental research tradition emphasizing the social aspects of knowledge acquisition (e.g., Bruner & Haste, 1987; Rogoff, 1990; Tomasello, 1999; Vygotsky, 1978).

In this chapter, we review somewhat disparate research relevant to learning via language in the first three years of life. Most of the studies are typically described in terms other than *learning*, but learning is nevertheless at the core of what they tell us about early development. Given the incongruent nature of the research reviewed, multiple kinds of methods for measuring language and its effects on learning and knowledge acquisition are highlighted.

TESTIMONY

Probably everyone reading this chapter knows that dolphins are not—contrary to their perceptual appearance, their close resemblance to sharks, and their sea-based existence—fish. How do we all have this belief? Because we were told by someone, sometime, either in person or in print, that even though dolphins look very much like fish, they are in fact mammals. Evidence supporting this assertion was presented—dolphins are warm-blooded, breathe air, and nurse their babies. We accepted the idea of dolphins as aquatic mammals, letting the testimony of others take precedence over our own observations.

The term *testimony* has long been used by philosophers with respect to the communication of information from one person to another (e.g., Coady, 1992; Reid, 1785/2002). As summarized by Harris (2002) and Harris and Koenig (2006), the 18th-century philosopher Thomas Reid proposed that humans are innately prepared to process information about the world that comes directly through their own senses and verbal information that is provided by other people. Bertrand Russell (1912/1997) made a similar distinction between "knowledge by acquaintance" and "knowledge by description."

Our willingness to accept the testimony of other people is presumably based on what two other philosophers have pointed out. Grice (1975) noted that listeners generally assume that speakers will attempt to be truthful (notable exceptions include adult expectations about the "testimony" of politicians and advertisers). Another relevant assumption is what Putnam (1973) called the *division of linguistic labor*. We routinely use words without knowing the specific criteria for their proper application. We might, for instance, insist on a platinum wedding band over a silver one without having any idea what actually distinguishes the two precious metals. Such distinctions, Putnam argued, are based on the assumption that such criteria exist and that some people know what they are.

In the present review, we adopt a liberal approach to what counts as "testimony"—much more liberal than what Reid (1785/2002) had in mind and even somewhat more liberal than that taken by Harris and Koenig (2006). We consider testimony to involve any information that is communicated by one person to another via language, emphasizing the absolutely central role it plays in the early development of knowledge. We review research on infants' and very young children's exploitation of adults' naming of objects or events as evidence for what they should be called, as well as what category they belong to and what properties they share with certain other entities. We also consider children's acceptance or rejection of adult testimony, including their use of what they hear to update their current knowledge. Although most of the research we review has to do with direct linguistic communication from adults to children, we also consider information provided by adults in the very common situation of joint parent–infant picture book interactions.

EFFECTS OF ADULT LABELING

Object Individuation

Some evidence for a very early effect of language on infants' conceptual world comes from research on the effect of labeling on object individuation. In an initial study by Xu and Carey (1996), 10- and 12-month-old infants watched as a toy duck emerged from behind one side of a screen and then returned behind the screen. Then a ball emerged from and disappeared behind the other side of the screen. To test whether the infants interpreted what they saw as two individual objects, the screen was removed, revealing either both of the objects or only one.

The older infants looked longer when there was only one object, indicating that they had expected there to be two and thereby showing that they had interpreted the scene as involving two individual objects. In contrast, the younger infants generally looked longer when the screen removal revealed two objects, indicating that they did not share the older infants' interpretation of two different objects moving back and forth in the display event.

In a subsequent study with 9-month-olds, Xu (2002) showed the same display, but in the crucial condition the two objects were labeled with two distinctly different names (*duck* and *ball*) as they appeared from behind the screen. These infants looked longer when only one object was revealed on the test, just like the 12-month-olds in the previous study. Control conditions established that the result was due to naming—other types of sounds had no effect.

Recently, Xu, Cote, and Baker (2005) reported that 12-month-old infants could use the number of labels they heard to infer how many unseen objects were concealed in a container. As the children watched, an adult looked into the opening of an opaque box and said either two different labels (e.g., "Look, a wug" and "Look, a fep") three times each or only one label ("Look, a zav") six times. Then the experimenter removed one item from the box and pushed the now empty box forward to enable the child to reach in. The infants searched more persistently in the empty box after hearing two labels than one. Thus, these infants appear to have formed a representation of multiple unseen objects based on hearing multiple labels.

This series of studies provides strong evidence that in the first year of life, testimony in the form of simple labels for objects has profound effects on infants' interpretation of their experience. Infants have fundamentally different interpretations of objects and events depending on what language accompanies them.

Category Formation

Substantial evidence exists that hearing labels applied to objects can profoundly influence category formation by infants (Balaban & Waxman, 1997). For example, in research by Waxman and Markow (1995), 12-month-olds saw several perceptually disparate exemplars from the same superordinate category (e.g., animals). Half the children heard all the exemplars referred to with a single label; the other children heard no labels. When the children were later shown an exemplar from that category and an exemplar from a different superordinate category (e.g., vehicle), those in the label condition showed greater interest in the member of the new superordinate category, whereas those in the no-label condition did not. Thus, hearing someone apply the same word to several different objects led children to interpret them as the same kind of thing.

Inductive Inference

Not only does hearing objects labeled influence the formation of categories by infants and very young children, but labeling also influences reasoning on the basis of category membership—specifically, inductive inferences. In an early study on this topic, Gelman and Coley (1990) showed 2-1/2-year-old children a typical exemplar from a familiar category and reminded them of a familiar property it possessed. For example, they might be shown a picture of a dog and told that it barks. The children were then presented with four test pictures, including one typical and one atypical member of the same category (e.g., Labrador and Chihuahua) and a typical and atypical member of a different category (e.g., a white lamb and a dog-like lamb). Each picture was either labeled appropriately (*dog* or *lamb*) or not labeled, and the children were asked whether it barks. In the no-label condition, the children relied on appearance to answer, inferring that the dog-like lamb would bark. However, when the same pictures were labeled, the children responded on the basis of the category label, claiming that both of the dogs barked but denying that either of the lambs did.

Evidence that even younger children are influenced by shared labels when drawing inductive inferences about invisible properties comes from recent work by Welder and Graham (2001) and Graham, Kilbreath, and Welder (2004). In this research, infants learned that certain target objects produced a sound when manipulated in a particular way. For example, squeezing an object of a given shape would produce a squeak. They were then presented with test objects that varied in physical similarity to the target objects. The target and test objects either were given the same label or were offered no labels.

The basic findings of this research were that, in the absence of labels, the infants relied on physical similarity to draw inferences between objects. Having learned that squeezing an object of a given shape produced an interesting sound, they squeezed a similar-looking test object in an attempt to elicit the sound. However, when the target and test objects were given a common label, the infants generalized on the basis of the shared label. Thus, hearing an adult give the same name to perceptually different objects led the infants to conclude that the objects belonged to the same category and were therefore likely to share the same non-obvious property.

Acceptance/Rejection of Testimony

The research reviewed so far reveals that infants and very young children are influenced by simple testimony in the form of object labels provided by an adult. A parallel line of research on adult testimony and young children concerns what factors influence children to accept or reject what someone else tells them. Pre-school children have been shown to be influenced by several factors, including the reliability of the past behavior of the individual offering information. They tend to accept testimony from someone who has been consistently right in the past in preference to one who has frequently provided wrong information (Koenig, Clément, & Harris, 2004; Koenig & Harris, 2005).

Very young children sometimes react skeptically to adult testimony, as shown by the report by Koenig and Echols (2003) that most 16-month-olds spontaneously attempted to correct an adult who referred to a very familiar object with the name of a different familiar object (objecting, for example, to the speaker calling a shoe a *ball*). In addition, Graham et al. (2004, Experiment 3) found that when 13-month-olds heard an adult refer to two very similar-looking objects with different labels, they nevertheless treated the objects as members of the same category. Apparently, the perceptual similarity of the two objects was salient enough to the infants that they ignored the fact that the adult had called them by different names.

Other research demonstrates that very young children can be swayed by adult testimony, even when it conflicts with their own knowledge. In research by Jaswal and Markman (2007), 24-month-olds watched an experimenter use small props to act out an activity associated with each of two familiar categories (e.g., a cat drinking milk and a dog chewing bones). They were then shown a hybrid prop that looked more like a member of one category than the other (e.g., a cat that had some dog features) and asked to show which activity it would engage in (e.g., drinking milk or eating bones). The hybrid was either not labeled at all or labeled with the counterintuitive label (e.g., the cat-like animal was referred to as "this dog").

The children behaved differently depending on whether the hybrid object was labeled or not. In the no-label condition, they generally acted out the activity associated with what the prop most looked like (e.g., if it looked more like a cat, they enacted drinking milk). In the label condition, they more often acted out the behavior associated with the category assigned to the prop by the experimenter.

This result shows that, based on what an adult tells them, very young children can be induced to recategorize an object from one known category to another. In using the adult's label to draw an inference about the test objects, the children discounted their own perceptual experience.

Research by Ma and Ganea (2008) provides an example of young children acceding to the adult testimony in one circumstance and rejecting the same testimony in another. In the initial study, 3-year-old children were induced to disregard their own experience of an event in deference to an adult's testimony. The children watched through a window as an experimenter hid a toy in one of three differently colored containers (box, bucket, bowl). Immediately afterward, the experimenter came into the room in which the child waited and announced that she had put the toy in a different container. For example, if the child had observed the toy being hidden in the box, she now heard that it was in the bucket.

The experimenter then invited the child to find the hidden toy. The majority (65%) of the 3-year-old children complied with the adult's testimony: Instead of searching in the container in which they had actually seen the toy being hidden, they based their search on the experimenter's false testimony. A different result occurred, however, if children were first given an opportunity to find a hidden toy in a searching game involving the same three containers. Having had experience searching successfully where they had seen the experimenter hide the toy, they ignored her false testimony. In this case, only 17% of the children searched where the experimenter told them the toy was hidden. Thus, the children's personal experience in the situation led them to rely on their own firsthand observation in preference to the false testimony offered by the adult.

Summary

From a very early age, infants and young children are influenced by various forms of testimony provided by adults, from simple labels for objects, events, and categories. Adult testimony can, in some conditions, influence children to ignore their own knowledge in deference to what they are told. It will be interesting to learn from future research more about the circumstances that make young children more and less susceptible to what they are told by others.

LEARNING FROM REFERENCES TO ABSENT OBJECTS

With infants, the object of parental discourse is typically present when it is referred to. However, the enormous power of language as a source of new knowledge derives from the fact that we can learn new information about entities that are not currently accessible. The first step in this crucial ability is being able to comprehend another person's reference to an absent object.

Comprehension of Reference to Absent Objects

Naturalistic observations conducted in the homes of infants (Huttenlocher, 1974; Lewis, 1936; Sachs, 1983) have established that the ability to understand another person's reference to something not in the environment is present as early as 13 months of age (Huttenlocher, 1974; Lewis, 1936). Thus, when an infant hears his or her father refer to *Mommy* or to *Prince*, the dog next door, the infant's mental representation of the corresponding familiar person or pet is activated.

Recent laboratory studies have furthered our understanding of the early development of the comprehension of absent reference. In particular, several studies have shown that this ability is not all-or-none; whether an infant responds to hearing an absent entity referred to depends on contextual factors. For example, Saylor (2004) established that children as young as 12 months of age are capable of responding to the mention of an absent entity when there is some reminder available of its existence. (Shimpi, 2005 has reported a similar result for slightly older children.)

Two recent studies provide further evidence of context effects. Saylor and Baldwin (2004) showed that infants as young as 15 months of age responded to hearing a reference to a highly familiar and valued person—the parent who had not accompanied them to a laboratory. However, 12-month-olds did not respond to hearing *Daddy*. In contrast, Ganea and Saylor (2006) showed that when the parent (or a sibling) of the participant had recently been present in the lab, hearing him or her referred to led even 13-month-olds to respond. Two factors may have contributed to the response of the young children in the latter study: The absent individual had been associated with the environment, and only 2 minutes had passed between the departure and when the child heard him or her referred to.

Ganea (2005) recently provided systematic evidence delineating the importance of contextual factors in early comprehension of absent reference. She taught 13- and 14-month-old infants a proper name—*Max*—for a novel stuffed animal, and the toy was then put out of sight. When the infants subsequently heard Max referred to, most of them (86%) did something to re-establish contact (either visual or physical) with the toy. Some simply looked to where the invisible toy was (concealed in a basket beside a nearby couch), sometimes also pointing toward it. Some children actually got up and went over to re-establish contact with the toy. Thus, by 13 months of age, hearing the newly learned name of an out-of-view object can bring the object to mind. Two subsequent studies revealed strong context effects: 13-month-olds reacted less often to the name of the absent object when the toy was slightly less accessible and when a delay had taken place since when they had last seen it.

These recent studies have established that at the beginning of their second year, infants take a crucial step toward mastery of one of the core features of language: the use of words to communicate beyond the here and now. However, whether they respond overtly to hearing an absent object referred to depends on the complex interaction of multiple representational and contextual factors (Ganea, 2005).

This developmental step inaugurates an enormous expansion in the extent to which an infant can share a focus of attention with another person. Eventually, the child can learn from adult testimony about entities that are not currently present and even ones the child has never directly experienced.

Updating Representations

The emergence early in the second year of life of the comprehension of references to absent objects sets the stage for the development of the vital ability to acquire new information about nonpresent entities and events. Often, when someone communicates information to us about a person (e.g., place, object, situation), the topic of the message is absent. We accommodate such information by updating our mental representation of the person with the recently received information. Thus, if we are told that our spouse had a fender bender with the family car, we update our representation of the car, regretfully incorporating the damage information into our mental representation of the car. (We may also update our representation of our spouse's driving skill.)

Young children hear information on a daily basis that could produce updating: "Mommy's getting her hair cut." "The cookies are done now." When are they capable of revising their existing mental representation of an object or situation based on what someone tells them has happened?

We are not aware of any existing research on this topic. Accordingly, Ganea, Shutts, Spelke, and DeLoache (2007) examined infants' ability to incorporate new information into their mental representation of a currently absent object. Our specific question concerned the modification of an existing mental representation of an absent object, based solely on hearing that something has happened to it.

To examine this topic, we first taught infants a proper name for a stuffed animal. Then—with the toy out of sight in another room—the infant was informed that the toy had undergone a change in state. What we wanted to know was whether the infants' mental representation of the toy would be modified to accommodate the change that they had been told about but had not witnessed. In this study, 19- and 22-month-old infants were initially shown three stuffed animals—for example, two identical frogs and one pig. One of the frogs was then put on a shelf, and the children learned a proper name—*Lucy*—for the remaining one. (As before, a proper name was taught so the toy could later be referred to in its absence.) The child and experimenter played for a while with Lucy and the pig (which was never given a name). Then the toys were left behind as the experimenter and child went to the adjoining room to read an unrelated picture book.

As they were engaged in the reading interaction, an assistant entered, carrying a bucket of water, and announced, "I'm going to go in the other room and wash the table." She went into the room in which the toys were located, closing the door behind her. About two minutes later, she returned and exclaimed in an agitated voice, "I'm so sorry—I spilled water on Lucy. Lucy's all wet!" Then the experimenter and child returned to the first room to "see Lucy."

Upon entering, the child saw the three toys on the table. One of the two frogs was sopping wet, as was the nameless pig. The child was asked to indicate which toy was Lucy. Our reasoning was that if the infants identified the thoroughly drenched frog as Lucy, it would indicate that hearing "Lucy's all wet" had (1) activated their mental representation of Lucy (a frog) and (2) (of primary importance for this study) led to the incorporation into that representation of what they heard had befallen Lucy. Thus, the young participants in this study were asked to use information about an unseen event involving an absent object to identify the object. Successful identification would provide evidence that the infants had updated their mental representation of the absent entity.

The majority (80%) of the 22-month-old children selected the correct toy (the wet frog) as Lucy (a rate significantly above chance). Thus, this age group showed evidence of being able to take in new information about an absent event or object and to incorporate that information into their existing representation of the object.

The 19-month-olds, however, did not perform above chance. They did remember the object–name relation, as shown by the fact that they always selected one of the two frogs, ignoring the pig, as being Lucy. Nevertheless, they did not use the information they had heard about the toy in its absence to identify which frog was Lucy.

To see if the younger children might be more successful if the task were simplified, a new group of 19-month-olds was given the same experience, but the test involved only the two identical animals—one wet and one dry. Even with this less demanding task, however, the children's selection of the correct toy was not above chance.

An additional study confirmed that the poor performance of the 19-month-olds was not due to a simple failure to understand what the experimenter said to them. A new group of 19-month-olds heard the same information about the spilling accident, but the two animals were in view when they heard it. The children were shown the two identical animals—one wet and one dry—and the experimenter told them that she had spilled water on Lucy. ("Look what happened! I spilled water all over Lucy.") The children were then asked to indicate which of the toys was Lucy. Thus, the need to update a representation of an absent object was eliminated. All that was needed to respond correctly was to understand what the experimenter said about the toys and to update their representation of a present object. The majority of these 19-month-olds (70%) selected the correct toy.

This result indicates that in the previous studies, the 19-month-old children's failure to use the information about the out-of-view toy was not due to difficulty understanding the experimenter's description of the spilling event. Rather, their poor performance can be attributed to difficulty incorporating new information into their existing representation of an absent toy.

The results of this series of studies suggest that the ability for updating an existing representation of an absent object may emerge quite rapidly in the second half of the second year (that is, between 19 and 22 months). However, it is also possible that 19-month-olds are capable of updating but that the manifestation of this ability depends on a complex interaction of representational and contextual factors (as is true for the comprehension of references to absent objects in general; Ganea, 2005). They might be capable of updating their representation of an absent object under less challenging conditions than those examined so far.

Future studies will be directed to further exploration of this emergent ability. One question concerns the extent to which prior experience might affect infants' ability to update a representation of an absent object. We suspect that updating may occur more readily for an object for which the infant already has a strong memory representation (Munakata, 2001; Munakata, McClelland, Johnson, & Siegler, 1997). Support for this prediction comes from evidence that young infants are more likely to search for a familiar hidden object than for a novel one (Shinskey & Munakata, 2005). Thus, 19-month-olds who failed to incorporate new information about a change to a recently encountered object in the initial study might succeed with a highly familiar one.

Temporal factors might also matter, with updating more likely for objects, whether familiar or new, that infants have recently interacted with than ones they have not seen for some time. The type of transformation might make a difference. For example, our intuition is that a change in the location of an object ("I moved Lucy to the couch.") should be easier to update than a change in the object itself.

It is also conceivable that some of the results predicted herein might actually turn out to be the opposite. Rather than updating being more likely for stronger mental representations of absent objects, it seems possible that updating might occur more readily for weaker representations. This is clearly a question for future research.

Summary

The emergence of the ability to comprehend references to absent objects early in the second year of life paves the way for the development of the ability to update mental representations based solely on the testimony of others.

LEARNING THROUGH PICTURE BOOK INTERACTIONS

A common opportunity that very young children have for learning indirectly comes in the form of joint picture book reading interactions with their parents, teachers, and older siblings. Such interactions are very frequent in American homes: Most children below the age of 3 are read to several times a week—the majority of them on a daily basis (Rideout, Vandewater, & Wartella, 2003). One reason that this type of interaction is so common is the fact that American parents generally think that books and reading are important for their young children's development (Gelman, Coley, Rosengren, Hartman, & Pappas, 1998; Rideout et al., 2003).

Parent-Infant Picture Book Reading

There is substantial evidence supporting these parents' general assumption—that is, evidence pointing to general benefits from early picture book experience. The most extensively documented benefit is enhanced vocabulary development. The amount of time that preschool children spend in picture book interactions with their parents is correlated with the size of their vocabulary (DeBaryshe, 1993; Fletcher & Reese, 2005; Karass & Braungart-Rieker, 2005; Sénéchal & Cornell, 1993; Whitehurst et al., 1994). Indeed, in one study, the best single predictor of receptive language in preschool children was the age at which their parents had started reading to them (DeBaryshe, 1993).

Another demonstrated gain from joint picture book reading is enhanced literacy skills and knowledge. Young children with substantial early book-reading experience enter school knowing more about the nature of books and how they are used than do children with less experience of this sort (Adams, 1990; Bialystok, 1995; Bus, van Ijzendoorn, & Pellegrini, 1995; Justice & Ezell, 2000; Mason, 1980; Sénéchal & LeFevre, 2001; Sulzby, 1985; Teale & Sulzby, 1986; Whitehurst & Lonigan, 1998). Furthermore, picture book reading has served as the basis for effective intervention programs with educationally at-risk young children (e.g., Lonigan & Whitehurst, 1998; Whitehurst et al., 1994; Whitehurst & Lonigan, 1998).

In a recent review of research on picture book reading with young children, Fletcher and Reese (2005) emphasized that three components of such interactions need to be considered: (1) the characteristics and behavior of the parent; (2) the nature of the book; and (3) the characteristics and behavior of the child. Relatively little attention has been paid to children's books and how they affect the nature of the interaction—a relative neglect the research described later in this section is designed to address.

Parent Behavior

A general feature of joint picture book interactions with very young children is that their parents expose them to novel words and concepts that rarely occur in parent–child conversations (DeTemple & Snow, 2003). Specifically, parents' speech to their children is more responsive and complex, and they label objects more often during joint reading than during joint play (Hoff-Ginsberg, 1991; Lewis & Gregory, 1987; Ninio & Bruner, 1978; Sorsby & Martlew, 1991).

A Vygotskian perspective underlies a substantial proportion of the research on early book interactions (e.g., Snow & Goldfield, 1982; Sulzby & Teale, 1987; van Kleeck, 2003), emphasizing the role of parents in scaffolding their child's participation in the book-reading interaction and thereby maximizing the benefit the child derives from it. Parents report that they modify their behavior based on their knowledge of their child's linguistic and cognitive abilities (DeLoache & DeMendoza, 1987; Martin, 1998; Martin & Reutzel, 1999), and parental input does indeed differ substantially as a function of the age of the child.

In book-reading interactions with children under 18 months, parents tend to devote a fair amount of time and effort to directing their child's attention (DeLoache & DeMendoza, 1987). They typically deviate from whatever text a book may contain in favor of simply labeling and commenting about the pictures in it: "That's a frog. Oh look, a bear." They rarely relate the depicted items to real ones, even if real objects of the same category are visible nearby (DeLoache & DeMendoza, 1987). Indeed, early picture book "reading" is essentially a labeling activity for parents and their young children (Fletcher & Reese, 2005).

With young children above 18 months, parents seek somewhat more active participation. They ask their child questions related to the book and often scaffold extended conversations about the pictures and stories (Goodsitt, Raitan, & Perlmutter, 1988; Martin, 1998; Murphy, 1978; Ninio, 1983; Sénéchal, Cornell, & Broda, 1995; van Kleeck, 2003; Wheeler, 1983). With older children, parents provide additional information in book-related interactions, often by drawing their child's attention to categorical relationships among depicted items (Gelman et al., 1998) or by orienting their child to the organizational theme of a book (Szechter & Liben, 2004).

Books

The nature of joint picture book interactions is also related to characteristics of the book itself. Picture books for young children typically fall into three categories: (1) alphabet or number/counting books, which tend to have relatively simple picture books with little or no text; (2) narrative books in which a story line accompanies the pictures; and (3) expository books with text and pictures designed to convey information (Fletcher & Reese, 2005). Simple alphabet and number/counting books are the most frequent choices for younger children (Sulzby & Teale, 1987).

The nature of the book has an impact on the parent–child interaction, as shown by the finding that very young children participate more actively in picture book interactions with simple books with a single picture per page than more complex books with multiple pictures per page (DeMendoza, 1995). In another study, 9- to 27-month-old children and their parents talked more when interacting with simpler, text-free books (Sénéchal et al., 1995).

Further evidence of the impact of the nature of books on parent–child interaction comes from a recent laboratory study in which mothers of 30- to 36-month-olds were asked to read different alphabet books with their child (Chiong & DeLoache, 2006). One of the books was a very simple, old-fashioned book with one picture per letter (A is for apple). The other was a manipulative book—that is, a book with features that invite children to interact physically with it (e.g., flaps to be lifted, levers to pull, textures to feel). The type of book affected the manner in which the mothers interacted with their children. They focused more on the educationally relevant information—the letters—with the plain book, pointing to them and labeling them more often than they did with the manipulative book. The children vocalized about the letters and pictures more often with the plain book. In contrast, the children physically interacted with the manipulative book more often than with the plain book, mainly by focusing on the manipulative elements. Thus, the plain book encouraged attention to the educationally relevant material, whereas the manipulative book engaged the children in exploring the educationally irrelevant manipulative features. The behavior of both the mothers and the children suggest that learning would be fostered better by the plain book than the manipulative one. These results reveal that the type of book can alter the nature of book-reading interactions with respect to both the parent and child.

Infant Behavior

From simply pointing and vocalizing in response to parental prompts, children become increasingly attentive to books and become increasingly active participants in picture book reading interactions over the first three years (Sénéchal et al., 1995). In addition, they take more responsibility for directing the interaction. One way they do so is by demanding that the same books be read over and over again. Although parents often despair when cajoled into reading, for example, *Machine in Space* for what seems like the millionth time, there is evidence that repeated reading of children's favorite books is associated with more active participation in the interactions (Goodsitt et al., 1988; Morrow, 1988; Phillips & McNaughton, 1990; Sulzby & Teale, 1987) and enhanced vocabulary acquisition (Ninio, 1983; Sénéchal, 1997; Snow & Goldfield, 1983).

Research on Learning from Picture Book Interactions

Given the extensive amount of time that American parents and their children spend in joint picture book interactions, an opportunity clearly exists for substantial learning to take place. However, there has been virtually no research on what children learn from picture book reading other than vocabulary words and literacy concepts. We have recently inaugurated a program of research examining the process of learning information through picture book interactions and assessing the extent to which infants and very young children extend what they learn from these interactions to the real world.

Suppose a toddler learns from a picture book interaction about an unfamiliar animal—a dolphin, for example. In addition to learning that the depicted animal is called a *dolphin*, the child learns that it lives in the sea, gives birth to babies, and sometimes performs tricks for children to enjoy. Now suppose that this child visits an aquarium a week later and sees a dolphin. Does the child know that the animal is called a *dolphin* and anticipate seeing it do a trick? In our initial study (Ganea, Bloom-Picard, & DeLoache, 2006), we examined 15- and 18-month-olds' learning of a novel name from a brief picture book interaction with an adult. Our first question was whether these very young children would extend the name learned for a depicted object from the book to the real object. The second question was whether they would generalize the newly learned label to a new instance of the object.

The third question was whether the nature of the pictures in the books would influence children's learning and generalization from them. To address it, we prepared simple books that contained color photographs, realistic drawings, or cartoons (Figure 8.1). Each book included pictures of several familiar objects (toy dog, ball, cup) and two novel objects. In a very natural picture book reading interaction, the experimenter and child looked through the book together. In the process, the experimenter labeled one of the novel objects several times—"Look, this is a *blicket*." The children were then tested to see if they (1) had learned the novel name for the novel depicted object, (2) would extend the name to the real object, and (3) would generalize the name to a novel exemplar.

The results indicated that both age groups learned the novel name from the brief picture book interaction, in that they correctly selected which of two pictures (of the novel objects in the picture book) was a *blicket*. Moreover, they correctly extended the name to the real novel object. When presented with the two novel objects that had been depicted in the book and asked which was the *blicket*, they chose correctly. The 18-month-olds, but not the 15-month-olds, also generalized the name to another new instance of the object (a differently colored exemplar). Thus, these very young children did apply a name that they learned from a picture book interaction to the real world, although the 18-month-olds did so to a greater extent than the 15-month-olds.

The results also revealed an effect for iconicity—the degree to which the pictures in the book looked like the real objects. Both age groups performed better when they had learned from the books with photographs and realistic drawings. This difference was especially pronounced for extension to a novel exemplar. Thus, the nature of the pictures in books for very young children affects the extent to which children apply the information they learn from the book to the real world.

A similar effect of iconicity appeared in a study of children's learning of actions from picture books (Simcock & DeLoache, 2006). The 18- and 30-month-old children in this research learned to imitate with novel objects a sequence of actions that was depicted in a book. Their subsequent imitation performance was better if the action sequence had been depicted with realistic photographs

(b) Drawings

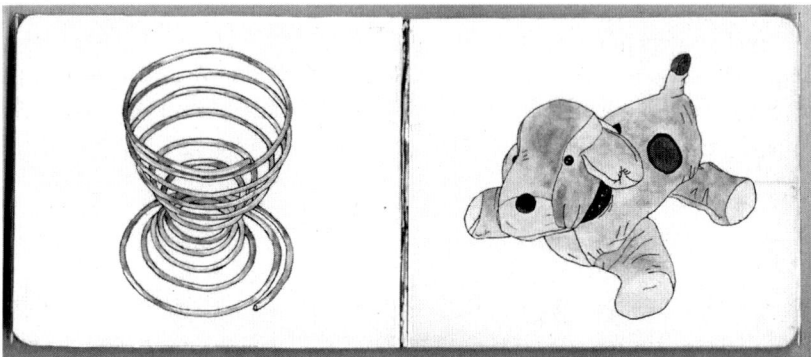

(c) Cartoons

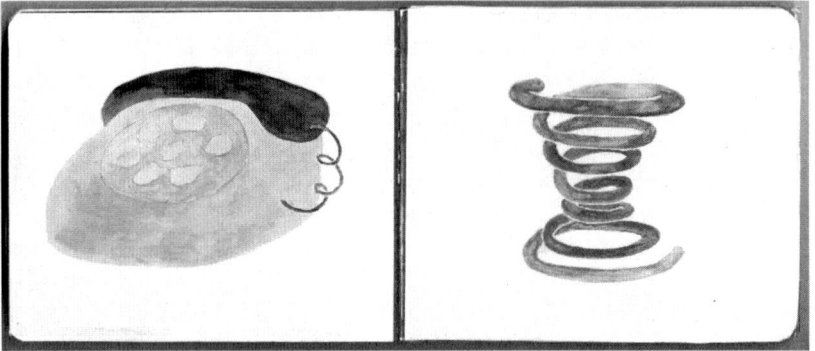

Figure 8.1   Sample pictures from the books of one of the novel objects and three of the familiar objects used in Ganea, Bloom-Pickard, & DeLoache (2008).

than with line drawings. Thus, the degree to which the pictures in a picture book resemble their real-world referents strongly affects whether children extend what they learn beyond the pages of a book.

A related finding concerns young children's interpretation of fantasy in books for very young children. Many of the books designed for very young children (perhaps the majority) are composed of cartoons depicting animals and inanimate objects engaged in human activities. Human motivation, emotion, and cognition are also attributed to these entities. Dogs drive cars, seals cook dinner, trains try very hard to make it up very steep hills, and all feel happy or sad depending on whether they succeed. This format is common even in books designed to teach young children information about the world.

Does the common use of cartoons in books for very young children matter? According to a study by Ganea, Richert, Bean, and DeLoache (2006), 2- and 3-year-old children are influenced by them. After being read to from fantasy cartoon books in their preschool classroom, the children were asked a series of questions about whether they thought, for example, cats can draw pictures or dogs can cook. Children who had recently experienced the fantasy cartoons were significantly more likely to attribute human powers to animals than was a control group that had not recently been exposed to fantasy books.

This series of studies on young children and picture books has important educational implications. For teaching young children new information about the world, books with more realistic pictures are better. In addition, fantasy (cartoon) formats may confuse children when the goal is to teach them accurate information. If a parent or teacher simply wants to amuse a child and have a positive interaction, the nature of the pictures in the book is not particularly important (other than that they be appealing to the child). However, if one wants children to learn and apply something beyond the pages of a picture book, it would be better to select a book with realistic pictures over one with cartoons. Unfortunately, cartoon books make up a substantial proportion of the books available for very young children.

Summary

Research on parent–child picture book interactions indicates that this extremely important activity has many important effects. In addition to earlier demonstrations of enhanced vocabulary acquisition and literacy knowledge, recent studies provide evidence of very young children learning specific content. The nature of the book with which the child interacts makes a difference in children's interpretation of the information in the book as well as in the extent to which they transfer what they learn from the pages of the book to the real world.

CONCLUSION

In the first years of life, children not only learn language but they also learn through language. The testimony of other people exerts a powerful influence on their knowledge and interpretation of the world. In the first year of life, hearing adults label objects and events leads infants not only to learn the names of things but also to form categories and to draw inductive inferences based on those categories. In their second year, infants become capable of learning new information simply by being told about objects that are not physically present—a momentous step that dramatically magnifies their opportunities for further learning. Very early picture book interactions introduce infants and young children to an especially powerful way of acquiring information.

The availability of testimony and the ability to comprehend it are fundamental to what it means to be human. The concept of the "wisdom of the ages" is meaningful only in the context of the uniquely human capacity for learning about the world from indirect experience.

REFERENCES

Adams, M. J. (1990). *Beginning to read: Thinking and learning about print*. Cambridge, MA: MIT Press.

Balaban, M. T. & Waxman, S. R. (1997). Do words facilitate object categorization in 9-month-old infants? *Journal of Experimental Psychology, 64*, 3–26.

Bialystok, E. (1995). Making concepts of print symbolic: Understanding how writing represents language. *First Language, 15*, 317–338.

Bruner, J. & Haste, H. (1987). *Making sense: The child's construction of the world*. New York: Methuen.

Bus, A. G., van IJzendoorn, M. H., & Pellegrini, A. D. (1995). Joint book reading makes for success in learning to read: A meta-analysis of intergenerational transmission of literacy. *Review of Educational Research, 65*(1), 1–21.

Chiong, C. & DeLoache, J. S. (2006). *Effects of book type on parent-child shared book reading*. Unpublished manuscript, University of Virginia.

Coady, C. A. J. (1992). *Testimony*. Oxford: Oxford University Press.

DeBaryshe, B. D. (1993). Joint picture-book reading correlates of early oral language skills. *Journal of Child Language, 20*, 455–461.

DeLoache, J. S. & DeMendoza, A. P. (1987). Joint picturebook interactions of mothers and 1-year-old children. *British Journal of Developmental Psychology, 5*, 111–123.

DeMendoza, P. (1995). Developmental changes and socioeconomic differences in mother-infant picture book reading, *European Journal of Psychology of Education 10*, 261–272.

DeTemple, J. & Snow, C. E. (2003). Learning words from books. In A. Van Kleek & S. A. Stahl (Eds.), *On reading books to children: Parents and teachers*. (pp. 16–36). Mahwah, NJ: Lawrence Erlbaum Associates.

Fletcher, K. L. & Reese, E. (2005). Picture book reading with young children: A conceptual framework. *Developmental Review, 25*, 64–103.

Ganea, P. A. (2005). Contextual factors affect absent reference comprehension in 14-month-olds. *Child Development, 76*, 989–998.

Ganea, P. A. & DeLoache, J. S. (2006). *From picture books to the real world: 15- and 18-month-olds generalize from depicted to real objects*. Manuscript in preparation.

Ganea, P. A. & Saylor, M. M. (2006). *Evidence for contextual effects on infants' absent reference comprehension*. Manuscript in preparation.

Ganea, P. A., Bloom, P. M., & DeLoache, J. S. (2008). Transfer between picture books and the real world by very young children. *Journal of Cognition and Development 9*, 46–66.

Ganea, P. A., Shutts, K., Spelke, E., & DeLoache, J. S. (2007). Thinking of things unseen: Infants' use of language to update object representations. *Psychological Science, 18*, 734–739.

Ganea, P. A., Richert, R. A., Bean, E., & DeLoache, J. S. (2006). *Fantasy picture books and young children's conceptions about reality*. Manuscript in preparation.

Gelman, S. A., Coley, J. D., Rosengren, K. S., Hartman, E., & Pappas, A. (1998). Beyond labeling: The role of maternal input in the acquisition of richly structured categories. *Monographs of the Society for Research in Child Development. Serial No. 253, 63*(1), 1–148.

Gelman, S. A. & Coley, J. D. (1990). The importance of knowing a dodo is a bird: Categories and inferences in 2-year-old children. *Developmental Psychology, 26*, 796–804.

Goodsitt, J., Raitan, J. G., & Perlmutter, M. (1988). Interaction between mothers and preschool children when reading a novel and familiar book. *International Journal of Behavioral Development, 11*(4), 489–505.

Graham, S. A., Kilbreath, C. S., & Welder, A. N. (2004). 13-month-olds rely on shared labels and shape similarity for inductive inferences. *Child Development, 75*, 409–427.

Grice, H. P. (1975). Logic and conversation. In P. Cole & J. L. Morgan (Eds.), *Syntax and semantics, Volume 3: Speech acts*. New York: Academic Press, pp. 41–58.

Harris, P. L. (2002). What do children learn from testimony? In P. Carruthers, M. Siegal, & S. Stich (Eds.), *Cognitive bases of science*. Cambridge, England: Cambridge University Press, pp. 316–334.

Harris, P. L. & Koenig, M. A. (2006). Trust in testimony: How children learn about science and religion. *Child Development, 77*, 505–524.

Hoff-Ginsberg, E. (1991). Mother-child conversations in different social classes and communicative settings. *Child Development, 62*, 782–796.

Huttenlocher, J. (1974). The origins of language comprehension. In R. Solso (Ed.), *Theories in cognitive psychology* (pp. 331–368). Hillsdale, NJ: Erlbaum.

Jaswal, V. K. & Markman, E. M. (2007). Looks aren't everything: 24-month-olds' willingness to accept unexpected labels. *Journal of Cognition and Development, 9*, 93–111.

Justice, L. M. & Ezell, H. K. (2000). Enhancing children's print and word awareness through home-based parent intervention. *American Journal of Speech and Language Pathology, 9*, 257–269.

Karass, J. & Braungart-Rieker, J. M. (2005). Parenting and temperament as interacting agents in early language development. *Parenting Science and Practice, 3*, 235–259.

Koenig, M., Clément, M., & Harris, P. L. (2004). Trust in testimony: Children's use of true and false statements. *Psychological Science, 15*, 694–698.

Koenig, M. A. & Echols, C. H. (2003). Infants' understanding of false labeling effects: The referential roles of words and the speakers who use them. *Cognition, 87*, 179–208.

Koenig, M. A. & Harris, P. L. (2005). Preschoolers mistrust ignorant and inaccurate speakers. *Child Development, 76*(6), 1261–1277.

Lewis, M. M. (1936). *Infant speech: A study of the beginnings of language.* New York: Harcourt, Brace and Company.

Lewis, C. & Gregory, S. (1987). Parents' talk to their infants: The importance of context. *First Language, 7,* 201–216.

Lonigan, C. J. (1994). Reading to preschoolers exposed: Is the emperor really naked? *Developmental Review, 14,* 303–323.

Lonigan, C. J., & Whitehurst, G. J. (1998). Relative efficacy of parent and teacher involvement in a shared-reading intervention for preschool children from low-income backgrounds. *Early Childhood Research Quarterly 17,* 265–292.

Ma, L. & Ganea, P. A. (2008). *Young children's reliance on first-hand observation versus testimony: The role of positive experience.* Unpublished manuscript, University of Virginia.

Martin, L. E. (1998). Early book reading: How mothers deviate from printed text for young children. *Reading Research and Instruction, 37,* 137–160.

Martin, L. E. & Reutzel, D. R. (1999). Sharing books: Examining how and why mothers deviate from the print. *Reading Research and Instruction, 39,* 39–70.

Mason, J. (1980). When do children begin to read? An exploration of four-year-old children's letter and word reading competencies. *Reading Research Quarterly, 15,* 203–227.

Morrow, L. M. (1988). Young children's responses to one-to-one story readings in school settings. *Reading Research Quarterly, 23,* 89–107.

Munakata, Y. (2001). Graded representations in behavioral dissociations. *Trends in Cognitive Sciences, 5,* 309–315.

Munakata, Y., McClelland, J. L., Johnson, M. H., & Siegler, R. S. (1997). Rethinking infant knowledge: Toward an adaptive processes account of success and failures in object permanence tasks. *Psychological Review, 104,* 686–713.

Murphy, C. M. (1978). Pointing in the context of a shared activity. *Child Development, 49,* 371–380.

Ninio, A. (1983). Joint book reading as a multiple vocabulary acquisition device. *Developmental Psychology, 19,* 445–451.

Ninio, A. & Bruner, J. (1978). The achievement and antecedents of labeling. *Journal of Child Language, 5,* 1–15.

Phillips, G. & McNaughton, S. (1990). The practice of storybook, reading to preschool children in mainstream New Zealand families. *Reading Research Quarterly, 25,* 196–212.

Putnam, H. (1973). Meaning and Reference. *Journal of Philosophy, 70*(19), 699–711.

Reid, T. (2002). *Essays on the intellectual powers of man: A critical edition.* University Park: Penn State University Press. (Original manuscript published 1785)

Rideout, V. J., Vandewater, E. A., & Wartella, E. A. (2003). Zero to six: Electronic media in the lives of infants, toddlers, and preschooler. Retrieved May 25, 2004 from The Henry J. Kaiser Family Foundation Web site, http://www.kff.org/entmedia/3378.cfm.

Rogoff, B. (1990). *Apprenticeship in thinking: cognitive development in social context.* New York: Oxford University Press.

Russell, B. (1997). *The problems of philosophy.* New York: Oxford University Press. (Original manuscript published 1912)

Sachs, J. (1983). Talking about the there and then: The emergence of displaced reference in parent-child discourse. In K. E. Nelson (Ed.), *Children's language.* Hillsdale, NJ: Erlbaum, pp. 3–28.

Saylor, M. M. (2004). 12- and 16-month-old infants recognize properties of mentioned absent things. *Developmental Science, 7,* 599–611.

Saylor, M. M. & Baldwin, D. A. (2004). Discussing those not present: Comprehension of references to absent caregivers. *Journal of Child Language, 31*, 537–560.

Sénéchal, M. (1997). The differential effect of storybook reading on preschoolers' acquisition of expressive and receptive vocabulary. *Journal of Child Language, 24*(1), 123–138.

Sénéchal, M. & Cornell, E. H. (1993). Vocabulary acquisition through shared reading experiences. *Reading Research Quarterly, 28*(4), 361–374.

Sénéchal, M., Cornell, E. H., & Broda, L. S. (1995). Age-related differences in the organization of parent-infant interactions during picture-book reading. *Early Childhood Research Quarterly, 10*, 317–337.

Sénéchal, M. & LeFevre, J.-A. (2001). Storybook reading and parent teaching: Links to language and literacy development. In P. R. Britto & J. Brooks-Gunn (Eds.), *The role of family literacy environments in promoting young children's emerging literacy skills. New directions for child and adolescent development* (pp. 39–52). San Francisco: Jossey-Bass.

Shimpi, P. M. (2005). *Infant sensitivity to associated object cues.* Poster presented at the 2005 meeting of the Cognitive Development Society, October, San Diego, CA.

Shinskey, J. L. & Munakata, Y. (2005). Familiarity breeds searching. Infants reverse their novelty preferences when reaching for hidden objects. *Psychological Science, 16*(8), 596–600.

Simcock, G. F. & DeLoache, J. S. (2006). Get the picture? The effect of iconicity on toddlers' reenactment from picture books. *Developmental Psychology, 42*(6), 1352–1357.

Snow, C. E. & Goldfield, B. A. (1983). Turn the page please: Situation-specific language acquisition. *Journal of Child Language* (10), 551–569.

Sorsby, A. J. & Martlew, M. (1991). Representational demands in mothers' talk to preschool children in two contexts: Picture book reading and a modeling task. *Journal of Child Language, 18*, 373–393.

Sulzby, E. (1985). Children's emergent reading of favorite storybooks: A developmental study. *Reading Research Quarterly, 20*, 458–481.

Sulzby, E. & Teale, W. H. (1987). Young Children's Storybook Reading: Longitudinal Study of Parent–Child Interaction and Children's Independent Functioning. Final Report.

Szechter, L. E. & Liben, L. S. (2004). Parental guidance in preschoolers' understanding of spatial-graphic representations. *Child Development, 75*(3), 869–885.

Teale, W. H. & Sulzby, E. (1986). *Emergent literacy: Writing and reading.* Norwood, NJ: Ablex.

Tomasello, M. (1999). *The cultural origins of human cognition.* Cambridge, MA: Harvard University Press.

van Kleeck, A. (2003). Research on book sharing: Another critical look. In A. v. Kleeck, S. A. Stahl, & E. Bauer (Eds.), *On reading books to children: Parents and teachers* (pp. 271–319). Mahwah, NJ: Erlbaum.

Vygotsky, L. (1978). *Mind in society: The development of higher psychological processes.* Cambridge, MA: Harvard University Press.

Waxman, S. R. & Markow, D. B. (1995). Words as invitations to form categories: Evidence from 12- to 13-month-old infants. *Cognitive Psychology, 29*, 257–302.

Welder, A. N., & Graham, S. A. (2001). The influence of shape similarity and shared labels on infants' inductive inferences about nonobvious object properties. *Child Development 72*, 1653–1673.

Welder, A. N. & Graham, S. A. (2006). Infants' categorization of objects with more or less obvious features. *Cognitive Psychology, 52*, 57–91.

Wheeler, M. P. (1983). Context-related age changes in mothers' speech: joint book reading. *Child Language, 10*, 259–263.

Whitehurst, G. J., Falco, F., Lonigan, C. J., Fischel, J. E., DeBaryshe, B. C., Valdez-Menchaca, M. C., et al. (1994). A picture book reading intervention in daycare and home for children from low-income families. *Developmental Psychology, 24,* 552–558.

Whitehurst, G. J. & Lonigan, C. J. (1998). Child development and emergent literacy. *Child Development, 69*(3), 848–872.

Xu, F. (2002). The role of language in acquiring object kind concepts in infancy. *Cognition, 85,* 223–250.

Xu, F. & Carey, S. (1996). Infants' metaphysics: The case of numerical identity. *Cognitive Psychology, 30,* 111–153.

Xu, F., Cote, M., & Baker, A. (2005). Labeling guides object individuation in 12-month-old infants. *Psychological Science, 16,* 372–377.

III

PREDICTORS OF LANGUAGE EMERGENCE

9

Early Attentional Predictors of Vocabulary in Childhood

JOHN COLOMBO, D. JILL SHADDY, OTILIA M.
BLAGA, CHRISTA J. ANDERSON, KATHLEEN
N. KANNASS, AND W. ALLEN RICHMAN

BACKGROUND

Forty years ago, Robert Fantz (1964) reported that the human infants' visual regard of simple stimuli habituated to repeated presentations and that such regard was redistributed to new or unfamiliar stimuli if they were made available. In many ways, this finding was the catalyst for the emergence of a science of infant cognition. Through the 1960s and 1970s, the visual habituation and novelty preference paradigms were used widely to demonstrate the breadth of young infants' sensory and cognitive abilities, from color vision (Bornstein, 1975), visual discrimination (Saayman, Ames, & Moffett, 1964), and categorization (Cohen & Strauss, 1979) to causal perception (Leslie & Keeble, 1987). These simple methods were followed by the development of operant conditioning techniques that allowed for the measurement of various phenomena around long-term memory (Rovee & Rovee, 1969). The last two decades have seen the development of many different and new methods for accessing infant cognitive function, including paradigms such as ocular reaction time and visual expectations (Haith, Hazan, & Goodman, 1988), statistical learning (Saffran, Aslin, & Newport, 1996), and short-term and working memory.

In the very late 1970s and early 1980s, a number of published reports (Fagan, 1981, 1982, 1984a, 1984c; Fagan & McGrath, 1981; Miller, Sinnott, Short, & Hains, 1976; Miller, Spiridigliozzi, Ryan, Callan, & McLaughlin, 1980; Miller et al., 1977, 1979; Sigman & Beckwith, 1980) suggested that laboratory measures of infant recognition memory were significantly correlated with performance on standardized intelligence tests later in toddlerhood and childhood. These findings were summarized and commented upon, and their theoretical implications were made plain in a series of papers published during that same period (Fagan 1984b, 1985, 1988; Fagan & Singer, 1983). These observations were regarded as highly significant, as they ran counter to the prevailing tenets of the time (best summarized in McCall, 1976, 1979, 1983), which held that measures taken during infancy (roughly from birth to 2 years) were largely irrelevant to the prediction of mature cognitive function. As such, in a seminal review, Bornstein and Sigman (1986) comprehensively summarized the extant evidence at the time and suggested that this tenet was in need of revision.

In response to this development, the late 1980s and 1990s saw a proliferation of longitudinal studies on the prediction of various measures of vocabulary and cognition from measures of cognitive function taken during infancy. These studies generally employed the basic techniques available for measuring infant recognition memory (the paired-comparison method; see Fantz, 1964) and visual attention and learning (the visual habituation paradigm; see Horowitz, Paden, Bhana, & Self, 1972), although the predominant method for studying infant operant learning and long-term memory (Fagen & Ohr, 1990) was also employed, as was a variant of the paired-comparison method that tapped infant recognition across different sensory modalities (Gottfried, Rose, & Bridger, 1977). One or more of these measures was typically administered to a sample of infants once or twice, and then the sample was followed longitudinally to toddlerhood or early childhood, although the occasional study (e.g., Sigman, Cohen, & Beckwith, 1997) has followed samples into near adulthood. These efforts are summarized in a series of reviews and commentaries published during that time (Bornstein, 1990; Bornstein, Slater, Brown, Roberts, & Barrett, 1997; Colombo, 1993, 1997; Colombo & Frick, 1999; McCall, 1994; McCall & Carriger, 1993; McCall & Mash, 1995; Rose, Feldman, & Jankowski, 2004; Sigman & Mundy, 1993). Generally, positive infant performance on these measures—expressed in the form of better recognition and long-term memory, better cross-modal recognition, and faster or more mature habituation (as reflected by shorter looking or rapid decrements in looking to a repetitive stimulus)—were found to be moderately related to later outcomes.

A recurring pattern with these studies was that an initial report—usually conducted with a relatively small sample—would be published showing an effect size accounting for one third to one half the variance in later outcomes (e.g., Fagan & Singer, 1983; Rose, Slater, & Perry, 1986; Rose & Wallace, 1985a, 1985b). Subsequent follow-up studies to these conducted with larger samples have provided evidence that was generally supportive of the initial reports but with effect sizes of much smaller magnitudes (e.g., Andersson, 1996; Laucht, Esser, & Schmidt, 1994; Rose, Feldman, & Wallace, 1992).

Colombo (1993) suggested that these early measures might account for as much as 15% to 20% of the variance in later outcomes. This work further suggested the amount of variance accounted for in later outcomes might approach

50% if researchers satisfactorily addressed the nagging issue of the unreliability of the infant measures. However, with some exceptions (Dougherty & Haith, 1997; Rose, Feldman, & Jankowski, 2005; Rose, Feldman, Wallace, & McCarton, 1991), recent studies suggest more modest effect sizes, with measures of infant cognition accounting for 4% to 10% of the variance in outcomes. The fact that these measures replicably account for more variance than would be expected by chance is notable, but such effect sizes do not necessarily allow for accurate prediction at the idiographic level. Initial reports of continuity generated significant enthusiasm among proponents of early identification and intervention (Rolfe, 1994; Vietze & Coates, 1986), but McCall (1994) cautioned us over a decade ago that these predictive relations were "more important theoretically than practically" (p. 107). This caution is now broadly appreciated.

This area of work has continued into the 21st century, but its emphasis has shifted toward more nomothetic concerns, such as the use of these measures as short-term outcomes in studies of groups at varying risk or advantage, in studies of the cognitive or attentional mechanisms underlying individual differences on these early measures, or in attempts to determine the mechanisms or pathways through which these measures exert whatever predictive validity that they do possess. Indeed, significant progress has been made in understanding the specific attentional processes that underlie some of the measures (Blaga & Colombo, 2006; Colombo, Richman, Shaddy, Greenhoot, & Maikranz, 2001; Frick, Colombo, & Saxon, 1999; Jankowski & Rose, 1997; Orlian & Rose, 1997; Rose, Feldman, Futterweit, & Jankowski, 1997, 1998; Rose, Futterweit, & Jankowski, 1999). The measures have proven sensitive to early interventions (Jankowski, Rose, & Feldman, 2001) or naturally occurring conditions of risk or advantage (e.g., Colombo, Kannass, et al., 2004; Landrey, Leslie, Fletcher, & Francis, 1985; McDonough & Cohen, 1982; Weir & Millar, 1997). Finally, a number of papers using sophisticated structural equation approaches have uniformly indicated that the relations between these measures and later outcomes are traced through indirect paths; that is, these measures do not relate to later outcomes simply through homotypic mechanisms (i.e., early recognition memory does not relate to later memory functions that appear on intelligence quotient [IQ] tests). Rather, individual differences on these measures appear to be catalysts in a series of *developmental cascades* in which accelerated or lagged lower-order cognitive abilities affect other higher-order functions over time, which then contribute variance to IQ (Bornstein et al., 2006; Rose & Feldman, 1997; Rose, Feldman, Wallace, & Cohen, 1991; Rose, Feldman, Jankowski, & Van Rossem, 2005).

This evidence suggests that early measures of cognitive function do not reflect simpler, preformed, or immature manifestations of later cognitive function. Rather, it is far more likely that some simpler functions contribute to the growth and development of higher-order functions in complex ways (see Wainwright &

Colombo, 2006). A further contribution to this point of view is the growing realization that predictive behavioral measures that we once believed to reflect a unitary construct of visual attention actually reflect multiple attentional mechanisms and processes (Colombo, 2001) and that some of these processes are active at some points during the early life span and less active at others (Colombo, 2002). Knowledge of the complexity of the developmental course of attention can be traced to the 1990s (e.g., Colombo, Harlan, & Mitchell, 1999); it had been known for some time that the developmental course of primary measures attention was distinctly nonlinear and could be affected by environmental factors (Colombo & Mitchell, 1990; see also Rose, Feldman, & Jankowski, 2001; Rose, Feldman, Jankowski, & Caro, 2002). At the same time, it was the case that nearly every study that had been published on this topic had examined linear relationships between single assessments and later outcomes. This was important, because a clear implication of our new working view was that such "snapshot" studies of prediction would not address the possibility that the developmental course of attention (which would capture the emergence of different attentional systems and functions) would be an important or better predictor of later lexical and cognitive status. As a result, we launched the Kansas Early Cognition Project (KECP), in which we intensively collected developmental profiles of attentional measures from habituation on a large sample of infants during the first year and then sought to relate those profiles to toddler and preschool outcomes. Initial reports on the project have appeared in a few venues so far (Colombo, Shaddy, Blaga, Anderson, & Kannass, in press; Colombo, Shaddy, Richman, Maikranz, & Blaga, 2004), but the findings and implications of this project for the long-term development of vocabulary and related cognitive measures have not been published. The remainder of this chapter explicates these findings.

THE KANSAS EARLY COGNITION PROJECT

From 1998 to 2003, the KECP was conducted at the University of Kansas Infant Cognition Laboratory. This longitudinal study examined the predictive value of measures of early attention for preschool language and cognitive development. More than 200 infants were recruited at 3 months of age and then were followed on a monthly basis until they were 9 months of age on measures of attention derived from habituation protocols.

Because the longitudinal sample was tested so intensively on attentional protocols during the first year, we included cross-sectional samples at every month from 4 to 9 months in order to assess the effects of repeated testing. Unlike past research projects on prediction, which collected only behavioral measures, we augmented these behavioral protocols with heart rate taken simultaneously with measures of looking. When infants turned 12 months, they were administered the Bayley Scales of Infant Development-Second Edition (BSID-II) and the MacArthur-Bates

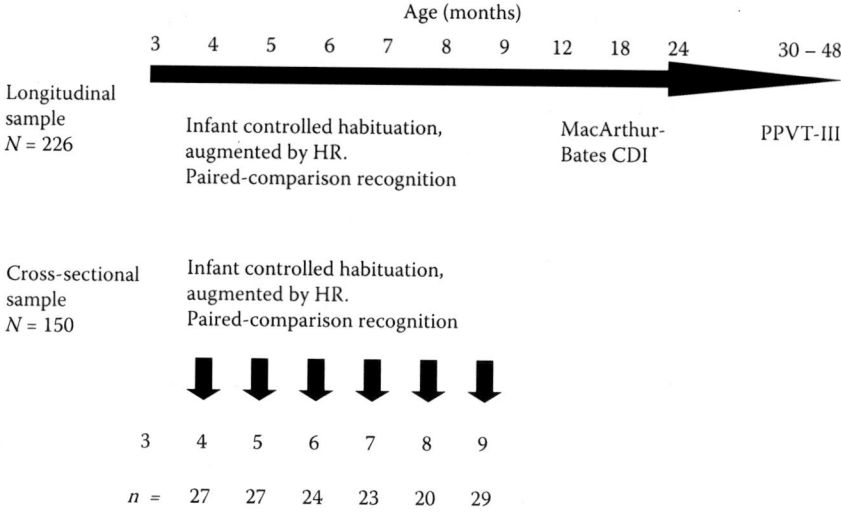

Figure 9.1   Schematic representation of the design and assessment schedule for the Kansas Early Cognition Project.

Communicative Development Inventory (MBCDI) semiannually until 30 months, at which point they were assessed with the Peabody Picture Vocabulary Test-Third Edition (PPVT-III) through age 4. The entire design and data collection sequence is represented in the schematic in Figure 9.1.

Attention Protocol Results

At each month from 3 to 9 months of age, participants were tested in a standard, infant-controlled visual habituation protocol. The protocols took place in a specially constructed room that was darkened; infants sat in a car seat placed directly in front of a screen on which the stimuli were presented. The stimuli were static, two-dimensional, chromatic slides of children's faces. Looks included as data were defined as being at least 1 second in length, and a look was terminated by a look away from the stimulus that was also at least 1 second in length. Stimuli were presented until infants' looking reached a criterion of two consecutive looks at 50% decrement from the previous longest look of the sequence. At the attainment of the criterion, the habituated stimulus was paired with a novel one for the assessment of immediate recognition memory.

Behavioral Data

Of primary interest from these protocols was the developmental course of the duration infants' looking. The case for the use of look duration as a sensitive measure of individual and developmental differences in infancy has been made in detail elsewhere (Colombo & Mitchell, 1990; Colombo, Mitchell, O'Brien, & Horowitz, 1987a, 1987b). Recent analyses of the developmental course of look duration across the first year of life (Colombo, 2002; Colombo & Cheatham, 2006; Courage, Reynolds, & Richards, 2006) suggest that the measure is influenced by different underlying processes at different age points (Colombo, 2001). Research over the past several decades indicate that the decline in look duration from 3 months of age to 6 or 7 months of age is attributable to improvements in the speed with which infants encode visual stimuli (e.g., Colombo, Mitchell, & Horowitz, 1988; Colombo, Mitchell, Coldren, & Freeseman, 1991), to improved facility with which infants become able to disengage attention from visual stimuli at midline (Blaga & Colombo, 2006; Frick et al., 1999), and possibly to some changes in face recognition (Colombo, Shaddy, et al., 2004). However, after the age-related drop in look duration reaches asymptote during the second half of the first year, some studies have observed the start of a gradual increase in look duration that continues into the second year (e.g., Courage et al., 2006; Saxon, Frick, & Colombo, 1997). Colombo and Cheatham (2006) suggested that this transition in the developmental course is related to the functional onset of a more volitional form of attention that is driven by internal ("endogenous") processes and, where attention, memory, and action become more broadly integrated, is probably due to the maturation of frontal areas. The normative developmental course for the duration of infants' peak look, including both cross-sectional and longitudinal data from the KECP, is presented in Figure 9.2.

Psychophysiological Data

Simultaneous with the collection of behavioral data on infants' looking to visual stimuli, heart-rate was collected using a triangular configuration of silver-silver chloride (Ag-AgCl) electrodes on the infant's abdomen. This yielded a digitized electrocardiogram (ECG) from which the time codes for r waves could be extracted and interbeat intervals could be calculated. The interbeat intervals were then interlaced with the time codes for various looking and stimulus events. The resulting record of infants' heart rate was then reduced, using Richards's framework (e.g., Richards & Casey, 1992) for identifying heart-rate-defined phases of attention. Based on the fact that infants show a robust and sustained parasympathetic response (i.e., heart-rate deceleration) during infants' looking, it is possible to parse infants' looking into one of three mutually exclusive phases. These three phases are anchored by the presence of *sustained attention* (SA), a phase reflected by a sustained deceleration in infants' heart rate while attending or looking at a stimulus or event. SA presumably represents the period during which infants are engaged and encoding the stimulus or event, and this contention is bolstered by more than a decade of Richards's research showing that stimuli presented

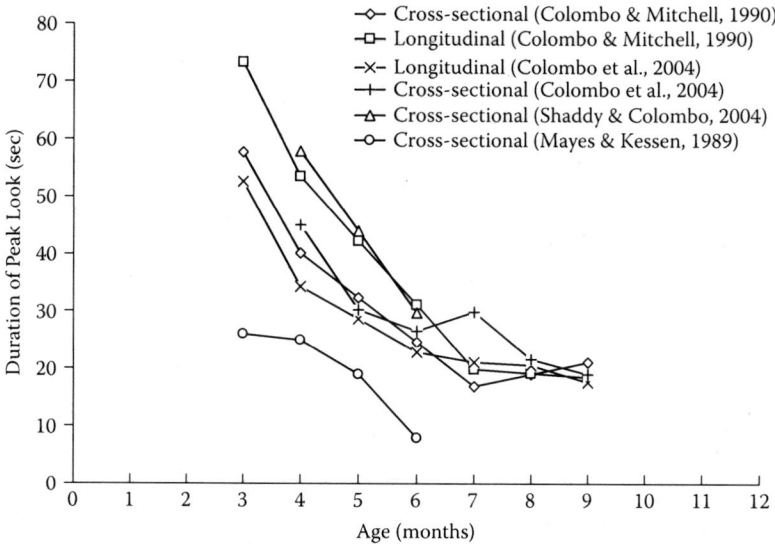

Figure 9.2   Data from various studies, showing the developmental course of look duration across the first year. Both cross-sectional and longitudinal data from the Kansas Early Cognition Project are shown on the graph. (From Colombo, J., Shaddy, D. J., et al., 2004, *Infancy*, 5, 1–38. With permission.)

during SA are encoded more efficiently (Frick & Richards, 2001; Richards, 1997) and that infants are more responsive to stimuli in the visual periphery during SA (see Richards, 2004, for a summary of this line of work). The period during which infants are looking but have not yet attained SA is called *orienting* (OR). It has been considered to be of theoretical importance, but this has yet to be definitively established; currently, it may be most safely regarded as the latency to attain the decelerative state. The phase during which the infant continues to look even though the decelerative phase (SA) has ended is called *attention termination* (AT). Richards (e.g., 1997) has suggested that infants are quite resistant to information processing during AT, and AT has also been used as an indirect measure of infants' ability to disengage attention (Colombo et al., 2001).

Despite their theoretical importance, the developmental course of these three phases has not previously been explicated. Data from the longitudinal database of the KECP on these phases are shown in Figure 9.3. When expressed in terms of the amount of time spent in these phases, the developmental patterns are strongly correlated with the duration of looking. As such, we express these data here in terms of the proportion of looking spent in each phase; in that way, the effects of any developmental change in look duration are removed. The developmental

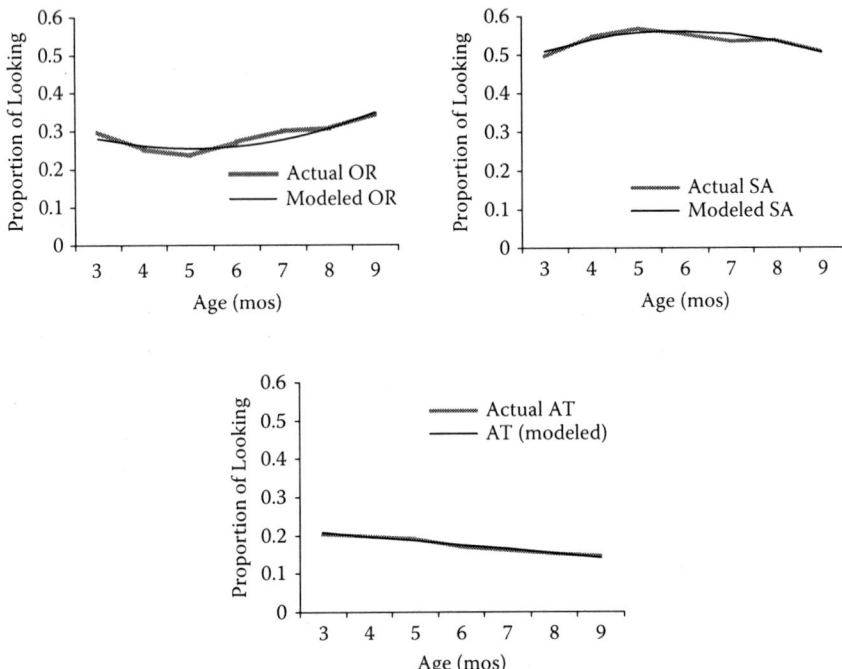

Figure 9.3   Normative developmental courses (showing actual and modeled data) for Richards's heart-rate defined phases of attention. Data taken from the longitudinal sample of the Kansas Early Cognition Project. (From Colombo, J., Shaddy, D. J., et al., 2004, *Infancy*, 5, 1–38. With permission.)

course for these measures was somewhat surprising. Two of the courses are decidedly nonlinear: OR shows a quadratic ($p < .01$) course, declining until 6 months and then increasing; SA also shows a quadratic ($p = .001$), inverted-U function, with a peak at about 6 months. As expected, that AT shows a linear ($p < .001$) decline across the first year.

Developmental Course: Individual Profiles and Outcomes

Given the developmental course of infant attention and prior work on individual differences in early attention and infant cognitive performance, it was expected that two groups of infants would be identified from the behavioral and psychophysiological data collected over the course of the first year of life. Both groups would show declines in look duration over the first year, but one group would show shorter looking than the other or an accelerated decline in looking across the period of measurements. It was also expected that both groups of infants

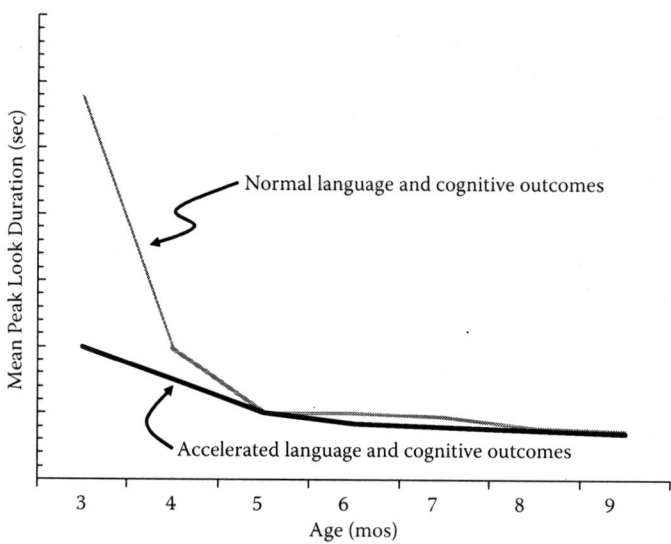

Figure 9.4   Expected variation in developmental course for look duration, with predicted outcomes from the Kansas Early Cognition Project. Since infants were recruited from a low-risk population, we did not expect poor outcomes. However, we expected more optimal language and cognitive outcomes for infants whose developmental courses were accelerated (i.e., briefer look durations overall, especially at earlier ages).

would perform adequately on outcome measures but that those infants showing shorter looking would, in fact, perform more optimally. Figure 9.4 shows the expected functions for development and the outcomes that were predicted to occur.

When data were collected, data from infants with complete sets (i.e., those who successfully completed all of the attention protocols from 3 to 9 months) were subjected to a hierarchical cluster analysis. In this analysis (see Colombo, Shaddy, et al., 2004), look durations were standardized within cases to maximize the influence of the shape of the individual developmental functions on the clustering. The clustering was conducted using Ward's method, which is shown to be the best of available methods (Milligan & Cooper, 1987). As previously noted, two clusters were anticipated, but instead the best fitting solution (based on criteria delineated in Green, 1990) involved four clusters. These clusters are shown in Figure 9.5(a–d), complete with both behavioral and psychophysiological data.

The expected clusters of normal and accelerated declines that had been predicted to emerge were indeed observed and are shown in Figure 9.5(a,b). The psychophysiological data for these two clusters were fairly straightforward. Both clusters show that SA comprises a majority of the time spent looking at stimuli (between 55% and 65%) and that this is constant across the first year; that is, longitudinal modeling of these data yielded no significant linear, quadratic, or cubic trends, and so the intercept for SA represents the function for both of these

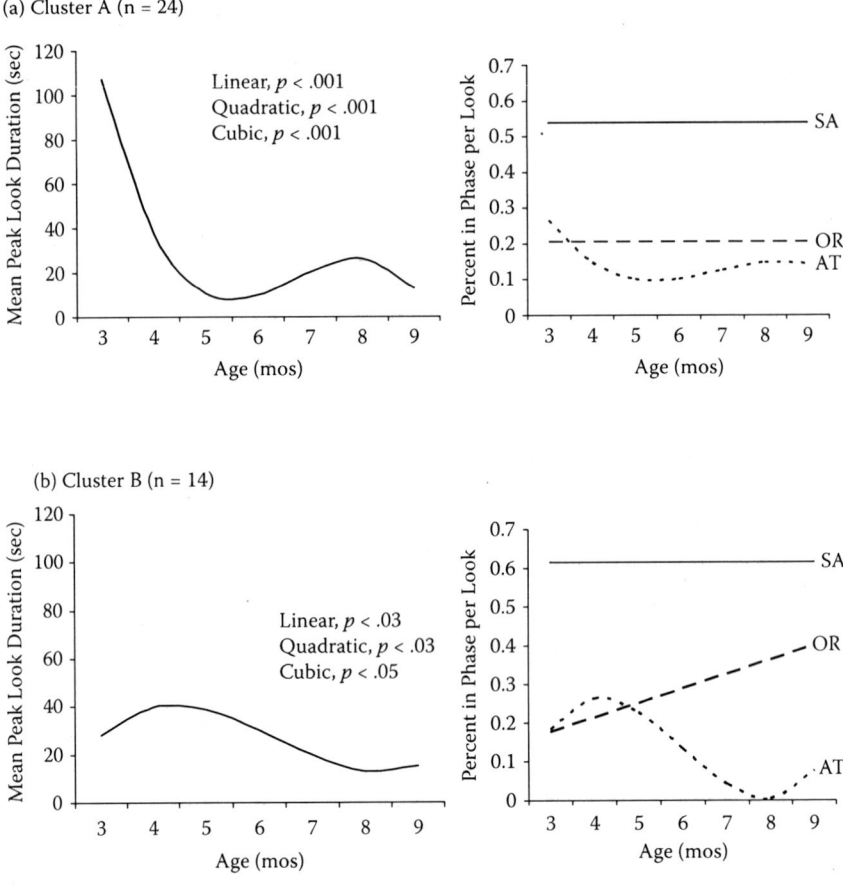

Figure 9.5   Clusters derived from analysis of look duration (peak look) at 3–9 months from attentional protocol. Behavioral data are presented at left for each cluster. To facilitate comparison, all data are presented on the same scale abscissa. The graph at right shows the proportion of looking spent in each of the heart-rate-defined phases of attention: sustained attention (SA), orienting (OR), and attention termination (AT): (a) Cluster A ($n = 24$); (b) Cluster B ($n = 14$); (c) Cluster C ($n = 18$); (d) Cluster D ($n = 21$).

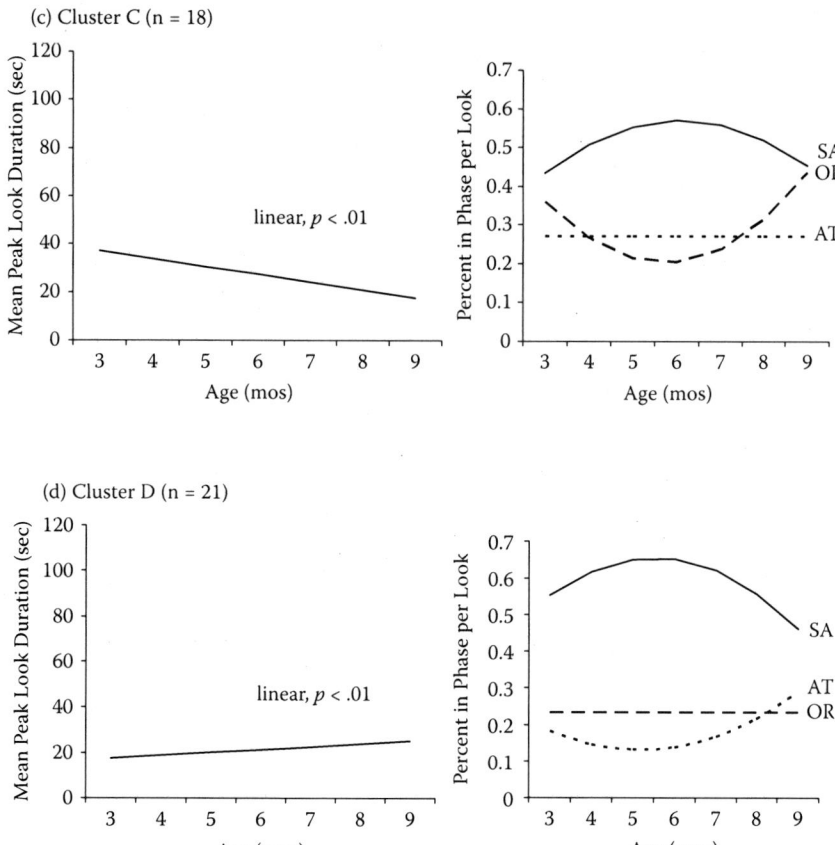

Figure 9.5 (*continued*)

figures. These two clusters diverge, however, in minor ways in which OR and AT are distributed, especially later in the first year. For the expected "normative" pattern shown in Cluster A, OR is constant across ages, but there is a drop in AT that occurs early and then attains asymptote, producing a significant cubic trend. In the "accelerated" normative pattern shown by Cluster B, AT drops precipitously from early infancy into the later months, and the drop in AT is supplanted by a linear increase in OR. In each of the cases, we expected a decline in AT, since AT presumably reflects an inefficient practice of looking after the completion of information processing, and we would expect that such inefficiency would decline with age. However, the increase in OR seen in Cluster B was somewhat surprising, and the theoretical significance of this remains somewhat uncertain. While this change may simply be an artifact or byproduct of the changes in AT, it may also be more meaningful. If, for example, as we have hypothesized elsewhere (Colombo & Cheatham, 2006; see also the following section), attention during the latter half of the first year becomes more endogenously controlled, then an increase in OR might reflect some volitional management over attentional engagement with visual stimuli. These alternatives will provide fuel for future inquiry on the development of attention.

We now turn our attention to the two other clusters that emerged from the analysis. These included groups of relatively short-looking infants with unexpected behavioral or psychophysiological profiles. Behaviorally, Cluster C (Figure 9.5[c]) shows a gradual linear drop in looking over the first year from a relatively low intercept. Cluster D (Figure 9.5[d]) also has a low intercept but actually shows a significant linear increase over time, which is highly unexpected. The psychophysiological profiles taken during looking for both of these clusters share an interesting commonality: SA shows quadratic (i.e., inverted-U) functions, with the proportion of SA decreasing toward the end of the first year. In the case of Cluster C, the drop in SA is supplanted by an increase in OR. In the case of Cluster D, however, the drop in SA is supplanted by an increase in AT.

Interpretation of Clusters

The first two clusters that emerged from these analyses were expected; Cluster A represents the expected norm for the development of look duration, showing a steep drop in look duration across ages from a relatively high level at 3 months. In addition, we saw Cluster B as an accelerated form of the normative curve, also showing a relatively steep drop in looking, although from a much shorter baseline of look duration in early infancy.

Clusters C and D represented groupings that we had not predicted on an a priori basis, but we found them to be interpretable from a theoretical framework we had been developing with respect to the emergence of endogenous attention toward the end of the first postnatal year (Colombo & Cheatham, 2006). These clusters represented short-looking infants, but with somewhat irregular behavioral and psychophysiological profiles. In Cluster C, the decline in looking is gradual rather than steep, while Cluster D shows an increase in looking. Most provocative, however, are the analyses of heart-rate-defined phases of attention. For both of these clusters, there is an unexpected decline in the proportion of time spent in SA during looking after 6 months of age, and for each of these clusters, the time spent looking in SA is displaced by other heart-rate-defined phases. Of special interest is Cluster D, where the proportion of looking spent in AT (a period during which looking continues after processing presumably has finished) actually increases with age (note that, from Figure 9.3, the normative course is for AT proportion to decrease linearly) and supplants the SA during looking. It is worth noting that Clusters C and D do not show disproportionately less SA overall than the other two "normative" clusters (Clusters A and B) but rather that the developmental function of SA and the dynamic interplay between attentional phases over time is quite different.

Colombo and Cheatham (2006) argued that major changes in attentional variables occur between 6 and 12 months of age and that most of these changes reflect the emergence of volitionally driven attentional functions powered by processes internal to the organism ("endogenous attention") related to self-regulation and higher-order cognitive functions that have long been theoretically related to vocabulary acquisition. For example, we have contended that the changes in attention and cognition that occur toward the end of the first year give rise to the emergence of true semantic networks. Such networks allow for perceptually based category information to be integrated with other types of information about objects and their function, and we have hypothesized that the emergence of endogenous attention toward the end of the first year will be directly related to various aspects of early language acquisition (see Booth & Waxman, 2002; Gopnik & Meltzoff, 1987; Waxman & Braun, 2005). Given that the somewhat atypical patterns seen in Clusters C and D appear to be traceable to changes occurring after 6 months, we posit here that the patterns seen in these two clusters likely reflect some uncharacteristic developmental course for endogenous attention and might be reflected in less-than-optimal vocabulary outcomes.

Toddler Outcomes and Cluster Membership

MBCDI Productive Vocabulary

The toddler developmental outcomes for these clusters has been previously reported in Colombo, Shaddy, et al. (2004), but those emphasizing the vocabulary/language measures will be briefly reviewed here. At 12, 18, and 24 months, the clusters were measured on the MBCDI, which is a parent-report measure of various language skills that has been reported to have reasonable psychometric properties and validity (Fenson et al., 1994). However, because the form of the MBCDI changes at 14 months and different variables are accessed across the two forms, the only constant variable available across the age range at which we assessed infants is productive vocabulary. The results on that variable as a function of cluster membership are shown in Figure 9.6.

A Cluster (4) × Age (4) mixed-design analysis of variance (ANOVA) on productive vocabulary counts yielded a statistically significant two-way interaction. The interaction may be broadly characterized as an increasing divergence between the two normative clusters (A and B) and the other clusters (C and D) in vocabulary. Interestingly, the clusters' vocabularies are not discriminable at 12 months, but they begin to diverge at 18 months and are clearly separable at 24 months. Although all clusters improve vocabulary across time, the accelerated

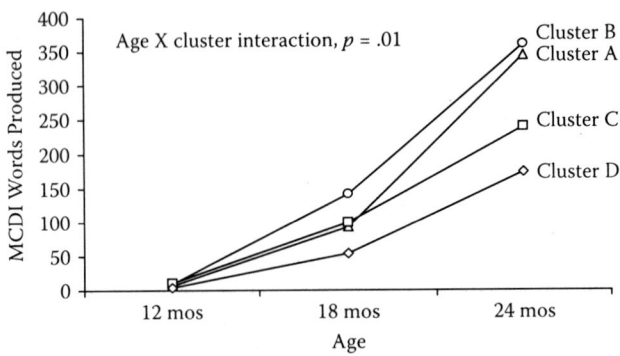

Figure 9.6 Developmental functions of the MBCDI productive vocabulary at 12, 18, and 24 months for each of the four clusters of infants.

cluster (B) shows an early vocabulary burst from 12 to 18 months, but the normative cluster (A) has its own burst between 18 and 24 months, such that by the final MBCDI assessment this cluster has basically caught up to the accelerated cluster, each showing an average productive vocabulary of about 350 words (i.e., the 60th percentile).

Vocabulary growth in Clusters C and D are slower, and neither shows any evidence of a strong burst or change in developmental trajectory as they approach the end of the second year. Although Cluster C is at the level of the larger normative cluster at 18 months, infants in that cluster grow slowly from 18 to 24 months and are at 250 words, which is on average 100 words behind the two normative clusters, and at the 38th percentile for this measure. Cluster D is significantly behind at 18 months and, on average, has attained about 175 words by 24 months, which approaches the lower quartile for this measure.

Other MBCDI Variables

In addition to productive vocabulary, the MBCDI provides data on a number of other continuous and dichotomous variables. The performance of the four clusters on these variables from the MBCDI is presented for 12 months in Figure 9.7, for 18 months in Figure 9.8, and for 24 months in Figure 9.9. Tests for significance were conducted using chi squares for dichotomous variables and one-way ANOVAs for continuous variables. Although the clusters are not significantly different on all of the variables across all ages, a consistent pattern emerges that essentially mirrors the changes seen in the productive vocabulary measure, with few differences early on and increasing divergence on theoretically important variables by the end of the second year.

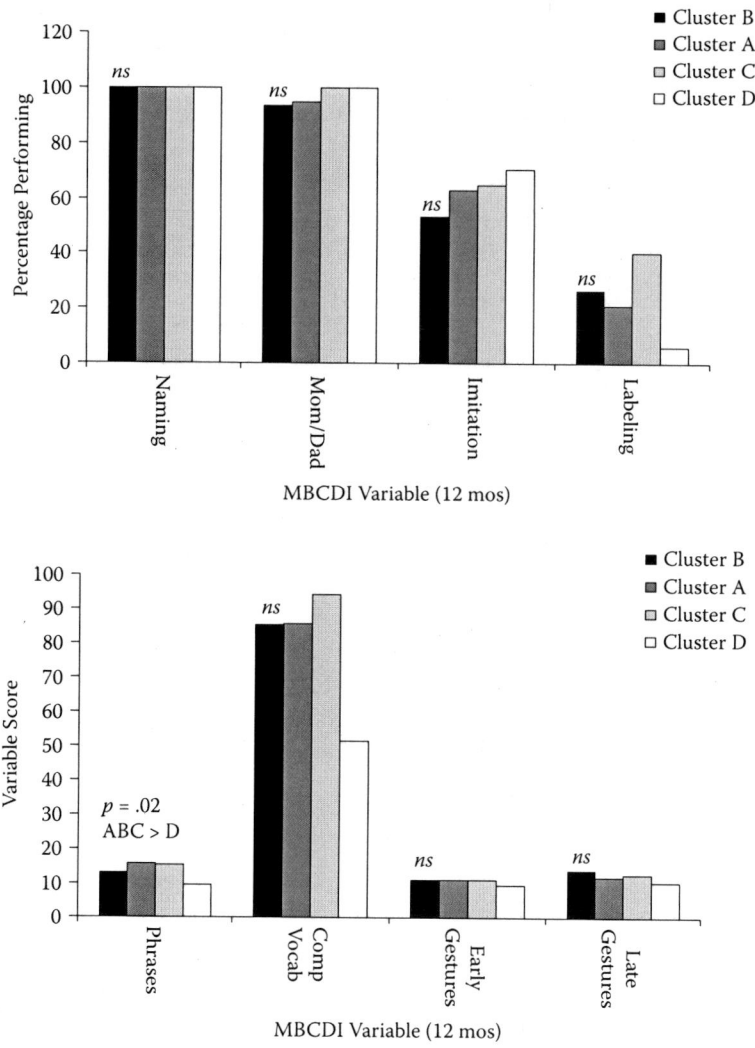

Figure 9.7 Dichotomous (top panel) and continuous (bottom panel) MBCDI variables at 12 months for the four clusters.

Early on, there are few significant differences as a function of cluster membership. Indeed, at 12 months, only the variable Phrases (i.e., the number of common phrases the infant understands) shows a difference, and here Cluster D lags behind the other three. At 18 months, the distance between the clusters is emerging, although the clusters are still only statistically significant on the dichotomous variable Combining (i.e., whether or not the infant has started combining

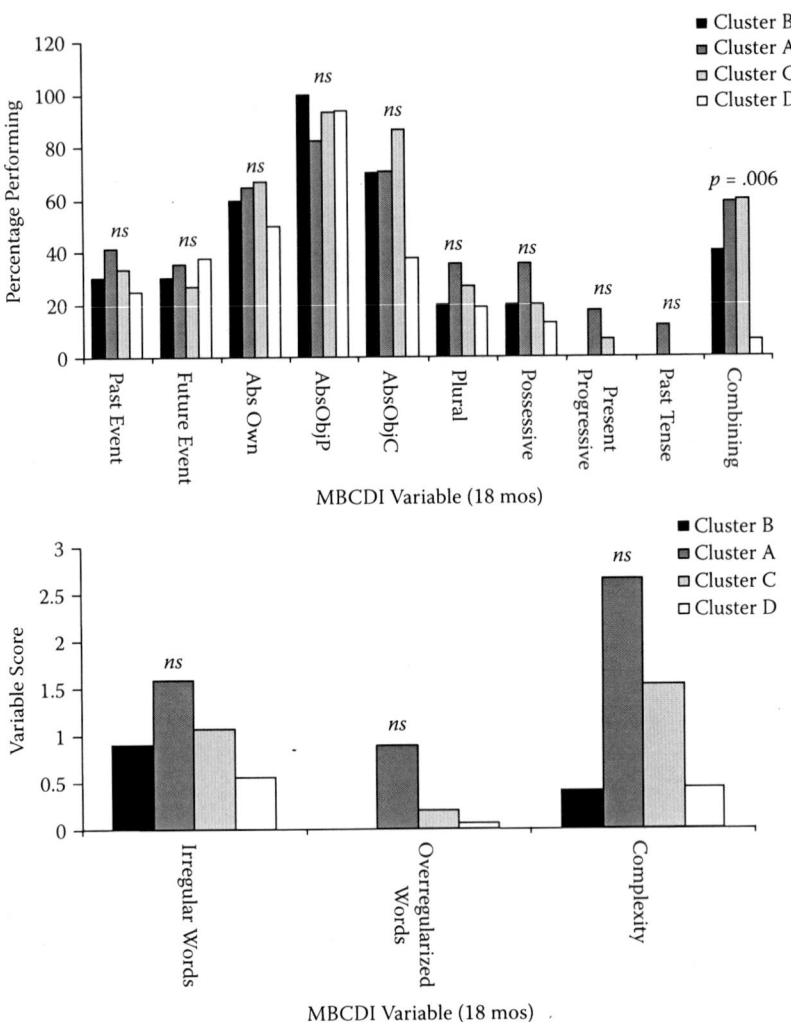

Figure 9.8 Dichotomous (top panel) and continuous (bottom panel) MBCDI variables at 18 months for the four clusters.

words). At 24 months, however, the Clusters A and B are statistically superior to clusters C and D on a number of important variables that extend beyond the lexicon and into the morphosyntactic realm. On dichotomous variables, marginally significant trends favor Cluster B on reference to past events and show the other three clusters diverging from Cluster D on reference to future events. Two other variables show statistically reliable effects: On the use of present progressive, Cluster B has pulled away ($p = .001$) from the other clusters, and on the

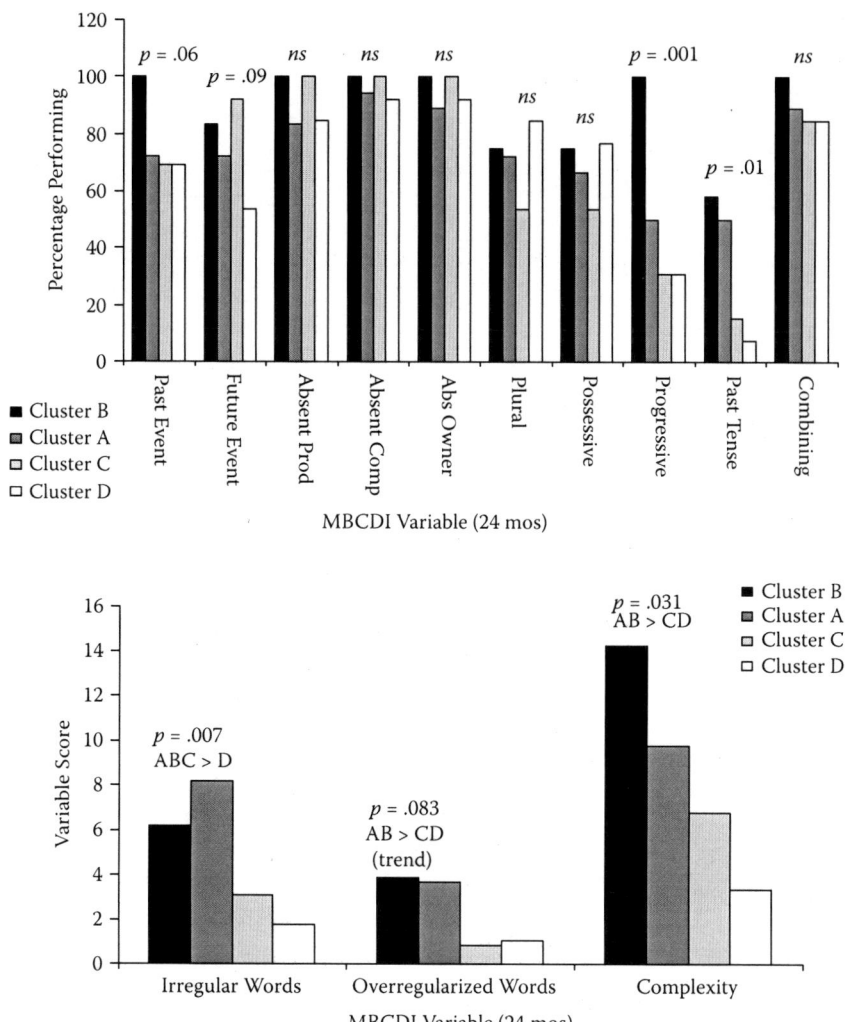

Figure 9.9   Dichotomous (top panel) and continuous (bottom panel) MBCDI variables at 24 months for the four clusters.

use of past tense, Clusters A and B have separated themselves ($p = .01$) from the other two clusters. The results from the continuous variables at 24 months are even stronger. Here, the two normative clusters (A and B) are reliably ahead on the variable Complexity ($p = .03$), and there is a similar marginal trend for both clusters to be ahead on the number of overregularized words. Finally, Cluster D lags behind all others on the number of irregular words ($p = .007$).

Preschool Outcomes and Cluster Membership

PPVT-III Performance

The PPVT-III, which is the predominant standardized instrument for measuring the receptive vocabulary of young children, was administered to participants remaining with the project during their third and fourth years, and this allowed us to determine the long-term predictive validity of cluster membership from measures taken during the first year. Data are presented here for measurements taken at 36 and 48 months of age, and raw scores from the PPVT-III are presented in Figure 9.10. In a similar pattern as that seen for the MBCDI, differences between the clusters emerge over time. At 36 months, the clusters are not discriminable from one another, but by 48 months there are significant differences ($p = .02$), which results in the significant Age × Cluster interaction depicted in Figure 9.10. At 48 months, Clusters A and B have once again significantly diverged from Clusters C and D.

SUMMARY AND DISCUSSION

The findings from this project indicate that parameters of attention during the first postnatal year may contribute in important ways to the development of various aspects of language in subsequent years. Using data from a large sample of longitudinally studied infants, cluster analyses revealed individual developmental profiles of change in visual attention over the first year of life; these profiles featured divergent psychophysiological concomitants. Furthermore, these various

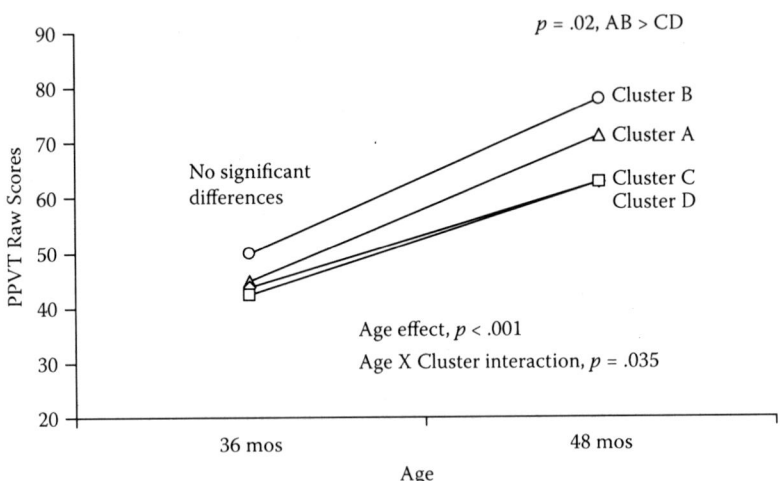

Figure 9.10   Developmental change in raw PPVT-III scores for the four clusters (A–D) at 3 and 4 years of age.

developmental courses were consistently related to the growth of productive vocabulary during the second year, to ancillary morphosyntactic variables at 2 years, and to receptive vocabulary at age 4.

Basic Overall Findings

These findings are in line with a larger literature indicating that individual differences in basic cognitive functions taken during the first year of life are correlated (at least a modest levels) with cognitive and language outcomes later in early and middle childhood. Language outcomes in toddlerhood and the preschool period were significantly predicted by specific developmental functions for attention collected during infancy. It is possible to reduce the findings as follows: Better language outcomes are observed for infants showing clear and precipitous declines in looking across the first year, where the proportion of SA is maintained across age and where the proportion of AT declines. Consistent with the extant literature, there is a small advantage on some variables for an accelerated cluster whose look durations are briefer, but by later ages differences between infants showing this profile and those showing a more normal pattern disappear. Less optimal language outcomes are seen for infants where the proportion of SA during looking declines during the latter half of the first year. Of these profiles, the least optimal outcomes are seen for infants where the proportion of SA is supplanted by an increase in AT. The current theoretical frame for the development of attention toward the end of the first year suggests that these latter two patterns reflect some irregularity in the emergence of endogenous attention.

Early Attention: A Reconsideration of Short Looking

These findings also provide important refinements to the interpretation of infant look duration during the first year. Much of the existing literature (e.g., Colombo, Frick, Ryther, & Gifford, 1996; Colombo et al., 1991; Colombo et al., 1988; Freeseman, Colombo, & Coldren, 1993) suggests that shorter look durations in infancy are advantageous relative to longer look durations. While there is much in the current database to support that contention in that the "accelerated" cluster (B) tends to be ahead on several measures, relative to the normative cluster (A), it is also the case that the current data indicate that all short looking is not alike and that, depending on the underlying attentional mechanisms (revealed here through concomitant analysis of psychophysiological measures), some short looking can also be related to less optimal outcomes. Clusters C and D would normally be characterized as short looking, but both show lags behind the more normative clusters. This underscores and emphasizes the importance of measurement of attention at multiple levels and also the importance of using a developmental approach in any predictive study.

Pathways to Early Language

While these findings do support previous work on the predictive nature of early attention, they also fit with recent revisions to the theory behind those findings of continuity in that they are less consistent with a *homotypic model* of development and prediction, where one expects that measures in infancy tap some emergent manifestation of an ability or skill that predicts the mature form of that ability or skill at maturity. Clearly, measures of attention in infancy cannot be considered to reflect early vocabulary learning or some morphosyntactic module. Instead, the findings are far more parsimoniously interpreted through a developmental cascade model, in which developmental status in different realms and at different points in the life span contribute in incremental and relatively indirect ways to developmental outcome. From these findings, it would seem more parsimonious to propose that the normal emergence or development of attention during the latter half of the first year (probably endogenous attention; Colombo & Cheatham, 2006) is related to vocabulary growth during the second year and beyond. It may also be that vocabulary growth in turn gives rise to progress in acquisition of morphosyntactic skills. It is worth noting that, throughout the explication of these findings, the analyses reveal prediction for *dynamic* aspects of the growth (i.e., developmental trajectories) of these language skills that are evident only from a longitudinal or developmental vantage point; these findings are not based on trait-level person effects that would be accessible at every or any point of measurement.

ACKNOWLEDGMENTS

This work was supported by R01HD35903 to John Colombo. We thank the families that participated in the Early Cognition Project and the staff and administration of the University of Kansas Edwards Campus.

REFERENCES

Andersson, H.W. (1996). The Fagan Test of Infant Intelligence: Predictive validity in a random sample. *Psychological Reports, 78*, 1015-1026.

Blaga, O.M. & Colombo, J. (2006). Visual processing and infant ocular latencies in the overlap paradigm. *Developmental Psychology, 42*, 1069–1076.

Booth, A. E. & Waxman, S. (2002). Object names and object functions serve as cues to categories for infants. *Developmental Psychology, 38*, 948–957.

Bornstein, M. H. (1975). Qualities of color vision in infancy. *Journal of Experimental Child Psychology, 19*, 401–419.

Bornstein, M. H. (1990). Attention in infancy and the prediction of cognitive capacities in childhood. In J. T. Enns (Ed.), *The development of attention: Research and theory. Advances in psychology*, (Vol. 69, pp. 3–19). Amsterdam: North Holland.

Bornstein, M. H., Hahn, C. S., Bell, C., Haynes, O. M., Slater, A., Golding, J., et al. (2006). Stability in cognition across early childhood: A developmental cascade. *Psychological Science. 17*, 151–158.

Bornstein, M. H. & Sigman, M. D. (1986). Continuity in mental development from infancy. *Child Development, 57,* 251–274.

Bornstein, M. H., Slater, A., Brown, E., Roberts, E., & Barrett, J. (1997). Stability of mental development from infancy to later childhood: Three "waves" of research. In G. Bremner, A. Slater, & G. Butterworth (Eds.), *Infant development: Recent advances.* (pp. 191–215). Hove, England: Psychology Press/Taylor & Francis.

Cohen, L. B. & Strauss, M. S. (1979). Concept acquisition in the human infant. *Child Development, 50,* 419–424.

Colombo, J. (1993). *Infant cognition: Predicting childhood intelligence.* Newbury Park, CA: Sage.

Colombo, J. (1997). Individual differences in infant cognition: Methods, measures and models. In J. Dobbing (Ed.), *Developing brain and behavior: The role of lipids in infant formulas* (Chapter text: pp. 339–372; Commentary and Author's replies: pp. 372–385). London: Academic Press.

Colombo, J. (2001). The development of visual attention in infancy. *Annual Review of Psychology, 52,* 337–367.

Colombo, J. (2002). Infant attention grows up: The emergence of a developmental cognitive neuroscience perspective. *Current Directions in Psychological Science, 11,* 196–199.

Colombo, J. & Cheatham, C. (2006). The emergence of endogenous attention in infancy and early childhood. In R. Kail (Ed.), *Advances in child development and behavior* (pp. 283–322). New York: Elsevier.

Colombo, J. & Frick, J. E. (1999). Recent advances and issues in the study of preverbal intelligence. In M. Anderson (Ed.), *Development of intelligence.* London: University College of London Press.

Colombo, J., Frick, J. E., Ryther, J. S., & Gifford, J. J. (1996). Individual differences in infant visual attention: Four-month-olds' recognition of forms connoted by complementary contour. *Infant Behavior and Development, 19,* 113–119.

Colombo, J., Harlan, J. E., & Mitchell, D. W. (1999, April). *The development of look duration in infancy: Evidence for a triphasic course.* Paper presented at the Biennial Meeting of the Society for Research in Child Development, Albuquerque, NM.

Colombo, J. & Mitchell, D. W. (1990). Individual and developmental differences in infant visual attention: Fixation time and information processing. In J. Colombo and J. W. Fagen (Eds.), Individual differences in infancy: Reliability, stability, and prediction (pp. 193–227). Hillsdale, NJ: Lawrence Erlbaum.

Colombo, J., Mitchell, D. W., Coldren, J. T., & Freeseman, L. J. (1991). Individual differences in infant attention: Are short lookers faster processors or feature processors? *Child Development, 62,* 1247–1257.

Colombo, J., Mitchell, D. W., & Horowitz, F. D. (1988). Infant visual behavior in the paired-comparison paradigm: Test-retest and attention-performance relations. *Child Development, 59,* 1198–1210.

Colombo, J., Kannass, K. N., Shaddy, D. J., Kundurthi, S., Anderson, C. J., Blaga, O. M., et al. (2004). Maternal DHA and the development of attention in infancy and toddlerhood. *Child Development, 75,* 1254–1267.

Colombo, J., Mitchell, D. W., O'Brien, M., & Horowitz, F. D. (1987a). Stability of infant visual habituation during the first year. *Child Development, 58,* 474–489.

Colombo, J., Mitchell, D. W., O'Brien, M., & Horowitz, F. D. (1987b). Stimulus and motoric influences on visual habituation at three months. *Infant Behavior and Development, 10,* 173–181.

Colombo, J., Richman, W. A., Shaddy, D. J., Greenhoot, A. F., & Maikranz, J. (2001). HR-Defined phases of attention, look duration, and infant performance in the paired-comparison paradigm. *Child Development, 72,* 1605–1616.

Colombo, J., Shaddy, D. J., Blaga, O. M., Anderson, C. J., & Kannass, K. N. (2007, in press). High cognitive ability in infancy. In F. Horowitz & D. Matthews (Eds.), *Concepts of giftedness in developmental theory and research.* Washington, DC: American Psychological Association Press.

Colombo, J., Shaddy, D. J., Richman, W. A., Maikranz, J. M., & Blaga, O. M. (2004). Developmental course of visual habituation and preschool cognitive and language outcome. *Infancy, 5,* 1–38.

Courage, M. L., Reynolds, G. D., & Richards, J. E. (2006). Infants' attention to patterned stimuli: developmental change from 3 to 12 months of age. *Child Development, 77,* 680–695.

Dougherty, T. M. & Haith, M. M. (1997). Infant expectations and reaction time as predictors of childhood speed of processing and IQ. *Developmental Psychology, 33,* 146–155.

Fagan, J. F. (1981). Infant intelligence. *Intelligence, 5,* 239–243.

Fagan, J. F. (1982). New evidence for the prediction of intelligence from infancy. *Infant Mental Health Journal, 3,* 219–228.

Fagan, J. F. (1984a). Recognition memory and intelligence. *Intelligence, 8,* 31–36.

Fagan, J. F. (1984b). The intelligent infant: Theoretical implications. *Intelligence, 8,* 1–9.

Fagan, J. F. (1984c). The relationship of novelty preferences during infancy to later intelligence and later recognition memory. *Intelligence, 8,* 339–346.

Fagan, J. F. (1985). A new look at infant intelligence. *Current Topics in Human Intelligence, 1,* 223–246.

Fagan, J. F. (1988). Evidence for the relationship between responsiveness to visual novelty during infancy and later intelligence: A summary. *Cahiers de Psychologie Cognitive/Current Psychology of Cognition, 8,* 469–475.

Fagan, J. F. & McGrath, S. K. (1981). Infant recognition memory and later intelligence. *Intelligence, 5,* 121–130.

Fagan, J. F. & Singer, L. T. (1983). Infant recognition memory as a measure of intelligence. *Advances in Infancy Research, 2,* 31–78.

Fagen, J. W. & Ohr, P. S. (1990). Individual differences in infant conditioning and memory. In J. Colombo & J. W. Fagen (Eds.), *Individual differences in infancy: Reliability, stability, prediction* (pp. 157–191). Hillsdale, NJ: Lawrence Erlbaum Associates, Inc.

Fantz, R. L. (1964). Visual experience in infants: Decreased attention familiar patterns relative to novel ones. *Science, 146,* 668–670.

Fenson, L., Dale, P. S., Reznick, J. S., Bates, E., Thal, D. J., & Pethick, S. J. (1994). Variability in early communicative development. *Monographs of the Society for Research in Child Development, 59*(242).

Freeseman, L. J., Colombo, J., & Coldren, J. T. (1993). Individual differences in infant visual attention: Discrimination and generalization of global and local stimulus properties. *Child Development, 64,* 1191–1203.

Frick, J. E., Colombo. J., & Saxon, T. F. (1999). Individual and developmental differences in disengagement of fixation in early infancy. *Child Development 70,* 537–548.

Frick, J. E. & Richards, J. E. (2001). Individual differences in infants' recognition of briefly presented visual stimuli. *Infancy, 2,* 331–352.

Gopnik, A. & Meltzoff, A. (1987). The development of categorization in the second year and its relation to other cognitive and linguistic developments. *Child Development, 58,* 1523–1531.

Gottfried, A. W., Rose, S. A., & Bridger, W. H. (1977). Cross-modal transfer in human infants. *Child Development, 48*, 118–123.

Green, J. A. (1990). Analyzing individual differences in development: Correlations and cluster analysis. In J. Colombo & J. W. Fagen (Eds.), *Individual differences in infancy: Reliability, stability, prediction.* (pp. 77–109). Hillsdale, NJ: Lawrence Erlbaum Associates, Inc.

Haith, M. M., Hazan, C., & Goodman, G. S. (1988). Expectation and anticipation of dynamic visual events by 3.5-month-old babies. *Child Development, 59*, 467–479.

Horowitz, F. D., Paden, L., Bhana, K., & Self, P. (1972). An infant-control procedure for studying infant visual fixations. *Developmental Psychology, 7*, 90.

Jankowski, J. J. & Rose, S. A. (1997). The distribution of visual attention in infants. *Journal of Experimental Child Psychology, 65*, 127–140.

Jankowski, J. J., Rose, S. A, & Feldman, J. F. (2001). Modifying the distribution of attention in infants. *Child Development, 72*, 339–351.

Landry, S. H., Leslie, N. A., Fletcher, J. M., & Francis, D. J. (1985). Visual attention skills of premature infants with and without intraventricular hemorrhage. *Infant Behavior and Development, 8*, 309–321.

Laucht, M., Esser, G., & Schmidt, M. H. (1994). Contrasting infant predictors of later cognitive functioning. *Journal of Child Psychology and Psychiatry, 35*, 649–662.

Leslie, A. M. & Keeble, S. (1987). Do six-month-old infants perceive causality? *Cognition, 25*, 265–288.

McCall, R. B. (1976). Toward an epigenetic conception of mental development in the first three years of life. In M. Lewis (Ed.), *Origins of intelligence* (pp. 97–122). New York: Plenum.

McCall, R. B. (1979). The development of intellectual functioning in infancy and the prediction of later IQ. In J. D. Osofsky (Ed.), *Handbook of infant development* (pp. 707–741). New York: Wiley.

McCall, R. B. (1983). A conceptual approach to early mental development. In M. Lewis (Ed.), *Origins of intelligence* (2d ed., pp. 67–106). New York: Plenum.

McCall, R. B. (1994). What process mediates prediction of childhood IQ from infant habituation and recognition memory? Speculations on the roles of inhibition and rate of information processing. *Intelligence, 18*, 107–124.

McCall, R. B. & Carriger, M. (1993). A meta-analysis of infant habituation and recognition memory performance as predictors of later IQ. *Child Development, 64*, 57–79.

McCall, R. B. & Mash, C. (1995). Infant cognition and its relation to mature intelligence. In G. Whitehurst (Ed.), *Annals of child development* (Vol. 11, pp. 27–56). Greenwich, CT: JAI.

McDonough, S. C. & Cohen, L. B. (1982). Attention and memory in cerebral palsied infants. *Infant Behavior and Development, 5*, 347–353.

Miller, D. J., Ryan, E. B., Aberger, E., McGuire, M. D., Short, E. J., & Kenny, D. A. (1979). Relationships between assessments of habituation and cognitive performance in the early years of life. *International Journal of Behavioral Development, 2*, 159–170.

Miller, D. J., Ryan, E. B., Short, E. J., Ries, P. G., McGuire, M. D., & Culler, M. P. (1977). Relationships between early habituation and later cognitive performance in infancy. *Child Development, 48*, 658–661.

Miller, D. J., Sinnott, J. P., Short, E. J., & Hains, A. A. (1976). Individual differences in habituation rates and object concept performance. *Child Development, 47*, 528–531.

Miller, D. J., Spiridigliozzi, G., Ryan, E. B., Callan, M. P., & McLaughlin, J. E. (1980). Habituation and cognitive performance: Relationships between measures at four years of age and earlier assessments. *International Journal of Behavioral Development, 3*, 131–146.

Milligan, G. W. & Cooper, M. C. (1987). Methodology review: Clustering methods. *Applied Psychological Measurement, 11*, 329–354.

Orlian, E. K. & Rose, S. A. (1997). Speed vs. thoroughness in infant visual information processing. *Infant Behavior and Development, 20*, 371–381.

Richards, J. E. (1997). Effects of attention on infants' preference for briefly exposed visual stimuli in the paired-comparison recognition-memory paradigm. *Developmental Psychology, 33*, 22–31.

Richards, J. E. (2004). The development of sustained attention in infants. In M. I. Posner (Ed.), *Cognitive neuroscience of attention* (pp. 342–356). New York: Guilford Press.

Richards, J. E. & Casey, B. J. (1992). Development of sustained visual attention in the human infant. In B. A. Campbell, H. Hayne, & R. Richardson (Eds.), *Attention and information processing in infants and adults: Perspectives from human and animal research* (pp. 30–60). Hillsdale, NJ: Erlbaum.

Rolfe, S. A. (1994). Does assessment of cognitive functioning in infancy hold the key to early detection of developmental disabilities? A review of research. *Australia and New Zealand Journal of Developmental Disabilities, 19*, 61–72.

Rose, D. H., Slater, A., & Perry, H. (1986). Prediction of childhood intelligence from habituation in early infancy. *Intelligence, 10*, 251–263.

Rose, S. A. & Feldman, J. F. (1997). Memory and speed: Their role in the relation of infant information processing to later IQ. *Child Development, 68*, 630–641.

Rose, S. A., Feldman, J. F., Futterweit, L. R., & Jankowski, J. J. (1997). Continuity in visual recognition memory: Infancy to 11 years. *Intelligence, 24*, 381–392.

Rose, S. A., Feldman, J. F., Futterweit, L. R., & Jankowski, J. J. (1998). Continuity in tactual-visual cross-modal transfer: Infancy to 11 years. *Developmental Psychology, 34*, 435–440.

Rose, S. A., Feldman, J. F., & Jankowski, J. J. (2001). Attention and recognition memory in the 1st year of life: A longitudinal study of preterm and full-term infants. *Developmental Psychology, 37*, 135–151.

Rose, S. A., Feldman, J. F., & Jankowski, J. J. (2004). Infant visual recognition memory. *Developmental Review, 24*, 74–100.

Rose, S. A., Feldman, J. F., & Jankowski, J. J. (2005). The structure of infant cognition at 1 year. *Intelligence, 33*, 231–250.

Rose, S. A., Feldman, J. F., Jankowski, J. J., & Caro, D. M. (2002). A longitudinal study of visual expectation and reaction time in the first year of life. *Child Development, 73*, 47–61.

Rose, S. A., Feldman, J. F., Jankowski, J. J., & Van Rossem R. (2005). Pathways from prematurity and infant abilities to later cognition. *Child Development, 76*, 1172–1184.

Rose, S. A., Feldman, J. F., & Wallace, I. F. (1992). Infant information processing in relation to six-year cognitive outcomes. *Child Development, 63*, 1126–1141.

Rose, S. A., Feldman, J. F., Wallace, I. F., & Cohen, P. (1991). Language: A partial link between infant attention and later intelligence. *Developmental Psychology, 27*, 798–805.

Rose, S. A., Feldman, J. F., Wallace, I. F., & McCarton, C. (1991). Information processing at 1 year: Relation to birth status and developmental outcome during the first 5 years. *Developmental Psychology, 27*, 723–737.

Rose, S. A., Futterweit, L. R., & Jankowski, J. J. (1999). The relation of affect to attention and learning in infancy. *Child Development, 70*, 549–559.

Rose, S. A. & Wallace, I. F. (1985a). Visual recognition memory: A predictor of later cognitive functioning in preterms. *Child Development, 56*, 843–852.

Rose, S. A. & Wallace, I. F. (1985b). Cross-modal and intramodal transfer as predictors of mental development in full-term and preterm infants. *Developmental Psychology, 21*, 949–962.

Rovee, C. K. & Rovee, D. T. (1969). Conjugate reinforcement of infant exploratory behavior. *Journal of Experimental Child Psychology, 8*, 33–39.

Saayman, G., Ames, E. W., & Moffett, A. (1964). Response to novelty as an indicator of visual discrimination in the human infant. *Journal of Experimental Child Psychology, 1*, 189–198.

Saffran, J. R., Aslin, R. N., & Newport, E. L. (1996). Statistical learning by 8-month-old infants. *Science, 274*, 1926–1928.

Saxon, T. F., Frick, J. E., & Colombo, J. (1997). Individual differences in infant visual fixation and maternal interactional styles. *Merrill-Palmer Quarterly, 43*, 48–66.

Sigman, M. D. & Beckwith, L. (1980). Infant visual attentiveness in relation to caregiver-infant interaction and developmental outcome. *Infant Behavior and Development, 3*, 141–154.

Sigman, M. D. & Mundy, P. (1993). Infant precursors of childhood intellectual and verbal abilities. In D. F. Hay & A. Angold (Eds.), *Precursors and causes in development and psychopathology* (pp. 123–144). Chichester, UK: John Wiley & Sons.

Sigman, M. D., Cohen, S. E., & Beckwith, L. (1997). Why does infant attention predict adolescent intelligence? *Infant Behavior and Development, 20*, 133–140.

Wainwright, P. E. & Colombo, J. (2006). Nutrition and the development of cognitive functions: interpretation of behavioral studies in animals and human infants. *American Journal of Clinical Nutrition, 84*, 961–970.

Waxman, S. R. & Braun, I. (2005). Consistent (but not variable) names as invitations to form object categories: New evidence from 12-month-old infants. *Cognition, 95*, B59–B68.

Weir, C. & Millar, W. S. (1997). The effects of neonatal jaundice and respiratory complications on learning and habituation in 5- to 11-month-old infants. *Journal of Child Psychology and Psychiatry, 38*, 199–206.

Vietze, P. M. & Coates, D. L. (1986). Using information processing strategies for early identification of mental retardation. *Topics in Early Childhood Special Education, 6*, 72–85.

10

Social Cognition and Language
The Role of Gaze Following
in Early Word Learning

Andrew N. Meltzoff and Rechele Brooks

INTRODUCTION

In the 1970s feminism was in the air. The zeitgeist can influence scientific theories (Kuhn, 1962). One could argue that feminism influenced theories of language acquisition. The dominant theory of language was Noam Chomsky's, which proposed that an innately structured *language-acquisition device* (LAD) controlled the timing and form of language growth. The 1970s brought a different approach to language acquisition rooted in the dynamics of parent–child interaction (e.g., Bates, Benigni, Bretherton, Camaioni, & Volterra, 1979; Bates, Camaioni & Volterra, 1975; Bruner, 1975a, 1975b; Bullowa, 1979; Halliday, 1975). Bruner (1983) codified the movement by proposing that Chomsky's LAD needed a *language-acquisition support system* (LASS). This was a social network that supported and scaffolded the child as he or she was initiated into the world of oral language. Ideas about the social foundations for language had already been articulated in philosophy (e.g., Austin, 1962; Grice, 1968; Searle, 1969) and psychology (e.g., de Laguna, 1927; Vygotsky, 1962), but the 1970s launched an unprecedented empirical investigation into the social factors that contribute to early language acquisition.

The movement launched in the 1970s is now coming to fruition. It is agreed by most current developmental scientists that Chomsky's *poverty of the stimulus argument* was brilliant in theory but that the language directed at children is not as impoverished as we once thought. For example, we now know that parents speak in different ways to their infants ("motherese") than they do to their spouses at the dinner table. Spousal speech is impoverished in ways that motherese is not. The syntax and semantics of child-directed speech are simplified (Ferguson, 1964), the pace is slowed (Fernald & Simon, 1984), the acoustics are attention getting (Fernald & Kuhl, 1987), and the vowels and consonants are exquisitely formed (hyperarticulated) to give infants a tutorial on the sound patterns of their mother tongue (Kuhl, 2004; Kuhl et al., 1997). Moreover, infants' own perceptual-cognitive abilities are well tuned to extract structure from the statistical regularities of parents' input (Aslin, Saffran, & Newport, 1998; Jusczyk, Luce, & Charles-Luce, 1994; Saffran, Aslin, & Newport, 1996). Other chapters in this volume address the perceptual, cognitive, and linguistic biases and capacities that infants bring to the problem of language acquisition. This chapter elaborates specific social factors that facilitate the infant's task (see also Golinkoff, & Hirsh-Pasek, 2006; Golinkoff et al., 2000; Tomasello, 2003).

For the scope of this chapter, we choose to concentrate on a crucial aspect of social cognition—gaze following—and its predictive links to language. It is easy to see why gaze following could contribute to word learning. In everyday settings, caretakers provide verbal labels for objects they are looking at (Tomasello & Farrar, 1986). Of course, language also refers to absent and hypothetical objects (Hockett, 1960), parents and children use nonnominal expressions (Gopnik, 1982, 1988; Gopnik & Meltzoff, 1985, 1986), and there is Quine's (1960) indeterminacy problem (Bloom, 2000; Eilan, Hoerl, McCormack, & Roessler, 2005; Markman, 1989). Nonetheless, empirical work shows that much of infant-directed speech is about here and now, whole objects—labeling the perceptually present ball, dog, or cup (Bruner, 1983; Harris, Jones, & Grant, 1983; Hart & Risley, 1999).

It has been argued that when several objects are perceptually available to the child, checking the speaker's gaze direction could help the child locate the object to which the speaker is referring (Baldwin, 1991, 1993, 1995; Bruner, 1975a; Butterworth & Jarrett, 1991; Hollich, Hirsh-Pasek, & Golinkoff, 2000; Meltzoff & Brooks, 2007; Tomasello, 1995). In Bruner's (1983) *initial word learning game,* if infants want to know what mom is labeling, they will get a big boost by following her eyes. She is probably not labeling what is behind her back or on the next page of the book or on the roof of the house. However, determining what mom is looking at is, itself, a developmental achievement. In this chapter we discuss the ontogeny of *gaze following,* carefully distinguishing it from the broader umbrella term of *joint visual attention* (JVA). After clarifying the definitional and methodological landscape, we discuss longitudinal work that examines the relation between gaze following and early vocabulary growth.

JOINT VISUAL ATTENTION: SHARPENING THE CONCEPT AND MEASURING INSTRUMENT

It is useful to distinguish gaze following from other closely aligned phenomena that have been bundled under the broader term of joint visual attention. Typical phenomena discussed under the JVA label are intersubjectivity, joint engagement, pointing, and gaze following. We will differentiate these concepts

and their attendant literatures. By doing so, the empirical and theoretical relation between gaze following per se and language will become clearer.

Intersubjectivity

The notion of infant intersubjectivity derives from philosophy (Gallagher, 2001;
Habermas, 1970; Husserl, 1977; Macmurray, 1961) and psychoanalytic theory
(Beebe, Rustin, Sorter, & Knoblauch, 2003; Beebe, Sorter, Rustin, & Knoblauch,
2003; Hobson, 1998, 2002). Two works by Trevarthen (1979; Trevarthen & Hubley, 1978) distinguished between primary intersubjectivity and secondary intersubjectivity. According to his analysis, primary intersubjectivity occurs when an
infant and mother show synchronized play that does not involve objects—for
example, turn-taking, with facial expressions, vocalizations, and body movements. These are the exquisitely timed, contingent "gestural dances" between
caretaker and infant (Bråten, 1998; Brazelton, Koslowski, & Main, 1974; Kaye
& Fogel, 1980; Jaffe, Beebe, Feldstein, Crown, & Jasnow, 2001; Papoušek, 2007;
Rochat, 2007; Stern, 1985). Secondary intersubjectivity marks a change from
the dyad to the inclusion of a third entity (person or object). For example, the
child picks up and bangs an object, and the mother contingently responds to that
object-directed act. The bulk of the work on infant intersubjectivity is ethologi-
cal/ethnographic rather than experimental, and it has contributed a rich literature about the nature of parent–child interaction.

Joint Engagement and Triadic Communication

Adamson and Bakeman (1985), Adamson and McArthur (1995), and Bakeman
and Adamson (1984, 1986) introduced the idea of *joint engagement*. Joint engagement refers to the fact that infants and caretakers often attend to and play with
the same toy. Bakeman and Adamson (1984) also call this *triadic communication* to indicate that the child and parent communicate about a shared object,
forming a triad. The notion of joint engagement has much in common with the
earlier notion of intersubjectivity, but while proponents of the latter built bridges
to philosophy of mind, the proponents of joint engagement operationalized their
concept and tested for empirical ties to language acquisition. For example, a key
component of *coordinated joint engagement* is that infants make eye contact with
their parent and alternate gaze back to the object (Bakeman & Adamson, 1984;
Carpenter, Nagell, & Tomasello, 1998; Rollins, 2003; Striano & Bertin, 2005;
Tomasello & Todd, 1983). The mother may in turn look at and verbally label the
object of shared attention (i.e., *follow-in labeling*).

Mothers differ in the propensity for follow-in labeling, and this seems to affect
their infants' language (Bornstein, Tamis-LeMonda, & Haynes, 1999; Masur,
Flynn, & Eichorst, 2005; Tomasello & Farrar, 1986; see also Hobson, Patrick,

Crandell, García Pérez, & Lee, 2004). Results suggest that maternal follow-in labeling for 9-month-olds predicts later vocabulary size (Carpenter et al., 1998; Masur et al., 2005; Rollins, 2003). For 12-month-olds, both mothers' follow-in labeling and infants' coordinated joint engagement (infants' alternating gaze between parent and toy) predict later receptive language (Carpenter et al., 1998; Rollins, 2003). At 14–15 months old, the tendency for an infant to initiate and maintain coordinated joint engagement predicts productive language (Carpenter et al., 1998; Laakso, Poikkeus, Eklund, & Lyytinen, 1999; Markus, Mundy, Morales, Delgado, & Yale, 2000; Smith, Adamson, & Bakeman, 1988).

Thus, measurements of joint engagement predict later language, but two points are noteworthy. First, part of the joint engagement concept concerns *maternal* behavior (e.g., maternal follow-in labeling); thus, in many cases the reported relationships between joint engagement and infant language simply show that one maternal style of verbal labeling is more favorable to language learning than another (Akhtar, Dunham, & Dunham, 1991). Second, the concept includes many behaviors *in addition to* infant gaze following. In this chapter, we seek to drill down on the role that gaze following per se plays in language learning. The joint engagement work, while often cited as an example of the relation between language and the umbrella terms *joint attention* or *preverbal communication,* does not isolate gaze following behavior in and of itself. It is fascinating that the types of preverbal interactions discussed in this literature are linked to language, but it would not require that infants gaze follow (see definitions that follow)—the chief topic of this chapter.

Pointing

Pointing is another component of the umbrella category of JVA, and it obviously does not implicate gaze following per se. The production of pointing has been tied to language (Bates et al., 1979; Camaioni, Castelli, Longobardi, & Volterra, 1991). Infants begin pointing to objects between 9 and 12 months (Butterworth & Morissette, 1996; Camaioni, Perucchini, Bellagamba, & Colonnesi, 2004; Carpenter et al., 1998; Ohgami, 2006). When infants point and look at their social partner, the points are called *communicative points;* points without a look at the adult are called *noncommunicative points* (Bates et al., 1979; Desrochers, Morissette, & Ricard, 1995). Empirical results suggest that the production of communicative points more strongly predicts subsequent language development than do noncommunicative points (Bates et al., 1979; Desrochers et al., 1995).

Another distinction that has been made is between protoimperative versus protodeclarative points (Bates et al., 1975; Camaioni et al., 2004; Franco & Butterworth, 1996; Henderson, Yoder, Yale, & McDuffie, 2002; Liszkowski, Carpenter, & Tomasello, 2007). The former concerns pointing because the child desires something: "Want that!" The latter concerns the child pointing to draw the

adult's attention to it: "Look at that!" Disagreements center on whether protoimperative pointing is developmentally prior to protodeclarative pointing and how
to reliably measure the difference between the two (Bates et al., 1975; Camaioni,
1997; Camaioni et al., 2004; Carpenter et al., 1998; Henderson et al., 2002; Liszkowski, Carpenter, Henning, Striano, & Tomasello, 2004). That said, in longitudinal studies relating pointing to language (Mundy, Fox, & Card, 2003; Mundy &
Gomes, 1998), there is some indication that infant protodeclarative points at 14
to 18 months predict later language (at 18 to 24 months), and the evidence is
much weaker for protoimperative points.

Gaze Following and Related Literature

We come, at last, to the gaze literature. There are several phenomena that suggest the
importance of gaze; we draw distinctions among them to help sharpen the issues.

Eye Preference

One oft cited literature concerns young infants' sensitivity to human eyes and preferences for face-like patterns containing eye spots (Baron-Cohen, 1995; Farroni,
Csibra, Simion, & Johnson, 2002; Farroni, Massaccesi, Pividori, & Johnson, 2004;
Haith, Bergman, & Moore, 1977; Hunnius & Geuze, 2004; Johnson & Morton,
1991; Maurer, 1985). This could be the "front end" of a gaze-following mechanism,
but, clearly, such perceptual biases and preferences are not evidence of gaze following per se. Nor have such preferences been linked to later language development.

Cued Looking to Periphery

Another literature concerns cued looking to peripheral targets (Driver et al., 1999;
Farroni, Johnson, Brockbank, & Simion, 2000; Farroni, Mansfield, Lai, & Johnson,
2003; Friesen, Moore, & Kingstone, 2005; Hood, Willen, & Driver, 1998; Langton,
Watt, & Bruce, 2000; MacPherson & Moore, 2007; Senju, Johnson, & Csibra, 2006;
Frischen, Bayliss, & Tipper, 2007). The classic stimulus used to measure this phenomenon is a digitized face with eyes that shift to one side before a target appears on
the right or left. The face is usually extinguished before the peripheral probes appear.
Adults and infants look with shorter latencies to the probe that has been cued —
if the cue shifts to the right side, infants will fixate a probe that appears on the
right faster than on the left.

These are fascinating effects, but they do not provide evidence about infants'
use of gaze following in biologically plausible settings. In the real world, when a
mother looks at and labels an object ("There's a dog!"), her face does not extin-
guish to free up infants' attentional resources. Moreover, the peripheral targets
do not pop into existence to attract attention immediately after the face has
extinguished (this is how the digitized stimuli work in the cuing studies). Rather,

in everyday settings the world stays stable, and the parental gaze spotlights a preexisting object.

In the gaze-following literature (to be discussed later), infants distinguish between an adult who is looking at an object with her eyes versus other control movements to the periphery. In contrast, in the cued-looking paradigm a range of directional cues to the periphery suffice—it need not involve gaze as a cue (e.g., Ristic, Friesen, & Kingstone, 2002). It is also noteworthy that cued-looking studies involving event-related potential (ERP) exclude any trials in which infants look to the side based on the adult's gaze (actual gaze following) (Senju et al., 2006). Most importantly, for the purposes of this chapter, there have been no studies to date suggesting that early responsivity to peripheral cuing is correlated with concurrent or subsequent language development, although such studies would be interesting to conduct.

We conclude that responding to adult directional cues may be a front-end precursor to true gaze following but that infants can succeed on tests of the former without demonstrating that they will follow the gaze of an adult. The reason we are focusing on gaze following is that in order for infants to use the adult's gaze to learn words they need to follow the adult's look to the distal object (i.e., perform the motor act); otherwise, they will not be able to use this signal as leverage for word learning.

Preferential Looking to Novelty

A third literature that is often cited derives from habituation studies (Woodward, 2003; Woodward & Guajardo, 2002). For example, Woodward (2003) found that infants habituated to a person looking to a ball on the left will dishabituate more to that person looking at a bear on the left (new object, same location) than to the person looking to the ball on the right (same object, new location). This suggests that infants have encoded the relationship between the looker and the object and that they dishabituate when the link is broken. Woodward's research shows that 12-month-olds succeed on this task but that younger infants typically fail (Woodward, 2003; but see also Johnson, Ok, & Luo, 2007).

Two points are noteworthy. First, the data chiefly document infants' recognition skills and their patterns of habituation–dishabituation. Infants are *recognizing* that another person is looking but are not required to *produce* a gaze-following act to succeed on the habituation–novelty–preference paradigm. Second, no studies have yet reported links between this perceptual parsing and later language acquisition. These dishabituation effects are important, but for the purposes of this chapter we distinguish them from data showing that infants turn to look where the adult is looking. Such productive gaze following by infants would be needed if gaze following were to play its role in word learning.

Composite Measures of Joint Visual Attention

Researchers have also created assessments of joint visual attention based on composite measures of gaze following, pointing, and responding to adult vocalizations. In these assessments infants observe an adult who both looks at a target and also uses a combination of other multimodal cues. For example Carpenter et al. (1998) defined attention following as a composite score based on infants' responses to two trials of an adult who looked and vocalized at distal targets and two trials in which the adult looked and pointed at the targets. They found that the age of emergence for such generic attention following was about 11.5 months old, and it predicted productive vocabulary size at 12 to 24 months.

Another composite measure comes from the Early Social Communication Scales (ESCS) developed by Mundy, Delgado, et al. (2003) and Seibert, Hogan, and Mundy (1982). ESCS is a semistructured assessment of infants' nonverbal social skills. For the purposes of this chapter, the most relevant subscale is the responding to joint attention (RJA), and that subscale itself is a composite based on an adult who presents a multimodal set of behaviors—looks, points, and vocalizations at a target. The results show that infant scores on RJA at 6 to 18 months predict vocabulary size at 24 to 30 months (Markus et al., 2000; Morales et al., 2000; Morales, Mundy, & Rojas, 1998; Mundy, Fox, et al., 2003; Mundy & Gomes, 1998; Mundy et al., 2007).

These composite measures reveal much about early foundations for language, but the combination of cues (gaze, point, and vocalization) makes it difficult to isolate (1) whether infants are following the adult's gaze or responding to the other cues and (2) which specific infant capacity is contributing to the language prediction. The correlations between infants' responding to these combined cues and later language may stem from an early linguistic sensitivity of the infant (because *the adult is vocalizing*). For example, in Mundy et al. (2007), the adult calls the infant's name during the adult's look to an object. Might the correlation with later language be influenced by the fact that the tests of the infants already involve their responsivity to adult language as part of the stimulus? (The same applies to Carpenter et al., 1998.)

Other Communicative and Cognitive Predictors of Language

Other approaches to predicting language growth are reviewed elsewhere in the volume; thus, only a few further examples will be mentioned here. Wetherby and Prizant (2002) developed a scale measuring early social, speech, and symbolic abilities and reported associations with later language (Wetherby, Allen, Cleary, Kublin, & Goldstein, 2002; Wetherby, Goldstein, Cleary, Allen, & Kublin, 2003). The MacArthur-Bates Communicative Developmental Inventory (MBCDI) contains gesture scales such as the *first communicative gestures* that have been shown to predict later language development in many laboratories (Bates, Thal, Whitesell, Fenson, & Oakes, 1989; Carpenter et al., 1998; Fenson et al., 1994). In a sample of Swedish infants, Heimann et al. (2006) found that measures of social communication coupled with measures of cognition (deferred imitation) significantly predicted scores on the Swedish MBCDI at 14 months of age, and a follow-up study showed that these infant measures predicted cognitive functioning as old as 4 years of age (Strid, Tjus, Smith, Meltzoff, & Heimann, 2006).

Finally, other authors in the current volume have uncovered other early predictors of subsequent language. Colombo, Shaddy, Richman, Maikranz, and Blaga (2004) and Colombo (this volume) discovered perceptual-cognitive predictors of later language; Liu, Kuhl, and Tsao (2003) and Kuhl (this volume) report aspects of early speech perception that predict later language; Goldin-Meadow (this volume) discusses the role of gesture in language learning; and Rice (this volume) analyzes environmental and biological factors associated with a slower than normal language course.

Without disputing a range of contributors to the pathway of language acquisition, this chapter focuses on the link between gaze following per se and language development—a topic that has not received sufficient empirical attention despite the theoretical reasons for thinking that gaze following may give an infant a leg up in word learning (e.g., Baldwin, 1995; Bruner, 1983; Golinkoff & Hirsh-Pasek, 2006; Tomasello, 1995).

DEFINING INFANT GAZE FOLLOWING

Basic gaze following occurs when two criteria are met—and more sophisticated forms entail a third feature. Here is our working definition:

1. The gaze follower looks *where* the gazer is looking.
2. The looking behavior of the gazer *causes* (is the *external stimulus for*) the gaze follower's response.
3. The gaze follower *seeks* what the gazer has looked at.

Criterion 1 excludes giving infants credit for gaze following if they simply look to a hemifield in space. Complete accuracy is perhaps not called for, but the experiment should include some attempt to show that infants are looking at/near the target specified by the adult's gaze. Moreover, it is not gaze following if the infant is merely following head or object movements to the side. The critical stimulus must involve *gaze*, which implies the eyes. *Movement following* is not *gaze following*.

Criterion 2 eliminates the possibility that infants happen to turn to an object by chance in synchrony with an adult. If there are dynamically changing objects in the field, infants may spot them independently of the adult's act. The environment might provide a stimulus that is the common cause for gazing by both adult and infant. A moving rattle or auditory bell could catch the attention of both adult and infant. Synchronous looking due to a common third cause is not gaze following, though it *results in* joint visual attention (and would be scored in most joint attention composite scales). Moreover, if the infant performs the first look to the object, and the mother follows, the causal arrow runs the wrong direction—it is *not* infant gaze following, although the mother and infant both end up fixating the same thing.

Criterion 3 is the Holy Grail of the gaze-following literature. It implies an effort to see what the other sees. This is what is meant by saying that infants treat the others' looking as referential. The other's look is interpreted to be "about" something, and infants seek to look at that something. Oftentimes the best evidence for Criterion 3 comes from converging measures that provide clues to infants' interpretation and motivation in turning to look at the target that was indicated by the adult looking. Infant points, vocalizations, checks back to the gazer, and other measures can be useful (Meltzoff, 2007).

MEASURING INFANT GAZE FOLLOWING

If an adult is speaking motherese and looking fervently back and forth between two objects, or scrutinizing a single object, it is likely that her accompanying speech refers to (some aspect of) these objects. When do infants begin to interpret an adult's gaze as more than an incidental bodily movement—a visual hiccup—and interpret it as referring to something beyond itself?

It is well established that young infants turn in the direction that an adult has turned, but there is a debate about the mechanism underlying this behavior (e.g., Butterworth, 2001; Csibra & Gergely, 2006; Eilan et al., 2005; Flom, Lee, & Muir, 2007; Moore & Dunham, 1995; Tomasello, Carpenter, Call, Behne, & Moll, 2005). One conservative proposal is that infants simply are attracted to the spatial hemifield indicated by the adult's head movement (Butterworth & Jarrett, 1991; Moore, 1999; Moore & Corkum, 1994). The infant is drawn in by the adult's large and salient head motion and in watching that head movement swings his or her own head to the correct half of space without processing the adult's gaze at all. In the leanest version, infants do not understand the adult as a perceiver of an external target but simply process the physical movements caused by the head. This would be an extremely blunt instrument with which to crack the naming game. On the one hand, infants would not necessarily fixate on the target (they would only be attracted to a hemifield); on the other, many head movements would lead infants down a blind alley, because they do not refer to external objects (e.g., sneezing, coughing, or turning over in one's sleep). The key is to follow the eyes, because the eyes are the organ of human visual perception—they point to what the interlocutor is looking at (and often talking about).

A Measurement Technique

We used a simple technique for measuring whether and when infants engage in genuine gaze following—the Gaze Following: Eyes Open/Closed test (Brooks & Meltzoff, 2002, 2005; Meltzoff & Brooks, 2007). It was designed to zero in on whether infants understand the primitive referential nature of adult gaze. Two identical objects were used, and the adult turned to look at one of them with no verbal or emotional cues. The principal manipulation was that the adult turned to the target object with *eyes open* for one group and with *eyes closed* for the other group. If infants relied simply on gross head motions, they should turn in both cases. If, however, infants understand that the eyes are relevant for connecting the agent and object, then they should differentiate the two conditions and turn to look at the target object in one situation and not the other.

Brooks and Meltzoff (2002) used the Gaze Following: Eyes Open/Closed test to assess 12-, 14-, and 18-month-old infants. Each infant at each age was randomly assigned to a condition in which the adult turned to the lateral targets with either open or closed eyes. There were no linguistic or emotional cues as to where to turn and no sound-localization cues because the targets were silent. Infants were given four trials (two to the left and two to the right).

Figure 10.1a shows a typical infant responding to the gaze following procedure; Figure 10.1b shows that infants at all ages looked significantly more often at the target when the adult turned with open than with closed eyes.

We also scored other behaviors beyond the traditional looking measure. We scored infants' average duration of correct looking—how long the infant stayed looking at a target once they gaze followed. This revealed that infants *inspected the target longer* when the adult turned to it with open versus closed eyes (i.e., the average duration of a look to the correct target was longer during the eyes open versus eyes closed condition). Also, more infants *vocalized* toward the correct target more in the open-eyes than closed-eyes condition. Finally, significantly more infants *pointed to the targets* in the open-eyes condition than in the closed-eyes condition (Figure 10.2). This pointing behavior is particularly striking because it is ostensive and done for the communicative partner. Infants are taking into account the perceptual status of the audience: They point when the social partner can see the objects but refrain when the partner cannot (eyes closed). We suggest that this is evidence of protodeclarative pointing in an experimental setting (Bates et al., 1975; Camaioni et al., 2004; Franco & Butterworth, 1996; Liszkowski et al., 2004).

This suite of dependent measures gathered in a controlled setting allows for strong inferences. The most conservative interpretation of the infant looking data has been that a visible movement simply drags infants' attention to a hemifield of space where they (happen to) see an interesting object. The current findings indicate that this does not provide a full explanation of the behavior of 12-month-olds, because head movement was controlled. Moreover, infants

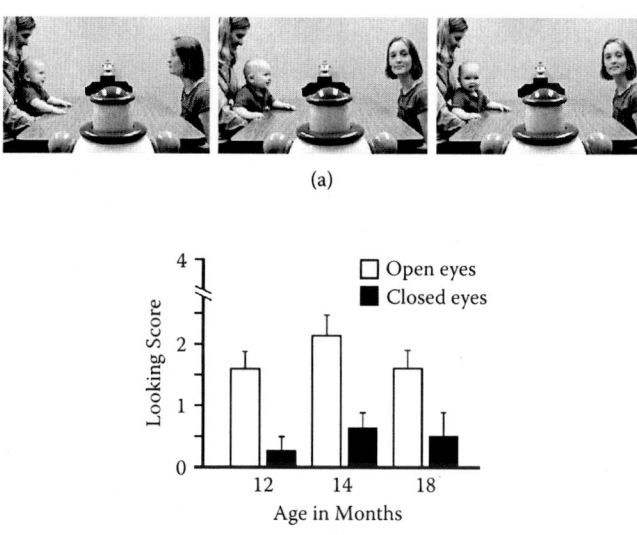

(a)

(b)

Figure 10.1   (a) A 12-month-old infant shows a gaze-following response. The adult turns in silence and does not point to the target. (b) Infants selectively gaze follow when the adult's eyes are open rather than closed. (Modified and reprinted from Brooks, R. & Meltzoff, A. N., 2002, *Developmental Psychology, 38*, 961 with permission from American Psychological Association.)

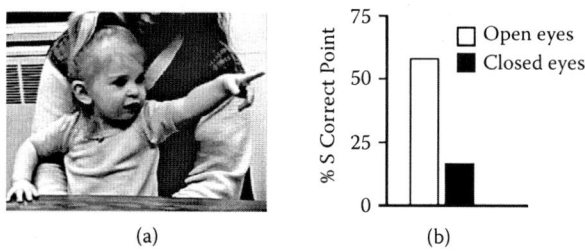

(a)   (b)

Figure 10.2   (a) An 18-month-old infant pointing at the correct target. (Modified and reprinted from Brooks, R. & Meltzoff, A. N., 2002, *Developmental Psychology, 38*, 962 with permission from American Psychological Association.) (b) Infants point when their social partner can see the pointing act (i.e., open-eyes condition) but rarely point when that person cannot (i.e., closed-eyes condition). We interpret this as evidence of communicative-referential pointing.

marshal other target-directed acts, such as pointing at the target and vocalizing toward it when the adult can see the target. Increased pointing and vocalizing at the target indicates that infants are not simply turning to a hemifield: Infants are generating communicative-referential acts *that the adult did not produce* and doing so significantly more often when the adult can see these acts. Finally, the average-duration-of-look measure is revealing. Evidently, the object takes on special valence when it is looked at by another person. It is as if having the adult shine her psychological spotlight on an inanimate object leaves a trace on that object. Infants are curious about the object and linger longer in their inspection of it, opening the door for parental verbal labeling (a possible mechanism by which gaze following and language may be related).

GAZE FOLLOWING DEVELOPS

The previous study showed that 12-month-olds follow adult gaze to distal targets and don't simply follow salient head movements in space. A developmental question remains: When does such gaze following begin? The Gaze Following: Eyes Open/Closed test provides a tool for investigating the ontogenesis of genuine gaze following (without input from other multimodal cues). Brooks and Meltzoff (2005) completed a study of infants from 9 months to 11 months of age. We used the same procedure as previously described, but tested infants within a tightly controlled age window. The infants were recruited to fall at three discrete ages: 9, 10, and 11 months old, with each infant ±1 week of the target age. This was the equivalent of a cross-sectional microgenetic study—we assessed infants at three moments over a 90-day growth period to see if we could capture a metamorphosis in behavior.

The results suggest that genuine gaze following emerges at about 10–11 months of age. As shown in Figure 10.3, 9-month-olds did not discriminate between the open-versus closed-eyes conditions. They turned equally often in both cases. However, there was a clear developmental shift 30 days later. For 10-month-olds, the looking scores in the open-eyes condition were significantly greater than in the closed-eyes condition, and a similar significant effect was also evident among 11-month-olds.

Note that it is not that the 9-month-olds fail to follow the adult's turn. Quite the contrary, in fact, *they follow too much;* they turn even when the adult turns with closed eyes. This is key for theory because it makes sense of the literature claiming that gaze following starts as early as 3 or 4 months old (e.g., Butterworth & Jarrett, 1991; D'Entremont, Hains, & Muir, 1997; Morales et al., 1998; Scaife & Bruner, 1975; Striano & Stahl, 2005). At first, these reports seem in contradiction to our claim about the development of gaze following at 10–11 months of age. But there is no contradiction. We believe that infants turn to follow the direction of *head movements and postural changes* at 9 months and younger but that they do

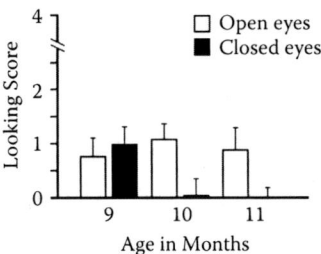

Figure 10.3   Developmental changes in gaze following. At 9-months-old infants turn regardless of whether the adult's eyes are open or closed. In contrast, 10- and 11-month-old infants gaze follow when the adult can see and refrain from turning when she cannot see. Modified and reprinted from Brooks, R. & Meltzoff, A. N., 2005, *Developmental Science, 8,* 538 with permission of Blackwell Publishing.)

not selectively *gaze follow,* properly so called (as shown by their indiscriminant turning to the closed-eyes condition). The problem is not a lack of turning; rather 9-month-olds turn even if the adult cannot possibly be looking at the target, and so they are not truly gaze following.

In sum, our interpretation is that following the visual line of regard of others is first manifest at 10–11 months. Whereas 9-month-olds may understand others as *body orienters,* older infants begin to understand others as *visually connected* to the external world and turn to follow the other's gaze (for a more extended argument, see Meltzoff & Brooks, 2007, pp. 232–238). This is an important step in understanding another as an intentional social agent (a looker, gazer, perceiver). This interpretation of others' gaze helps infants narrow down the referent of a verbal label uttered by an interacting adult.

INFANT GAZE FOLLOWING PREDICTS LATER WORD LEARNING: GROWTH-CURVE MODELING

On theoretical grounds, there is good reason for thinking that gaze following provides social support for word learning, an element in Bruner's LASS. Infants who understand adult gaze as a referential act are in a better position to use everyday interactions with adults to learn words as labels for objects (e.g., Baldwin, 1995; Baldwin & Moses, 1994, 2001; Bruner, 1983; Carpenter et al., 1998; Hollich et al., 2000; Moore, Angelopoulos, & Bennett, 1999; Tomasello, 1995, 2003). In order to test this conjecture empirically within our own data set, we conducted a longitudinal follow-up of the same children who came into the lab at 10–11 months of age (the age when infants first responded with clear evidence of gaze following).

There were 32 infants who were followed longitudinally through the next 14 months, with language assessments at 10–11, 14, 18, and 24 months. The infants were recruited from primarily English-speaking families; mothers' median education was a college degree with a range from high school to advanced degrees. Parents completed the MBCDI using the "Words and Gestures" form when their infants were 10 to 18 months old and the "Words and Sentences" form after 18 months (Fenson et al., 1994). From the forms, we tallied the number of words each child produced at each age.

To analyze individual differences in vocabulary growth, we used growth-curve analysis, the technique of choice for longitudinal data (Raudenbush & Bryk, 2002; Singer & Willett, 2003, 2005). Often called hierarchical linear modeling or multilevel modeling, growth curves provide a powerful statistical tool to examine vocabulary development. The statistical approach models the change in children's vocabulary size with age. Each individual child has a trajectory of change. For vocabulary development, this is a great advantage because individual children vary in the rate that they add words to their vocabularies (Dale & Goodman, 2005).

In order to apply growth-curve modeling, one needs to select a growth pattern that typifies the trajectories of change within the domain under test. Based on previous work, we used a quadratic curve (e.g., Huttenlocher, Haight, Bryk, Seltzer, & Lyons, 1991). The analyses confirmed that a quadratic curve significantly fit our obtained language data (Brooks & Meltzoff, 2008). The quadratic curve is expressed in terms of infants' age in months^2 which is also called *acceleration of growth* (Raudenbush & Bryk, 2002). In our sample, productive vocabulary growth accelerated with age at the rate of 10.2 words per month at 14 months, 30.6 words per month at 18 months, and 61.2 words per month at 24 months. An average child in our sample had a productive vocabulary of 367 words at 24 months and had a growth trajectory that was within the normal range, moderately above the 50th percentile of the norms for the MDCDI (Fenson et al., 2007; see Brooks & Meltzoff, 2008, for further statistical analyses).

Using standard growth-curve modeling procedures (Singer & Willett, 2003) we tested whether gaze-following behavior from 10 to 11 months of age predicted the subsequent growth of productive vocabulary. The results showed that the average duration of correct looking at 10–11 months was a highly significant predictor of accelerated vocabulary growth ($p < .0001$), explaining 33% more of the variance in accelerated growth *than infant age alone*. When children had a "high" gaze-following score (looks at the correct target that were +1 standard deviation (*SD*) above the mean duration at 10–11 months old), they had a rapidly accelerating growth curve, resulting in an estimated 458-word vocabulary at 24 months old. When children had a "low" gaze-following score (–1 *SD* below the mean duration at 10–11 months old), they had a slower acceleration in their vocabulary growth curve, yielding 272 words by 24 months. Not only do these trajectories and 2-year-old outcomes differ from each other, but they also follow a consistent pattern in comparison with the Fenson et al. (2007) norms. The high gaze followers were consistently above the 50th percentile of the norms for the MBCDI, and the low gaze followers were consistently below the 50th percentile (Figure 10.4a). A 2 × 2 chi-square test of the infant gaze following scores at 10–11 months (high versus low) confirmed that 92% of infants from the high gaze following group had 24-month vocabulary scores above the Fenson et al. 50th percentile, in contrast to 33% of the infants from the low gaze following group ($p < .05$).

Next, we examined whether infants' spontaneous pointing predicted accelerated vocabulary growth. Pointing to distal locations (e.g., targets or experimenter in the room) explained additional variance in accelerated growth over and above age alone. We then investigated whether pointing added to the gaze-following model of accelerated vocabulary growth and found that it did.

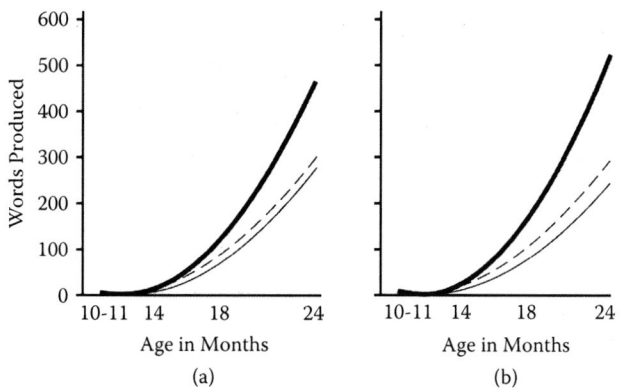

Figure 10.4   (a) Gaze-following model of productive vocabulary growth. The thick, solid line represents the trajectory for infants with high gaze-following scores (+1 *SD* average duration of correct looking). The thin, solid line represents the trajectory for infants with low gaze-following scores (–1 *SD*). The dashed line represents the 50th percentile for the MBCDI. (From Fenson, L., et al., 2007, *MacArthur-Bates Communicative Development Inventories: User's guide and technical manual* (2d ed.), Baltimore, MD: Brookes. With permission.). (b) Gaze-following and pointing model of productive vocabulary growth (controlling for maternal education). The thick, solid line represents the trajectory for infants with high gaze-following scores (+1 *SD*) who also point. The thin, solid line shows the trajectory for infants with low gaze-following scores (–1 *SD*) who also do not point. The dashed line is the 50th percentile for the MBCDI. Modified from Brooks, R. & Meltzoff, A. N., 2008, *Journal of Child Language, 35*, 214. With permission.)

The next question was whether these social-cognitive factors (gaze following and pointing) would still hold predictive power when maternal education was taken into account. When maternal education was added to the nonverbal predictors, it significantly improved the statistical model, explaining 22.8% more of the variance than the model with infant gaze following, pointing, and age. As expected, as the number of years of maternal education increased there was an increase in the rate of vocabulary growth. Importantly, however, the gaze following and pointing predictors remained significant *over and above the contributions of maternal education* (see Brooks & Meltzoff, 2008, for details).

This final growth-curve model simultaneously takes into account infants' gaze following and pointing at 10–11 months as well as maternal education. Figure 10.4b shows that after accounting for maternal education both social-cognitive factors have a strong effect on the pattern of vocabulary growth through 24 months old. For high gaze followers who also pointed, the prototypical or average trajectory had a rapid acceleration, resulting in an estimated 517 words at 24 months. For low gaze followers who did not point, the trajectory had a slow acceleration, staying consistently below the 50th percentile across age and resulting in an estimated 243-word vocabulary at 24 months. Overall, our final model explained 49% more of the variance in accelerated vocabulary growth than infant age alone.

CONCLUSIONS: GAZE FOLLOWING ON THE PATHWAY TO LANGUAGE

As expected, productive vocabulary in our sample of children grew rapidly after age 14 months. The new finding is that infants' gaze-following behavior at 10 and 11 months significantly predicted accelerated growth through 24 months of age, even after accounting for the expected effects of age and maternal education. This is the first demonstration that following an adult's look (rather than a composite of vocalizing, pointing, and looking) relates to faster vocabulary growth (Figure 10.4a, Figure 10.4b).

Another interesting finding was that infant gaze following and pointing each separately and significantly predicted lexical development. As seen in some (Mundy & Gomes, 1998; Striano & Bertin, 2005) but not all (Carpenter et al., 1998) of the previous work, gaze following did not correlate with pointing. In our study, the individual infants who were high gaze followers were not necessarily the same infants who spontaneously pointed. Nonetheless, being a high gaze follower who points resulted in the fastest vocabulary growth. This latter pattern was associated with a vocabulary size of 517 words at 2 years old, near the 80th percentile of norms (Fenson et al., 2007). Thus, having a rigorous definition of gaze following and pointing coupled with a good laboratory assessment before the first birthday supports very strong predictions about subsequent vocabulary growth (see Brooks & Meltzoff, 2005, 2008, for detailed definitions and analyses).

It is worth considering the potential meaning of these predictors. First, all of the infants had visual access to the two identical targets, which did not move or make sound. Yet infants examined a target longer when an adult was looking at it. It is as though the target acquired a special valence from the adult's gaze and infants were curious to scrutinize it themselves. Infants who react in this way may be "ready" to accept a label for the object; they have individuated it from the surroundings based on the spotlight provide by the adult's gaze. Second, only a subset of the 10–11 month olds (34%) spontaneously pointed in our laboratory session. In a review of the recordings, we found that infants usually looked at the adult before pointing at distal targets. This is the context that others use as a marker for protodeclarative pointing (Bates et al., 1979; Camaioni et al., 2004; Franco & Butterworth, 1996). Thus, our data support the suggestion that communicative-referential pointing by infants is a good predictor of subsequent language—perhaps, because it measures an infant's early tendency to want to "refer to" or "share" a perceptual event with a partner and perhaps because it invites parents to provide "follow-in" labeling for infants.

One consideration is that infants who are advanced in gaze following and pointing may simply have more advanced social-perceptual-cognitive skills, which generally contribute to language development. However, a general early advantage does not match the current findings of this type, because individual children's gaze following did not correlate with their pointing and not all gaze-following behaviors related to language development (see also Mundy et al., 2007, for similar findings). For example, we found that a short latency to look at the adult's target was not correlated with accelerated vocabulary growth.

Clearly, early gaze following and pointing are not the only factors supporting word learning. Linguistic input from infants' parents (Hart & Risley, 1995; Hoff, 2006; Huttenlocher et al., 1991; Pan, Rowe, Singer, & Snow, 2005) as well as infants' own linguistic, social, and cognitive abilities are also implicated (Booth & Waxman, 2003; Booth, Waxman, & Huang, 2005; Bornstein, Haynes, & Painter, 1998; Colombo et al., 2004; Gopnik & Meltzoff, 1986, 1987, 1997; Liu et al., 2003; and multiple chapters in this volume). In addition, individual differences in infant speech processing predict later language learning (e.g., Fernald, Perfors, & Marchman, 2006; Kuhl, Conboy, Padden, Nelson, & Pruitt, 2005). Our current growth-curve modeling adds to the literature by showing that infant gaze following and spontaneous pointing are powerful nonverbal predictors of later variations in lexical development through 2 years of age.

The current research supports the theory that infant gaze following relates to subsequent language development (e.g., Baldwin, 1993, 1995; Carpenter et al., 1998; Mundy, Fox et al., 2003; Tomasello, 1995). Although past work has shown that infants' sensitivity to a composite of multimodal cues (looking, vocalizing, and pointing at an object) positively correlates with language development (e.g.,

Morales et al., 1998, 2000; Mundy & Gomes, 1998), the current work shows that reactions to a purely nonverbal gaze stimulus (an adult who looks but does not vocalize or point) is important on its own.

Infant Gaze Following and Pointing Creates Conditions for Word Learning

Gaze-following behavior provides infants with a tool for decoding speakers' intended referents. Moreover, through the act of gaze following infants may *create* the conditions for their own word learning. When infants engage in prolonged visual inspection of the objects looked at by adults they are "inviting" parents to provide a verbal label. The motivation to follow the adult's gaze and point to what one sees thus gives infants an advantage in Bruner's (1983) word-learning game. Social cognition and early language development are inextricably intertwined. The pathway to spoken language is paved by the intentions of other people.

ACKNOWLEDGMENTS

Work on this chapter was supported by the National Institutes of Health (NIH) (HD-22514), the National Science Foundation (#SBE-0354453), and the Tamaki Foundation. We gratefully acknowledge the helpful contributions of Pat Kuhl, Alison Gopnik, Craig Harris, Calle Fisher, and Jacque Mullen, and we thank Barbara Conboy, John Colombo, and Peggy McCardle for feedback on an earlier draft.

REFERENCES

Adamson, L. B. & Bakeman, R. (1985). Affect and attention: Infants observed with mothers and peers. *Child Development, 56,* 582–593.

Adamson, L. B. & McArthur, D. (1995). Joint attention, affect, and culture. In C. Moore & P. J. Dunham (Eds.), *Joint attention: Its origins and role in development* (pp. 205–221). Hillsdale, NJ: Erlbaum.

Akhtar, N., Dunham, F., & Dunham, P. J. (1991). Directive interactions and early vocabulary development: The role of joint attentional focus. *Journal of Child Language, 18,* 41–49.

Aslin, R. N., Saffran, J. R., & Newport, E. L. (1998). Computation of conditional probability statistics by 8-month-old infants. *Psychological Science, 9,* 321–324.

Austin, J. L. (1962). *How to do things with words.* Cambridge, MA: Harvard University Press.

Bakeman, R. & Adamson, L. B. (1984). Coordinating attention to people and objects in mother-infant and peer-infant interaction. *Child Development, 55,* 1278–1289.

Bakeman, R. & Adamson, L. B. (1986). Infants' conventionalized acts: Gestures and words with mothers and peers. *Infant Behavior & Development, 9,* 215–230.

Baldwin, D. A. (1991). Infants' contribution to the achievement of joint reference. *Child Development, 62,* 875–890.

Baldwin, D. A. (1993). Early referential understanding: Infants' ability to recognize referential acts for what they are. *Developmental Psychology, 29,* 832–843.

Baldwin, D. A. (1995). Understanding the link between joint attention and language. In C. Moore & P. J. Dunham (Eds.), *Joint attention: Its origins and role in development* (pp. 131–158). Hillsdale, NJ: Erlbaum.

Baldwin, D. A. & Moses, L. J. (1994). Early understanding of referential intent and attentional focus: Evidence from language and emotion. In C. Lewis & P. Mitchell (Eds.), *Children's early understanding of mind: Origins and development* (pp. 133–156). Hillsdale, NJ: Erlbaum.

Baldwin, D. A. & Moses, L. J. (2001). Links between social understanding and early word learning: Challenges to current accounts. *Social Development, 10,* 309–329.

Baron-Cohen, S. (1995). *Mindblindness: An essay on autism and theory of mind.* Cambridge, MA: MIT Press.

Bates, E., Benigni, L., Bretherton, I., Camaioni, L., & Volterra, V. (1979). *The emergence of symbols: Cognition and communication in infancy.* New York: Academic Press.

Bates, E., Camaioni, L., & Volterra, V. (1975). The acquisition of performatives prior to speech. *Merrill-Palmer Quarterly, 21,* 205–226.

Bates, E., Thal, D., Whitesell, K., Fenson, L., & Oakes, L. (1989). Integrating language and gesture in infancy. *Developmental Psychology, 25,* 1004–1019.

Beebe, B., Rustin, J., Sorter, D., & Knoblauch, S. (2003). An expanded view of intersubjectivity in infancy and its application to psychoanalysis. *Psychoanalytic Dialogues, 13,* 805–841.

Beebe, B., Sorter, D., Rustin, J., & Knoblauch, S. (2003). A comparison of Meltzoff, Trevarthen, and Stern. *Psychoanalytic Dialogues, 13,* 777–804.

Bloom, P. (2000). *How children learn the meanings of words.* Cambridge, MA: MIT Press.

Booth, A. E. & Waxman, S. R. (2003). Mapping words to the world in infancy: Infants' expectations for count nouns and adjectives. *Journal of Cognition and Development, 4,* 357–381.

Booth, A. E., Waxman, S. R. & Huang, Y. T. (2005). Conceptual information permeates word learning in infancy. *Developmental Psychology, 41,* 491–505.

Bornstein, M. H., Haynes, M. O., & Painter, K. M. (1998). Sources of child vocabulary competence: A multivariate model. *Journal of Child Language, 25,* 367–393.

Bornstein, M. H., Tamis-LeMonda, C. S., & Haynes, O. M. (1999). First words in the second year: Continuity, stability, and models of concurrent and predictive correspondence in vocabulary and verbal responsiveness across age and context. *Infant Behavior & Development, 22,* 65–85.

Bråten, S. (Ed.). (1998). *Intersubjective communication and emotion in early ontogeny.* Cambridge, UK: Cambridge University Press.

Brazelton, T. B., Koslowski, B., & Main, M. (1974). The origins of reciprocity: The early mother-infant interaction. In M. Lewis & L. A. Rosenblum (Eds.), *The effect of the infant on its caregiver* (pp. 49–76). New York: Wiley.

Brooks, R. & Meltzoff, A. N. (2002). The importance of eyes: How infants interpret adult looking behavior. *Developmental Psychology, 38,* 958–966.

Brooks, R. & Meltzoff, A. N. (2005). The development of gaze following and its relation to language. *Developmental Science, 8,* 535–543.

Brooks, R. & Meltzoff, A. N. (2008). Infant gaze following and pointing predict accelerated vocabulary growth through two years of age: A longitudinal, growth curve modeling study. *Journal of Child Language, 35,* 207–220.

Bruner, J. S. (1975a). From communication to language—A psychological perspective. *Cognition, 3,* 255–287.

Bruner, J. S. (1975b). The ontogenesis of speech acts. *Journal of Child Language, 2,* 1–19.

Bruner, J. S. (1983). *Child's talk: Learning to use language.* New York: Norton.

Bullowa, M. (Ed.) (1979). *Before speech: The beginning of interpersonal communication.* New York: Cambridge University Press.

Butterworth, G. (2001). Joint visual attention in infancy. In G. Bremner & A. Fogel (Eds.), *Blackwell handbook of infant development* (pp. 213–240). Oxford: Blackwell.

Butterworth, G. & Jarrett, N. (1991). What minds have in common is space: Spatial mechanisms serving joint visual attention in infancy. *British Journal of Developmental Psychology, 9,* 55–72.

Butterworth, G. & Morissette, P. (1996). Onset of pointing and the acquisition of language in infancy. *Journal of Reproductive and Infant Psychology, 14,* 219–231.

Camaioni, L. (1997). The emergence of intentional communication in ontogeny, phylogeny, and pathology. *European Psychologist, 2,* 216–225.

Camaioni, L., Castelli, M. C., Longobardi, E., & Volterra, V. (1991). A parent report instrument for early language assessment. *First language, 11,* 345–359.

Camaioni, L., Perucchini, P., Bellagamba, F., & Colonnesi, C. (2004). The role of declarative pointing in developing a theory of mind. *Infancy, 5,* 291–308.

Carpenter, M., Nagell, K., & Tomasello, M. (1998). Social cognition, joint attention, and communicative competence from 9 to 15 months of age. *Monographs of the Society for Research in Child Development, 63*(4, Serial No. 255).

Colombo, J., Shaddy, D. J., Richman, W. A., Maikranz, J. M., & Blaga, O., M. (2004). The developmental course of habituation in infancy and preschool outcome. *Infancy, 5,* 1–38.

Csibra, G. & Gergely, G. I. (2006). Social learning and social cognition: The case for pedagogy. In Y. Munakata & M. H. Johnson (Eds.), *Processes of change in brain and cognitive development. Attention and performance, XXI* (pp. 249–274). Oxford: Oxford University Press.

Dale, P. S. & Goodman, J. C. (2005). Commonality and individual differences in vocabulary growth. In M. Tomasello & D. I. Slobin (Eds.), *Beyond nature-nurture: Essays in honor of Elizabeth Bates* (pp. 41–78). Mahwah, NJ: Lawrence Erlbaum.

de Laguna, G. A. (1927). *Speech: Its function and development.* New Haven, CT: Yale University Press.

D'Entremont, B., Hains, S. M. J., & Muir, D. W. (1997). A demonstration of gaze following in 3- to 6-month-olds. *Infant Behavior & Development, 20,* 569–572.

Desrochers, S., Morissette, P., & Ricard, M. (1995). Two perspectives on pointing in infancy. In C. Moore & P. J. Dunham (Eds.), *Joint attention: Its origins and role in development* (pp. 85–101). Hillsdale, NJ: Erlbaum.

Driver, J., Davis, G., Ricciardelli, P., Kidd, P., Maxwell, E., & Baron-Cohen, S. (1999). Gaze perception triggers reflexive visuospatial orienting. *Visual Cognition, 6,* 509–540.

Eilan, N., Hoerl, C., McCormack, T., & Roessler, J. (Eds.) (2005). *Joint attention: Communication and other minds: Issues in philosophy and psychology.* New York: Oxford University Press.

Farroni, T., Csibra, G., Simion, F., & Johnson, M. H. (2002). Eye contact detection in humans from birth. *Proceedings of the National Academy of Sciences, 99,* 9602–9605.

Farroni, T., Johnson, M. H., Brockbank, M., & Simion, F. (2000). Infants' use of gaze direction to cue attention: The importance of perceived motion. *Visual Cognition, 7,* 705–718.

Farroni, T., Mansfield, E. M., Lai, C., & Johnson, M. H. (2003). Infants perceiving and acting on the eyes: Tests of an evolutionary hypothesis. *Journal of Experimental Child Psychology, 85,* 199–212.

Farroni, T., Massaccesi, S., Pividori, D., & Johnson, M. H. (2004). Gaze following in new-borns. *Infancy, 5,* 39–60.

Fenson, L., Dale, P. S., Reznick, J. S., Bates, E., Thal, D. J., & Pethick, S. J. (1994). Variability in early communicative development. *Monographs of the Society for Research in Child Development, 59*(5, Serial No. 242).

Fenson, L., Marchman, V. A., Thal, D. J., Dale, P. S., Reznick, J. S., & Bates, E. (2007). *MacArthur-Bates Communicative Development Inventories: User's guide and technical manual* (2d ed.). Baltimore, MD: Brookes.

Ferguson, C. A. (1964). Baby talk in six languages. *American Anthropologist, 66,* 103–114.

Fernald, A. & Kuhl, P. K. (1987). Acoustic determinants of infant preference for moth-erese speech. *Infant Behavior & Development, 10,* 279–293.

Fernald, A., Perfors, A., & Marchman, V. A. (2006). Picking up speed in understanding: Speech processing efficiency and vocabulary growth across the 2nd year. *Developmental Psychology, 42,* 98–116.

Fernald, A. & Simon, T. (1984). Expanded intonation contours in mothers' speech to new-borns. *Developmental Psychology, 20,* 104–113.

Flom, R., Lee, K., & Muir, D. (Eds.) (2007). *Gaze-following: Its development and significance.* Mahwah, NJ: Erlbaum.

Franco, F. & Butterworth, G. (1996). Pointing and social awareness: Declaring and requesting in the second year. *Journal of Child Language, 23,* 307–336.

Friesen, C. K., Moore, C., & Kingstone, A. (2005). Does gaze direction really trigger a reflexive shift of spatial attention? *Brain and Cognition, 57,* 66–69.

Frischen, A., Bayliss, A. P., & Tipper, S. P. (2007). Gaze cueing of attention: Visual attention, social cognition, and individual differences. *Psychological Bulletin, 133,* 694–724.

Gallagher, S. (2001). The practice of mind: Theory, simulation or primary interaction? *Journal of Consciousness Studies, 8,* 83–108.

Golinkoff, R. M. & Hirsh-Pasek, K. (2006). Baby wordsmith: From associationist to social sophisticate. *Current Directions in Psychological Science, 15,* 30–33.

Golinkoff, R. M., Hirsh-Pasek, K., Bloom, L., Smith, L. B., Woodward, A. L., Akhtar, N., et al. (2000). *Becoming a word learner: A debate on lexical acquisition.* New York: Oxford University Press.

Gopnik, A. (1982). Words and plans: Early language and the development of intelligent action. *Journal of Child Language, 9,* 303–318.

Gopnik, A. (1988). Three types of early word: The emergence of social words, names and cognitive-relational words in the one-word stage and their relation to cognitive development. *First Language, 8,* 49–70.

Gopnik, A. & Meltzoff, A. N. (1985). From people, to plans, to objects: Changes in the meaning of early words and their relation to cognitive development. *Journal of Pragmatics, 9,* 495–512.

Gopnik, A. & Meltzoff, A. N. (1986). Relations between semantic and cognitive development in the one-word stage: The specificity hypothesis. *Child Development, 57,* 1040–1053.

Gopnik, A. & Meltzoff, A. N. (1987). The development of categorization in the second year and its relation to other cognitive and linguistic developments. *Child Development, 58,* 1523–1531.

Gopnik, A. & Meltzoff, A. N. (1997). *Words, thoughts, and theories.* Cambridge, MA: MIT Press.

Grice, H. P. (1968). Utterer's meaning, sentence-meaning and word-meaning. *Foundations of Language, 4*, 225–242.

Habermas, J. (1970). Towards a theory of communicative competence. *Inquiry: An Interdisciplinary Journal of Philosophy, 13*, 360–375.

Haith, M. M., Bergman, T., & Moore, M. J. (1977). Eye contact and face scanning in early infancy. *Science, 198*, 853–855.

Halliday, M. A. K. (1975). *Learning how to mean: Explorations in the development of language*. London: Edward Arnold.

Harris, M., Jones, D., & Grant, J. (1983). The nonverbal context of mothers' speech to infants. *First Language, 4*, 21–30.

Hart, B. & Risley, T. R. (1995). *Meaningful differences in the everyday experience of young American children*. Baltimore, MD: Brookes.

Hart, B. & Risley, T. R. (1999). *The social world of children: Learning to talk*. Baltimore, MD: Brookes.

Heimann, M., Strid, K., Smith, L., Tjus, T., Ulvund, S. E., & Meltzoff, A. N. (2006). Exploring the relation between memory, gestural communication, and the emergence of language in infancy: A longitudinal study. *Infant and Child Development, 15*, 233–249.

Henderson, L. M., Yoder, P. J., Yale, M. E., & McDuffie, A. (2002). Getting the point: electrophysiological correlates of protodeclarative pointing. *International Journal of Developmental Neuroscience, 20*, 449–458.

Hobson, R. P. (1998). The intersubjective foundations of thought. In S. Bråten (Ed.), *Intersubjective communication and emotion in early ontogeny* (pp. 283–296). Cambridge, UK: Cambridge University Press.

Hobson, R. P. (2002). *The cradle of thought: Exploring the origins of thought*. London: Macmillan.

Hobson, R. P., Patrick, M. P. H., Crandell, L. E., García Pérez, R. M., & Lee, A. (2004). Maternal sensitivity and infant triadic communication. *Journal of Child Psychology and Psychiatry, 45*, 470–480.

Hockett, C. F. (1960). Logical considerations in the study of animal communication. In W. E. Lanyon & W. N. Tavolga (Eds.), *Animal sounds and communication* (pp. 392–430). Washington, DC: American Institute of Biological Sciences.

Hoff, E. (2006). How social contexts support and shape language development. *Developmental Review, 26*, 55–88.

Hollich, G. J., Hirsh-Pasek, K., & Golinkoff, R. M. (2000). Breaking the language barrier: An emergentist coalition model of the origins of word learning. *Monographs of the Society for Research in Child Development, 65*(3, Serial No. 262).

Hood, B. M., Willen, J. D., & Driver, J. (1998). Adult's eyes trigger shifts of visual attention in human infants. *Psychological Science, 9*, 131–134.

Hunnius, S. & Geuze, R. H. (2004). Developmental changes in visual scanning of dynamic faces and abstract stimuli in infants: A longitudinal study. *Infancy, 6*, 231–255.

Husserl, E. (1977). *Phenomenological psychology: Lectures, summer semester, 1925* (J. Scanlon, Trans.). The Hague, Netherlands: Martinus Nijhoff. (Original work published 1962)

Huttenlocher, J., Haight, W., Bryk, A., Seltzer, M., & Lyons, T. (1991). Early vocabulary growth: Relation to language input and gender. *Developmental Psychology, 27*, 236–248.

Jaffe, J., Beebe, B., Feldstein, S., Crown, C., & Jasnow, M. D. (2001). Rhythms of dialogue in infancy: Coordinated timing in development. *Monographs of the Society for Research in Child Development, 66*(2, Serial No. 265).

Johnson, M. H. & Morton, J. (1991). *Biology and cognitive development: The case of face recognition.* Oxford: Blackwell.

Johnson, S. C., Ok, S.-J., Luo,Y. (2007). The attribution of attention: 9-month-olds' interpretation of gaze as goal-directed action. *Developmental Science, 10,* 530–537.

Jusczyk, P. W., Luce, P. A., & Charles-Luce, J. (1994). Infant's sensitivity to phonotactic patterns in the native language. *Journal of Memory & Language, 33,* 630–645.

Kaye, K. & Fogel, A. (1980). The temporal structure of face-to-face communication between mothers and infants. *Developmental Psychology, 16,* 454–464.

Kuhl, P. K. (2004). Early language acquisition: Cracking the speech code. *Nature Reviews Neuroscience, 5,* 831–843.

Kuhl, P. K., Conboy, B. T., Padden, D., Nelson, T., & Pruitt, J. (2005). Early speech perception and later language development: Implications for the "critical period." *Language Learning and Development, 1,* 237–264.

Kuhl, P. K., Andruski, J. E., Chistovich, I. A., Chistovich, L. A., Kozhevnikova, E. V., Ryskina, V. L., et al. (1997). Cross-language analysis of phonetic units in language addressed to infants. *Science, 277,* 684–686.

Kuhn, T. S. (1962). *The structure of scientific revolutions.* Chicago: University of Chicago Press.

Laakso, M.-L., Poikkeus, A.-M., Eklund, K., & Lyytinen, P. (1999). Social interactional behaviors and symbolic play competence as predictors of language development and their associations with maternal attention-directing strategies. *Infant Behavior & Development, 22,* 541–556.

Langton, S. R. H., Watt, R. J., & Bruce, V. (2000). Do the eyes have it? Cues to the direction of social attention. *Trends in Cognitive Sciences, 4,* 50–59.

Liszkowski, U., Carpenter, M., Henning, A., Striano, T., & Tomasello, M. (2004). Twelve-month-olds point to share attention and interest. *Developmental Science, 7,* 297–307.

Liszkowski, U., Carpenter, M., & Tomasello, M. (2007). Reference and attitude in infant pointing. *Journal of Child Language, 34,* 1–20.

Liu, H.-M., Kuhl, P. K., & Tsao, F.-M. (2003). An association between mothers' speech clarity and infants' speech discrimination skills. *Developmental Science, 6,* F1–F10.

Macmurray, J. (1961). *Persons in relation.* London: Faber and Faber.

MacPherson, A. C. & Moore, C. (2007). Attentional control by gaze cues in infancy. In R. Flom, K. Lee, & D. Muir (Eds.), *Gaze-following: Its development and significance* (pp. 53–75). Mahwah, NJ: Erlbaum.

Markman, E. M. (1989). *Categorization and naming in children: Problems of induction.* Cambridge, MA: MIT Press.

Markus, J., Mundy, P., Morales, M., Delgado, C. E. F., & Yale, M. (2000). Individual differences in infant skills as predictors of child-caregiver joint attention and language. *Social Development, 9,* 302–315.

Masur, E. F., Flynn, V., & Eichorst, D. L. (2005). Maternal responsive and directive behaviours and utterances as predictors of children's lexical development. *Journal of Child Language, 32,* 63–91.

Maurer, D. (1985). Infants' perceptions of facedness. In T. M. Field & N. A. Fox (Eds.), *Social perception in infants* (pp. 73–100). Norwood, NJ: Ablex.

Meltzoff, A. N. (2007). "Like me": A foundation for social cognition. *Developmental Science, 10,* 126–134.

Meltzoff, A. N. & Brooks, R. (2007). Eyes wide shut: The importance of eyes in infant gaze following and understanding other minds. In R. Flom, K. Lee, & D. Muir (Eds.), *Gaze following: Its development and significance* (pp. 217–241). Mahwah, NJ: Erlbaum.

Moore, C. (1999). Gaze following and the control of attention. In P. Rochat (Ed.), *Early social cognition: Understanding others in the first months of life* (pp. 241–256). Mahwah, NJ: Erlbaum.

Moore, C., Angelopoulos, M., & Bennett, P. (1999). Word learning in the context of referential and salience cues. *Developmental Psychology, 35,* 60–68.

Moore, C. & Corkum, V. (1994). Social understanding at the end of the first year of life. *Developmental Review, 14,* 349–372.

Moore, C. & Dunham, P. J. (Eds.). (1995). *Joint attention: Its origins and role in development.* Hillsdale, NJ: Erlbaum.

Morales, M., Mundy, P., Delgado, C. E. F., Yale, M., Messinger, D., Neal, R., et al. (2000). Responding to joint attention across the 6- through 24-month age period and early language acquisition. *Journal of Applied Developmental Psychology, 21,* 283–298.

Morales, M., Mundy, P., & Rojas, J. (1998). Following the direction of gaze and language development in 6-month-olds. *Infant Behavior & Development, 21,* 373–377.

Mundy, P., Block, J., Delgado, C., Pomares, Y., Van Hecke, A. V., & Parlade, M. V. (2007). Individual differences and the development of joint attention in infancy. *Child Development, 78,* 938–954.

Mundy, P., Delgado, C., Block, J., Venezia, M., Hogan, A., & Seibert, J. (2003). *A manual for the abridged Early Social Communicative Scales (ESCS).* Coral Gables, FL: University of Miami, Department of Psychology.

Mundy, P., Fox, N., & Card, J. (2003). EEG coherence, joint attention and language development in the second year. *Developmental Science, 6,* 48–54.

Mundy, P. & Gomes, A. (1998). Individual differences in joint attention skill development in the second year. *Infant Behavior & Development, 21,* 469–482.

Ohgami, H. (2006, June). *Developmental trajectory of social cognition in infancy: Longitudinal survey from 8 months to 5 years old.* Poster presented at the biennial meeting of the International Conference on Infant Studies, Kyoto, Japan.

Pan, B. A., Rowe, M. L., Singer, J. D., & Snow, C. E. (2005). Maternal correlates of growth in toddler vocabulary production in low-income families. *Child Development, 76,* 763–782.

Papoušek, M. (2007). Communication in early infancy: An arena of intersubjective learning. *Infant Behavior & Development, 30,* 258–266.

Quine, W. V. O. (1960). *Word and object.* Cambridge, MA: MIT Press.

Raudenbush, S. W. & Bryk, A. S. (2002). *Hierarchical linear models: Applications and data analysis methods* (2d ed.). Thousand Oaks, CA: Sage.

Ristic, J., Friesen, C. K., & Kingstone, A. (2002). Are eyes special? It depends on how you look at it. *Psychonomic Bulletin & Review, 9,* 507–513.

Rochat, P. (2007). Intentional action arises from early reciprocal exchanges. *Acta Psychologica, 124,* 8–25.

Rollins, P. R. (2003). Caregivers' contingent comments to 9-month-old infants: Relationships with later language. *Applied Psycholinguistics, 24,* 221–234.

Saffran, J. R., Aslin, R. N., & Newport, E. L. (1996). Statistical learning by 8-month-old infants. *Science, 274,* 1926–1928.

Scaife, M. & Bruner, J. S. (1975). The capacity for joint visual attention in the infant. *Nature, 253,* 265–266.

Searle, J. R. (1969). *Speech acts: An essay in the philosophy of language.* New York: Cambridge University Press.

Seibert, J. M., Hogan, A. E., & Mundy, P. C. (1982). Assessing interactional competencies: The early social-communication scales. *Infant Mental Health Journal, 3,* 244–258.

Senju, A., Johnson, M. H., & Csibra, G. (2006). The development and neural basis of referential gaze perception. *Social Neuroscience, 1,* 220–234.

Singer, J. D. & Willett, J. B. (2003). *Applied longitudinal data analysis: Modeling change and event occurrence.* New York: Oxford University Press.

Singer, J. & Willett, J. B. (2005, April), *Longitudinal research: Current status and future prospects.* Invited talk presented at the Biennial Meeting of the Society for Research in Child Development, Atlanta, GA.

Smith, C. B., Adamson, L. B., & Bakeman, R. (1988). Interactional predictors of early language. *First Language, 8,* 143–156.

Stern, D. N. (1985). *The interpersonal world of the infant: A view from psychoanalysis and developmental psychology.* New York: Basic Books.

Striano, T. & Bertin, E. (2005). Social-cognitive skills between 5 and 10 months of age. *British Journal of Developmental Psychology, 23,* 559–568.

Striano, T. & Stahl, D. (2005). Sensitivity to triadic attention in early infancy. *Developmental Science, 8,* 333–343.

Strid, K., Tjus, T., Smith, L., Meltzoff, A. N., & Heimann, M. (2006). Infant recall memory and communication predicts later cognitive development. *Infant Behavior & Development, 29,* 545–553.

Tomasello, M. (1995). Joint attention as social cognition. In C. Moore & P. J. Dunham (Eds.), *Joint attention: Its origins and role in development* (pp. 103–130). Hillsdale, NJ: Erlbaum.

Tomasello, M. (2003). *Constructing a language: A usage-based theory of language acquisition.* Cambridge, MA: Harvard University Press.

Tomasello, M., Carpenter, M., Call, J., Behne, T., & Moll, H. (2005). Understanding and sharing intentions: The origins of cultural cognition. *Behavioral and Brain Sciences, 28,* 675–691.

Tomasello, M. & Farrar, M. J. (1986). Joint attention and early language. *Child Development, 57,* 1454–1463.

Tomasello, M. & Todd, J. (1983). Joint attention and lexical acquisition style. *First Language, 4,* 197–211.

Trevarthen, C. (1979). Communication and cooperation in early infancy: a description of primary intersubjectivity. In M. Bullowa (Ed.), *Before speech: The beginning of interpersonal communication* (pp. 321–347). New York: Cambridge University Press.

Trevarthen, C. & Hubley, P. (1978). Secondary intersubjectivity: Confidence, confiding and acts of meaning in the first year. In A. Lock (Ed.), *Action, gesture, and symbol: The emergence of language* (pp. 183–229). London: Academic Press.

Vygotsky, L. S. (1962). *Thought and language* (E. Hanfmann & G. Vakar, Trans.). Cambridge, MA: MIT Press. (Original work published 1934)

Wetherby, A. M., Allen, L., Cleary, J., Kublin, K., & Goldstein, H. (2002). Validity and reliability of the communication and symbolic behavior scales developmental profile with very young children. *Journal of Speech, Language, and Hearing Research, 45,* 1202–1218.

Wetherby, A. M., Goldstein, H., Cleary, J., Allen, L., & Kublin, K. (2003). Early identification of children with communication disorders: Concurrent and predictive validity of the CSBS developmental profile. *Infants and Young Children, 16,* 161–174.

Wetherby, A. M. & Prizant, B. M. (2002). *Communication and Symbolic Behavior Scales Developmental Profile.* Baltimore, MD: Brookes.

Woodward, A. L. (2003). Infants' developing understanding of the link between looker and object. *Developmental Science, 6,* 297–311.

Woodward, A. L. & Guajardo, J. J. (2002). Infants' understanding of the point gesture as an object-directed action. *Cognitive Development, 17,* 1061–1084.

11

Using the Hands to Study How Children Learn Language

SUSAN GOLDIN-MEADOW

Gesture provides privileged access to information that language-learning children know but do not say. For example, young children who are not yet able to produce two-word sentences ("mommy's hat") are nevertheless able to express sentence-like ideas using gesture and speech ("mommy" + point at hat). Importantly, children who produce these gesture + speech "sentences" will utter their first two-word utterance before children who have not yet produced a gesture + speech combination of this sort. Children's gestures can thus identify them as ready to take the next step on the path toward language acquisition (Iverson & Goldin-Meadow, 2005; Ozcaliskan & Goldin-Meadow, 2005). In addition, evidence is mounting that gesture can do more than identify the next cognitive step a child is about to take. Gesture can actually play a role in helping the child take that step (Goldin-Meadow & Wagner, 2005).

Moreover, gesture has the potential to provide insight into other aspects of the language-learning process—it can offer a window onto the linguistic preconceptions that children bring to language learning. Deaf children whose hearing losses prevent them from acquiring a spoken language and whose hearing parents have not exposed them to a sign language use gesture to communicate with the hearing individuals in their worlds. Despite the fact that these children have not been exposed to a conventional language model, their gestures take on many of the structures found in natural languages (Goldin-Meadow, 2003b). Gesture can thus shed light on properties of language that are robust enough to be invented by a child in the absence of linguistic input.

This chapter explores these two ways that gesture can be used within the language-learning domain:

1. As a tool to explore the predispositions children bring to language-learning before exposure to a language model
2. As a tool to track the early steps children take when learning the language of their community.

My goal is to illustrate the unique information that can be gleaned about language learning from watching how children use their hands to communicate.

GESTURE CAN TELL US ABOUT THE SKILLS CHILDREN BRING TO LANGUAGE

When deaf children are exposed to sign language from birth, they learn that language as naturally as hearing children learn spoken language (Newport & Meier, 1985). However, 90% of deaf children are not born to deaf parents who could provide early access to sign language. Instead, they are born to hearing parents who often choose to expose their children solely to speech (Hoffmeister & Wilbur, 1980). Unfortunately, it is uncommon for deaf children with profound hearing losses to acquire spoken language, even with specialized instruction (Conrad, 1979; Mayberry, 1992).

My colleagues and I have studied 10 profoundly deaf children in the United States and four in Taiwan whose hearing losses prevented them from acquiring spoken language and whose hearing parents had decided to educate them in oral schools where sign language was neither taught nor encouraged (Feldman, Goldin-Meadow, & Gleitman, 1978; Goldin-Meadow & Feldman, 1977; Goldin-Meadow & Mylander, 1984, 1998). The children had made little progress in oral language and, in addition, had not been exposed to sign language in or out of school. As a result, the children had no usable model for a conventional language, neither signed nor spoken. Nevertheless, the children spontaneously used gestures to communicate. What is particularly surprising is that the children's gestures displayed many of the structural properties characteristic of natural language. I have called the linguistic properties that deaf children introduced into their gesture systems *resilient* properties of language (Goldin-Meadow, 1982; 2003a). Table 11.1 lists properties of language identified in deaf children's gesture systems thus far.

This chapter focuses on the structural aspects of deaf children's gesture systems, specifically, on word- and sentence-level structures. However, it is important to note that the children used their gesture systems for a wide variety of linguistic functions:

- To make requests, comments, and queries about things and events happening at the moment, that is, to communicate about the here and now (Goldin-Meadow & Mylander, 1984)
- To communicate about objects and events taking place in the past, in the future, or in a hypothetical world, that is, to communicate about the nonpresent (Butcher, Mylander, & Goldin-Meadow, 1991; Morford & Goldin-Meadow, 1997)
- To make category-broad generic statements about objects, particularly about natural kinds (Goldin-Meadow, Gelman, & Mylander, 2005)

Table 11.1   The Resilient Properties of Language

The Resilient Property	As Instantiated in Deaf Children's Gesture Systems
Words	
Stability	Gesture forms are stable and do not change capriciously with changing situations.
Paradigms	Gestures consist of smaller parts that can be recombined to produce new gestures with different meanings.
Categories	The parts of gestures are composed of a limited set of forms, each associated with a particular meaning.
Arbitrariness	The relation between gesture form and meaning, although essentially transparent (i.e., it is easy to guess its meaning from its form), has arbitrary aspects.
Grammatical functions	Gestures are differentiated by the noun, verb, and adjective grammatical functions they serve.
Sentences	
Underlying frames	Frames organized around the act predicate underlie gesture sentences.
Deletion	Consistent production and deletion of gestures within a sentence mark particular thematic roles.
Word Order	Consistent orderings of gestures within a sentence mark particular thematic roles.
Inflections	Consistent inflections on gestures mark particular thematic roles.
Recursion	Complex gesture sentences are created by recursion.
Redundancy reduction	Gestures are produced for redundant semantic elements in complex sentences less often than for nonredundant semantic elements.
Language Use	
Here-and-now talk	Gesturing is used to make requests, comments, and queries about the present.
Displaced talk	Gesturing is used to communicate about the past, future, and hypothetical.
Narrative	Gesturing is used to tell stories about self and others.
Self-talk	Gesturing is used to communicate with oneself
Generic statements	Gesturing is used to make generic statements, particularly about animate objects
Metalanguage	Gesturing is used to refer to one's own and others' gestures.

- To tell stories about themselves and others (Phillips, Goldin-Meadow, & Miller, 2001);
- To communicate not only with others but also with themselves
- To refer to their own or to others' gestures, that is, to communicate about communication (Goldin-Meadow, 1993)

Words

Deaf children's gesture words have a number of properties found in all natural languages. The gestures are stable in form, although they need not be. It would be easy for a child to make up a new gesture to fit every new situation. Indeed, hearing speakers appear to do just that when they gesture along with their speech (McNeill, 1992). But that's not what deaf children do; they develop a stable store of forms that they use in a range of situations (Goldin-Meadow, Butcher, Mylander, & Dodge, 1994)—they develop a lexicon, an essential component of all languages.

Moreover, the gestures deaf children develop are composed of parts that form paradigms or systems of contrasts (Goldin-Meadow, Mylander, & Butcher, 1995; Goldin-Meadow, Mylander, & Franklin, 2007). When deaf children invent a gesture form, they do so with two goals in mind: The form must not only capture the meaning they intend (a gesture-to-world relation) but must also contrast in a systematic way with other forms in their repertoire (a gesture-to-gesture relation). In addition, the parts that form these paradigms are categorical. The manual modality can easily support a system of analog representation, with hands and motions reflecting precisely the positions and trajectories used to act on objects in the real world. But, again, these children do not choose this route. They develop categories of meanings that, although essentially iconic, have hints of arbitrariness about them (they do not, for example, all share the same form–meaning pairings for handshapes).

Finally, the gestures that deaf children develop are differentiated by grammatical function (Goldin-Meadow et al., 1994). Some serve as nouns, some as verbs, some as adjectives. As in natural languages, when the same gesture is used for more than one grammatical function, that gesture is marked (morphologically and syntactically) according to the function it plays in the particular sentence.

Sentences

Deaf children's gesture sentences also have properties found in all natural languages. Underlying each sentence is a predicate frame that determines how many arguments can appear along with the verb in the surface structure of that sentence (Goldin-Meadow, 1985).[1] Moreover, the arguments of each sentence are marked according to the thematic role they play. Three types of markings have been identified as resilient (Feldman et al., 1978; Goldin-Meadow et al., 1994):

1. Deletion: The children consistently produce and delete gestures for arguments as a function of thematic role; for example, in describing a soldier beating a drum, the children are likely to produce a gesture for the patient (*drum*) but not for the actor (*soldier*).
2. Word order: The children consistently order gestures for arguments as a function of thematic role; for example, the children tend to produce gestures for patients (*drum*) before gestures for the act (*beat*).
3. Inflection: The children mark with inflections gestures for arguments as a function of thematic role; for example, the children mark the *beat* gesture by producing it near the drum, thus identifying *drum* as the patient.

In addition, the children form complex gesture sentences out of simple ones. They combine the predicate frames underlying each simple sentence, following systematic, and language-like, principles. When there are semantic elements that appear in both propositions of a complex sentence, the children have a systematic way of reducing redundancy, a property shared with all natural languages. Thus, recursion, which gives natural languages their generative capacity, is a resilient property of language (Goldin-Meadow, 1982).

The resilient properties of language listed in Table 11.1 are found in all natural languages and in the gesture systems spontaneously generated by deaf children. But, interestingly, they are *not* found in the communication systems of nonhumans. Even chimpanzees who have been explicitly taught a communication system by humans do not display the array of structural properties seen in Table 11.1. Moreover, a skill as simple as communicating about the nonpresent seems to be beyond the chimpanzee. For example, Kanzi, the most proficient of the language-trained chimps, uses his symbols to make requests 96% of the time (Greenfield & Savage-Rumbaugh, 1991, p. 243)—he very rarely comments on the here and now, let alone the distant past or future. Thus, the linguistic properties displayed in Table 11.1 are resilient in humans but not in any other species—indeed, there appear to be *no* conditions under which other species will develop the set of properties listed in Table 11.1.

Children Transform the Gestures They See to Create Language

The deaf children in our studies were not exposed to sign language. They were, however, exposed to the gestures that their hearing parents produced as they spoke. These gestures could have served as input to the children's gesture systems.

To explore this possibility, we looked at the gestures that the hearing mothers produced when talking to their deaf children. However, we looked at them not as they were meant to be experienced (i.e., with speech) but as a deaf child would look at them—we turned off the sound and analyzed the mothers' gestures using the same analytic tools that we used to describe the children's gestures. We found that the hearing mothers' gestures did *not* have the language-like structures found in their deaf children's gestures (e.g., Goldin-Meadow & Mylander, 1983, 1998)—indeed, they were no different from the gestures that all hearing speakers produce when they talk. The deaf children thus received as input gestures that were not language-like in form but they produced as output gestures that resembled language.

Why didn't the resilient properties of language appear in the hearing mothers' gestures? The mothers wanted their deaf children to learn to talk and, as a result, always spoke as they gestured. We hypothesized that the mothers' gestures (like the gestures of all hearing speakers; Goldin-Meadow, 2003a; Kendon, 1980; McNeill, 1992) were integrated with the words they accompanied and thus were not free to assume the language-like properties found in their children's gestures. This hypothesis leads to the following prediction: Hearing adults' gestures should look more like those of the deaf children if they are produced without talking. We tested this prediction experimentally.

We asked English speakers who had no experience with sign language to describe videotaped scenes using their hands and not their mouths. We then compared the resulting gestures with gestures these same adults produced when asked to describe the scenes using speech (Gershkoff-Stowe & Goldin-Meadow, 2002; Goldin-Meadow, McNeill, & Singleton, 1996). When using gesture with speech, the adults rarely combined gestures into strings, and when they did, those gestures were not consistently ordered. In contrast, when using gesture on its own, the adults often combined gestures into strings characterized by order, and, interestingly, this order did not follow canonical English word order—it appeared to be invented on the spot.

To summarize thus far, when gesture is called upon to fulfill all of the communicative functions of speech, it takes on word and sentence properties characteristic of speech. This "transformation" happens in deaf children not exposed to a linguistic model and also in hearing adults asked on the spot to communicate only with their hands. The appearance of these properties is particularly striking given that they are not found in the gestures that hearing adults routinely produce when they talk. I turn next to the gestures that young hearing children produce, exploring what those gestures might be able to tell us about how children go about acquiring the spoken language of their community.

GESTURE CAN TELL US WHEN CHILDREN ARE READY TO TAKE THEIR FIRST STEPS IN LEARNING A LANGUAGE

Young children communicate using gestures before they are able to speak. Children typically produce their first gestures between 9 and 12 months, usually points used to indicate objects in the here and now environment (Bates, 1976; Bates, Benigni, Bretherton, Camaioni, & Volterra, 1979). Even after they begin to produce words, children continue to produce gestures in combination with their words (e.g., point at cup while saying *cup*; e.g., Greenfield & Smith, 1976), and these gesture + word combinations precede production of two-word combinations. Gesture development thus predates language development. The question I focus on here is whether these gestures are fundamentally tied to language development.

The gestures that children produce early in language development provide a way for them to communicate information that they cannot yet express verbally. For example, pointing gestures (e.g., point at cup) offer children a technique for referring to objects before they have words for those objects. Moreover, gesture + word combinations offer children a technique for communicating two pieces of information within a single utterance before they can produce two-word utterances (e.g., point at cup while saying *mine*; Butcher & Goldin-Meadow, 2000; Capirci, Iverson, Pizzuto, & Volterra, 1996; Goldin-Meadow & Butcher, 2003). The fact that gesture allows children to communicate meanings that they may have difficulty expressing verbally opens up the possibility that gesture might play a role in the language-learning process. If so, changes in gesture should not only predate but should also predict changes in language at both word and sentence levels.

Words

If gesture serves a facilitating function in lexical development, we might expect an individual lexical item to enter a child's repertoire first in gesture and then, over time, to transfer to speech. Iverson and Goldin-Meadow (2005) explored this possibility in 10 children as they made the transition from one-word to two-word speech. We focused on the gestures and words that the children used to refer to objects, people, and places—that is, on deictic gestures (e.g., point at ball) and noun words (e.g., *ball*). We identified lexical items that a child used in multiple sessions and classified those items into four categories as a function of the modality in which they were produced over time: (1) the lexical item appeared initially in speech and remained in speech; (2) the lexical item appeared initially in gesture and remained in gesture; (3) the lexical item appeared initially in speech and transferred or spread to gesture; (4) the lexical item appeared initially in gesture and transferred or spread to speech. Items that appeared initially in speech and gesture were excluded from the analysis.

We found that modality had a clear impact on lexical development. Significantly more lexical items were produced initially in gesture (.75) than in speech (.25). However, over half (.59) of the lexical items did not remain in the modality in which they were initially produced but instead transferred or spread to the other modality. Importantly, the lexical items that were initially produced in gesture moved to speech (.50) significantly more often than the lexical items that were initially produced in speech moved to gesture (.09). Thus, overall, lexical items that the children produced initially in gesture were more likely to move to speech (.67) than the lexical items that the children produced initially in speech were to move to gesture (.36). On average, children produced a gesture to indicate a particular object 3.0 months (standard deviation [SD] = .54, range 2.3 to 3.9 months) before they produced the word for that object.

Thus, consistent with the gestural facilitation hypothesis, we are able to predict a large proportion of the lexical items that eventually appear in a child's verbal repertoire from looking at that child's earlier gestures. Because the relation between a deictic gesture and its referent is more transparent than the arbitrary relation between most words and their referents, gesture seems to be able to provide children with a temporary way to communicate about objects, one that allows them to circumvent difficulties related to producing speech (Acredolo & Goodwyn, 1988; Werner & Kaplan, 1963). Gesture may thus serve as a transitional device in early lexical development.

Sentences

Iverson and Goldin-Meadow (2005) examined the role of gesture in the acquisition of two-word sentences in the same 10 children. All of the children combined single gestures with single words and did so several months before producing their first two-word utterances. Moreover, all 10 children produced two kinds of gesture + speech combinations before the onset of two-word utterances (*bird nap*): (1) supplementary combination in which gesture adds information to the information conveyed in speech (e.g., point at bird while saying "nap"); and (2) complementary combinations in which the information conveyed in gesture is redundant with the information conveyed in speech (e.g., point at bird while saying "bird"). The mean interval between the onset of supplementary gesture + word combinations and the onset of two-word utterances was 2.3 months (*SD* = 1.66); the corresponding interval for complementary gesture + word combinations and the onset of two-word combinations was 4.7 months (*SD* = 2.2).

Note that like two-word combinations, supplementary gesture + word combinations communicate two semantic elements within a single communicative act. If gesture facilitates the emergence of early speech combinations, we might expect children who produce supplementary gesture + word combinations to be the first to make the transition to two-word speech. And, indeed, we found a significant correlation between age of onset of supplementary gesture + word combinations and age of onset of two-word combinations (Figure 11.1, left graph; Spearman $r_s = .94$, $p < .001$).

Unlike supplementary gesture + word combinations, complementary combinations convey a single semantic element. We therefore would not expect the onset of this type of gesture + word combination to predict the onset of two-word utterances, and, indeed, it did not. The correlation between age of onset of complementary gesture + word combinations and age of onset of two-word combinations was low and not reliable (Figure 11.1, right graph; Spearman $r_s = .24$, ns). Thus, it is the ability to combine two different semantic elements within a single communicative act, one in gesture and the other in speech—not simply the ability to produce gesture and speech together—that reliably predicts the onset of two-word speech.

Gesture May Play an Active Role in the Early Stages of Language Learning

We now know that gesture reflects skills that are involved in language learning. But gesture has the potential to do more—it could be part of the learning mechanism itself. In other words, gesture might not only signal that a child is ready to build his or her vocabulary or sentences; it might also play a role in the

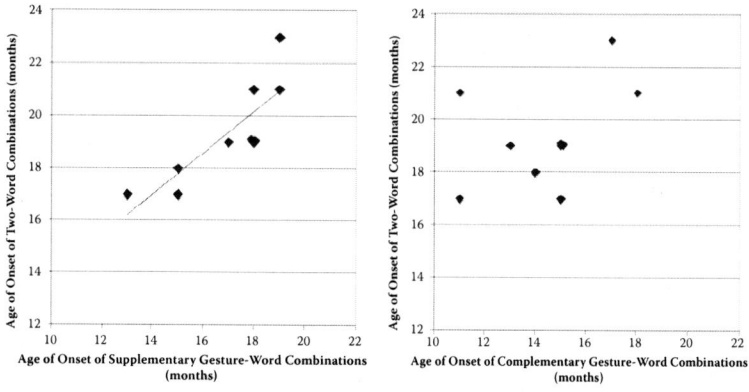

Figure 11.1   Scatterplots displaying the relation between age of onset of supplementary gesture + word combinations and age of onset of two-word combinations (left graph), and age of onset of complementary gesture + word combinations and age of onset of two-word combinations (right graph).

actual building. Gesture could play a causal role in language learning in two nonmutually exclusive ways, outlined in the next two sections.

Gesture Can Play a Role in Language Learning through Its Communicative Effects

The gestures children produce in the early stages of language learning reflect their readiness to progress to the next linguistic level. This insight into a child's cognitive state is accessible to researchers armed with video cameras and instant replay. But the insight is also accessible to adults interacting with their children on a daily basis. Perhaps adults respond in a targeted way to the gestures that their children produce, providing children with just the right input to take the next step on the road to learning to speak English.

Goldin-Meadow, Goodrich, Sauer, and Iverson (2007) explored this hypothesis in the same 10 children as the previously mentioned studies. We identified all of the times the children produced gestures, either without speech (e.g., point at bird) or with speech but conveying different information from that speech (e.g., point at bird + *nap*), and calculated the proportion of times the mothers translated those gestures into words. We found that mothers translated a third of their children's gestures into speech (e.g., producing the word *bird* after the child pointed at a bird). The more important result, however, is that the mothers translated gestures whose verbal equivalents *became* part of the child's spoken vocabulary during our observation sessions (.36) significantly more often than they translated gestures whose verbal equivalents *did not become* part of the child's vocabulary (.20). In other words, when mother translated her child's gestures into words, those words tended to become part of the child's spoken vocabulary. Thus, when mothers produced words in response to the gestures that their children produced without speech, the children added those words to their vocabularies. The children's gestures thus provided a signal to the mothers, who responded accordingly.

We asked next whether mothers were similarly responsive to their children's gesture + word combinations. If mothers understand both the gestural and verbal elements in a child's supplementary gesture + word combination, they might be expected to reproduce both elements in their response, thus producing a relatively long sentence. To explore this possibility, we calculated mean length of utterances (MLUs) for sentences that mother produced in response to her child's supplementary combinations and compared them with MLUs for sentences produced in response to the child's complementary combinations. We found that mothers' MLUs were significantly higher in their responses to children's supplementary combinations (3.7) than in their responses to children's complementary combinations (3.0; Goldin-Meadow, Goodrich, et al., 2007).

This effect is even more striking if we look at the kinds of sentences the mothers produced in response to their children's supplementary combinations. The mothers' MLUs differed as a function of the type of response they gave to the child's supplementary combinations. MLU was significantly longer when mothers incorporated *both* the child's word and a translation of the child's gestures into their utterances (5.7, e.g., saying, "the *bird* is taking a *nap*" after the child says *nap* and points at a bird) than when they reproduced the information found only in the child's gesture (3.8, "it's just like grandma's *bird*") or only in the child's word (2.5, "it's time for your *nap*"), and than when they reproduced none of the information conveyed by the child (2.6, "let's read the other book"). Sentences identified as containing semantic elements conveyed in the child's word *and* gesture must, of course, have a minimum MLU of 2.0. Note, however, that the mothers embellished the two-element information they gleaned from their children, producing their most complex sentences (with MLUs of 5.7, which were much larger than 2.0) at just those moments when they appeared to grasp the sentence-like nature of their children's thoughts.

Importantly, mothers' increased MLUs were targeted to particular utterances that their child produced and not to the child's state overall. Mothers might have begun producing longer utterances when they sensed that their child was ready to hear them—that is, around the time that the child first produced supplementary gesture + word combinations. But, in fact, mothers' MLUs overall were no higher after their children began producing supplementary combinations than they were before. Mothers increased the length of their sentences selectively in response to particular gesture + speech combinations that their children produced.

But do these translations play a role in the child's transition to two-word speech? A multiple linear regression analysis of the data from the 10 mothers provides tentative evidence that mothers' translations of child gesture might contribute to the onset of two-word utterances. We used two factors—(1) the proportion of supplementary combinations to which mother responded with a gesture translation and (2) the age at which each child first produced supplementary combinations—to try to predict the age at which the child first produced two-word utterances. As the findings reported earlier would lead us to expect, the onset of children's supplementary combinations (i.e., child gesture) accounted for a significant proportion of the variance in the onset of two-word utterances ($r^2 = .68$). But the proportion of gesture translations that the mothers produced (i.e., adult responses to child gesture) also contributed, accounting for an additional 11% of the variance in the age at which children produced their first two-word utterance.

Mothers thus translate their child's gestures into words, providing timely input for the child's acquisition of both object names and multiword sentences.

In previous work, experimenters have tried to target responses to child utterances, responding to a child's utterance with an expansion of that utterance (Nelson, 1989). Expansions of this sort have sometimes led to learning (Nelson, 1977; Nelson, Carskaddan, & Bonvillian, 1973) but not always (Cazden, 1965), perhaps because it is often difficult to know what a child has in mind when he or she produces an incomplete utterance. By using a child's gestures to narrow down the range of possible expansions for a given utterance, both experimenters and mothers may be better able to target input to the child, thus making that input particularly effective.[2]

Gesture Can Play a Role in Language Learning through Its Cognitive Effects
The results described in the previous section suggest that gesture can play a role in learning through its communicative effects—learners signal through their gestures that they are in a particular cognitive state, and listeners adjust their responses accordingly. But gesture also has the potential to play a role in learning through its cognitive effects (cf. Goldin-Meadow & Wagner, 2005). Take as an example children learning how to solve a mathematical equivalence problem. Encouraging children to produce gestures that convey a correct strategy for solving the problem increases the likelihood that those children will learn to solve the problem correctly. Findings such as these suggest that the act of gesturing may itself play a role in learning (Broaders, Cook, Mitchell, & Goldin-Meadow, 2007; Cook & Goldin-Meadow, 2006; Cook, Mitchell, & Goldin-Meadow, 2008).

There is indeed evidence within the language-learning domain that children's own gestures might be setting the stage for their subsequent vocabulary learning. We observed 54 English-learning children at home once every four months interacting naturally with their caregivers during the period from 14 to 30 months (Rowe, Ozcaliskan, & Goldin-Meadow, 2006; see also Rowe & Goldin-Meadow, in press; Rowe, Ozcaliskan, & Goldin-Meadow, 2008). As expected, children showed substantial growth in their productive vocabularies over this time period. On average, children produced 14 different spoken words at 14 months and 207 at 30 months, an increase of more than 190 words in a 16-month period. There was, moreover, large variation in the rate at which children increased their spoken vocabularies during this period. The interesting result from the point of view of the discussion here is that the children's own gesture production explained some of this variability—controlling for the number of different spoken words that the children and their mothers produced at 14 months, we found that the number of gestures the children produced at 14 months accounted for 28% of the variance in vocabulary growth. As a specific example of this relation, children who produced more gestures at 14 months used an estimated 38 more spoken words at 26 months than children who produced fewer gestures at 14 months.

There is thus growing evidence that gesture can promote language learning not only by allowing children to elicit timely input from their language-learning environments but also by influencing their own cognitive state.

GESTURE AS A TOOL FOR CHILDREN AND RESEARCHERS

When gesture assumes the full burden of communication, acting on its own without speech (as in the deaf children described here), it takes on language-like form; for example, structure at both word and sentence levels (see Table 11.1). Gesture can thus provide the raw materials out of which a child who has not been exposed to a language model can construct language.

However, when children are exposed to input from a language model (as are all young hearing children), gesture can serve as a stepping stone to language, particularly at the earliest stages of the learning process. Although not language-like in structure when it accompanies speech, gesture nevertheless forms an important part of language, providing young language learners with the means to convey word-like and sentence-like thoughts that they are not yet able to express entirely within speech.

Gesture is thus a useful tool for children when they are forced to invent their own communication system and when they are attempting to learn the communication system of their elders. But precisely because gesture taps into important aspects of the language-learning process, it can also serve as a useful tool for language researchers. Gesture offers researchers two unique perspectives on language learning—a window into the linguistic properties that a young language creator deems essential to communication and a window into the earliest steps that a young language learner takes en route to language (it may even provide insight into the mechanism responsible for those steps). For these reasons, gesture belongs in every language researcher's tool kit.

ENDNOTES

1. According to Bickerton (1998), having predicate frames is what distinguishes language from its evolutionary precursor, protolanguage.
2. Note that child gaze can also tell mothers what to focus on. If mother is attentive to where her child is looking, she can follow her child's gaze and establish joint attention with the child—a situation that turns out to be good for word learning (Tomasello & Farrar, 1986). The advantage gesture has over gaze is that, by gesturing, the child makes it clear that she is interested in communicating; mother can thus calibrate her words to a child who is ready to hear them.

REFERENCES

Acredolo, L.A. & Goodwyn, S. (1988). Symbolic gesturing in normal infants. *Child Development, 59,* 450–466.

Bates, E. (1976). *Language and context.* New York: Academic Press.

Bates, E., Benigni, L., Bretherton, I., Camaioni, L., & Volterra, V. (1979). *The emergence of symbols: Cognition and communication in infancy.* New York: Academic Press.

Bickerton, D. (1998). Catastrophic evolution: The case for a single step from protolanguage to full human language. In J. R. Hurford, M. Studdert-Kennedy, & C. Knight (Eds.), *Approaches to the evolution of language* (pp. 341–358). Cambridge, UK: Cambridge University Press.

Butcher, C. & Goldin-Meaodw, S. (2000). Gesture and the transition from one-to two-word speech: When hand and mouth come together. In D. McNeill (Ed.), *Language and gesture* (pp. 235–257). Cambridge, UK: Cambridge University Press.

Butcher, C., Mylander, C., & Goldin-Meadow, S. (1991). Displaced communication in a self-styled gesture system: Pointing at the non-present. *Cognitive Development, 6,* 315–342, 420–435.

Broaders, S., Cook, S. W., Mitchell, Z., & Goldin-Meadow, S. (2007). Making children gesture brings out implicit knowledge and leads to learning. *Journal of Experimental Psychology: General, 136,* 539–550.

Capirci, O., Iverson, J. M., Pizzuto, E., & Volterra, V. (1996). Communicative gestures during the transition to two-word speech. *Journal of Child Language, 23,* 645–673.

Cazden, C. B. (1965). *Environmental assistance to the child's acquisition of grammar.* Unpublished doctoral dissertation, Harvard University, Cambridge, MA.

Conrad, R. (1979). *The deaf child.* London: Harper & Row.

Cook, S. W. & Goldin-Meadow, S. (2006). The role of gesture in learning: Do children use their hands to change their minds? *Journal of Cognition and Development, 7,* 211–232.

Cook, S. W., Mitchell, Z., & Goldin-Meadow, S. (2008). Gesturing makes learning last. *Cognition, 106,* 1047–1058.

Feldman, H., Goldin-Meadow, S., & Gleitman, L. (1978). Beyond Herodotus: The creation of language by linguistically deprived deaf children. In A. Lock (Ed.), *Action, symbol, and gesture: The emergence of language.* New York: Academic Press.

Gershkoff-Stowe, L. & Goldin-Meadow, S. (2002). Is there a natural order for expressing semantic relations? *Cognitive Psychology, 45*(3), 375–412.

Goldin-Meadow, S. (1982). The resilience of recursion: A study of a communication system developed without a conventional language model. In E. Wanner & L. R. Gleitman (Eds.), *Language acquisition: The state of the art* (pp. 51–77). New York: Cambridge University Press.

Goldin-Meadow, S. (1985). Language development under atypical learning conditions: Replication and implications of a study of deaf children of hearing parents. In K. Nelson (Ed.), *Children's language* (Vol. 5, pp. 197–245). Hillsdale, NJ: Lawrence Erlbaum & Associates.

Goldin-Meadow, S. (1993). When does gesture become language? A study of gesture used as a primary communication system by deaf children of hearing parents. In K. R. Gibson & T. Ingold (Eds.), *Tools, language and cognition in human evolution* (pp. 63–85). New York: Cambridge University Press.

Goldin-Meadow, S. (2003a). *Hearing Gesture.* Cambridge, MA: Harvard University Press.

Goldin-Meadow, S. (2003b). *Resilience of language*. New York: Psychology Press.

Goldin-Meadow, S. & Butcher, C. (2003). Pointing toward two-word speech in young children. In S. Kita (Ed.), *Pointing: Where language, culture, and cognition meet* (pp. 85–107). Mahwah, NJ: Lawrence Erlbaum Associates.

Goldin-Meadow, S., Butcher, C., Mylander, C. & Dodge, M. (1994). Nouns and verbs in a self-styled gesture system: What's in a name? *Cognitive Psychology, 27*, 259–319.

Goldin-Meadow, S. & Feldman, H. (1977). The development of language-like communication without a language model. *Science, 197*, 401–403.

Goldin-Meadow, S., Gelman, S., & Mylander, C. (2005). Expressing generic concepts with and without a language model. *Cognition, 96*, 109–126.

Goldin-Meadow, S., Goodrich, W., Sauer, E., & Iverson, J. (2007). Young children use their hands to tell their mothers what to say. *Developmental Science, 10*, 778–785.

Goldin-Meadow, S., McNeill, D., & Singleton, J. (1996). Silence is liberating: Removing the handcuffs on grammatical expression in the manual modality. *Psychological Review, 103*, 34–55.

Goldin-Meadow, S. & Mylander, C. (1983). Gestural communication in deaf children: The non-effects of parental input on language development. *Science, 221*, 372–374.

Goldin-Meadow, S. & Mylander, C. (1984). Gestural communication in deaf children: The effects and non-effects of parental input on early language development. *Monographs of the Society for Research in Child Development, 49*, 1–121.

Goldin-Meadow, S. & Mylander, C. (1998). Spontaneous sign systems created by deaf children in two cultures. *Nature, 91*, 279–281.

Goldin-Meadow, S., Mylander, C., & Butcher, C. (1995). The resilience of combinatorial structure at the word level: Morphology in self-styled gesture systems. *Cognition, 56*, 195–262.

Goldin-Meadow, S., Mylander, C., & Franklin, A. (2007). How children make language out of gesture: Morphological structure in gesture systems developed by American and Chinese deaf children. *Cognitive Psychology, 55*, 87–135.

Goldin-Meadow, S. & Wagner, S. M. (2005). How our hands help us learn. *Trends in Cognitive Science, 9*, 234–241.

Greenfield, P. M. & Savage-Rumbaugh, E. S. (1991). Imitation, grammatical development, and the invention of protogrammar by an ape. In N. A. Krasnegor, D. M. Rumbaugh, R. L. Schiefelbusch, & M. Studdert-Kennedy (Eds.), *Biological and behavioral determinants of language development* (pp. 235–262). Hillsdale, NJ: Earlbaum Associates.

Greenfield, P. & Smith, J. (1976). *The structure of communication in early language development*. New York: Academic Press.

Hoffmeister, R. & Wilbur, R. (1980). Developmental: The acquisition of sign language. In H. Lane & F. Grosjean (Eds.), *Recent perspectives on American Sign Language* (pp. 61–78). Hillsdale, NJ: Earlbaum Associates.

Kendon, A. (1980). Gesticulation and speech: Two aspects of the process of utterance. In M. R. Key (Ed.), *Relationship of verbal and nonverbal communication* (pp. 207–228). The Hague: Mouton.

Iverson, J. M. & Goldin-Meadow, S. (2005). Gesture paves the way for language development. *Psychological Science, 16*, 368–371.

Mayberry, R. I. (1992). The cognitive development of deaf children: Recent insights. In S. Segalowitz & I. Rapin (Eds.), *Child neuropsychology, volume 7, handbook of neuropsychology* (pp. 51–68), F. Boller & J. Graffman (Series Eds.). Amsterdam: Elsevier.

McNeill, D. (1992). *Hand and mind*. Chicago: University of Chicago Press.

Morford, J. P. & Goldin-Meadow, S. (1997). From here to there and now to then: The development of displaced reference in homesign and English. *Child Development*, 68, 420–435.

Nelson, K. E. (1977). Facilitating children's syntax acquisition. *Developmental Psychology*, 13, 101–107.

Nelson, K. E. (1989). Strategies for first language teaching. In M. L. Rice & R. L. Schiefelbusch (Eds.), *The teachability of language* (pp. 263–310). Baltimore, MD: Paul H. Brookes Publishing Co.

Nelson, K., Carskaddan, G., & Bonvillian, J. (1973). Syntax acquisition: Impact of experimental variation in adult verbal interaction with the child. *Child Development, 44,* 497–504.

Newport, E. L. & Meier, R. P. (1985). The acquisition of American Sign Language. In D. I. Slobin (Ed.), *The cross-linguistic study of language acquisition, vol. 1: The data.* Hillsdale, NJ: Erlbaum.

Ozcaliskan, S. & Goldin-Meadow, S. (2005). Gesture is at the cutting edge of early language development. *Cognition, 96,* B01–113.

Phillips, S. B. V. D., Goldin-Meadow, S., & Miller, P. J. (2001). Enacting stories, seeing worlds: Similarities and differences in the cross-cultural narrative development of linguistically isolated deaf children. *Human Development, 44,* 311–336.

Rowe, M., Ozcaliskan, S., & Goldin-Meadow, S. (2006). The added value of gesture in predicting vocabulary growth. In D. Bamman, T. Magnitskaia, & C. Zaller (Eds.), *Proceedings of the 30th Annual Boston University Conference on Language Development* (pp. 501–512). Somerville, MA: Cascadilla Press.

Rowe, M., Ozcaliskan, S. & Goldin-Meadow, S. (2008). Learning words by hand: Gesture's role in predicting vocabulary development. *First Language, 28,* 185–203.

Rowe, M., & Goldin-Meadow, S. (in press). Early gesture selectively predicts later language learning. *Developmental Science.*

Werner, H. & Kaplan, B. (1963). *Symbol formation.* New York: Wiley.

Tomasello, M. & Farrar, M., (1986). Joint attention and early language. *Child Development, 57,* 1454–1463.

IV

MODELS AND METHODS TO STUDY INFANT LANGUAGE

12

Linking Infant Speech Perception to Language Acquisition
Phonetic Learning Predicts Language Growth

PATRICIA K. KUHL

INTRODUCTION

A lively conference on language processing was held at Massachusetts Institute of Technology (MIT) in 1976, when Denis Klatt, Peter Eimas, and Peter Jusczyk were still living (Perkell & Klatt, 1976). A specific question raised by Eimas resonated among the attendees regarding the fast-growing literature on infants' perception of speech: Infants show exquisite processing of speech in the first year of life—what role does it play in language development? Does resolution of a 10 ms difference in voice onset time (VOT) (to differentiate /ba/ from /pa/; see Eimas, Siqueland, Jusczyk, & Vigorito, 1971) assist the acquisition of language? Jusczyk and Klatt wondered similarly about prosody and its role in language acquisition, and Jusczyk's work over the next two decades made that connection (Jusczyk, 1997).

Thirty years after the conference, the question about continuity between speech and language is gaining momentum. Janet Werker's group is examining toddlers' use of phonetic detail in their early word representations (Werker & Yeung, 2005; Werker, this volume); Swingley and Aslin (2002, 2007) pursued this question, and so has Kim Plunkett's group (Ballem & Plunkett, 2005). These studies attempt to link speech perception and language acquisition.

Studies in my laboratory have taken a different approach. We have been examining Eimas's question in another way by asking if an infant's early speech perception skill predicts that child's later language ability. A considerable literature indicates an association between deficits in speech perception and specific language impairment in children, as described herein, but such studies do not prove that a relationship can be established between early speech perception and later language in typically developing children.

Prospective experimental studies conducted in the last few years in my laboratory suggest that infants' early speech perception abilities do predict language growth (Kuhl, Conboy, Padden, Nelson, & Pruitt, 2005; Kuhl et al., 2008; Rivera-Gaxiola, Klarman, Garcia-Sierra, & Kuhl, 2005; Tsao, Liu, & Kuhl, 2004). The data make an important point: What we once considered "noise"—the variance observed in phonetic perception in typically developing infants—is meaningful. Individual differences in infants' speech perception abilities predict the variance in their developmental growth patterns for language.

This chapter summarizes these studies, discusses their implications, and describes the Native Language Magnet-Expanded (NLM-e) model, which explains how linguistic, social, and cognitive skills contribute to the early development of speech perception and speech production and how this early learning affects second language learning.

RETROSPECTIVE STUDIES AND THE ROLE OF PHONETIC PROCESSING IN LANGUAGE IMPAIRMENT

Before any prospective studies demonstrated associations between early speech perception performance and later language abilities, retrospective and concurrent studies revealed a link between reduced phonetic perception and language impairment. Early pioneers in this work were Dennis Molfese and his colleagues who showed, in children between the ages of 3 and 8, that classification into high- versus low-functioning language groups could be predicted by their event-related potential (ERP) responses to speech syllables as newborns (Molfese, 2000; Molfese & Molfese, 1985, 1997). The authors' discriminant function analyses of the children's brain waves as newborns predicted their classification with about 80% accuracy into normal- and low-language performance groups, based on standardized tests.

These data are buttressed by a large body of literature on the phonetic abilities of children diagnosed with reading disorders, learning disabilities, or language impairment in the form of specific language impairment (SLI). Studies confirm that children with reading disabilities show deficits in speech perception when compared with age-matched controls (Reed, 1989). Performance differences between children with dyslexia and controls were reported for tests of speech perception in several studies (Godfrey, Syrdal-Lasky, Millay, & Knox, 1981; Manis et al., 1997; Reed, 1989; Werker & Tees, 1987). Similar findings, using both brain and behavioral measures, have been reported for children with various forms of learning disabilities (Bradlow et al., 1999; Kraus et al., 1996).

Links between deficiencies in speech perception and poor language skills are particularly strong in school-age children with SLI (Leonard, McGregor, & Allen, 1992; Stark & Heinz, 1996; Sussman, 1993; Tallal & Piercy, 1974). SLI children perform significantly poorer than age-matched controls in the perception of consonantal acoustic cues such as formant transitions, VOT, and frication noise (Leonard et al., 1992; Tallal & Piercy, 1974; Tallal & Stark, 1981).

PROSPECTIVE STUDIES: ASSOCIATIONS BETWEEN EARLY PHONETIC PERCEPTION AND LATER LANGUAGE

Prospective studies looking at the association between speech discrimination skills in typically developing infants and their future language skills began in my laboratory with the publication of a study showing that vowel discrimination predicted language during the first two years of life. Tsao et al. (2004) tested 6-month-old infants' performance on a standard measure of speech perception, the head-turn (HT) conditioning task, and a simple vowel contrast (the vowels in *tea* and *two*). He assessed the same infants' language skills at 13, 16, and 24 months of age using the MacArthur-Bates Communicative Development Inventory (CDI) (Fenson et al., 1994, 2000). Significant correlations between individual infants' speech perception skills at 6 months and word understanding, word production, and phrase understanding were seen at 13, 16, and 24 months of age. The findings demonstrated, for the first time, that a standard measure of native language speech perception at 6 months of age—the ability to discriminate two vowels—prospectively predicted language outcomes in typically developing infants at three ages over the next 18 months. Parental socioeconomic variables (education, profession, and income level) for both the mother and the father were measured and shown to be unrelated to either the infants' early speech perception skills or their later language abilities (Tsao et al., 2004).

Tsao et al. (2004) argued that phonetic perception per se was related to later language but raised two alternative accounts for the association they observed between native language speech perception and later language—infants' general auditory abilities or general cognitive abilities. Infants who performed better in the phonetic perception tasks might have had better listening skills or might have been cognitively advanced. If so, the observed relationship between speech and language would not link infants' *phonetic abilities* to later language but rather link them to infants' more general hearing and cognitive skills. The next studies in my laboratory examined these alternatives and tested a specific hypotheses generated by the NLM-e model.

PROSPECTIVE STUDIES USING BOTH NATIVE AND NONNATIVE PHONETIC UNITS

Behavioral Studies Examining Native and Nonnative Contrasts

To advance theory, we designed prospective tests using native as well as nonnative phonetic units to examine their predictive value for later language. A revision of the original Native Language Magnet (NLM) model (NLM-e, described following) made specific predictions regarding how native and nonnative perception should relate to later language (Kuhl, 2004; Kuhl et al., 2008). We argue that language acquisition depends on native language *neural commitment*, the development of neural circuitry dedicated to the analysis of the statistical and prosodic patterns in native language speech. The degree to which infants remain able to detect *nonnative* phonetic contrasts reflects the degree to which the brain remains in an earlier, more immature state of phonetic perception (Phase 1)—still "open" and uncommitted to native language speech patterns. According to the model, early native language speech perception is required for advancement toward language. Therefore, native perception skill should positively predict language growth. Nonnative phonetic skill, on the other hand, is predicted to correlate negatively with later language learning: An open system reflects uncommitted circuitry.

Kuhl, Conboy, et. al. (2005), conducted the first study using both native and nonnative contrasts. They utilized a standard behavioral measure of speech perception (HT conditioning; see Polka, Jusczyk, & Rvachew, 1995 for procedural details). We tested 20 infants at 7 months of age on the discrimination of the native stop contrast /pa-ta/ and the nonnative Mandarin affricate-fricative contrast / t6ʰi-6i/, counterbalanced across subjects. The Mandarin contrast has been used in previous research in our laboratory (Kuhl, Tsao, & Liu, 2003; Tsao, Liu, & Kuhl, 2006).

The HT task provides a sensitive measure of individual infants' speech perception skill and has been used in many studies. It provides an absolute performance measure, both percent correct and d-prime (d'), for individual infants. The CDI was used to measure language outcomes at 14, 18, 24, and 30 months of age.

Two results were noteworthy. First, there was an association between performance on the native and nonnative contrasts at 7.5 months of age. We found a significant negative correlation for the native and nonnative contrasts ($r = -.481$, $p = .030$, $n = 16$). Infants with higher d' scores for the English native contrast tended to have lower d' scores for the Mandarin Chinese nonnative contrast.

Second, we examined whether native or nonnative phonetic perception predicted future language ability and, if so, the direction of the effects. As hypothesized, both native and nonnative d' measures of speech discrimination at 7 months predicted later language, but differentially. Native language phonetic discrimination was positively correlated with word production at 18 months ($r = .503$, $p = .017$, $n = 17$), sentence complexity at 24 months ($r = .423$, $p = .046$,

n = 17), and the mean of the three longest utterances (M3L) at 24 months (r = .492, p = .023, n = 17) (Figure 12.1a). In contrast, nonnative language phonetic discrimination in the same infants was negatively correlated with word production at 18 months (r = -.507, p = .023, n = 16), word production at 24 months (r = -.532, p = .017, n = 16), and sentence complexity at 24 months (r = -.699, p = .001, n = 16) (Figure 12.1b).

Vocabulary was measured at all four CDI test ages, allowing examination of the vocabulary growth patterns over time. The differential relationship between native and nonnative phonetic discrimination and vocabulary growth can be seen by comparing vocabulary growth in infants whose d′ scores are above or below the median (Figure 12.2).

Perception of native (Figure 12.2[a]) and nonnative phonetic contrasts (Figure 12.2[b]) at 7 months of age differentially affects the pattern of later vocabulary growth. For the *native* language contrast, infants with a d′ above the median showed faster vocabulary growth than infants with d′ values below the median. For the *nonnative* contrast, the pattern was reversed: Infants with d′ values above the median showed slower vocabulary growth than those with d′ values below the median.

Differences in vocabulary for subjects above and below the d′ median are most pronounced at 18 and 24 months of age. Group effects for the native predictor approach significance at 18 months (t(15) = -2.045, p = .059). Repeated measures analysis of variance (ANOVA) with the native predictor as a between subjects variable reveals the expected significant age effect for number of words produced (F(1,14) = 64.170, p = .000). Main effects for the native predictor and the native predictor by age interaction were not significant. Group effects for the nonnative predictor are significant at 24 months (t(14) = 2.858, p = .013). Repeated measures ANOVA with the nonnative predictor as a between subjects variable also reveals the expected significant age effect for number of words produced (F(1,13) = 76.653, p = .000). The main effect for the nonnative predictor is significant (F(1,13) = 5.046, p = .043). Moreover, the nonnative predictor by age interaction is significant (F(1,13) = 4.600, p = .05).

After 24 months the vocabulary growth differences between native and nonnative predictors dissipate. Given the fact that the infant participants in the study are all typically developing infants who are expected to achieve normal language skills, it is not surprising that the curves merge over time.

Brain Measures of Phonetic Perception as Prospective Predictors of Future Language

We reasoned that the use of brain measures would advance this work because pre-attentive event ERPs reduce the role of cognitive factors, such as attention, on

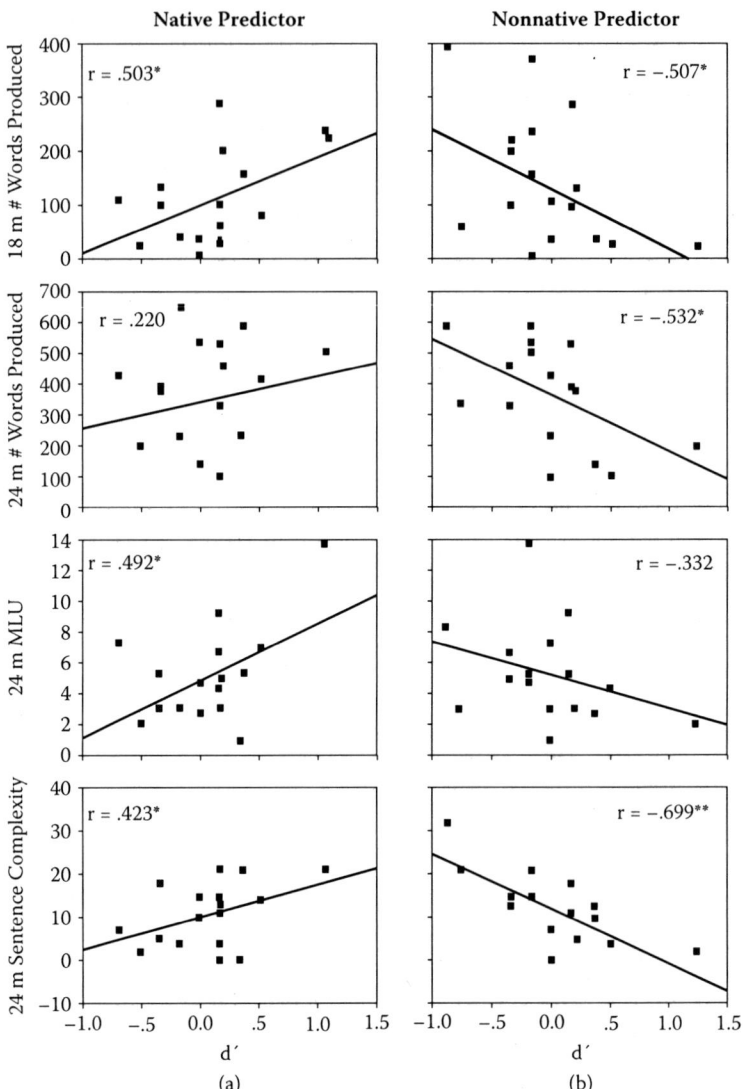

Figure 12.1 Scatterplots showing the relationship between native (left) and nonnative (right) phonetic perception at 7.5 months and language measures taken in the second and third year of life. (Modified from Kuhl, Conboy, et al., 2005, *Language Learning and Development, 1*, 248. With permission.)

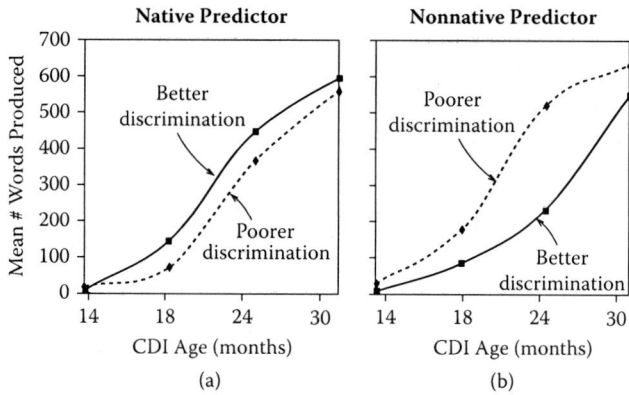

Figure 12.2   Vocabulary growth curves (median number of words produced) for participants with phonetic discrimination at or above (solid line) versus below (dashed line) the median for the native-language contrast (a) and the nonnative language contrast (b). (Modified from Kuhl, Conboy, et al., 2005, *Language Learning and Development, 1*, 249. With permission.)

discrimination. In Kuhl, et al., 2008, we used ERPs to test the same native place contrast (/pa-ta/) and either the nonnative contrast (Mandarin /t6ʰi-6i/) used in the earlier behavioral tests (Kuhl, Conboy, et al., 2005) or a new nonnative contrast (Spanish voiced-voiceless). Native and nonnative contrasts were presented in counterbalanced order. The use of two nonnative contrasts allowed us to examine whether the predictive relationship we had observed in the behavioral study between early speech and later language would obtain with ERPs and a new nonnative contrast. The classic "oddball" paradigm was used, which has been shown to provide discriminative responses to phonetic changes in the form of mismatch negativity (MMN) in adults (Näätänen et al., 1997) and an MMN-like response in infants (Cheour et al., 1998; Pang et al., 1998; Rivera-Gaxiola, Silva-Pereyra, & Kuhl, 2005).

ERPs were recorded in 30 (14 female) monolingual full-term infants at 7.5 months of age in response to the native and nonnative phonetic contrasts. In our ERP task (Kuhl et al., 2008), infants listened to the syllables passively while an experimenter entertained them with quiet toys. The oddball paradigm was used with 85% standards and 15% deviants. An EEG was collected continuously with a sampling rate of 250 Hz and was band-pass filtered from 0.1 to 60 Hz at 16 electrode sites using Electro-caps with standard international 10/20 placements. Data collected from eight lateral electrode sites (F7/8, F3/4, T3/4, C3/4) were used in the analysis. Participants heard approximately 500 syllables (standard deviation [SD] = 39) and 60 deviant trials (SD = 14) for each contrast. Mean amplitude of the deviant minus standard difference wave (the MMN) between

300 and 500 ms after the onset of the deviant was measured. Usable ERP data were obtained from 24 of the 30 participants for the native contrast and 22 of the 30 participants for the nonnative contrast (15 to Mandarin and 7 to Spanish). Of the 30 participants, 21 had acceptable ERP data for both native and nonnative contrasts (15 with the Mandarin nonnative contrast and 6 with the Spanish non-native contrast).

Average waveforms for the standards and deviants obtained for the native and nonnative contrasts at the eight electrode sites were analyzed for each child, and the mean amplitude of the MMN (Näätänen et al., 1997) was calculated at each site. The MMN is a negative wave that is observed in response to the deviant at approximately 250 ms (adults) and slightly later (300–500) for infants (Cheour et al., 1998; Rivera-Gaxiola, Silva-Pereyra, et al., 2005). Better discrimination is indicated by larger amplitudes of the negativity, which can be measured either as a peak value or as a mean amplitude value (Kraus et al., 1996). Separate repeated measures ANOVAs, conducted for each contrast (native, Spanish, and Mandarin), indicated no interactions of stimulus (standard vs. deviant) by hemisphere (left vs. right) by site ($N = 8$) for the native ($F(3,66) = 0.229$, $p = 0.844$, $n = 23$), the Mandarin ($F(3,39) = 0.265$, $p = 0.817$, $n = 14$), or the Spanish ($F(3,18) = 1.309$, $p = 0.305$, $n = 7$) contrast. Based on the broad distributions of the MMNs, a single MMN mean amplitude difference value (deviant[minus standard at 300–500 ms) was calculated for each infant's native and nonnative contrast by averaging values across hemisphere and electrode site.

We observed a significant negative correlation between infants' ERPs to native and nonnative contrasts; this was true when the Mandarin nonnative contrast was correlated with the native contrast ($r = -0.741$, $p = 0.046$, $n = 6$), and with the combined data ($r = -0.631$, $p = 0.001$, $n = 21$). Infants with more negative MMN values (indicating better discrimination) for the native /p-t/ contrast tended to have less negative values for the nonnative contrast (either Mandarin or Spanish), while infants with less negative values for the native contrast showed more negative values for the nonnative. This relationship replicates the findings of our previous behavioral study (Kuhl, Conboy, et al., 2005) and extends the pattern of results to a brain measure and a new nonnative contrast.

As we had hypothesized, analysis of the CDI data revealed that both native and nonnative neural measures predicted future language and in opposing directions (Figure 12.3). Better native language discrimination was associated with more advanced language skills measured over the next two years. The native language MMN at 7.5 months significantly predicted the number of words produced at 18 months ($r = -0.430$, $p = 0.020$), the number of words produced at 24 months ($r = -0.611$, $p = 0.001$), higher sentence complexity at 24 months ($r = -0.643$, $p = 0.001$), and a longer M3L at 24 months ($r = -0.632$, $p = 0.001$), as well as at 30 months ($r = -0.487$, $p = 0.017$) (see Figure 12.3[a] for examples). In all cases,

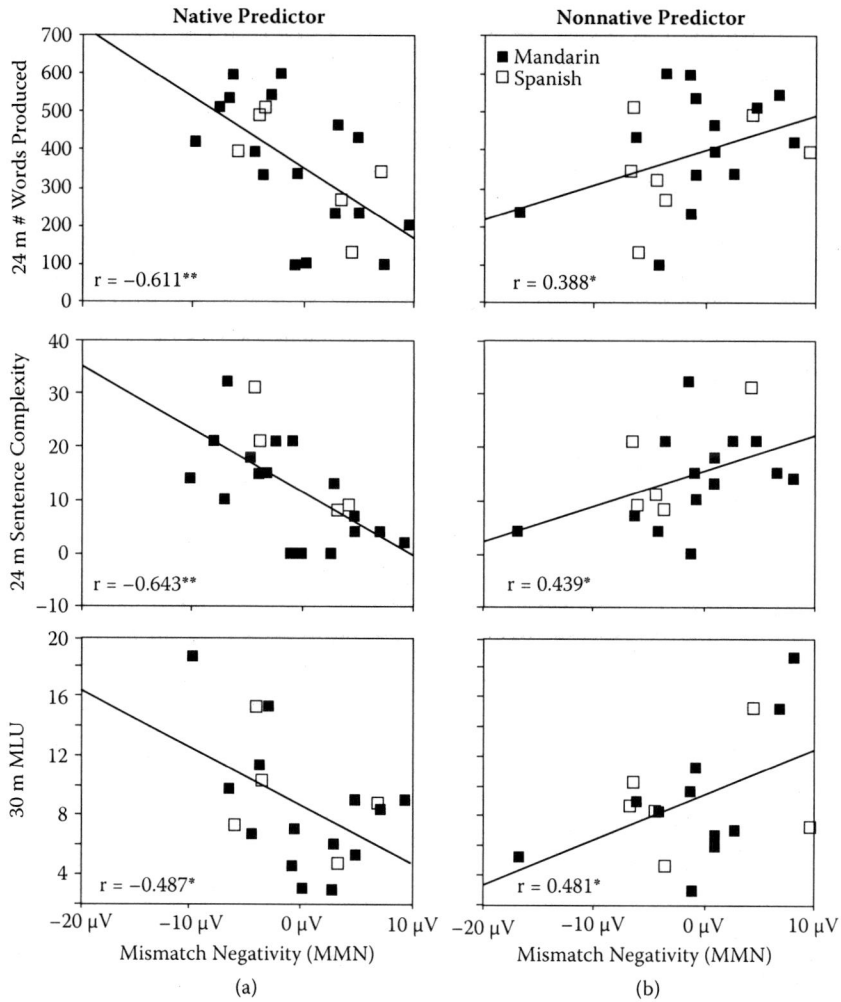

Figure 12.3   Scatterplots show significant correlations between infants' phonetic discrimination, as measured by ERPs (the infant MMN), at 7.5 months for native (left) as opposed to nonnative (right) phonetic contrasts and their later language abilities. (Filled = Mandarin, Open = Spanish). (From Kuhl et al., 2008, *Philosophical Transactions of the Royal Society B*, p. 987. With permission.)

more negative MMN values (indicating better discrimination) are associated with higher language scores, producing negative correlations.

A very different pattern of prediction was observed when infants' MMN measures of nonnative perception were used to predict future language skills

(Figure 12.3[b]). Better discrimination of the nonnative contrast is associated with less advanced language skills. More negative MMNs to nonnative phonetic contrasts (better discrimination) at 7.5 months predicted fewer words produced at 24 months ($r = 0.388$, $p = 0.041$), lower sentence complexity at 24 months ($r = 0.439$, $p = 0.030$), and a shorter M3L at 30 months ($r = 0.481$, $p = 0.025$). Thus, both native and nonnative phonetic units predict later language, but in different directions. This pattern of associations replicates the effects seen in our earlier behavioral study (Kuhl, Conboy, et al., 2005) and extends the pattern to a new nonnative contrast.

Hierarchical Linear Growth-Curve Modeling

Acceleration in expressive vocabulary growth during the second year characterizes learning in many of the world's languages (Bornstein & Cote, 2005; D'Odorico, Carubbi, Salerni, & Calvo, 2001; Fenson et al., 1994; Huttenlocher, Haight, Bryk, Seltzer, & Lyons, 1991). To examine whether brain responses to speech sounds at 7.5 months predicted rates of expressive vocabulary development from 14 to 30 months, Kuhl et al. (2008) used the Hierarchical Linear Models (HLMs) program HLM 6 (Raudenbush, Bryk, & Congdon, 2005)(Figure 12.4).

In multilevel modeling, repeated measurements of vocabulary size are used to estimate growth functions for each individual child, and the resultant growth parameters for each individual are modeled as random with variance predicted by a between subjects variable. Inspection of individual children's data indicated that variation across children was observed from 14 to 30 months. Of the 23 children for whom at least 3 data points were available, approximately half ($n = 12$) showed rapid initial growth, reaching close to 400 words or more by 24 months (range, 393–597). From 24 to 30 months, the slopes were flatter in these children, which may be at least partially an artifact of the vocabulary measure (their 30-month vocabulary sizes ranged from 555 to 673 and the CDI ceiling is 680 words). The remaining children evidenced lesser gains in vocabulary size up to 24 months, although their scores were still within the normal range at 24 months (97–343 words) and 30 months (207–678 words).

Separate analyses were conducted for the native and nonnative contrast ERP data in children with artifact-free data at 7.5 months ($n = 24$ and $n = 22$, respectively, with 21 children participating in both analyses). At the first level of each analysis, we estimated individual growth curves for each child using a quadratic equation with the intercept centered at 18 months (due to the small sample sizes we used restricted maximum likelihood). Several reports on expressive vocabulary development in this age range have indicated that quadratic models capture typical growth patterns—both a steady increase and acceleration (Fernald, Perfors, & Marchman, 2006; Ganger & Brent, 2004; Huttenlocher et al., 1991). Centering at 18 months allowed us to evaluate individual differences in vocabulary size at an age

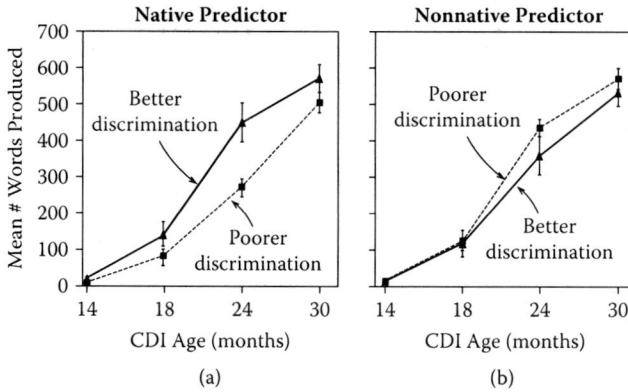

Figure 12.4   A median split of infants whose MMNs indicate better (solid line) versus poorer (dotted line) discrimination of native (a) and nonnative (b) phonetic contrasts is shown along with their corresponding longitudinal growth-curve functions for the number of words between 14 and 30 months of age. (From Kuhl et al., 2008, *Philosophical Transactions of the Royal Society B*, p. 988. With permission.)

that has previously been associated with rapid growth ("vocabulary spurt") as well as differences in rates of growth across the whole period.

For each sample of children, unconditional models indicated individual variation in the random effects for the intercept (18-month vocabulary size), linear slope, and quadratic component. Covariance estimates indicated high degrees of collinearity between the linear and quadratic components for each sample. For both the native and nonnative MMN samples, the intercepts and linear slopes were highly positively correlated at .99, indicating that children with higher 18-month vocabulary sizes tended to have faster growth throughout the 14–30-month period. For both samples, the intercepts and quadratic components were highly negatively correlated (native tau = −.95, nonnative tau = −.99), and the slopes and quadratic components were highly negatively correlated (native tau = −.89, nonnative tau = −.97), which likely reflects the fact that children whose vocabulary sizes reached higher levels by 18 months and had overall faster growth had a leveling off function toward 30 months as they reached the CDI ceiling.

At the second level of analysis, child-level variations in the intercepts (i.e., 18-month vocabulary sizes) and in the slopes of the growth functions were modeled as a function of the 7.5-month native and nonnative MMN values. The quadratic growth-curve model indicated that the average native contrast MMN was significantly related to the intercept (18-month vocabulary size) ($t(22) = -4.15$, $p < 0.001$), the linear slope component ($t(22) = -4.07$, $p < 0.001$), and the quadratic component of the growth function ($t(22) = 3.32$, $p = 0.003$).

To illustrate this relationship, Figure 12.4(a) shows the growth patterns for children whose 7.5-month *native* MMNs were below and above the median. The children with better native discrimination skills (more negative mean MMN amplitude values, solid curve) showed faster vocabulary growth. In contrast, children with poorer native discrimination skills (more positive mean MMN values, dotted curve) showed slower growth in the number of words.

As predicted by our hypothesis, the opposite pattern was obtained for the nonnative language contrast (Figure 12.4[b]). Children with better non-native discrimination skills (more negative mean MMN amplitude values, solid curve) showed slower vocabulary growth, while children with poorer nonnative discrimination skills (more positive mean MMN values, dotted curve) showed faster growth in the number of words. The quadratic growth-curve model showed that the average nonnative contrast MMN values were significantly related to the intercept ($t(20) = 2.27$, $p = 0.03$) and the linear slope component ($t(20) = 2.63$, $p = 0.02$). There was a trend for the interaction between nonnative MMN size and the quadratic component of the growth function ($t(20) = -1.97$, $p = 0.06$). Thus, greater discrimination of the nonnative contrast at 7.5 months was associated with slower vocabulary growth. In contrast, infants showing poorer discrimination evidenced faster growth in vocabulary size.

EXPLAINING THE LINK BETWEEN SPEECH AND LANGUAGE

Our tests show that both native and nonnative phonetic discrimination abilities at around 7 months predict children's language abilities at the age of 30 months. Using both behavioral and brain measures, we show that better *native* phonetic abilities predict faster advancement in language, whereas better *nonnative* phonetic abilities predict slower linguistic advancement.

Additional studies from our laboratory show a similar pattern of prediction for native and nonnative phonetic abilities and later language. Rivera-Gaxiola, Klarman, et al., (2005) measured ERPs in response to native and nonnative English–Spanish contrasts in 11-month-old infants and measured their language skills with the CDI at 18, 22, 25, 27, and 30 months of age. Infants were categorized into two groups depending on the latency and polarity of their *nonnative* contrast responses; infants with prominent negativities between 250 and 600 ms after stimulus onset (good discrimination) at 11 months produced significantly fewer words at each age when compared with infants who did not show this negativity. While infants ERPs were measured differently by Kuhl et al. (in press) and Rivera-Gaxiola, Klarman, et al., (2005), both focus on the degree to which infants produce a strong negativity (indicating good discrimination) in response to a change in phonetic contrasts, and both studies show that good discrimination of the nonnative contrast after 7.5 months of age predicts slower language development.

Using the Rivera-Gaxiola, Klarman, et al. (2005) stimuli and a new double-target behavioral measure to relate concurrent language abilities and speech perception in 11-month-old infants, Conboy, Rivera-Gaxiola, Klarman, Aksoylu, and Kuhl (2005) showed that the degree to which infants' d′ scores to native contrasts exceeded their performance on nonnative contrasts predicted the number of words they comprehended at that age. In other words, a bigger difference between native and nonnative performance predicted faster language growth. This result is consistent with the idea that better performance on native phonetic tasks is an indicator of faster language growth while better performance on nonnative phonetic tasks is an indicator of slower growth in language.

Finally, a study of Finnish 7- and 11-month-old infants replicates this pattern (Silven, Kouvo, Haapakoski, Lahteenmaki, & Kuhl, 2004). Monolingual infants tested on a native Finnish and a nonnative Russian contrast at the two ages and followed up with the Finnish version of the CDI at 14 months showed a significant positive correlation between native language and future language perception at 7 months and a significant negative correlation between nonnative perception at 11 months and future language, a pattern of results that is consistent with what we observed in the English-learning infants (Kuhl, Conboy, et al., 2005; Kuhl et al., 2005).

Thus, a number of studies of typically developing infants between 6 and 12 months of age using different phonetic contrasts in different countries show that better native language speech perception skill, measured either behaviorally or neurally, predicts rapid advancement of language, whereas better nonnative phonetic skill, measured in the same way at the same age, is an indicator of slower language growth. It is important to note that these results are for monolingual infants who have not had any experience with the foreign language being tested. Expectations for bilingual infants are discussed following.

What accounts for the continuity between speech perception and later language? The NLM model (Kuhl, 1992, 1994) has recently been revised. The new Native Language Magnet expanded (NLM-e) model indicates a potential pathway by which phonetic learning advances language development (Kuhl et al., 2008). NLM-e is described briefly here, because it offers an account of the results of our prediction experiments. NLM-e suggests how auditory, cognitive, and social factors interact during phonetic learning, and indicates how early phonetic learning affects second-language learning later in life.

Native Language Magnet-Expanded

The NLM-e model is shown in Figure 12.5. Phase 2, neural *commitment*, is the heart of the model and is most relevant to the experiments discussed here that show a differential relationship between native and nonnative phonetic perception in infancy as predictors of later language. The model is described next.

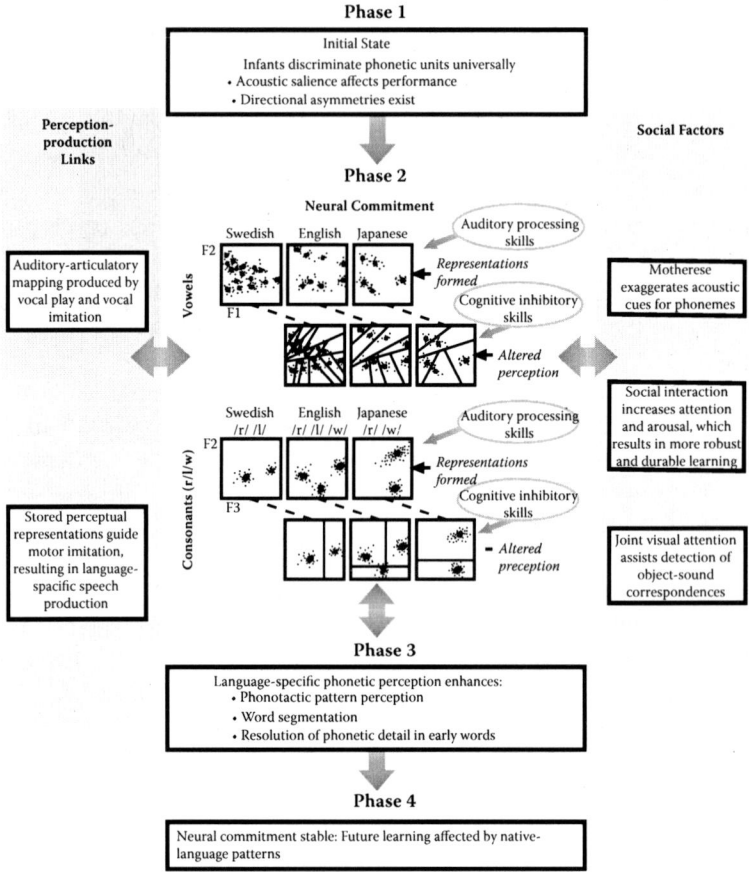

Figure 12.5   NLM-e is shown in four phases (see text for description). The representations of native language input for vowels and consonants are drawn roughly to reflect existing data for Swedish (Fant, 1973; Lacerda, 2006), English (Dalston, 1975; Flege, Takagi, & Mann, 1995; Hillenbrand, Getty, Clark, & Wheeler, 1995) and Japanese (Iverson et al., 2003; Lotto, Sato, & Diehl, 2004). (From Kuhl et al., 2008, *Philosophical Transactions of the Royal Society B*, p. 989. With permission.)

NLM-e: Phase 1

Phase 1 of the model indicates that infants discriminate all phonetic units in the world's languages, though contrasts differ in difficulty and directional effects exist for both consonants (Kuhl et al., 2006) and vowels (Polka & Bohn, 2003). Studies demonstrate that the acoustic salience of a phonetic contrast impacts performance; fricatives, for example, have been shown to be more difficult to discriminate due to their low amplitude (Eilers, Wilson, & Moore, 1977; Kuhl, 1980; Nittrouer, 2001; see also Burnham, 1986). Moreover, studies show that discrimination performance in infants and young children is above chance but far below that shown by adult native listeners (Kuhl et al., 2006; Nittrouer, 2001; Sundara, Polka, & Genesee, 2006). Infants' initial performance thus leaves room for substantial improvement, especially for those contrasts that are acoustically fragile. The model stipulates that in Phase 1, infants' phonetic abilities are relatively crude (see Kuhl, 2000 for cross-species comparisons), reflecting general auditory perceptual constraints or learning in utero (Moon, Cooper, & Fifer, 1993). Infants begin life with a capacity to discriminate the acoustic cues that differentiate phonetic units, an ability that is helpful in Phase 2.

NLM-e: Phase 2

Phase 2 represents the core of the NLM-e model, describing how neural commitment to native language patterns ensues. At this stage in development, phonetic learning is produced through infants' sensitivity to the distributional patterns of language input to the child (Kuhl, Williams, Lacerda, Stevens, & Lindblom, 1992; Maye, Werker, & Gerken, 2002) and the exaggerated cues of infant-directed speech (Burnham, Kitamura, & Vollmer-Conner, 2002; Kuhl et al., 1997; Liu, Kuhl, & Tsao, 2003; Liu, Tsao, & Kuhl, 2007). We argue that distributional cues are exaggerated by infant-directed speech, and therefore that the two factors work in concert as agents of change in phonetic perception during Phase 2. Recent data show prominent distributional differences across languages (Werker et al., 2007). As diagrammed in NLM-e, infants form phonetic representations that are stored in memory based on the distributional patterns (exaggerated by infant-directed speech) contained in language input.

Phonetic learning for various contrasts will vary depending on the availability of information about the contrast in language input. As diagrammed, phonetic learning occurs earlier for vowels than consonants (e.g., Best & McRoberts, 2003; Kuhl et al., 1992; Polka & Werker, 1994; Werker & Tees, 1984), a difference that could reflect the availability of exaggerated cues in infant-directed speech—consonants are not as easily exaggerated as vowels, because exaggeration can change the category (e.g., stretching the formant transitions of /b/ eventually produces /w/). Alternatively, there may be differences in the availability or prominence of distributional differences for consonants (e.g., consonants like /th/ occur in function words, which are lower in energy and do not capture infant attention; see Sundara et al., 2006). Individual infants should be affected by the quantity and quality of language input they hear and its exact properties. Detailed studies will need to be done to test these hypotheses.

Our findings suggest that phonetic *learning*, as described in Phase 2—rather than infants' simpler abilities in Phase 1—is the factor associated with advanced language. Infants whose native language perception skills increase are learning from language input, whereas infants who remain good at nonnative perception have not yet begun the phonetic learning process. Group data show that native language speech perception increases between 6 and 12 months of age but also that variability exists (Kuhl et al., 2006; Tsao et al., 2006)—exploiting the variability revealed that infants who learn native language patterns more quickly also advance more rapidly toward language.

What causes the substantial variability we observed in the onset of phonetic learning? One possibility is that maturational factors are responsible. We have argued that the "opening" of the critical period for phonetic learning may reflect a maturational component, and this could vary across infants (Kuhl, Conboy, et al., 2005; Kuhl et al., 2008). Maturation of the human auditory cortex between the middle of the first year of life and 3 years of age shows the development of axons entering the deeper cortical layers from the subcortical white matter—neurofilament-expressing axons appear for the first time in the temporal lobe, with projections to the deep cortical layers of the brain; these axons would provide the first highly processed auditory input from the brainstem to higher auditory cortical areas (Moore & Guan, 2001). The temporal coincidence between this cytoarchitectual change and infants' phonetic learning provides a possible maturational cause for the onset of phonetic learning, and its timing could vary across infants.

Environmental factors could also play a role in the variance seen in the onset of initial phonetic learning. Liu et al. (2003; see also Liu et al., 2007) established an association between mothers' use of the exaggerated pronunciation of speech typical of infant-directed speech and infants' abilities to discriminate phonetic contrasts. The association was observed with two independent samples of mother-infant dyads, one with infants aged 6–8 and a second with infants at 10–12 months of age. We posit, therefore, that infants' phonetic learning skills could also depend on the linguistic environment in which infants are developing; those with richer linguistic environments should advance toward language more quickly.

What role do auditory and cognitive factors play in phonetic learning? Good auditory resolution of the cues that underpin phonetic contrasts is essential to native language phonetic learning. An auditory skill that has been suggested as critical to language is rapid auditory processing (RAP), and relative skill has been shown to predict language disabilities as well as language development in typical children (Benasich & Leevers, 2002; Benasich & Tallal, 2002). It is important to note, however, that a basic auditory skill like RAP cannot explain our differential future language predictions using native and nonnative phonetic contrasts. If better auditory resolution alone were responsible, native and nonnative phonetic perception would predict later language in the same direction. The phonetic prediction effects we have seen must therefore go beyond auditory skills. The NLM model posits a role for auditory resolution in the ability to hear the relevant phonetic differences in native language speech in Phase 2; the fact that infant-directed speech increases the acoustic distance between native language phonetic units should make it easier for infants to do so (Burnham et al., 2002; Kuhl et al., 1997; Liu et al., 2003, 2007).

Similarly, cognitive abilities are linked to various aspects of communicative development (e.g., Bates & Snyder, 1987; Gopnik & Meltzoff, 1987; Thal, 1991; Tomasello & Farrar, 1984), and research suggests that cognitive abilities that tap attentional or inhibitory control are specifically related to performance on nonnative (but not native) speech perception tasks (Conboy, Sommerville, & Kuhl, in press; Diamond, Werker, & Lalonde, 1994; Lalonde & Werker, 1995). Infants' capacity to discriminate nonnative contrasts declines but remains above chance at the end of the first year (Kuhl et al., 2006; Rivera-Gaxiola, Silva-Perayra, et al., 2005; Tsao et al., 2006)—cognitive control may explain how infants refrain from attending to nonnative contrasts that they can discriminate (see Conboy et al., in press for discussion). We note that bilingual children, whose language environments require them to "switch" between languages, develop inhibitory control to a greater extent than monolingual children (Bialystok, 1999; Carlson & Meltzoff, 2008). Early speech perception may be one mechanism through which this "bilingual advantage" emerges.

Social Factors in Phonetic Learning

Social interaction is posited to play a major role in phonetic learning in Phase 2 of NLM-e, placing early language learning in a neurobiological context. Mimicking effects seen in songbirds (see Doupe & Kuhl, 1999 for review), we have shown that social interaction is effective in enhancing phonetic learning in infancy (Kuhl et al., 2003). We used a foreign-language intervention design to examine the role of social interaction in phonetic learning. The study showed that infants exposed to a second language in a social setting for the first time at 9 months showed extraordinary ability to learn over 12 sessions. However, the study also showed that infants did not learn via a conventional TV or audio recording. Infants showed no learning when exposed to the same material. Learning in the social condition was robust and durable. Behavioral tests of infant learning were conducted 2–12 days (median = 6 days) after the final language-exposure session, and ERP tests were conducted between 12 and 30 days (median = 15 days) after the final exposure session, with no observable differences in infant performance as a function of the delay (Kuhl, Coffey-Corina, & Padden, 2007).

In further tests using exposure to Spanish, ERPs were used to test learning of both phonetic units and words in 11-month-old infants after exposure to Spanish speakers in natural play sessions (Conboy & Kuhl, 2007). The results show learning of both Spanish phonemes and words. Moreover, the study was designed to test the hypothesis that social interaction between the infants and their Spanish tutors during the exposure sessions would predict the degree to which individual infants learned phonemes and words (Conboy, Brooks, Taylor, Meltzoff, & Kuhl, 2008). This hypothesis was also confirmed. Infants' overall attention during the exposure sessions and specific measures of shared visual attention between the infant and tutor surrounding the introduction of new toys predicted the degree to which individual infants' ERPs reflected learning of Spanish phonemes and Spanish words. Attention also plays a role in simpler distributional learning experiments in the laboratory (Yoshida, Pons, Cady, & Werker, 2006), and joint visual attention predicts aspects of language, such as the number of words produced (Baldwin, 1995; Baldwin & Markman, 1989; Brooks & Meltzoff, 2005; Meltzoff & Brooks, this volume; Tomasello & Farrar, 1986). The results of Kuhl et al. (2003), Kuhl & Conboy (2007), and Conboy et al. (2008) suggest that social interaction may be critical to phonetic learning in early infancy. In complex natural communicative settings, social interaction may effectively "gate" the computational mechanisms underlying learning (Kuhl, 2007).

The Spanish exposure experiment also provides support for the idea that cognitive control skills can be advanced by exposure to a second language (Bialystok, 2001; Carlson & Meltzoff, 2006). In our study, pre- and post-exposure cognitive control comparisons showed that 12 sessions of Spanish exposure improved cognitive control skills in the infants whose ERPs demonstrated phonetic learning (Conboy & Kuhl, 2007). Understanding how complex systems—linguistic, social, and cognitive—interact in language learning will be a challenge for language research during the next decade.

Exploring how multiple factors affect infants' developing language skills has practical implications. Measures of speech perception, both phonetic abilities and a social interest in speech, may provide early markers of language disorders, such as autism (Kuhl, Coffey-Corina, Padden, & Dawson, 2005). Understanding how early measures, alone and in concert, predict future language will require a comprehensive study that measures simultaneously a variety of skills in infants—basic auditory abilities, cognitive skills, social understanding, phonetic perception, and the ability to detect distributional patterns and statistical cues—in a longitudinal study that examines the individual and joint effects of these factors on language development and on brain development. Multiple factors are expected to play a role in language acquisition (Hollich, Hirsh-Pasek, & Golinkoff, 2000). A comprehensive study using multiple measures on a large cohort of infants is now warranted given the results of these studies showing continuity between early speech perception and later language skills.

NLM-e also indicates a link to speech production that is forged during Phase 2 (see Kuhl et al., 2008, for details). Infants develop connections between speech production and the auditory signals it causes during development as they practice and play with vocalizations and imitate those they hear (Kuhl & Meltzoff, 1996). As speech production improves, imitation of the learned patterns stored in memory leads to language-specific speech production. Our new work on infants uses infant magnetoencephalography (MEG) to explore the linkage between speech perception and production (see also Dehaene et al., 2006; Imada et al., 2006).

By the end of Phase 2, infant perception is altered; native language phonetic learning has begun the neural commitment process, and this propels infants forward toward more complex forms of language.

NLM-e: Phase 3

In Phase 3, enhanced speech perception abilities could advance language by improving three interdependent skills that promote word learning:

1. The detection of phonotactic patterns (Friederici & Wessels, 1993; Mattys, Jusczyk, Luce, & Morgan, 1999)
2. The detection of transitional probabilities between segments and syllables (Goodsitt, Morgan, & Kuhl, 1993; Newport & Aslin, 2004; Saffran, Aslin, & Newport, 1996)
3. The association between sound patterns and objects (Stager & Werker, 1997; Werker, Fennell, Corcoran, & Stager, 2002)

At this stage, phonetic learning would assist the detection of word patterns, and the learning of phonetically close words would be expected to sharpen awareness of phonetic distinctions (see Swingley & Aslin, 2007). Each of these skills— detection of phonotactic patterns, detection of word-like units, and the resolution of phonetic detail in early words—may themselves predict future language, and recent studies provide some retrospective data (Newman, Bernstein Ratner, Jusczyk, Jusczyk, & Dow, 2006).

NLM-e: Phase 4

By Phase 4, the model indicates that analysis of incoming language has produced relatively stable neural representations—that is, new utterances do not cause shifts in the distributional properties coded neurally. In early infancy, neural networks are not stable, and learning is not restricted. Infants are thus capable of learning from multiple languages, as shown in most of the world's countries and also as shown by experimental interventions (Conboy & Kuhl, 2007; Kuhl et al., 2003; Maye et al., 2002). In adulthood, representations are stable, and new learning is more difficult—unlike in infancy, exposure to a new language does not automatically produce learning. The principle underlying the model is that the degree of "plasticity" in learning the phonetics of a second language depends on the stability of the underlying perceptual representations.

The model raises interesting questions about our current language prediction data. Learning and flexibility are in a trading relationship; infants who move more quickly toward native language phonetic learning are becoming less flexible in the process (though early neural commitment to native language patterns is unstable and therefore forms a relatively soft constraint on learning). The model predicts that all learning affects the system's future capacity to learn, and the effect is predicted to work in both directions; infants who are slower to learn native language patterns remain more flexible and may more readily learn from second-language exposure.

PREDICTIONS OF THE NLM-E MODEL

Predictions for Bilingual Learners

The NLM-e model predicts that phonetic development follows the same principles for two languages that it does for a single language. Bilingual infants learn through the exaggerated acoustic cues provided by infant-directed speech and through the distributional properties of the two languages, as do monolingual infants. Phonetic exaggeration and the distributional properties of the two languages differ, and these properties would provide infants a means of separating the two streams of input.

According to the model, the development of representations in Phase 2 could require a longer period of time for bilingual learners than for the monolingual case. Infants learning two first languages simultaneously might thus be expected to reach the developmental change in perception at a later point than infants learning either language monolingually. Bilingual infants could remain in Phase 2 for a longer period of time because it takes longer to experience enough data from both languages to permit alteration of infant perception; this could depend on factors such as the number of people in the infants' environment producing the two languages in speech directed toward the child and the amount and quality of the infant-directed speech they provide.

As in the case of monolingual exposure, social factors would be expected to play a role in bilingual learning and could in fact be argued to assist learning. In some cases of simultaneous bilingualism, different people speak the two languages to which the infant is exposed. If the social settings in which exposure to the two languages occurs also differ, greater separation between the distributional properties of the two inputs would be achieved. At present there is no evidence of an advantage for such "one person, one language" approaches to bilingual language socialization over approaches in which infants hear both languages from the same people or over situations in which parents frequently code-switch between languages; this is clearly a matter for future research. Code-switching and mixing are common practices in many bilingual communities, and it has been shown that a strict separation of languages is difficult for many families (Goodz, 1989). Even in mixed-language situations, infant-directed speech could exaggerate different aspects of the two languages, assisting infants' mapping of features that are relevant for each of the two languages. We note that the differential effects we observed in predicting future language from infants' early native and nonnative speech perception would also be expected to apply to bilingual infants, though to see the pattern of predictive correlations that we observed, a third language to which the infants have not been exposed would have to be tested. Phonetic contrasts from both languages to which bilingual infants are exposed should correlate positively with later language; a third language, to which infants are not exposed, would be expected to show the opposite pattern.

There are little data on speech perception in infants exposed to two languages simultaneously early in development, and the data are mixed with regard to the question about the timing of the transition in perception. Some studies show later acquisition of language-specific phonetic skills (Bosch & Sebastian-Galles, 2003a, 2003b). This is especially the case when infants are tested on contrasts that are phonemic in only one of the two languages; this has been shown both for vowels (Bosch & Sebastian-Galles, 2003b) and consonants (Bosch & Sebastian-Galles, 2003a). However, other studies report no delay in the development of phonetic skills in the two languages of bilingual infants (Burns, Yoshida, Hill, & Werker, 2007; Sundara, Polka & Molnar, in press). Data from an ERP study of Spanish–English bilingual infants show that at both 6–9 and 9–12 months of age, bilingual infants show negativities in response to both Spanish and English phonetic contrasts (Rivera-Gaxiola & Romo, 2006), distinguishing them from English-learning monolingual infants who no longer respond to the Spanish contrast at the later age (Rivera-Gaxiola, Silva-Pereyra, et al., 2005).

An experiment that will help answer the question with regard to whether bilingual infants take longer to show the developmental transition in phonetic perception is a study on bilingual infants that mirrors our recent studies on monolingual infants (e.g., Kuhl, Conboy, et al., 2005; Kuhl et al., 2008). In the monolingual studies, an increase in native language performance and a decline in nonnative phonetic performance serve to indicate that infants are no longer in the initial phase of development in which all phonetic distinctions are treated similarly (ibid.). To show a decline in bilingual infants a third phonetic contrast, one to which the bilingual children have not been exposed, must be used at the 10–12-month-old age to test the hypothesis that the bilingual infants are no longer in Phase 1 of development. If tests on bilingual infants at 10–12 months reveal the decline typically observed in response to contrasts to which the infant is not exposed, it would signal that bilingual children transition from the initial phase (Phase 1) to Phase 2 at the same point in development as monolingual children. However, if a decline is not observed in the third phonetic contrast, it would indicate that bilingual infants remain in Phase 1 of development—phonetically "open" for a longer period of time, due perhaps to the fact that it takes longer to map two distinct sets of phonetic cues (see Kuhl et al., 2008 for discussion). Such studies are now under way in our laboratory.

Predictions on the Durability and Robustness of Learning

The NLM-e model posits that social interaction results in learning in natural settings that is more robust and durable; in other words, we suggest that learning in social settings is in some sense more potent and enduring. There are two reasons to suggest that social factors affect learning in this way. First, our own data suggest some degree of durability; infants in the Mandarin exposure studies (Kuhl et al., 2003) returned to the laboratory between 2 and 12 days (median = 6 days) after the final exposure session to complete their behavioral Mandarin discrimination tests and between 12 and 30 days (median = 15 days) to complete their ERP tests (Kuhl et al., 2007). Analysis showed that delays of this magnitude had no effect on infants' performance. These data suggest that natural language exposure produced durable effects, with a month-long delay in the measures of learning showing no change.

Infants in the exposure experiment would nonetheless be expected to show a "forgetting function" eventually, because 5 hours of listening experience to a new language would not be sufficient to undo the representations built up over the previous 9 months of life. Memory for the 1-month experience of Mandarin could, however, prompt more rapid learning later in life than would be the case if never exposed to Mandarin. Neural modelers suggest that short-term learning of new phonetic contrasts is initially perceptually separated and therefore produces learning without undoing the representations formed by long-term listening to one's primary language (Vallabha & McClelland, 2007).

Adopting a neurobiological framework, song learning in birds also indicates that social interaction extends the period of learning and produces learning that is more robust and durable. Richer social environments extend the duration of the sensitive period for learning in owls and songbirds (Baptista & Petrinovich, 1986; Brainard & Knudsen, 1998). Social contexts affect the rate, quality, and retention of song elements in songbirds' repertoires (West & King, 1988). The idea that social interaction affects learning in this way can be experimentally assessed by systematically measuring the "forgetting function" for learning under conditions in which the complexity of the input (conversational language from multiple talkers as opposed to 2-minute syllable presentations in the laboratory) as well as the degree of social interaction that the learning paradigm incorporates, will allow us to test this hypothesis.

Predictions Regarding the Mechanism Underlying a "Critical Period" at the Phonetic Level

Language and the "critical period" have long been associated (Bialystok & Hakuta, 1994; Birdsong & Molis, 2001; Flege, Yeni-Komshian, & Liu, 1999; Johnson & Newport, 1989; Lenneberg, 1967; Newport, Bavelier, & Neville, 2001; Weber-Fox & Neville, 1999; Werker & Tees, 2005; Yeni-Komshian, Flege, & Liu, 1999). As described in recent publications, the views laid out in NLM-e may provide a clue to the mechanisms underlying a "critical period" at the phonetic level for language (Kuhl, Conboy, et al., 2005). NLM-e indicates that phonetic learning is associated with a decline in phonetic flexibility, suggesting that *experience*, not simply *time*, is a critical factor driving phonetic learning and perception.

Bruer (2006) recently discussed the need to separate studies that focus on identifying the phenomena and optimum periods of learning in various domains (see also Bateson & Hinde, 1987; Hess, 1973; Lorenz, 1957) from experimental tests that explore the explanatory causal mechanism that underlies a critical period for language. Thus far, our work (Kuhl, Conboy, et al., 2005; Kuhl et al., 2008) has focused on the mechanism question, which requires a different kind of experiment—one that differentiates the role of maturation and the role of experience. Both the maturational view (Bialystok & Hakuta, 1994; Birdsong & Molis, 2001; Flege et al., 1999; Johnson & Newport, 1989; Lenneberg, 1967; Newport et al., 2001; Weber-Fox & Neville, 1999; Yeni-Komshian et al., 1999) and the experience/interference view (Iverson et al., 2003; Kuhl, 1998, 2000, 2004; Seidenberg & Zevin, 2006) are supported by experimental data on first- and second-language learning.

Our data link native language phonetic learning and nonnative decline—both brain and behavioral measures show that the two are significantly negatively correlated, indicating that as native learning ensues nonnative perception is correspondingly reduced in individual infants (Kuhl, Conboy, et al., 2005; Kuhl et al., 2008). What explains this association?

We are exploring two possibilities. If phonetic features form an oppositional network, as is the case in vision, native language phonetic learning could directly inhibit nonnative learning. Testing this hypothesis requires testing a number of different native and nonnative contrasts to examine the generality of our findings. Thus far, the negative correlation has been confirmed for one native contrast (stop consonant place) and two different nonnative contrasts (a Mandarin affricate-fricative and a Spanish voicing contrast), but more contrasts need to be tested. Another possibility is that at a particular point in time infants are sensitive to the distributional cues in language input and this explains the patterns of correlation we have observed. Both explanations would also produce the dissociation between native and nonnative contrasts that we have observed. Further work at the phonetic level will be necessary to determine how learning the set of phonetic contrasts appropriate for one language affects future learning of the phonetic contrasts of a new language, and this will contribute to our understanding of the mechanisms underlying critical period phenomena at the phonetic level of language with potential implications for other levels of language.

CONCLUSIONS

The studies reviewed here suggest continuity between infants' early speech perception skills and their later language abilities. Infants' early abilities to discern differences between native language phonetic contrasts predict their rate of growth for words, phrases, and sentences, suggesting that the variability observed in infants' phonetic skills are not "noise" and instead represent meaningful differences in early linguistic skills that provide a pathway toward language. The fact that our studies show that both native and nonnative speech perception predict later language, but in opposing directions suggests that it is neither infants' general auditory nor their general cognitive skills but instead their phonetic learning abilities that affect language growth. These findings have both theoretical and practical value. A theoretical model, NLM-e, uses the concept of *neural commitment* to explain early speech perception development and makes predictions about bilingual learning and the roles of social and cognitive factors on the mechanisms of phonetic learning. From a practical standpoint, the results suggest that infants' phonetic perception skills may serve as early markers for various disorders of language, including autism, dyslexia, and specific language impairment.

ACKNOWLEDGMENTS

Funding for the research was provided by a grant to the author from the National Institutes of Health (HD37954) and by funding to the University of Washington LIFE Center by the National Science Foundation (NSF) Science of Learning program. This chapter is based on a presentation at a conference sponsored by the Merrill Advanced Studies Institute in Tempe, Arizona, in September 2005 on "Infant Pathways to Language."

REFERENCES

Baldwin, D. A. (1995). Understanding the link between joint attention and language. In C. Moore & Dunham, P.J. (Eds.), *Joint attention: Its origins and role in development* (pp. 131–158). Hillsdale, NJ: Lawrence Erlbaum Associates.

Baldwin, D. A. & Markman, E. M. (1989). Establishing word-object relations: A first step. *Child Development, 60,* 381–398.

Ballem, K. D. & Plunkett, K. (2005). Phonological specificity in children at 1:2. *Journal of Child Language, 32,* 159–173.

Baptista, L. F. & Petrinovich, L. (1986). Song development in the white-crowned sparrow: Social factors and sex differences. *Animal Behavior, 34,* 1359–1371.

Bates, E. & Snyder, L. (1987). The cognitive hypothesis in language development. In I. Uzgiris & J. M. Hunt (Eds.), *Research with scales of psychological development in infancy* (pp. 168–206). Champaign: University of Illinois Press.

Bateson, P. & Hinde, R. A. (1987). Developmental changes in sensitivity to experience. In M. H. Bornstein (Ed.), *Sensitive periods in development* (pp. 19–34). Hillsdale, NJ: Erlbaum.

Benasich, A. & Leevers, H. J. (2002). Processing of rapidly presented auditory cues in infancy: Implications for later language development. In J. Fagan & H. Haynes (Eds.), *Progress in Infancy Research* (Vol. 3, pp. 245–288). Mahwah, NJ: Lawrence Erlbaum Associates, Inc.

Benasich, A. & Tallal, P. (2002). Infant discrimination of rapid auditory cues predicts later language impairment. *Behavioral Brain Research, 136,* 31–49.

Best, C. & McRoberts, G. (2003). Infant perception of non-native consonant contrasts that adults assimilate in different ways. *Language & Speech, 46,* 183–216.

Bialystok, E. (1999). Cognition and language: Cognitive complexity and attentional control in the bilingual mind. *Child Development, 70,* 636–644.

Bialystok, E. (2001). *Bilingualism in development: Language, literacy, and cognition.* New York: Cambridge University Press.

Bialystok, E. & Hakuta, K. (1994). *In other words: The science and psychology of second-language acquisition.* New York: Basic Books.

Birdsong, D. & Molis, M. (2001). On the evidence for maturational constraints in second-language acquisition. *Journal of Memory and Language, 44,* 235–249.

Bornstein, M. H. & Cote, L. R. (2005). Expressive vocabulary in language learners from two ecological settings in three language communities. *Infancy, 7,* 299–316.

Bosch, L. & Sebastián-Gallés, N. (2003a). Language experience and the perception of a voicing contrast in fricatives: Infant and adult data. In M. J. Solé, D. Recasens, & J. Romero (Eds.), *International Congress of Phonetic Sciences* (pp. 1987–1990). Barcelona, Spain.

Bosch, L. & Sebastián-Gallés, N. (2003b). Simultaneous bilingualism and the perception of a language-specific vowel contrast in the first year of life. *Language & Speech, 46,* 217–243.

Bradlow, A., Kraus, N., Nicol, T., McGee, T., Cunningham, J., Zecker, S., et al. (1999). Effects of lengthened formant transition duration on discrimination and neural representation of synthetic CV syllables by normal and learning-disabled children. *Journal of the Acoustical Society of America, 106,* 2086–2096.

Brainard, M. S. & Knudsen, E. I. (1998). Sensitive periods for visual calibration of the auditory space map in the barn owl optic tectum. *Journal of Neuroscience, 18,* 3929–3942.

Brooks, R. & Meltzoff, A. (2005). The development of gaze following and its relation to language. *Developmental Science, 8,* 535–543.

Bruer, J. T. (in press). Critical periods: Phenomena versus theories. In M. Mody & E. Silliman (Eds.), *Language impairment and reading disability: Interactions among brain, behavior, and experience*. New York: Guilford Press.

Burnham, D. K. (1986). Developmental loss of speech perception: Exposure to and experience with a first language. *Applied Psycholinguistics, 7*, 207–239.

Burnham, D. K., Kitamura, C., & Vollmer-Conner, U. (2002). What's new pussycat? On talking to babies and animals. *Science, 296*, 1435–1435.

Burns, T. C., Yoshida, K. A., Hill, K., & Werker, J. F. (2007). The development of phonetic representation in bilingual and monolingual infants. *Applied Psycholinguisics, 28*, 455–474.

Carlson, S. M, & Meltzoff, A. N. (2008). Bilingual experience and executive functioning in young children. *Developmental Science, 11*, 282–298.

Cheour, M., Ceponiene, R., Lehtokoski, A., Luuk, A., Allik, J., Alho, K., et al. (1998). Development of language-specific phoneme representations in the infant brain. *Nature Reviews Neuroscience 1*, 351–353.

Conboy, B. T. & Kuhl, P. K. (2007, April). ERP mismatch negativity effects in 11-month-old infants after exposure to Spanish. Paper presented at the Society for Research in Child Development Biennial Meeting, Boston, MA.

Conboy, B., Brooks, R., Taylor, M., Meltzoff, A., & Kuhl, P. (2008, March). *Joint engagement with language tutors predicts brain and behavioral responses to second-language phonetic stimuli.* Poster presented at the meeting of the International Conference on Infant Studies, Vancouver, BC.

Conboy, B. T., Rivera-Gaxiola, M., Klarman, L., Aksoylu, E., & Kuhl, P. K. (2005). Associations between native and nonnative speech sound discrimination and language development at the end of the first year. In A. Brugos, M. R. Clark-Cotton, & S. Ha (Eds.), *Supplement to the Proceedings of the 29th Boston University Conference on Language Development.* http://www.bu.edu//linguistics/appliedBUCLD/supp29.html

Conboy, B. T., Sommerville, J., & Kuhl, P. K. (in press). Cognitive control factors in speech perception at 11 months. *Developmental Science.*

D'Odorico, L., Carubbi, S., Salerni, N., & Calvo, V. (2001). Vocabulary development in Italian children: A longitudinal evaluation of quantitative and qualitative aspects. *Journal of Child Language, 28*, 351–372.

Dalston, R. M. (1975). Acoustic characteristics of English /w,r,l/ spoken correctly by young children and adults. *Journal of the Acoustical Society of America, 57*, 462–469.

Dehaene-Lambertz, G., Hertz-Pannier, L., Dubois, J., Meriaux, S., Roche, A., Sigman, M., et al. (2006). Functional organization of perisylvian activation during presentation of sentences in preverbal infants. *Proceedings of the National Academy of Sciences USA, 103*, 14240–14245.

Diamond, A., Werker, J. F., & Lalonde, C. (1994). Toward understanding commonalities in the development of object search, detour navigation, categorization, and speech perception. In G. Dawson & K. W. Fischer (Eds.), *Human behavior and the developing brain* (pp. 380–426). New York: Guilford Press.

Doupe, A. J. & Kuhl, P. K. (1999). Birdsong and human speech: Common themes and mechanisms. *Annual Review of Neuroscience, 22*, 567–631.

Eimas, P., Siqueland, E., Jusczyk, P., & Vigorito, J. (1971). Speech perception in infants. *Science, 171*, 303–306.

Eilers, R. E., Wilson, W. R., & Moore, J. M. (1977). Developmental changes in speech discrimination in infants. *Journal of Speech and Hearing Research, 20*, 766–780.

Fant, G. (1973). *Speech sounds and features.* Cambridge, MA: MIT Press.

Fenson, L., Bates, E., Dale, P., Goodman, J., Reznick, J. S., & Thal, D. (2000). Measuring variability in early child language: Don't shoot the messenger. *Child Development, 71*, 323–328.

Fenson, L., Dale, P., Reznick, J., Bates, E., Thal, D., & Pethick, S. (1994). Variability in early communicative development. *Monographs of the Society for Research in Child Development, Serial, 59*(5, Serial No. 242).

Fernald, A., Perfors, A., & Marchman, V. A. (2006). Picking up speed in understanding: Speech processing efficiency and vocabulary growth across the 2nd year. *Developmental Psychology, 42*, 98–116.

Flege, J. E., Takagi, N., & Mann, V. (1995). Japanese adults can learn to produce English /r/ and /l/ accurately. *Language & Speech, 38*, 25–55.

Flege, J. E., Yeni-Komshian, G., & Liu, S. (1999). Age constraints on second-language acquisition. *Journal of Memory and Language, 41*, 78–104.

Friederici, A. D. & Wessels, J. M. I. (1993). Phonotactic knowledge of word boundaries and its use in infant speech perception. *Perception & Psychophysics, 54*, 287–295.

Ganger, J. & Brent, M. R. (2004). Reexamining the vocabulary spurt. *Developmental Psychology, 40*, 621–632.

Godfrey, J., Syrdal-Lasky, A., Millay, K., & Knox, C. (1981). Performance of dyslexic children on speech perception tests. *Journal of Experimental Child Psychology, 32*, 401–424.

Goodsitt, J., Morgan, J., & Kuhl, P. K. (1993). Perceptual strategies in prelingual speech segmentation. *Journal of Child Language, 20*, 229–252.

Goodz, N. S. (1989). Parental language mixing in bilingual families. *Infant Mental Health Journal, 10*, 25–44.

Gopnik, A. & Meltzoff, A. N. (1987). The development of categorization in the second year and its relation to other cognitive and linguistic developments. *Child Development, 58*, 1523–1531.

Hess, E. H. (1973). *Imprinting: Early experience and the developmental psychobiology of attachment.* New York: Von Nostrand Reinhold Company.

Hillenbrand, J., Getty, L., Clark, M., & Wheeler, K. (1995). Acoustic characteristics of American English vowels. *Journal of the Acoustical Society of America, 97*, 3099–3111.

Hollich, G., Hirsh-Pasek, K., & Golinkoff, R. (2000). Breaking the language barrier: An emergentist coalition model for the origins of word learning. *Monographs of the Society for Research in Child Development, Serial, 65*(3, Serial No. 262).

Huttenlocher, J., Haight, W., Bryk, A., Seltzer, M., & Lyons, T. (1991). Early vocabulary growth: Relation to language input and gender. *Developmental Psychology, 27*, 236–248.

Imada, T., Zhang, Y. Cheour, M., Taulu, S., Ahonen, A., & Kuhl, P. K. (2006). Infant speech perception activates Broca's area: A developmental magnetoenceohalography study. *Neuroreport, 17*, 957–962.

Iverson, P., Kuhl, P. K., Akahane-Yamada, R., Diesch, E., Tohkura, Y. Kettermann, A., et al. (2003). A perceptual interference account of acquisition difficulties for non-native phonemes. *Cognition, 87*, B47–B57.

Johnson, J. & Newport, E. (1989). Critical period effects in second language learning: The influence of maturation state on the acquisition of English as a second language. *Cognitive Psychology, 21*, 60–99.

Jusczyk, P. (1997). *The discovery of spoken language.* Cambridge, MA: MIT Press.

Kraus, N., McGee, T., Carrell, T., Zecker, S., Nicol, T., & Koch, D. (1996). Auditory neurophysiologic responses and discrimination deficits in children with learning problems. *Science, 273,* 971–973.

Kuhl, P. K. (1980). Perceptual constancy for speech-sound categories in early infancy. In G. H. Yeni-Komshian, J. F. Kavanagh, & C. A. Ferguson (Eds.), *Child Phonology: Vol. 2. Perception* (pp. 41–66). New York: Academic Press.

Kuhl, P. K. (1992). Psychoacoustics and speech perception: Internal standards, perceptual anchors, and prototypes. In L. A. Werner & E. W. Rubel (Eds.), *Developmental psychoacoustics* (pp. 293–332). Washington, DC: American Psychological Association.

Kuhl, P. K. (1994). Learning and representation in speech and language. *Current Opinion in Neurobiology, 4,* 812–822.

Kuhl, P. K. (1998). The development of speech and language. In T. J. Carew, R. Menzel, & C. J. Shatz (Eds.), *Mechanistic relationships between development and learning* (pp. 53–73). New York: Wiley.

Kuhl, P. K. (2000). A new view of language acquisition. *Proceedings of the National Academy of Sciences USA, 97*(22), 11850–11857.

Kuhl, P. K. (2004). Early language acquisition: Cracking the speech code. *Nature Reviews Neuroscience, 5,* 831–843.

Kuhl, P. K. (2007). Is speech learning "gated" by the social brain? *Developmental Science, 10,* 110–120.

Kuhl, P. K., Andruski, J., Christovich, I., Chistovich, L., Kozhevnikova, E., Ryskina, V., et al. (1997). Cross-language analysis of phonetic units in language addressed to infants. *Science, 277,* 684–686.

Kuhl, P. K., Coffey-Corina, S., Padden, D., & Dawson, G. (2005). Links between social and linguistic processing of speech in preschool children with autism: Behavioral and electrophysiological evidence. *Developmental Science, 8,* 1–12.

Kuhl, P. K., Coffey-Corina, S., & Padden, D. (2007). Effects of short-term foreign-language exposure on brain measures of phonetic perception in infants. Manuscript in preparation.

Kuhl, P. K., Conboy, B. T., Coffey-Corina, S., Padden, D., Rivera-Gaxiola, M., & Nelson, T. (2008). Phonetic learning as a pathway to language: New data and native language magnet theory expanded (NLM-e). *Philosophical Transactions of the Royal Society B, 363,* 979–1000.

Kuhl, P. K., Conboy, B. T., Padden, D., Nelson, T., & Pruitt, J. (2005). Early speech perception and later language development: Implications for the "critical period." *Language Learning and Development, 1,* 237–264.

Kuhl, P. K. & Meltzoff, A. N. (1996). Infant vocalizations in response to speech: Vocal imitation and developmental change. *Journal of the Acoustic Society of America, 100,* 2425–2438.

Kuhl, P. K., Stevens, E., Hayashi, A., Deguchi, T., Kiritani, S., & Iverson, P. (2006). Infants show facilitation for native language phonetic perception between 6 and 12 months. *Developmental Science, 9,* 13–21.

Kuhl, P. K., Tsao, F.-M., & Liu, H.-M. (2003). Foreign-language experience in infancy: Effects of short-term exposure and social interaction on phonetic learning. *Proceedings of the National Academy of Science USA, 100,* 9096–9101.

Kuhl, P. K., Williams, K. A., Lacerda, F., Stevens, K. N., & Lindblom, B. (1992). Linguistic experience alters phonetic perception in infants by 6 months of age. *Science, 255,* 606–608.

Lacerda, F. (2006). Acoustic analysis of standard central Swedish /r/ and /l/. Manuscript in preparation.

Lalonde, C. & Werker, J. (1995). Cognitive influence on cross-language speech perception in infancy. *Infant Behavior and Development, 18,* 495–475.

Lenneberg, E. (1967). *Biological foundations of language.* New York: John Wiley & Sons.

Leonard, L., McGregor, K., & Allen, G. (1992). Grammatical morphology and speech perception in children with specific language impairment. *Journal of Speech and Hearing Research, 35,* 1076–1085.

Liu, H. -M., Kuhl, P. K., & Tsao, F.-M. (2003). An association between mothers' speech clarity and infants' speech discrimination skills. *Developmental Science, 6,* F1–F10.

Liu, H.-M, Tsao, F.-M., & Kuhl, P. K. (2007). Acoustic analysis of lexical tone in Mandarin infant-directed speech. *Developmental Psychology, 43,* 912–917.

Lotto, A. J., Sato, M., & Diehl, R. (2004). Mapping the task for the second language learner: The case of Japanese acquisition of /r/ and /l/. In J. Slitka, S. Manuel, & M. Matthies (Eds.), *From sound to sense: 50+ years of discoveries in speech communication* (pp. C381–C386). Cambridge, MA: MIT Press.

Lorenz, K. (1957). Companionship in bird life. In C. H. Schiller (Ed.), *Instinctive behavior: The development of a modern concept* (pp. 83–128). New York: International Universities Press.

Manis, R., McBride-Chang, C., Seidenberg, M., Keating, P., Doi, L., Munson, B., et al. (1997). Are speech perception deficits associated with developmental dyslexia? *Journal of Experimental Child Psychology, 66,* 211–235.

Mattys, S., Jusczyk, P., Luce, P., & Morgan, J. (1999). Phonotatic and prosodic effects on word segmentation in infants. *Cognitive Psychology, 38,* 465–494.

Maye, J., Werker, J., & Gerken, L. (2002). Infant sensitivity to distributional information can affect phonetic discrimination. *Cognition, 82,* B101–B111.

Molfese, D. (2000). Predicting dyslexia at 8 years of age using neonatal brain responses. *Brain and Language, 72,* 238–245.

Molfese, D. & Molfese, V. (1985). Electrophysiological indices of auditory discrimination in newborn infants: The bases for predicting later language development? *Infant Behavior and Development, 8,* 197–211.

Molfese, D. & Molfese, V. (1997). Discrimination of language skills at five years of age using event-related potentials recorded at birth. *Developmental Neuropsychology, 13,* 135–156.

Moon, C., Cooper, R. P., & Fifer, W. P. (1993). 2-day-olds prefer their native language. *Infant Behavior & Development, 16,* 495–500.

Moore, J. K. & Guan, Y. L. (2001). Cytoarchitectural and axonal maturation in human auditory cortex. *Journal of the Association for Research in Otolaryngology, 2,* 297–311.

Näätänen, R., Lehtokoski, A., Lennes, M., Cheour, M., Huotilainen, M., Iivonen, A., et al. (1997). Language-specific phoneme representations revealed by electric and magnetic brain responses. *Nature, 385,* 432– 434.

Newman, R. S., Bernstein Ratner, N., Jusczyk, A., Jusczyk, P. W., & Dow, K. A. (2006). Infants' early ability to segment the conversational speech signal predicts later language development: A retrospective analysis. *Developmental Psychology, 42,* 643–655.

Newport, E. L. & Aslin, R. N. (2004). Learning at a distance I. Statistical learning of non-adjacent dependencies. *Cognitive Psychology, 48*, 127–162.

Newport, E. L., Bavelier, D., & Neville, H. J. (2001). Critical thinking about critical periods: Perspectives on a critical period for language acquisition. In E. Dupoux (Ed.), *Language, brain, and cognitive development: Essays in honor of Jacques Mehlter* (pp. 481–502). Cambridge, MA: MIT Press.

Nittrouer, S. (2001). Challenging the notion of innate phonetic boundaries. *Journal of the Acoustical Society of America, 110*, 1598–1605.

Pang, E., Edmonds, G., Desjardins, R., Khan, S., Trainor, L., & Taylor, M. (1998). Mismatch negativity to speech stimuli in 8-month-old infants and adults. *International Journal of Psychophysiology, 29*, 227–236.

Perkell, J. S. & Klatt, D. H. (1976). *Invariance and variability in speech processes.* Hillsdale, NJ: Lawrence Erlbaum Associates.

Polka, L. & Bohn, O. S. (2003). Asymmetries in vowel perception. *Speech Communication, 41*, 221–231.

Polka, L., Jusczyk, P., & Rvachew, S. (1995). Methods for studying speech perception in infants and children. In W. Strange (Ed.), *Speech perception and linguistic experience: Issues in cross-language research* (pp. 49–89). Timonium, MD: York Press.

Polka, L. & Werker, J. F. (1994). Developmental changes in perception of nonnative vowel contrasts. *Journal of Experimental Psychology: Human Perception and Performance, 20*, 421–435.

Raudenbush, S. W., Bryk, A. S., & Congdon, R. (2005). *HLM-6: Hierarchical Linear and Nonlinear Modeling.* Lincolnwood, IL: Scientific Software International, Inc.

Reed, M. (1989). Speech perception and the discrimination of brief auditory cues in dyslexic children. *Journal of Experimental Child Psychology, 48*, 270–292.

Rivera-Gaxiola, M., Klarman, L., Garcia-Sierra, A., & Kuhl, P. K. (2005). Neural patterns to speech and vocabulary growth in American infants. *NeuroReport, 16*, 495–498.

Rivera-Gaxiola, M., & Romo, H. (2006, October). *Infant head-start learners: Brain and behavioral measures and family assessments.* Paper presented at From Synapse to Schoolroom: The Science of Learning. NSF Science of Learning Centers Satellite Symposium, Society for Neuroscience Annual Meeting, Atlanta, GA.

Rivera-Gaxiola, M., Silva-Pereyra, J., & Kuhl, P. K. (2005). Brain potentials to native- and non-native speech contrasts in seven and eleven-month-old American infants. *Developmental Science, 8*, 162–172.

Saffran, J., Aslin, R., & Newport, E. (1996). Statistical learning by 8-month old infants. *Science, 274*, 1926–1928.

Seidenberg, M.S. & Zevlin, J. D. (2006). Connectionist models in developmental cognitive neuroscience: Critical periods and the paradox of success. In Y. Munakata & M. Johnson (Eds.), *Attention & performance XXI: Processes of change in brain and cognitive development* (pp. 585–612). Oxford, England: Oxford University Press.

Silven, M., Kouvo, A., Haapakoski, M., Lahteenmaki, V., & Kuhl, P. K. (2004, July). *Language learning in infants from mono- and bilingual families.* Paper presented at the 18th Biennal International Society for the Study of Behavioral Development (ISSBD) Conference, Ghent, Belgium.

Stager, C. & Werker, J. (1997). Infants listen for more phonetic detail in speech perception than in word-learning tasks. *Nature, 388*, 381–382.

Stark, R. & Heinz, J. (1996). Perception of stop consonants in children with expressive and receptive-expressive language impairments. *Journal of Speech and Hearing Research, 39*, 676–686.

Sundara, M., Polka, L., & Genesee, F. (2006). Language-experience facilitates discrimination of /d-ðethe/ in monolingual and bilingual acquisition of English. *Cognition, 100*, 369–388.

Sundara, M., Polka, L., & Molnar, M. (in press). Development of coronal stop perception: Bilingual infants keep pace with their monolingual peers. *Cognition.*

Sussman, J. (1993). Perception of formant transition cues to place of articulation in children with language impairments. *Journal of Speech and Hearing Research, 36*, 1286–1299.

Swingley, D. & Aslin, R. N. (2002). Lexical neighborhoods and the word-form representations of 14-month-olds. *Psychological Science, 13*, 480–484.

Swingley, D. & Aslin, R. N. (2007). Lexical competition in young children's word learning. *Cognitive Psychology, 54*, 99–132

Tallal, P. & Piercy, M. (1974). Developmental aphasia: Rate of auditory processing and selective impairment of consonant perception. *Neuropsychologia, 12*, 83–93.

Tallal, P. & Stark, R. (1981). Speech acoustic cue discrimination abilities of normally developing and language impaired children. *Journal of the Acoustical Society of America, 69*, 568–574.

Thal, D. (1991). Language and cognition in normal and late-talking toddlers. *Topics in Language Disorders, 11*, 33–42.

Tomasello, M. & Farrar, M. J. (1984). Cognitive bases of lexical development: Object permanence and relational words. *Journal of Child Language, 11*, 477–493.

Tomasello, M. & Farrar, M. J. (1986). Joint attention and early language. *Child Development, 57*, 1454–1463.

Tsao, F.-M., Liu, H.-M., & Kuhl, P. K. (2004). Speech perception in infancy predicts language development in the second year of life: a longitudinal study. *Child Development, 75*, 1067–1084.

Tsao, F.-M., Liu, H.-M., & Kuhl, P. K. (2006). Perception of native and nonnative affricate-fricative contrasts: Cross-language tests on adults and infants. *Journal of the Acoustical Society of America. 120*, 2285–2294.

Vallabha, G. K. & McClelland, J. L. (2007). Success and failure of new speech category learning in adulthood: Consequences of learned Hebbian attractors in topographic maps. *Cognitive, Affective, & Behavioral Neuroscience, 7*, 53–73.

Weber-Fox, C. M. & Neville, H. J. (1999). Functional neural subsystems are differentially affected by delays in second language immersion: ERP and behavioral evidence in bilinguals. In D. Birdsong (Ed.), *Second language acquisition and the critical period hypothesis*, pp. 23–38. Mahwah, NJ: Lawrence Erlbaum and Associates.

Werker, J., Fennell, C., Corcoran, K., & Stager, C. (2002). Infant's ability to learn phonetically similar words: Effects of age and vocabulary size. *Infancy, 3*, 1–30.

Werker, J. F., Pons, F., Dietrich, C., Sachiyo, K., Fais, L., & Amano, S. (2007). Infant-directed speech supports phonetic category learning in English and Japanese. *Cognition, 103*, 147–162.

Werker, J. & Tees, R. (1984). Cross-language speech perception: Evidence for perceptual reorganization during the first year of life. *Infant Behavior and Development, 7*, 49–63.

Werker, J. & Tees, R. (1987). Speech perception in severely disabled and average reading children. *Canadian Journal of Psychology, 41*, 48–61.

Werker, J. & Tees, R. C. (2005). Speech perception as a window for understanding plasticity and commitment in language systems of the brain. *Developmental Psychobiology, 46*, 233–234.

Werker, J. & Yeung, H. H. (2005). Infant speech perception bootstraps word learning. *Trends in Cognitive Sciences, 9*, 519–527.

West, M. & King, A. (1988). Female visual displays affect the development of male song in the cowbird. *Nature, 334*, 244–246.

Yeni-Komshian, G., Flege, J. E., & Liu, S. (1999). Pronunciation proficiency in the first and second languages of Korean–English bilinguals. *Bilingualism: Language and Cognition, 3*, 131–150.

Yoshida, K. A., Pons, F., Cady, J. C., & Werker, J. F. (2006, June). Distributional learning and attention in phonological development. Paper presented at International Conference on Infant Studies, Kyoto Japan.

13

Early Word Learning and Categorization
Methodological Issues and Recent Empirical Evidence

Leslie B. Cohen and Jason Brunt

The ability to use words to stand for object categories is one of the most fundamental language-related behaviors. It is an ability upon which the use of language is founded, and it is one of the first signs of language development that parents witness in their children. Infants may use their first words as early as 12 months of age, and by 24 months of age most children are masters of this ability. They may then make their first forays into more complex linguistic behaviors like sentence construction that depend on the ability to assign words to object categories. It may be surprising, then, that the ability of researchers to experimentally explore the earliest stages of the relationship between words and categories has itself been so late in developing.

METHODS OF ASSESSING WORD–OBJECT ASSOCIATIONS

Within the last decade, two complementary methods have been used to explore infants' ability to associate labels[1] with objects below the age of (18) months: the switch design (Werker, Cohen, Lloyd, Casasola, & Stager, 1998) and the intermodal preferential looking paradigm (Schafer & Plunkett, 1998). Werker et al. employed the switch design to test infants' ability to associate words with objects.

The Switch Design

In the switch design, infants are habituated to two word–object pairs, one pair per trial. Once they are fully habituated to the two pairs (i.e., looking time falls below a predefined criterion), they are shown a novel pairing that consists of a word from one of the habituation pairs and the object from the other pair.

If infants' looking time increases to this novel pairing it must be because during habituation, they successfully associated the words and objects that were paired together. Werker et al. (1998) found that 14-month-olds but not 12-month-olds would recover attention to the switched pair.

The Intermodal Preferential Looking Paradigm

Schafer and Plunkett (1998) employed the second design, the intermodal preferential looking (IPL) paradigm with 15-month-olds to test for the ability to associate a word with an object. This design consists of a familiarization phase in which two objects are repeatedly paired with a different label, followed by a test phase in which the two objects are simultaneously presented to the infants while one of the familiar labels is presented. Preferential looking by the infants toward the familiar object previously paired with that label during the test phase is usually interpreted as evidence that they successfully associated the word and object.

Although these studies, and many others that use variations of these paradigms, indicate that infants can associate a word with an individual object by simple repetitive pairing of the two in a controlled laboratory situation, they do not directly inform us as to the types of relationships infants can form between words and whole categories. Exploration of this issue is the focus of this chapter.

TYPES OF WORD–CATEGORY RELATIONSHIPS

One of the traditional, fundamental assumptions about labels is that most refer to categories (Markman, 1992). However, a recent explosion in early word-learning research illustrates that this simple assumption is not quite sufficient for a description of early language behavior. There are, in fact, different types of categories to which labels can be applied. Several researchers have explored (or begun to explore) the developing relationship between labels and a variety of categories, including the following:

- Categories of properties (Waxman, 1999; Waxman & Booth, 2001; Waxman & Markow, 1998)
- Categories of actions (Casasola & Cohen, 2000; Golinkoff, Jacquet, Hirsh-Pasek, & Nandakumar, 1996; Tomasello & Kruger, 1992)
- Categories of spatial relationships, such as the following:
  - Support and containment (Casasola, 2005)
  - Tight and loose fit (McDonough, Choi, & Mandler, 2002)
  - Object individuation (Xu, 2002; Xu, Cote, & Baker, 2005)

The studies described herein focus on what is the most common interpretation of an early word–category relationship, the relationship between a word and a category of objects (see also Balaban & Waxman, 1997; Booth & Waxman, 2002; Fulkerson & Haaf, 2003; Nazzi & Gopnik, 2001; Roberts, 1997; Roberts & Jacob, 1991; Waxman & Markow, 1998).

THE RELATIONSHIP BETWEEN WORDS AND OBJECT CATEGORIES

Infant research on the relationship between words and object categories has tended to examine one of two types of issues: (1) how the presence of labels affects the ability of infants to categorize; and (2) how infants learn to associate labels with categories. We shall discuss each in turn.

How Labels Affect Categorization

A few researchers have investigated how the mere presence of labels influences an infant's ability to form categories. Some have argued that the mere presence of labels may direct the attention of infants as young as 9 months of age toward what is common among a set of objects, thereby facilitating categorization (Balaban & Waxman, 1997; Roberts, 1997). Robinson and Sloutsky (2004), on the other hand, hypothesize a dominant role for auditory processing in infancy and suggest that the presence of labels will draw attention away from a visual processing task, thereby inhibiting categorization. Evaluating these two hypotheses and investigating contexts in which either might be correct is a task for present-day research. Later in this chapter we present the results from a set of recent experiments that examine this issue directly.

How Labels and Categories of Objects Become Associated

The other issue relates to the attachment of labels (i.e., words) to object categories. Werker et al. (1998) in their habituation switch studies have mentioned the distinction between association and reference. There is an important difference, the authors argue, between learning that a word is associated with a category of objects and learning that a word stands for, or refers to, an object. The former can arguably be performed with general learning mechanisms; the latter involves something more linguistic in nature. Researchers are only very recently attempting to arrive at methods for distinguishing between these two types of relationships and how they might change with development. Later in this chapter we also discuss recent research we have been conducting related to this issue.

METHODOLOGICAL ISSUES IN INFANT LABELING RESEARCH

Before we describe either type of study, we must mention some important methodological issues confronting infant word learning researchers and how we chose to deal with them.

Ecological Validity versus Experimental Control

Among the studies of infant label learning, researchers have developed methods that vary greatly along the continuum between ecological validity and experimental control. Leaning toward the end of ecological validity, Woodward and Hoyne (1999) employed an interactive technique to study the role that both words and sounds might play for infants at 13 months and 20 months in a labeling situation. In their procedure, real objects that infants could hold and manipulate were used as stimuli. Training trials were interspersed with trials that used familiar objects, and experimenters continued a relatively constant dialogue with the participants. Test trials were embedded in a natural play setting. Woodward and Hoyne found that 13-month-olds learned both word–object and sound–object correspondences. On the other hand, 20-month-olds learned only the word–object correspondences.

An interactive procedure, like the one used by Woodward and Hoyne (1999), has obvious advantages, providing a variety of cues during both training and testing phases with which infants would be familiar and upon which to base their learning and judgments. Infants can pay attention to the experimenter's hand movements, eye gaze, and voice inflection to decide when and where to direct their own attention during the training phase and have a similar set of cues to determine when to respond during the test phase. In addition, the natural play setting and experimenter involvement can help to regulate infants' attention and mood, allowing them to remain involved in a task through completion. However, even with careful counterbalancing of object presentation, and with scripts for controlling experimenter voicing, the experimental manipulations aren't as controlled as they might otherwise be. The experimenter, of necessity, is producing the experimental manipulation and inadvertent experimenter bias is at least a possibility.

At the other end of the validity spectrum, some researchers opt for more highly controlled, though perhaps less ecologically valid, methods. Balaban and Waxman (1997), for instance, used a highly controlled familiarization–preferential looking technique to test the effects of labels on infant categorization. They presented 9-month-old infants with a series of slides upon which were depicted line drawings of different exemplars of a single category (e.g., rabbits). Infants heard either a label or a tone during this phase. In a test phase, infants were presented with two slides: (1) a novel exemplar of the trained category; and (2) an exemplar from a new category. Their results suggested that the presence of labels, but not tones, facilitated categorization. In this procedure, visual stimuli were presented on slides, and auditory stimuli were presented via prerecorded voice. In this way, all infants with all experimenters received the same stimuli, presented in the same manner. An experimental setting such as this allows for great control and isolation of the experimental factors of interest. For Balaban and Waxman, this was repeated association of labels and objects. Such control does not come without cost, however. This cost is ecological validity. It is highly unlikely that infants will encounter a word-learning situation like this outside of a psychological laboratory. If factors are additive (such as has been suggested of social cues and associative repetition; Baldwin, Markman, Bill, Desjardins, et al., 1996) or are otherwise dependent on complex environmental cues, then an effect may be difficult to find, and the procedure may underestimate the infants' ability. Nevertheless, in our own research we have chosen to be conservative and have opted for procedures that emphasize tight experimental control.

The Importance of Social Referencing

A second methodological issue confronting researchers of infant label learning is that of social referencing. Baldwin et al. (1996), in particular, argued for the necessity of a social role in label learning by infants. They argued that temporal contiguity alone will not be enough for infants to build a label–object relationship. Infants understand the social nature of language, they argued, and any label learning task would necessarily involve a person delivering the label in the physical presence of the infant learner. This seems to be at odds with both Werker et al. (1998) and Schafer and Plunkett (1998), who found that infants aged 14 and 15 months could associate a label with an object even when the label was delivered by computer, without a human labeler in the room. Others have found that between the ages of 12 and 20 months, infants come increasingly to depend on humans in a labeling situation as a source of input (Fulkerson & Haaf, 2003; Woodward & Hoyne, 1999) and for direction of attention (Hollich, Hirsh-Pasek, Tucker, & Golinkoff, 2000). So though the value of social interaction in label-learning tasks is still an open question for young infants and is an issue in need of more research, researchers can safely use paradigms that isolate factors such as temporal contiguity, stimulus salience, and prior knowledge, remaining confident that infants can learn label–object associations in the stripped-down experimental setting. Researchers should keep in mind, however, that it is possible to examine social referencing factors, as Briganti and Cohen (2007) and Houston-Price, Plunkett, and Duffy (2006) are doing, even in a highly controlled experimental setting.

Novelty versus Familiarity Effects

Another methodological issue, disentangling familiarity from novelty effects, has plagued infant researchers for years. At the root of problem lies the fact that unless infants are sufficiently familiarized or habituated to a stimulus during the training phase of an experiment, one cannot predict if they will respond more to a novel or to a familiar stimulus in the test phase. Some studies simply want to demonstrate that infants can discriminate between two test items. For these studies a significant preference for either the familiar or the novel test item is sufficient. Infant categorization studies, however, are a bit more complicated. It is presumed (or sometimes specifically tested) that infants can discriminate between both within-category and out-of-category items from one another. Nevertheless, when infants are sufficiently trained with multiple instances of items from within a single category and then are tested for generalization with a novel within-category item versus a novel out-of-category item, it is assumed they will respond more to the out-of-category item. Such a response indicates the infant has learned the category and is treating the within-category test item as equivalent to the other within-category training items. Thus, a demonstration of infant categorization presumes the infants are sufficiently trained that they will exhibit a preference for novelty and will respond more to an out-of-category novel stimulus than to a within-category novel stimulus. One can then conduct a study that includes labels, sounds, and music during the training phase to see if the categorization is facilitated or impeded (e.g., Balaban & Waxman, 1997; Fulkerson & Half, 2003; Roberts, 1997).

One additional complication should be addressed. Inclusion of, for example, a word or sound during training may not only influence the infants' categorization; it may also come to refer to the category being trained. If that word or sound is also presented in the test phase, it could serve as an instruction to the infant to look at the novel *within-category* item. If that happens, it would counteract the infant's normal tendency to look longer at the novel out-of-category item, and it could obscure any evidence of categorization. One of our experiments to be presented later in this chapter examines how, over age and over trials, this referential function of a word can come to obscure evidence of categorization.

Category Knowledge Prior to the Experiment

A final methodological issue, infants' prior experience with object categories, is one we feel is potentially of vital importance, but it is rarely mentioned in the literature. This is somewhat surprising given that many studies purport to measure infants' ability to form categories of training stimuli or to generalize a feature from a training category to a new member of that category. Any knowledge infants already have of that category before they enter into the experiment is a potential source of interference for learning new information about that category. Therefore, a primary question that should be answered before designing any study on this topic is whether learning the category will be something the infants are expected to do during the task or is something infants should have done before coming into the laboratory. There are at least two relatively simple methods with which researchers can deal with this issue. One is to use artificial categories. This is an approach taken by Hollich et al. (2000). By designing their own stimuli, a researcher can be certain that participants will not have encountered them before and that any categorization will be done during the task. We describe in detail one such study shortly. Researchers also run the risk, however, of creating stimuli that do not reflect real-world complexity and category variation—a step away from ecological validity. A second method for dealing with past experience is to attempt to assess infants' prior exposure to categories. Schafer, Plunkett, and Harris (1999) employed a parent-response questionnaire to assess infants' prior experience with a set of objects. They were interested in the effect of label possession on infants' attentional preferences. They were able to choose from a single set of objects two objects for each participant with which that participant had approximately equal levels of experience. Having controlled for past experience, they were more secure in their finding that infants were more likely to look toward an object for which they also possessed a label than to an object for which they did not possess a label. Later in this chapter we describe a more elaborate version of this parental questionnaire, called the Baby Label and Object Category Knowledge (BLOCK) inventory, which we are developing and have begun to use to assess infants prior experience with categories and their knowledge of labels for those categories.

RECENT RESEARCH EVIDENCE

The Effects of Labels on Infant Categorization

As we mentioned earlier, some debate continues regarding the effect of presenting labels during infant category learning. Balaban and Waxman (1997), Waxman (2003), and Waxman and Markow (1995) maintain that labels highlight the commonalities between objects thus facilitating the categorization process. In fact, these works state that words serve as "invitations" to form new categories and concepts. Robinson and Sloutsky (2004), on the other hand, provide evidence that auditory processing predominates in infancy and thus the presence of labels, particularly novel ones, should interfere with visual categorization. Even if labels facilitate infant categorization, what is the locus of that facilitation? Does the presence of labels merely increase the general attentiveness of the infants, or does it have a more specific effect on category learning? Furthermore, in previous label-categorization studies the visual stimuli have been animals or objects that infants may have seen before, making it difficult to determine if the familiarization process produced entirely new categories for the infant or merely reactivated existing categories.

Plunkett, Hu, and Cohen (2008) recently completed a series of studies that address these issues. These studies were based on a classic set of experiments reported 20 years earlier by Younger (1985). Younger had examined 10-month-old infants using a visual preferential looking design. Her infants were familiarized to a set of line drawings of animals such as those shown as training stimuli in Figure 13.1. The animals differed from one another on four features: spread of ears, length of neck, width of tail, and length of legs. An individual infant was familiarized to either the set representing the broad condition or the set representing the narrow condition. In the broad condition the values of the four features were uncorrelated. That is, wide ears were just as likely to occur with a long neck as a short neck and with a wide or narrow tail and with long and short legs. In the narrow condition these values were correlated so that narrow ears tended to go with a long neck, a wide tail, and short legs and vice versa. Younger hypothesized that infants in the broad condition should form one general category that encompasses all eight training animals, whereas infants in the narrow condition should form two specific categories that take into account the pattern of correlations among the eight training animals. Younger predicted that if infants had formed one general category, then when given preference trials with the test stimuli shown in Figure 13.1, they should find animal 3333 to be the most familiar, since it would be the average and most representative animal in the set, and therefore they should look longer at either 1111 or 5555 than at 3333. On the other hand, if infants had formed two more specific categories, then 1111

Training Stimuli

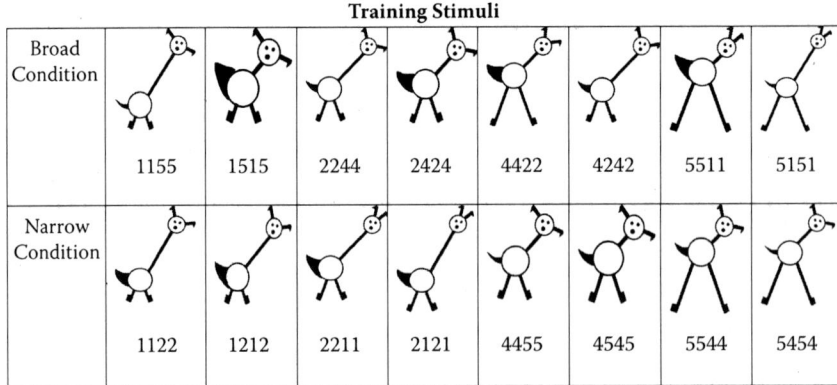

Test Stimuli

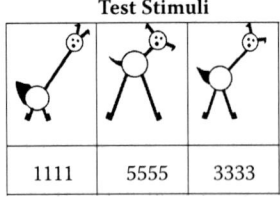

Figure 13.1 Stimuli used in categorization study.

and 5555 would be more representative of one of those categories. In this case 3333 should fall between the two categories, should be more novel, and should be looked at longer than 1111 or 5555. Those were just the results Younger obtained, and they showed unequivocally that one could train 10-month-old infants in a single, short, experimental session to learn either one or two object categories depending upon the correlational structure of the items in the categories.

Plunkett et al.'s (2008) first step was an attempt to replicate Younger's (1985) results some 20 years later, using more sophisticated stimulus presentation methods and more precise looking-time measures. Testing 10-month-old infants with the same animal pictures Younger had used, Plunkett et al. also found that if the infants had been given the broad training condition (Experiment 1), they looked significantly less in the test (44.39%) at 3333 than at 1111 or 5555, but if given the narrow training condition (Experiment 2) the infants looked significantly greater at (56.14%) at 3333 in the test. Thus, the present results, as had Younger's original data, demonstrated that 10-month-old infants can learn either one or two new perceptual categories in a single experimental session depending upon the correlations among feature values of the items.

The next step was to see if adding labels during the training phase would affect this learning. In Experiment 3, Plunkett et al. (2008) replicated Experiment 2 but added the phrases, "Look dax" and "Look rif," presented in infant-directed speech during each familiarization trial. Each label was correlated with one of the two narrow categories and was meant to signify that category. No labels were presented on the test trials. The results were essentially the same as in Experiment 2. Infants looked significantly greater than chance (54.35%) at 3333, indicating that they had formed two categories. There was no direct evidence that the presence of a label during familiarization facilitated their categorization since the infants performed the same as they had in Experiment 2 when there was no label. But the evidence from Experiment 3 does run counter to the Robinson and Sloutsky (2004) position that the presence of novel auditory labels should interfere with object categorization.

Experiment 4 was the same as Experiment 3 except that the two labels were uncorrelated with the object categories. Infants still heard, "Look dax" or "Look rif," on each familiarization trial, but which of the two labels they heard was decided randomly and not a function of the category assignment of the object. In this case the labels did disrupt or interfere with categorization and infants' test performance dropped to chance (50.23%).

Finally, in Experiment 5 infants received the same "narrow" stimuli as in Experiments 2, 3, and 4, but in this case they just heard a single label throughout all familiarization. In this case, they reversed what they had done in Experiments 2 and 3 and looked significantly less (45.75%) at 3333. In other words, they performed as the infants had in Experiment 1. The presence of a single label seemed to produce a single broad category even though the visual objects met the conditions for two narrow categories. These results provide a strong indication that the presence of novel labels can have a major influence on 10-month-old infants' acquisition of new object categories. The labels controlled whether the infants formed two narrow categories, no category at all, or one broad category, and it should be remembered that these results all occurred within one highly controlled 10-minute laboratory session. Thus, even before infants start to produce their first words, labeling can have a decisive impact on the way they learn novel categories. This impact goes beyond simply increasing infants' attentiveness; it shows they were sensitive to the correlation between words and category structure at 10 months of age.

The Effects of Past Experience on Label Assignment

Another issue potentially related to the relationship between labels and categorization is infants' past experience with a category for which a label is to be learned. We've already seen that the presence of a novel label can have a major effect on the categorization behavior of infants and that processing categories and processing labels are not completely independent processes. It stands to reason, then, that if infants enter into a word-learning task having already become familiar with the categories they will encounter, then the task with which they will be confronted may be qualitatively different from one in which labels and categories are to be learned simultaneously. Generally, the approach to this issue has been to try to control for past experience, usually by using novel objects and categories. Very few attempts have been made to measure past experience with test objects or to treat past experience as an independent variable in tests of labeling and categorization. Sufficient familiarity with stimulus categories may reduce task demands and may lessen the effects of auditory interference that were suggested by Robinson and Sloutsky (2004), increasing the likelihood that infants will learn to associate novel labels with the category. On the other hand, if an infant comes into a word-learning test already possessing a label for the object category, then according to some word-learning principles it may be more difficult to associate another novel label with that same category (Markman, 1992).

Brunt, Gora, and Cohen (2005) recently developed the BLOCK parent questionnaire to measure infants' prior experience with a set of objects and possession of labels for those objects. We then ran two experiments to test for the effects of prior experience on infants' ability to notice changes in either the object or a simultaneously presented novel label and their ability to associate novel labels with those objects.

The BLOCK questionnaire consists of 3 questions for each of 45 object categories. The questions and items are arranged such that parents answer 2 experience questions for each of the 45 items and then answer a label question for each item. The 2 questions of experience that parents answer are designed to measure both the frequency with which a child encounters members of a given object category and the variation among the members within a category that a child encounters. In addition, parents respond whether their infant comprehends a label for each of the categories.

For each infant, the BLOCK gave us a measure of past experience with each of 45 categories of objects. We were then able to treat past experience as a true independent variable in a set of word-learning experiments by randomly assigning infants to different levels of previous experience and then by selecting exemplars from our set of 45 object categories that matched the criteria defining a given experience level. One of the key features for the BLOCK is its deliverability over the World Wide Web. Parents with Internet access completed the questionnaire from home at their convenience, and the investigators coded data and individualized stimulus sets before participants arrived at the laboratory. This increased the ease and convenience of participation and greatly reduced the amount of time parents spent at the laboratory.

The first study that was run in conjunction with the BLOCK was a habituation switch type of experiment designed to test whether prior experience with categories and possession of labels for the same categories would affect the ability of 13-month-old infants to associate novel labels with those categories. Infants were randomly assigned to one of three levels of prior experience: (1) high experience with a category and possession of a label for that category; (2) high experience with no label; and (3) low experience without a label. Parents then completed the BLOCK, and 2 objects from the list of 45 were chosen for each infant that fit the randomly assigned level of experience.

During the test, infants were habituated to two photographs (one each of the two stimulus objects) presented one at a time on a computer monitor. Each object was paired with a different novel label. When infant looking time fell below a preset criterion, infants were presented with three critical test trials: (1) a familiar object–label pairing from habituation; (2) a switch trial in which an object from one of the habituation pairs was paired with the label from the other pair; and (3) a final novel pair in which neither object nor label were familiar. As shown in the left-hand bars of Figure 13.2, the only group of infants that reliably increased looking time to the switch trial was the one that habituated quickly and had entered the task with both prior experience with the test objects and a label for those objects. If infants did not have prior experience with the test objects or did not already possess a label for the objects, they did not notice the switch in object–label pairing.

A second study was then run in an attempt to determine why some infants did not respond to the switch-test trial. In a habituation switch design, there are

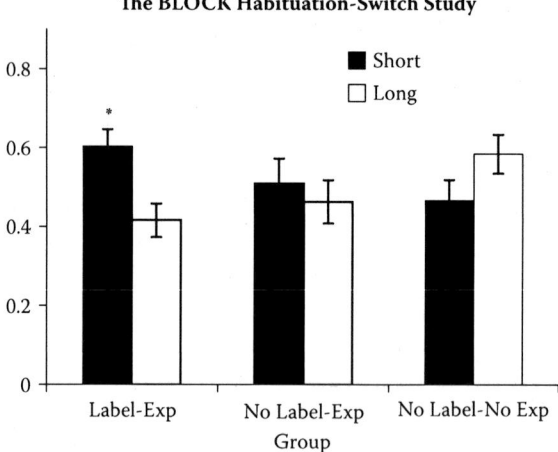

Figure 13.2   The BLOCK habituation switch study. Mean preference for novel versus familiar object for infants taking a short or long time to habituate in each of three levels of experience. Means designated with * are significantly above chance.

two reasons that infants might not respond to the switch trial. It may be because they did not notice the new combination of familiar parts (i.e., label and object), or it may be that they were no longer paying attention to one or the other of the parts. This second study was a simpler, habituation-change experiment. Infants were again randomly assigned to levels of previous experience, and stimulus objects were chosen on an individual basis according to parents' responses on the BLOCK. Three items were chosen for each infant for this experiment. Infants were habituated to two object–label pairs, just as in the first experiment. They were then tested with a familiar object–label pair, and a novel pairing in which either the label or the object from a habituation pair was replaced by a novel label or novel object. As can be seen in Figure 13.3, the only infants who looked reliably longer (greater than 50%) at a change in either the label or the object were those who entered the task with both prior experience with the objects and possession of a label for the objects. If infants entered the task without prior experience or without a label for the objects, then they did not notice the change in either the label or the object.

We interpret the results of these studies as indicative of an influence of prior experience on labeling behavior. Past experience with a category (perhaps importantly, past labeling experience with a category) may facilitate processing of labeling events related to exemplars of that category. As Schafer and Plunkett (1998) suggested, possession of a label for an object may add an extra dimension to the object, attracting processing resources.

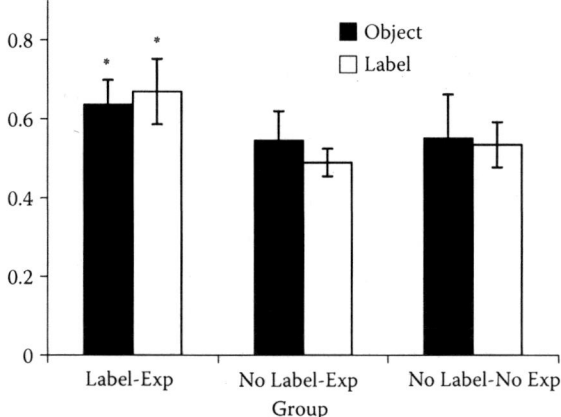

Figure 13.3   The habituation change study. Mean preference for novel versus familiar object for infants presented with an object change or a label change in each of
three levels of experience. Means designated with * are significantly above chance.

Novelty and Familiarity Effects and Labeling

In ongoing research to disentangle the effects of intermodal matching and
familiarity and novelty, we (Brunt & Cohen, 2006) have been using a method of
repeated paired comparisons similar to that used by Fantz (1964). We've taken
a cross-sectional approach to the study, selecting infants at 13 and 18 months of
age. Infants at these ages either are just younger than or are several months older
than the youngest of those who reliably learn labels in laboratory settings (Schafer
& Plunkett, 1998; Werker et al., 1998). In this study, we presented infants of both
ages with a different pair of objects on each of 20 8-second trials. One of the
objects on each trial was from a single category. The particular item changed from
trial to trial, but it was always an exemplar from that category. This, then, became
a familiar category item as the trials progressed. The other object on each trial
was drawn from a different category on every trial and thus remained novel. We
measured infants' preference for looking at the novel versus the familiar category
item across the 20 trials under one of 3 different acoustic stimulation conditions.
One third of the infants viewed the objects in silence, one third heard the same
novel label repeated during each trial, and one third heard a novel, nonlinguistic
noise repeated during each trial.

The results for both 13- and 18-month-olds are plotted in Figure 13.4. The
data represented in these figures are grouped into blocks of four trials. Across the
five blocks of trials, 13-month-olds developed a novelty preference, suggesting
that they were learning to treat the set of familiar items as a category. They did

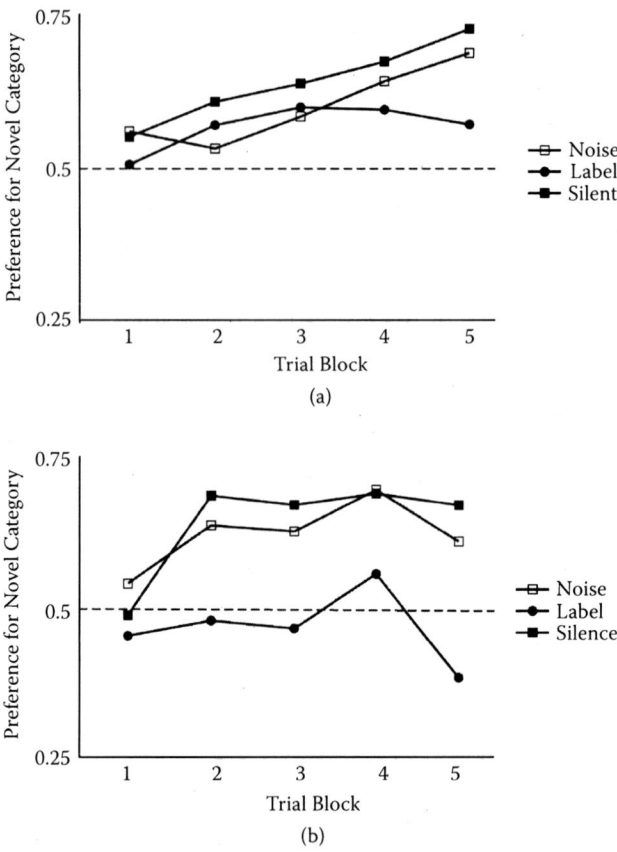

Figure 13.4 Novelty preference study with (A) 13-month-old and (B) 18-month-old infants. Mean preference for novel object across five blocks of four trials each for 13-month-old infants (A) and 18-month-old infants (B) in noise, label, and silence conditions.

not, however, show an overall difference between acoustic conditions. Looking preference does seem to diverge between groups in the last few of the 20 trials, so that on the final block (Trials 16 through 20), the difference between conditions is significant ($p < .05$) but doesn't seem to be very robust.

The 18-month-olds developed a novelty preference quite early—but only in the silence and noise conditions, not in the label condition. Furthermore, by the last block of trials, they exhibit a preference for the familiar object in the label condition (though this preference does not reach significance). The difference between groups was not only significant across the five blocks of trials ($p < .01$); it developed as early as the second block of four trials ($p < .05$).

These two studies present evidence that labeling can have a strong effect on novelty and familiarity preferences. The 18-months-olds, who are in the age range of the so-called word-learning spurt (Bates, Dale, & Thal, 1995), treated the presence of labels as a special case and adjusted their looking behavior accordingly. Furthermore, they treated the labeling situation differently from the noise situation, suggesting that by 18 months infants understand that labels play a special role in their environment. We (Brunt & Cohen, 2008) recently completed an additional study indicating that the lack of novelty preference by the 18-month-olds in the label condition was a more a result of referential assignment than of interference due to the complexity of the task.

The Importance of Social Referencing in Infant Word Learning

Word learning, by definition, is a social phenomenon, since words are themselves social stimuli. Some, however, would argue that word learning is much more of an interactive social process with social referencing cues (e.g., gaze, gesture, emotion, intonation) generated by parents and others playing major, if not essential, roles in how infants learn words and the referents for those words (e.g., Baldwin, 1991; Baldwin et al., 1996; Moore, Angelopoulos, & Bennett, 1999). On the other hand, others would assert that although these social referencing factors may be helpful to the infant they are by no means necessary for word learning (e.g. Bloom, 2000) and that associating words with objects or categories of objects follows domain general learning mechanisms that apply in both social and nonsocial situations (e.g., Houston-Price et al., 2006).

We believe resolution of this controversy will depend on an understanding of the myriad ways social cues produced by an adult can influence infants in word-learning tasks. First, the presence and interest of an adult may simply enhance an infant's attention to whatever situation currently is being experienced. Thus, it may indirectly facilitate word–object associations, if the infant happens to be highly attentive and in a learning state while in that type of task. Second, social cues such as an adult's direction of gaze or gesture can focus and direct an infant's attention to a particular location or object and can signify to the infant that the object in that location is important. Once again, this social facilitation may indirectly affect word learning. If a label or word happens to occur and is correlated with the presence of that object, this co-occurrence can facilitate the word–object association. Finally, social referencing factors such as looking and gesturing at an object in the presence of a word can have a more direct influence on word learning. These factors may not only signify that a particular object is important and where it is located but also may indicate that the word being presented refers specifically that particular object or object category.

Since this type of social referencing usually involves active social interaction between an adult and an infant, one might assume it would be very difficult, if not impossible, to differentiate among these potential influences in an experimental word-learning situation. Furthermore, the adult who is interacting with the infant in these situations usually knows the presumed effect of that interaction as well as the hypotheses being tested. Therefore, it is possible for subtle cues to be transmitted to the infant inadvertently that could affect the infant's performance in the word-learning task. Nevertheless, as we stated earlier, we believe one can design tightly controlled experimental procedures that eliminate any potential for experimenter bias yet at the same time that allow us to examine these different types of social influences in infant word learning.

Briganti and Cohen (2007) currently explores one such experiment using a variation of the IPL procedure. In this experiment 14- and 18-month-old infants are given 12 familiarization trials followed by 4 test trials. During each 11-second trial, on a plasma screen infants are shown two different novel rotating objects—one on the left and one on the right. During the familiarization trials they see an adult in the center of the screen turning, looking, and pointing at one of the objects, and they hear the phrase, "Look, lif," or "Look, neem." During the test trials the adult remains stationary and does not point at either of the objects. Direction of pointing and presentation of the novel labels are counterbalanced across both familiarization and test trials. Figure 13.5 provides examples of the stimuli presented to the infants.

Infants at each age are randomly assigned to one of two conditions. In the consistent condition, during familiarization a particular label is always associated with the adult's pointing at a particular object (e.g., *lif* occurs whenever the adult points to the yellow and green block, and *neem* occurs whenever the adult points to the red pointed object). In the inconsistent condition infants view exactly the same videos and hear the same labels, but the particular label presented on each trial is uncorrelated with object pointed to by the adult.

If social referencing (i.e., looking and pointing) actually facilitates word learning, in the test infants in the consistent condition should tend to look longer at the object being labeled than should infants in the inconsistent condition. On the other hand, if social referencing during familiarization merely heightens infants' attention or directs infants to look at a particular object on each trial, then there should be no difference between consistent and inconsistent conditions in the test.

By considering infants' behavior during familiarization we can also distinguish between the social referencing functions of generalized attention versus directing attention to specific objects. If social referencing is directing attention to one of the two objects on each trial, then during the familiarization phase, in both consistent and inconsistent conditions, infants should tend to look longer at the object the adult is pointing to than at the other object.

Training Stimuli
"Look Neem"

"Look Lif"

Test Stimulus
"Look Lif"

Figure 13.5   Social referencing experiment.

This study is still ongoing, but the preliminary results are already quite interesting. During the familiarization phase, at both 14 months of age (.570, $p < .05$) and at 18 months of age (.551, $p < .05$) infants look a greater proportion of time at the objects to which the adult points than at the other object. So at both ages the infants clearly are paying attention to the adult and are basing their behavior on the adult's actions. Nevertheless, it is only at 18 months that the infants show any evidence in the test of looking longer at the labeled object in the consistent condition than in the inconsistent condition.

Once we have completed this social referencing study, an obvious extension will be to repeat it at 14 and 18 months of age—but with unfamiliar categories of objects, as determined by the BLOCK, rather than with just the two unfamiliar objects shown in Figure 13.5.

SUMMARY AND CONCLUSIONS

Investigating the relationship between early word learning and categorization may seem relatively straightforward. However, as we have indicated in this chapter, it really is quite a complex problem, and several issues should be resolved before any study should be conducted on this topic. First, there are actually two distinct accomplishments that can be investigated: (1) learning how the presence of words affects categorization; and (2) learning how knowledge of a category affects word learning. Each accomplishment is significant, yet each follows its own developmental sequence.

The second issue is choice of the most appropriate testing environment. The decision must be made whether to use a naturalistic setting in which an adult actually speaks to an infant who, in turn, interacts with real objects, or to use a more artificial, tightly controlled experimental setting in which infants receive identical auditory and visual stimuli while their looking time to some type of video monitor is recorded. As can be seen from the experiments described in this chapter, we tend to prefer the more tightly, controlled experimental studies because of their precision, their ease of replication, and their avoidance of potential inadvertent bias. Furthermore, the abilities and the ages we have found in our studies tend to be remarkably similar to those reported in looser, more naturalistic studies. Thus, we are reinforcing the findings reported in the more naturalistic studies while at the same time demonstrating the external validity of our more tightly controlled artificial studies.

Third, whether one is examining infant categorization or infant word learning, it is essential to know the infant's past experience with the objects or categories being used in those studies. For example, in an investigation of the effects of labels on categorization, if the labels seem to have a positive effect, is it because their presence facilitates the acquisition of a new category, or are they just helping to reactivate an existing category? One solution is to use novel, artificial categories and even to manipulate the breadth of the category experimentally, as we reported in Plunkett et al. (2008). That set of studies clearly indicates that by 10 months of age infants can take advantage of the correlation between labels and category features to build either one or two categories or to prevent a category from being formed.

It is equally important to know the infant's prior experience with the objects or categories when investigating infant word learning. Several of studies on this topic have devised totally novel objects and then have attempted to teach infants the relationship between nonsense labels and these objects (e.g., Schafer & Plunkett, 1998; Werker et al., 1998). Almost all of these studies tested the association of a particular label with a single novel object rather than that label with an entire category of novel objects. One reason is that although it is relatively simple to invent one or two novel objects, it is much more difficult to come up with an entire set of related novel objects that represents a coherent novel category.

It is for this reason that our laboratory has been developing the BLOCK, an online questionnaire that parents complete to indicate their infant's prior experience with real object categories as well as their understanding of labels for those categories. In this chapter we also reported the results of two initial word-learning studies that used the BLOCK to experimentally manipulate whether 14-month-old infants were being taught to associate novel labels with a novel category item, with a category item for which they had prior experience but no prior labels, or with a category item for which they had both experience and a prior label. Contrary to what one might expect from a "mutual exclusivity" point of view, the infants learned the new label best when they already had both experience and an old label for the category item. We want to be cautious on how much we generalize from this study. Our primary conclusion at this point is that the BLOCK has considerable potential in future word-learning studies to control for the effects of an infant's prior category experience.

The final two studies presented in this chapter shared several commonalities, although they addressed rather different methodological issues. Both examined some aspect of infant word learning, both used an unconventional, albeit different, version of the IPL paradigm, and both reported significant developmental changes between 14 and 18 months of age.

The novelty preference study contrasted two competing tendencies; infants' natural propensity to look longer at an object from a novel category than at one from a familiar category with their propensity to look longer at a familiar object when the label for that object has been mentioned. Both 14- and 18-month-olds displayed the general novelty preference, but only the 18-month-olds reduced or reversed that preference when the word was presented, thus indicating that the presence of the word made the task qualitatively different.

The social referencing study compared different possible functions of having an adult look at and point to an object while the infant heard the name of that object being mentioned. At both 14 and 18 months of age infants were responsive to the social stimulation and tended to look at the object to which the adult was pointing. However, in the test phase when the adult was no longer looking or pointing at the object, only the 18-month-olds looked longer at it than at a contrasting object.

It is important to note that in both the novelty preference and social referencing studies the 14-month-old infants were not simply overwhelmed by the task. They were processing the information and responding appropriately, either showing a novelty preference or looking at the location the adult was referencing. It is just that in both tasks the infants had to be 18 months of age before they responded as if the word they heard was somehow different in that it referred to a particular object or category of objects. At the age of 18 months is when most researchers of early language agree that words clearly have become "special" to the infant, and it is the age when, for most infants, the so-called naming explosion begins. Thus, our recent results seem to us to be not only quite informative but also consistent with much of the evidence in this area.

ENDNOTE

1. We recognize that the terms "label" and "word" may not be entirely synonymous. For example, a label can be an entire phrase or a string of novel letters that have no meaning, and what may be considered a meaningful word to an adult may not be meaningful to an infant. Nevertheless, we will use the terms "label" and "word" interchangeably in this chapter.

REFERENCES

Balaban, M. & Waxman, S. (1997). Do words facilitate object categorization in 9-month-old infants? *Journal of Experimental Child Psychology, 64*, 3–26.

Baldwin, D., Markman, E., Bill, B., Desjardins, R., Irwin, J., & Tidball, G. (1996). Infants' reliance on a social criterion for establishing word-object relations. *Child Development, 67*, 3135–3153.

Baldwin, D. A. (1991). Infants' contribution to the achievement of joint reference. *Child Development, 62*, 875–890.

Bates, E., Dale, P., & Thal, D. (1995). Individual differences and their implications for theories of language development. In P. Fletcher & B. MacWhinney (Eds.), *Handbook of child language* (pp. 95–151). Oxford: Basil Blackwell.

Bloom, P. (2000). *How children learn the meanings of words.* Cambridge, MA: MIT Press.

Booth, A. E. & Waxman, S. (2002). Object names and object functions serve as cues to categories for infants. *Developmental Psychology, 38*, 948–957.

Briganti, A. M. & Cohen, L. B. (2007, March), *Examining the role of social cues in early word learning.* Poster presented at Society for Research in Child Development Meeting, Boston.

Brunt, R. J., Gora, K., & Cohen, L. B. (2005, April). *Building BLOCK for the Investigation of early word learning and experience.* Poster session presented at the 2005 Biennial Meeting of the Society for Research in Child Development, Atlanta, GA.

Brunt, R. J. & Cohen, L. B. (2006, July). *Tracking attentional and labeling influences on looking behavior of 13- and 18-month-olds.* Poster presented at International Conference on Infant Studies. Kyoto.

Casasola, M. & Cohen, L.B. (2000). Infants' association of linguistic labels with causal actions. *Developmental Psychology.* 36, 155–168.

Casasola, M. (2005). Can language do the driving? The effect of linguistic input on infants' categorization of support spatial relations. *Developmental Psychology, 41*, 183–192.

Fantz, R. L. (1964). Visual experience in infants: Decreased attention familiar patterns relative to novel ones. *Science, 146*, 668–670.

Fulkerson, A. & Haaf, R. (2003). The influence of labels, non-labeling sounds, and source of auditory input on 9- and 15-month-olds' object categorization. *Infancy, 4*, 349–369.

Golinkoff, R. M., Jacquet, R. C., Hirsh-Pasek, K., & Nandakumar, R. (1996). Lexical principles may underlie the learning of verbs. *Child Development, 67*(6), 3101–3119.

Hollich, G., Hirsh-Pasek, K., Tucker, M., & Golinkoff, R. (2000). The change is afoot: Emergentist thinking in language acquisition. In P. Anderson, C. Emmeche, N. Finnemann, & P. Christiansen (Eds.), *Downward causation* (pp. 143–178). Oakville, CT: Aarhus University Press.

Houston-Price, C., Plunkett, K., & Duffy, H. (2006). The use of social and salience cues in early word learning. *Journal of Experimental Child Psychology, 95*, 27–55.

Markman, E. (1992). Constraints on word learning: Speculations about their nature, origins, and domain specificity. In M. R. Gunnar & M. P. Maratsos (Eds.), *Modularity and constraints in language and cognition: The Minnesota Symposia on Child Psychology* (Vol. 25, pp. 59–101). Hillsdale, NJ: Erlbaum.

McDonough, L., Choi, S., & Mandler, J. M. (2002). Understanding spatial relations: Flexible infants, lexical adults. *Cognitive Psychology, 46*, 229–259.

Moore, C., Angelopoulos, M., & Bennett, P. (1999). Word learning in the context of referential and salience cues. *Developmental Psychology, 35*(1), 60–68.

Nazzi, T. & Gopnik, A. (2001). Linguistic and cognitive abilities in infancy: When does language become a tool for categorization. *Cognition, 80*, B11–B20.

Plunkett, K., Hu, J., & Cohen, L. B. (2008). Labels can override perceptual categories in early infancy. *Cognition, 106*, 665–681.

Roberts, K. (1997). Linguistic and nonlinguistic factors influencing infant categorization: Studies of the relationship between cognition and language. *Advances in Infancy Research, 11*, 45–107.

Roberts, K. & Jacob, M. (1991). Linguistic versus attentional influences on nonlinguistic categorization in 15-month-old infants. *Cognitive Development, 6*, 355–375.

Robinson, S. & Sloutsky, V. (2004). The effect of stimulus familiarity on modality dominance. In K. Forbus, D. Gentner, & T. Regier (Eds.), *Proceedings of the XXVI Annual Conference of the Cognitive Science Society* (pp. 1167–1172). Mahwah, NJ: Erlbaum.

Schafer, G. & Plunkett, K (1998). Rapid word learning by 15-month-olds under tightly controlled conditions. *Child Development, 69*(2), 309–320.

Schafer, G., Plunkett, K., & Harris, P. (1999). What's in a name? Lexical knowledge drives infants' visual preferences in the absence of referential input. *Developmental Science, 2*(2), 188–195.

Tomasello, M. & Kruger, A. C. (1992). Joint attention on actions: acquiring verbs in ostensive and non-ostensive contexts. *Journal of Child Language, 19*(2), 311–333.

Waxman, S. (2003). Links between object categorization and naming: Origins and emergence in human infants. In D. Rakison & L. Oakes (Eds.), *Early concept and category development* (pp. 213–241). Oxford: Oxford University Press.

Waxman, S. & Markow, D. (1995). Words as invitations to form categories: Evidence from 12- to 13-month-old infants. *Cognitive Psychology, 29*, 257–302.

Waxman, S. & Markow, D. (1998). Object properties and object kind: Twenty-one-month-old infants' extension of novel adjectives. *Child Development, 69*, 1313–1329.

Waxman, S. R. (1999). Specifying the scope of 13-month-olds' expectations for novel words. *Cognition, 70*(3), B35–B50.

Waxman, S. R. & Booth, A. E. (2001). Seeing pink elephants: Fourteen-month-olds' interpretations of novel nouns and adjectives. *Cognitive Psychology, 43*, 217–242.

Waxman, S. R. & Booth, A. E. (2003). The origins and evolution of links between word learning and conceptual organization: new evidence from 11-month-olds. *Developmental Science, 6*(2), 128–135.

Werker, J., Cohen, L., Lloyd, V., Casasola, M., & Stager, C. (1998). Acquisition of word-object associations by 14-month-old infants. *Developmental Psychology, 34*(6), 1289–1309.

Woodward, A. & Hoyne, K. (1999). Infants' learning about words and sounds in relation to objects. *Child Development, 70*(1), 65–77.

Xu, F. (2002). The role of language in acquiring object kind concepts in infancy. *Cognition, 85,* 223–250.

Xu, F., Cote, M., & Baker, A. (2005). Labeling guides object individuation in 12-month-old infants *Psychological Science, 16*(5), 372–377.

Younger, B. A. (1985). The segregation of items into categories by ten-month-old infants. *Child Development, 56,* 1547–1583.

14

Language Acquisition, Domain Specificity, and Descent with Modification

Gary F. Marcus and Hugh Rabagliati

Research in language acquisition has, to a remarkable degree, been defined around a single vexing question: To what extent is the machinery for acquiring language *specific* to language? Even when people claim to be arguing about innateness (or a lack thereof), what they typically have in mind is really the question of domain specificity—of whether the capacity to acquire language depends on machinery that is specially adapted for language or whether whatever we come to know about language might merely be the product of some sort of general learning mechanisms.

The domain-specificity view is captured by Pinker's (1994) suggestion that "language is not just a solution thought up by a generally brainy species" (p. 45), which might be contrasted to Elman et al.'s (1996) position that "domain-specific representations ... emerge from domain-general architectures and learning algorithms [with] modularization as the end product of development rather than its starting point" (p. 115).

The canonical strong empiricist view holds that the innate endowment is absolutely minimal, consisting only of domain-general learning mechanisms and no language-specific prior knowledge. Information about how to perceive speech, how syntax should be structured, and so forth would be acquired in exactly the same way as all other kinds of knowledge; learning about relative clauses would use very similar computations to learning about the social behavior of kin and conspecifics. Crucially, on this view, it follows that the only reason language would be learned differently from any other material (if at all) would be due to idiosyncrasies in either the input or (for example) a transducer such as the ear.

The canonical nativist, in contrast, holds that the human mind *is* endowed with a significant amount of innate knowledge or structure that can be brought to bear on learning from particular domains, such as language. Although in principle one could imagine a nativist position in which the only thing that was innate was an intricate yet domain-general learning mechanism, the debate has really been about whether there might be contributions that are not only innate but are also domain specific. To the extent that language acquisition depended largely on domain-specific mechanisms, one would expect the acquisition of language to be relatively independent of other cognitive abilities.

Although the canonical views—empiricist and nativist—are strikingly different and would appear to make very different predictions, there has been a notorious lack of consensus, even after several decades of research (Cosmides & Tooby, 1994; Crain, 1991; Elman et al., 1996; Karmiloff-Smith, 2000; Pinker, 1997, 2002; van der Lely, 2005). In our view, the problem is not that the two theories don't actually differ (as some cynics have suggested) or that either side lacks evidence. Rather, both sides have an embarrassment of riches: Language *does* dissociate from cognition, *and* it does overlap with cognition. How can that be the case? Before we can suggest a way out of this puzzle, it is necessary to examine in some detail both sorts of evidence: that which points to dissociation and that which points to comorbidity.

EVIDENCE FOR BOTH COMORBIDITY AND DISSOCIATION

There are at least three reasons to believe that there is some sort of dissociation between language and cognition. First, there is evidence from studies of developmental disorders, such as in the contrast between specific language impairment (SLI) and Williams syndrome. People with Williams syndrome show significantly impaired and unusual cognition (Bellugi, Lichtenberger, Jones, Lai, & St. George, 2000; Mervis, Morris, Bertrand, & Robinson, 1999). For instance, they exhibit very low performance on tasks requiring them to reason spatially (e.g., copying a drawing; Bellugi et al., 2000), frequently failing to put the components of their model in the correct spatial relation. Likewise, they have difficulty reasoning about the taxonomic structures underlying everyday folk biology (Johnson & Carey, 1998). In contrast, their language is relatively intact. Intriguingly, these dissociations extend to a remarkably fine grain. For instance, despite their poor reasoning about spatial relations, people with Williams Syndrome display relative mastery of prepositions (Landau & Hoffman, 2005), and their knowledge of syntax is far greater than is seen in other disorders (such as Down syndrome) with similar levels of mental retardation.

Children with SLI, in contrast, have by definition normal to nearly normal cognitive capacities yet display significant impairments in at least one element of language production or comprehension (The SLI Consortium, 2002). Whereas Williams syndrome leads to (comparatively) intact language in the face of large-scale cognitive disabilities, SLI appears to have the opposite pattern. A particularly striking example of dissociation has come from Heather van der Lely's work on grammatical SLI (G-SLI) (van der Lely, 2005; van der Lely, Rosen, & McClelland, 1998), a form of language impairment that appears specifically targeted at the development of grammar. Affected individuals exhibit an extreme deficit in the comprehension and production of grammatical relations in sentences but otherwise normal cognitive and metalinguistic skills (e.g., pragmatics). For example, the 10-year-old child AZ examined in van der Lely et al. (1998) demonstrated auditory processing, analogical, and logical reasoning indistinguishable from age-matched controls. At the same time his knowledge and use of syntax was poor. He frequently omitted agreement morphemes (e.g., the plural –s) and could not use or understand complex sentence structures without the aid of a context. AZ was at chance when deciding on the referents of *him* or *himself* in sentences like, "Mowgli says Baloo is tickling him," or "Mowgli says Balooo is tickling himself," which are completely transparent to normal readers. At the same time, he could easily use the available context to understand sentences such as, "Grandpa says Granny is tickling him," or "Grandpa says Granny is tickling herself." The strong dissociation between linguistic and nonlinguistic skills led van der Lely and colleagues (1998) to conclude, "The case of AZ provides evidence supporting the existence of a genetically determined, specialised mechanism that is necessary for the normal development of human language" (p. 1253).

A second line of evidence suggests that language dissociates from cognition even in the pattern of normal development. Whereas language is acquired quickly and robustly across a broad range of cultural conditions, before children start formal schooling and without any specific instruction (Lenneberg, 1967; Pinker, 1994), the acquisition of systems like mathematics or logical reasoning takes many years of instruction, is often tied to literacy, and is only found in some cultures (Gordon, 2004; Luria, 1979; Pica, Lemer, Izard, & Dehaene, 2004). Recently observed cases of children developing their own languages (Goldin-Meadow, 2003; Goldin-Meadow & Mylander, 1998; Senghas & Coppola, 2001) do not appear to find a parallel in mathematical or formal reasoning ability. (It is likewise striking that language seems to be somewhat self-contained—in that children can acquire it with relatively little real-world background knowledge,—in contrast to, say, rules of social interaction or global politics.)

Third, language can be acquired—and indeed is best acquired—early in life, even before many other cognitive abilities have matured, and thus appears temporally dissociated from a general maturation of cognitive skills (Johnson & Newport, 1989; Newport, 1990). The fluency with which both first and second languages are acquired decreases with increasing age. This doesn't mean that language is unique in having a "critical" or sensitive period (cf., e.g., musical ability; Schlaug, 2001), but it does further the notion that language (but not, e.g., rules for card games) can be acquired in a way that dissociates from a number of other cognitive systems.

Such findings are all an embarrassment for a strong empiricist learning theory yet fit naturally with a strong nativist theory. Were this recounting sufficient to exhaust the evidence one might wonder why any controversy remains. However, an entirely different set of facts points in the opposite direction.

First, across the population as a whole, disorders in language are correlated with disorders in cognition and motor control. Although strong dissociations are possible, comorbidity is actually the more typical situation. Across SLI children taken as a whole, cases such as van der Lely's G-SLI (van der Lely, 2005; van der Lely, Rosen, & McClelland, 1998) are comparatively rare. Disorders of language are rarely isolated—frequently co-occurring with impairments in, for example, motor control (Hill, 2001)—and language abilities tend to correlate with general intelligence (Colledge et al., 2002). Furthermore, language disorders with strong dissociations are rare relative to disorders that impair both language and general cognitive ability. Whereas Williams syndrome occurs once every 20,000 births (Morris & Mervis, 2000), Down syndrome occurs once every 800 births (Nadel, 1999). Conversely, verbal and nonverbal skills, as measured for example by SAT verbal and SAT math, are significantly correlated across the normal population (Frey & Detterman, 2004).

Second, evidence from neuropsychology and brain imaging suggests that many of the neural substrates that contribute to language also contribute to other aspects of cognition. Whereas the textbook view attributes linguistic function largely to two areas that were once thought to be essentially unique to language— Broca's and Wernicke's area—it is now clear that regions such as the cerebellum and basal ganglia (once thought to be of little significance for language) also play important roles. Meanwhile, those same previously unique areas are now implicated in numerous nonlinguistic processes, such as music perception (Maess, Koelsch, Gunter, & Friederici, 2001) and motoric imitation (Iacoboni et al., 1999).

Genetic evidence also hints at a common substrate for language and cognition. The human genome differs by only a small percentage (less than 1.5% measured by nucleotides) from the chimpanzee genome, which suggests that cognitive differences between the two species must be limited. Similarly, multivariate genetic research—the analysis of covariation between traits—consistently points to links between the genetic influences on different domains (Kovas & Plomin, 2006). That is, tasks such as reading and mathematics, or different tests of general cognitive ability, show highly heritable covariation with language, suggesting a common genetic basis (Plomin & Kovas, 2005).

To sum up, there is both striking evidence for dissociation and for comorbidity. The nativist can point to evidence for dissociation and the empiricist to evidence for comorbidity. Yet neither camp should really be satisfied: The nativist has no ready account of the facts pointing to comorbidity, and the empiricist has no ready account of the facts pointing to dissociation. The real challenge, clearly, lies in reconciling the two.

THE EVOLUTION OF A LANGUAGE-ACQUISITION
DEVICE—AND A WAY OUT OF THE PARADOX

The key, we suggest, to resolving this apparent paradox—the juxtaposition of comorbidity and dissociation—lies in evolutionary theory, but not in the ways that theory has been typically applied to psychology.

Our account begins with the observation that cognitive scientists often assume (habitually, but not necessarily explicitly) that if two neural or cognitive mechanisms subserve different systems, they are separate not only in their current function but also in their evolutionary history. For example, the evolutionary psychologists Cosmides and Tooby (1994) argue, "The human mind can be expected to include a number of functionally distinct cognitive adaptive specializations…. Both empirically and theoretically, there is no more reason to expect any two cognitive mechanisms to be alike than to expect the eye and the spleen, or the pancreas and the pituitary to be alike" (p. 92).

We beg to differ. Even where two different neural systems are dedicated (or become specialized) in two different ways, they may well share evolutionary history. Whereas the eye and the spleen diverged roughly 500 million years ago, language evolved quite recently (perhaps in the last several hundred thousand years). As the Nobel Laureate François Jacob (1977) put it, evolution is a tinkerer, who "often without knowing what he is going to produce … uses what ever he finds around him, old cardboards, pieces of strings, fragments of wood or metal, to make some kind of workable object … [The result is] a patchwork of odd sets pieced together when and where the opportunity arose" (pp. 1163–1166). Marcus (2006) suggested that the rapid evolution of language suggests it should be seen in similar terms, as more of a "tinkering" with preexisting systems rather than as a wholesale innovation from new cloth.

Two things follow from this. First, phylogeny does not necessarily map transparently onto ontogeny. The hand and the foot, for example, are, in contemporary organisms, functionally and anatomically distinct ("modules," if you will) yet are transparently evolved from a common source. Second, contemporary systems that are physically (or behaviorally) separate may derive from common ancestry. The hand and the foot subserve different functions but depend in part (although not exclusively) on a large number of overlapping genes. What we are suggesting is that "cognitive modules" or "linguistic modules" be viewed in a similar fashion. Comorbidity follows from common ancestry;

dissociation follows from a divergence during that portion of evolutionary history that separates systems that derive from a once common origin. In Charles Darwin's terminology, we are describing the consequence of the process that he called "descent with modification."

Figure 14.1 schematizes this relationship (Figure 14.1[c]) and its comparisons with the strong nativist (Figure 14.1[a]) and empiricist (Figure 14.1[b]) accounts. The area of each oval represents a set of mechanisms; in Figure 14.1(a) these are distributed between mechanisms specified for language and those specialized for other forms of cognition. In Figure 14.1(b), language represents a subset of general cognitive mechanisms. Our proposal, Figure 14.1(c), is that language relies on a set of mechanisms mainly shared across multiple domains but with some additional adaptation for a particular task, resulting in a mental organ of a manner analogous with the hand or foot. Neither Figure 14.1(a) nor Figure 14.1(b) is compatible with the evolution of physical organs; we consider it unlikely they should describe the evolution of a mental one.

This perspective can cast immediate light on the apparently paradoxical conclusion that language is both domain general and domain specific and that it is both dissociable from other cognitive abilities and comorbid with them. Any distinct cognitive system must have evolved from a prior structure. The genes (and neural/cognitive circuitry) that underlie linguistic ability are descendents, presumably with modification, of genes (and neural/cognitive circuitry) that contributed to other, evolutionarily prior, abilities. Comorbidity comes from descent—from those substrates of language that are shared with or descended from other cognitive systems. Dissociation comes from divergence—from the ways language's substrates have been modified as it diverged and developed into its current unique form.

In some ways, our position is close to Bates's (2004) suggestion that language is "a new machine that Nature has constructed out of old parts" (p. 250), but with a pair of important differences. First, Bates considered that relevant evolutionary changes were likely to have been quantitative rather than qualitative in character,

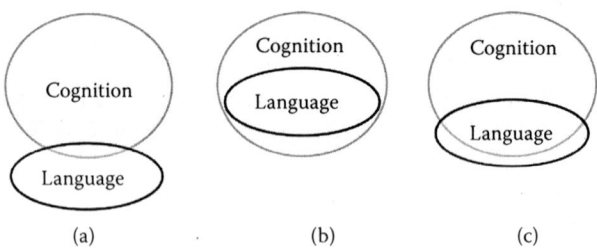

(a)　　　　　　(b)　　　　　　(c)

Figure 14.1   The relationship between language and cognition under three evolutionary scenarios.

likening the evolution of language to the evolution of the giraffe's neck. Bates's analysis of the giraffe's neck—"possible because of quantitative changes in the general-purpose vertebrate neck plan [yet still used] for the older purposes that necks serve in other species: turning the head with its associated sense organs, sending food down, sending air and blood in both directions" (ibid.)—seems correct. But the notion that the "uniquely human capacity for language, culture and technology may have been acquired across the course of evolution by a similar process—quantitative changes in primate abilities that bring about and insure a qualitative leap in cognition and communication" (ibid.) excludes, without argument, the possibility of *qualitative* change.

In truth, evolution is capable of both sorts of change; we see qualitative change, for example, in the transition from monochromatic vision to di- (and ultimately tri-) chromatic vision, and in the infrequent but powerful process by which wholly new neural pathways are constructed (Nishikawa, 1997, 2002). Human language, at least superficially, seems like a case where qualitative (as well as quantitative) change might be involved. No other species, for example, seems to be able to acquire such an open-ended vocabulary or to use recursion in the service of constructing complex sentences with complex meanings (Hauser, 1996). Even if those abilities depend at least in part on reconfigurations of "old parts," the reconfigurations themselves may be without precedent.

Whether language evolution depended on quantitative change, qualitative change, or some mix of the two (as seems most plausible to us), there is a deeper way in which Bates (2004) appears to have something rather different in mind. As best we can tell, her positions really seems to have been closer to what is depicted in Figure 14.1b, to wit, that language is a *subset* of a nonspecific "human capacity for language, culture and technology." In Bates's (2004) view, at least as we understand it (given, e.g., remarks about how language should be seen only as the end product of modularization), all of the evolutionary action in the origin of the human species was in changes to a domain-general cognitive system. Again, we see nothing in the data or evolutionary record to suggest that change must have been restricted in this way; we would concur that domain-general mechanisms may have changed in ways that are necessary for linguistic evolution: Memory and posture both come to mind—the former for computational reasons, the latter because of what could follow in the vocal tract. But why *only* these? In our view, one ought to find hallmarks of adaptation both in "general" cognitive capacities and in whatever novel circuitry contributes (along with preexisting circuitry) to language.

Bates (2004), in short, seems to have put her weight on descent (a new machine from old parts) but to have underemphasized the importance of modification (the ways new parts could diverge qualitatively from ancestral elements); we believe the weight should be approximately equal and that any account of language ought duly to take into account both what we might we expect from descent and what novel contributions might arise through modification.

LANGUAGE ACQUISITION

If language is, as we have argued, likely to be a mix of the domain general and the domain specific, what is language acquisition? The general perspective that we are advocating leads to a particular view of language acquisition—neither as a sui generis unified module nor as some general-purpose learning mechanism constrained only by the input data but rather as an orchestrated set of components whose arrangement (and initial state) is a result of evolution.

This view motivates a particularly structured approach to researching and understanding language acquisition. If the language faculty consists of a large group of organized components, rather than a simple statistical learning mechanism or monolithic set of innate grammatical rules, then the correct way to understand the process of language acquisition is to identify each of these component mechanisms and then ask what about them (if anything) is specialized for language acquisition and how they are interrelated. More pointedly, it suggests that the question of whether language acquisition is domain specific or domain general is too coarse; the real question should be which contributors to language acquisition are domain specific and which are domain general. The question of domain specificity thus becomes both piecemeal (since we might expect different elements to have different evolutionary histories) and empirical, to be answered separately for each underlying mechanism.

§

Unfortunately, the database for evaluating this hypothesis is surprisingly sparse: Research in language acquisition is rarely about the mechanisms of language learning; instead, many studies simply characterize what children know at particular points in development, providing a series of snapshots that help to illuminate children's grasp of language and how it improves over time. Still, a smaller but now thriving strand has tried to directly characterize *how* children acquire language—by teaching them aspects of language (e.g., a word or rudimentary syntactic construction) within some laboratory context—and from these studies we can gain some preliminary insight.

In particular, research thus far suggests that children might possess several distinct learning mechanisms, including machinery for recognizing categorical distinctions, for recognizing associations between sound and meaning, for noting statistical regularities, and for acquiring rules. It is quite possible that all of these mechanisms play a genuine role in language acquisition, and there may well be many others. Yet, crucially, it need not be the case that all have the same evolutionary history—or that all should reflect similar degrees of specialization for language.

A good place to begin is with the once-popular notion that "categorical perception" of speech might be a language-specific phenomenon and presumably a human-unique contribution to language learning. This began with the discovery by Liberman, Harris, Hoffman, and Griffith (1957) that humans perceive speech in a categorical manner—that is, adults perceive phonemes that differ by, say, voicing (e.g., *b* and *p*) as falling into bounded categories. Variation of voicing within these bounds results in perception of the same phoneme; the same variation between those bounds results in the perception of different phonemes. Prelinguistic infants were later discovered to perceive the same contrasts (Eimas, Siqueland, Jusczyk, & Vigorito, 1971), all of which led Liberman, Cooper, Shankweiler, and Studdert-Kennedy (1967) to suggest that humans are specialized to perceive speech in a distinct manner, innately tuned to recognize spoken language. In other words, "speech is special."

This theory was challenged, however, by later evidence showing categorical perception as neither specific to speech nor to humans. Numerous results demonstrate categorical perception of nonspeech, such as musical intervals (Burns & Ward, 1978). Indeed, faces are also perceived as falling into categories, even when they are manipulated to vary over continuous dimensions (Beale & Keil, 1995). More strikingly, animals with no linguistic skills (chinchillas) are able to perceive the categorical contrasts in human speech and to respond based upon them using the same metrics as humans (Kuhl & Miller, 1975). One need not assume that categorical perception is unimportant for language—we presume in fact that it is essential—or even that speech is not special in some way; plainly, however, categorical perception is not uniquely tied either to humans or to language.

A more recent example comes from the notion of *fast mapping* (Carey & Bartlett, 1978), defined as an early developing ability to quickly and accurately map a word to its referent, even with limited exposure (one or two examples) to the link between the two. For example, preschool children could learn a novel adjective about an object (e.g., that a particular colored tray was "the *chromium* one") through only two nonostensive repetitions of the word. Fast mapping was uncovered as an attempt to explain the remarkably rapid growth in vocabulary among young children, and it was generally assumed to be a language-specific effect.

Twenty years later these assumptions have been substantially revised. Markson and Bloom (1997) tested whether children learned names for objects (e.g., "Let's use the *koba* to …") more easily than they learned facts about objects. These facts included descriptions (e.g., "Let's use the one my uncle gave me") and instructions (e.g., where on an object a sticker should be placed). Children who were 3 and 4 years old were able to recall the descriptions as accurately as the names (instructions were harder to learn) even one month after training, suggesting that fast mapping is not domain specific. More recently, Kaminski, Call, and Fischer (2004) claimed to demonstrate fast mapping in a well-trained domestic dog. Their Border Collie subject not only demonstrated a vocabulary of more than 200 items but could also succeed in a fast-mapping task similar to that of Carey and Bartlett (1978), retaining labels for items for at least a month. As with categorical perception, fast mapping appears unique to neither language nor humans.

Statistical learning (Saffran, Aslin, & Newport, 1996a; Saffran, Johnson, Aslin, & Newport, 1999) seems to be following a parallel track. The term *statistical learning,* as studied in developmental psychology, refers to an ability to learn transitional probabilities, the likelihood with which a particular element follows any other particular element (for much more detail see Chapter 2 and Chapter 3 in this volume). For example, in the syllable sequence *PaBiKuTiBuDoGoLaTu-TiBuDo, Bu* follows *Ti* with 100% probability, but the syllable *Ti* only precedes *Ku* with 50% probability. By comparing the transitional probabilities between the elements of the sequence, it is possible to determine and isolate consistent groupings (Saffran, Aslin, & Newport, 1996b), and by 8 months of age human infants can perform this task, learning the distributions of syllables in a speech stream with only 2 minutes exposure (Saffran et al., 1996a). This may be important for learning a language, allowing the infant to parse individual words from sentences and to learn language-specific regularities such as phonotactics.

Nonetheless, an analysis of the task requirements in statistical learning suggests that it may not be specifically evolved for language learning. In particular, transitional probability learning is no more than learning feature co-occurrences over time. The ability to learn feature co-occurrences is clearly vital for learning the perceptual structure of visual categories and is present for this task in infancy (Younger & Cohen, 1983). It may also be useful for learning about other visual structures of the world (Fiser & Aslin, 2002).

As predicted, the ability to track co-occurrences over time appears to act generally—infants track the transitional probabilities between elements as different from speech as musical tones or pictures presented in sequence (Kirkham, Slemmer, & Johnson, 2002; Saffran et al., 1999). Learning surface arrangements like phonotactics seems to require the same mechanisms useful for learning about the surface features of a number of domains, from categories to music. Studies using the same logic as Saffran et al.'s (1996) speech study previously described—but with different stimuli, such as sequences of looming shapes or musical notes— consistently show that human adults and infants are able to learn the consistent groupings and patterns. Again, these abilities are also not specific to humans. Animals as distinct as apes and rats track statistics in speech over time similarly to human infants (Hauser, Newport, & Aslin, 2002; Toro & Trobalón, 2005).

More broadly, none of these mechanisms seems to be unique to humans, and none seems to be unique to language. Yet only humans acquire language. While

Bates's (2004) notion that evolution has produced only quantitative differences cannot yet be ruled out with certainty, the analysis here and the array of data on the dissociation of language and cognition suggest that it would not be surprising if at least some mechanisms were specially suited to language.

§

Our laboratory has been investigating one candidate mechanism: infants' ability to learn abstract rules. By abstract rules we mean structures that define a particular linguistic form and can be applied to any new constituents, such as novel names or verbs (Marcus, Vijiyan Bandi Rao, and Vishton (1999)). A simple example would be a rule, such as is found in English, that phrases are produced with the structure SUBJECT–VERB–OBJECT (e.g., John loves Mary) rather than SUBJECT–OBJECT–VERB, as is found in, e.g., Japanese. This abstract rule ensures that an infinite variety of novel sentences can be produced by plugging the particular constituents into the correct placeholders.

Marcus et al. (1999) showed that 7-month-old infants were able to learn such abstract structures from streams of computer-synthesized speech. Infants were familiarized to 2 minutes of 3-syllable sentences, patterned after a simple grammar, such as AAB (e.g., *wo wo fe, la la ta, ga ga na*). After familiarization, infants were tested to see if they were able to transfer this previously heard structure to sentences with novel elements, which would imply that they had parsed the training strings into an abstract grammar. Using a familiarization preference procedure, the infants were given short trials consisting of the novel sounds combined using either a novel or a familiar grammar. Infants overwhelmingly preferred to listen to the novel grammar.

Given the important differences between our abstract rules and Saffran et al.'s transitional probability learning, we wanted to test whether the same domain-general application held true for abstract rule learning, too. In fact, we (Marcus, Fernandes, & Johnson, 2007) found the opposite: results that argue for the presence of an early-appearing, language-privileging mechanism for learning abstractions.

In the first experiment, we tried to replicate Saffran and colleagues' (1996) success with learning from tones. Could 7-month-olds learn abstract patterns from tones and apply those to new tones? In a further comparison with speech, the tone pattern was replaced with a pattern of sung syllables, matched for pitch and contour.

Following the procedures outlined in Marcus et al. (1999), infants sat in a testing chamber with speakers and visual accompaniment on either side. Infants were familiarized with 50 presentations of 16 different sequences following a particular grammar (ABA, ABB, or AAB), with a .25 second gap between individual sounds and a 1 second gap between sequences, presented from both sides equally. The dependent measure was the amount of time spent looking in the direction of speakers presenting those stimuli following familiarization. Familiarization rule (ABB vs. ABA or ABB vs. AAB), order of test sequence presentation (consistent vs. inconsistent first), and side of presentation (left vs. right side first at test) were counterbalanced across infants in each condition. There were no reliable effects of these variables, or of test trial, in preliminary statistical analyses.

For the tones condition, infants were presented with 16 sequences, composed of piano notes. Half of the sequences had a rising contour, and half had a falling contour; in this way, the infant had to learn the rule by transposing the identity relations of the notes rather than matching a melody. For the sung syllables condition, each syllable was produced at a particular note within the fifth octave of a standard keyboard matching the pitches and contours in the Tones condition.

Our results diverged significantly from Saffran et al. (1996, 1999). Looking times were entered into a 2 (condition: Tones vs. Sung Syllables) × 2 (test pattern: consistent vs. inconsistent) mixed analysis of variance (ANOVA), which yielded a reliable main effect of test pattern ($F(1,30) = 5.67, p = .024$ [$p_{rep} = .919, d = .416$]) and a reliable condition × test pattern interaction ($F(1,30) = 4.99, p = .033$ [$p_{rep} = .903$]). Simple effects tests revealed a strong preference for the inconsistent pattern in the Sung Syllables condition ($F(1,30) = 10.65, p = .0028$ [$p_{rep} = .975, d = .886$]) but no significant preference in the Tones condition ($F(1,30) = .01, ns$; Figure 14.1).

While infants are able to extract transitional probabilities from tonal sequences and can identify distinct melodies in different transpositions, they do not appear to extract any notion of abstract reduplicative structure from music. However, when the training items were sets of syllables sung at the same pitches, infants easily extracted the rule.

To confirm this surprising dissociation, we performed three further tests. First, to ensure that the failure with the tones was not due to an inability to encode the items or to confusion caused by the differences in melodic contour, we constructed an analogous set of stimuli using the same note (middle C) played on instruments varying in timbre (e.g. piano, violin, French horn). Previous studies (Trainor et al., 2004) had shown that infants easily encode the differences in sounds varying in timbre, but in our work they again failed to extract and generalize the identities of the timbres. In an ABB versus AAB condition, the infants showed no preference for novel strings following either a familiar or novel rule (Figure 14.2).

To confirm this failure, we tested a second contrast—ABB versus ABA—using the same timbre stimuli. Again, infants failed to generalize this simple identity rule. Finally, to guard against the possibility that our musical materials did not saliently differ or were somehow ecologically inappropriate, we created a set of stimuli using animal calls (from, e.g., cat, hen, dog). Again testing an ABB versus AAB contrast, we found no significant differences in looking time to novel items patterned after a familiar or unfamiliar rule.

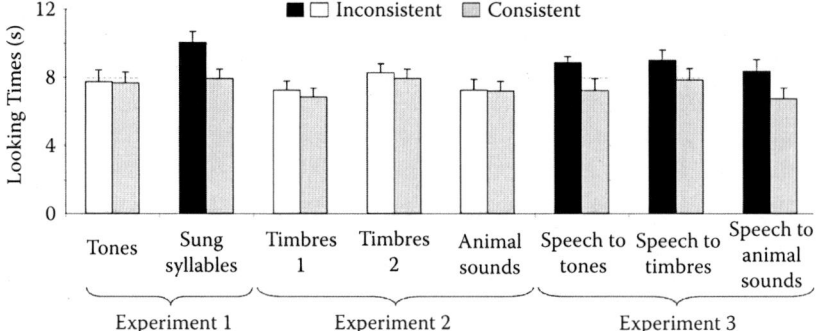

Figure 14.2 Mean looking times for inconsistent and consistent test items in each of the eight conditions. Dark-gray bars denote conditions in which familiarization consisted of speech sounds; light-gray bars denote conditions in which familiarization sounds consisted of sequences of nonspeech stimuli.

We reasoned that this failure could be explained in three ways. First, it could be a simple materials artifact—the differences between the stimuli were not salient enough, ensuring the patterns were indistinct to the infants. Second, the infants might have been unable to extract the rules from the training sequences. Third, the infants might have been able to extract a rule from the training sequences but were not able to apply this rule to the test sequences. Based on a distinction between rule extraction and rule generalization (e.g., Anderson, 1983) we designed a simple "crossover" experiment to test among these three possibilities. Infants were familiarized with speech, as in Marcus et al. (1999), and then tested on the same aforementioned nonspeech materials—tones, timbre sounds, and animal calls. If infants were unable to generalize the rule to the test stimuli or if a materials artifact prevented them from doing so, we would not expect the same lack of discrimination we saw in our earlier experiments. Alternately, if the results were a failure of rule extraction rather than generalization or materials, we might expect the infants to use the rule extracted from speech in examining the nonspeech sounds and therefore to show discrimination.

Tested over three conditions (Speech Training to Tones, Speech to Timbre, Speech to Animal Calls) infants showed a reliable main effect of looking time to test pattern ($F(1,45) = 19.96$, $p = .000053$); planned comparisons revealed that each condition led to a reliable effect of test pattern. If infants possessed an abstract rule, they could apply it to any stimuli—the difficulty appeared to lie in extracting abstractions.

Therefore, while infants easily learn and generalize simple rules from speech, they fail to do so under comparable circumstances from a wide range of nonlinguistic materials. The failure appears to be one of rule extraction—infants are able to understand the nonlinguistic stimuli in terms of previously learned rules but are unable to extract novel rules from the same stimuli. The instinct to learn rules is thus preferentially evoked by speech stimuli. This conclusion is substantially reinforced when performances across all experiments are analyzed together, in a 2 (familiarization stimulus: speech vs. nonspeech) × 2 (test pattern: consistent vs. inconsistent) mixed ANOVA. The general preference for speech is reflected in a reliable effect of familiarization stimulus ($F(1,126) = 3.92$, $p = .049$ $[p_{rep} = .879, d = .349]$), and a reliable effect of test pattern is driven by the success when speech is used ($F(1,126) = 17.81$, $p < .001$ $[p_{rep} = .997, d = .364]$). A significant interaction between familiarization stimulus and test pattern ($F(1,126) = 10.29$, $p = .002$ $[p_{rep} = .981]$) indicates that the familiarization conditions have very different results. The speech-familiarization condition shows a reliable effect of test pattern ($F(1,126) = 27.58$, $p < .001$ $[p_{rep} > .999, d = .640]$). In contrast, combining all conditions where infants were familiarized with nonspeech sounds produced nothing even close to a reliable preference ($F(1,126) = .51$, ns).

DISCUSSION

It would be too strong to suggest that infants are altogether unable to extract rules from nonlinguistic input. Adult humans can extract statistics and rules from a variety of domains (Altmann, 1995), though perhaps not equally from all domains (see Conway & Christiansen, 2005), and at least some evidence suggests that infants can extract rules from visual stimuli that are presented cotemporally such that a child could apprehend the relevant pattern in a single glance (Saffran, Pollak, Seibel, & Shkolnik, 2006; Tyrell, Stauffer, & Snowman, 1991; Tyrrell, Zingaro, & Minard, 1993). Instead, the bias for speech might inhere only in sequences presented *over time*—which inherently require infants to establish memory traces of individual elements within and across trials (Oakes & Ribar, 2005). Consistent with this notion, infants appear to have difficulty acquiring rules from sequentially presented visual stimuli (Johnson et al., in press). It would be similarly too strong to suggest that rule learning is the unique province of humans. Adults of at least two other species can extract at least some rules: Honeybees can extract and generalize a simple rule of identity (Giurfa, Zhang, Jenett, Menzel, & Srinivasan, 2001), and cottontop tamarins can extract and generalize rules in speech (Hauser, Weiss, & Marcus, 2002).

Yet in comparison with the extraction of transition probabilities, which appears to be content neutral, it is striking that infants privilege speech in extracting rules from temporal streams of speech. We do not yet know why; infants may analyze speech more deeply than other signals because it is highly familiar or highly salient, because it is produced by humans, because it is inherently capable of bearing meaning, or because speech bears some not-yet-identified acoustic property that draws the attention of the rule-induction system. Infants prefer listening to speech relative to closely matched controls from the time of birth (Vouloumanos & Werker, 2004, 2007), and the rule-learning bias could in some way be an extension of that initial, profound interest in speech. Regardless of its origin, the selectivity of rule learning in infancy may hold important clues into why children show a special facility for acquiring language relative to other complex cognitive systems.

CONCLUSIONS

Humans are alone in their capacity to acquire a language, but it does not follow that the machinery they use to acquire language is without precedent. Evolutionary biology suggests that even the most apparently novel systems descended with modification from ancestral systems, and we see no reason to think that language should be any different in this respect.

On the presumption that the evolution of language follows from the same sorts of evolutionary processes as other systems, it follows that the classical division between domain-specific and domain-general approaches to language acquisition is likely misplaced. Where humans are the only species capable of acquiring language, it would be quite surprising if the canonical empiricist view were correct, yet the view of language as a wholly separate module seems too coarse. What we have argued instead is that the machinery for acquiring language may be a novel orchestration of parts old and new; we should expect both qualitative and quantitative change relative to our ancestors, but also continuity.

On this perspective, the question of domain specificity becomes very much piecemeal and empirical: piecemeal in that different elements of the language apparatus may have evolved in different ways, and empirical in the sense that each component must be explored separately, through explorations of applicability and ancestry. To date, most of the learning mechanisms that have been uncovered appear to be domain general and not unique to humans. Rule learning may be a partial exception—a mechanism that is not unique to humans but that (at least in humans) appears to be initially tuned toward the analysis of speech. We anticipate that other mechanisms tuned toward—or even solely devoted to—language will yet be uncovered, yet even those most specially tied to language will have roots in ancestral nonlinguistic mechanisms. We expect considerable progress as the field moves past simple dichotomies and into a sophisticated understanding of how the evolutionarily ancient works together with the evolutionarily more recent.

REFERENCES

Altmann, G. T. (1995). Modality independence of implicitly learned grammatical knowledge. *Journal of Experimental Psychology: Learning, Memory and Cognition, 21,* 899–912.

Anderson, J. R. (1983). *The architecture of cognition.* Cambridge, MA: Harvard University Press.

Bates, E. A. (2004). Explaining and interpreting deficits in language development across clinical groups: Where do we go from here? *Brain and Language, 88,* 248–253.

Beale, J. M. & Keil, F. C. (1995). Categorical effects in the perception of faces. *Cognition, 57,* 217–239.

Bellugi, U., Lichtenberger, L., Jones, W., Lai, Z., & St. George, M. (2000). I. The neurocognitive profile of Williams Syndrome: a complex pattern of strengths and weaknesses. *Journal of Cognitive Neuroscience, 12*(Suppl 1), 7–29.

Burns, E. M. & Ward, W. D. (1978). Categorical perception—phenomenon or epiphenomenon: evidence from experiments in the perception of melodic musical intervals. *Journal of the Acoustical Society of America, 63,* 456–468.

Carey, S. & Bartlett, E. J. (1978). Acquiring a single new word. *Papers and Reports on Child Language Development, 15,* 15–29.

Colledge, E., Bishop, D. V., Koeppen-Schomerus, G., Price, T. S., Happe, F. G., Eley, T. C., et al. (2002). The structure of language abilities at 4 years: a twin study. *Developmental Psychology, 38,* 749–757.

Conway, C. M. & Christiansen, M. H. (2005). Modality-constrained statistical learning of tactile, visual, and auditory sequences. *Journal of Experimental Psychology-Learning Memory and Cognition, 31,* 24–39.

Cosmides, L. & Tooby, J. (1994). Origins of domain specificity: The evolution of functional organization. In L. A. Hirschfeld & S. A. Gelman (Eds.), *Mapping the mind: Domain specificity in cognition and culture* (pp. 85–116). Cambridge, UK: Cambridge University Press.

Crain, S. (1991). Language acquisition in the absence of experience. *Behavioral and Brain Sciences, 14,* 597–650.

Eimas, P. D., Siqueland, E. R., Jusczyk, P., & Vigorito, J. (1971). Speech perception in infants. *Science, 171,* 303–306.

Elman, J. L., Bates, E., Johnson, M. H., Karmiloff-Smith, A., Parisi, D., & Plunkett, K. (1996). *Rethinking innateness: A connectionist perspective on development.* Cambridge, MA: MIT Press.

Fiser, J. & Aslin, R. N. (2002). Statistical learning of new visual feature combinations by infants. *Proceedings of the National Academy of Sciences of the USA, 99,* 15822–15826.

Frey, M. C. & Detterman, D. K. (2004). Scholastic assessment or g? The relationship between the Scholastic Assessment Test and general cognitive ability. *Psychological Science, 15,* 373–378.

Giurfa, M., Zhang, S., Jenett, A., Menzel, R., & Srinivasan, M. V. (2001). The concepts of "sameness" and "difference" in an insect. *Nature, 410,* 930–933.

Goldin-Meadow, S. (2003). *The resilience of language: What gesture creation in deaf children can tell us about how all children learn language.* London: Psychology Press.

Goldin-Meadow, S. & Mylander, C. (1998). Spontaneous sign systems created by deaf children in two cultures. *Nature, 391,* 279–281.

Gordon, P. (2004). Numerical cognition without words: evidence from Amazonia. *Science, 306,* 496–499.

Hauser, M. D. (1996). *The evolution of communication.* Cambridge, MA: MIT Press.

Hauser, M. D., Newport, E. L., & Aslin, R. N. (2002). Segmentation of the speech stream in a non-human primate: statistical learning in cotton-top tamarins. *Cognition, 78,* B53–64.

Hauser, M. D., Weiss, D., & Marcus, G. (2002). Rule learning by cotton-top tamarins. *Cognition, 86,* B15.

Hill, E. L. (2001). Non-specific nature of specific language impairment: a review of the literature with regard to concomitant motor impairments. *International Journal of Language and Communication Disorders, 36,* 149–171.

Iacoboni, M., Woods, R. P., Brass, M., Bekkering, H., Mazziotta, J. C., & Rizzolatti, G. (1999). Cortical mechanisms of human imitation. *Science, 286,* 2526–2528.

Jacob, F. (1977). Evolution and tinkering. *Science, 196,* 1161–1166.

Johnson, S. C. & Carey, S. (1998). Knowledge enrichment and conceptual change in folkbiology: Evidence from Williams syndrome. *Cognitive Psychology, 37,* 156–200.

Johnson, S. P., Fernandes, K. J., Frank, M. C., Kirkham, N. Z., Marcus, G. F., Rabagliati, H., and Slemmer, J. A. (in press), Development of Abstract Rule Learning in Infancy, *Infancy.*

Johnson, J. S. & Newport, E. L. (1989). Critical period effects in second language learning: the influence of maturational state on the acquisition of English as second language. *Cognitive Psychology, 21,* 60–99.

Kaminski, J., Call, J., & Fischer, J. (2004). Word learning in a domestic dog: evidence for "fast mapping." *Science, 304,* 1682–1683.

Karmiloff-Smith, A. (2000). Why babies' brains are not Swiss army knives. In H. Rose & S. P. R. Rose (Eds.), *Alas, poor Darwin: Arguments against evolutionary psychology* (pp. 144–156). London: Jonathan Cape.

Kirkham, N. Z., Slemmer, J. A., & Johnson, S. P. (2002). Visual statistical learning in infancy: Evidence for a domain general learning mechanism. *Cognition, 83,* B35–42.

Kovas, Y. & Plomin, R. (2006). Generalist genes: implications for the cognitive sciences. *Trends in Cognitive Science, 10,* 198–203.

Kuhl, P. K. & Miller, J. D. (1975). Speech perception by the chinchilla: Voiced-voiceless distinction in alveolar plosive consonants. *Science, 190,* 69–72.

Landau, B. & Hoffman, J. E. (2005). Parallels between spatial cognition and spatial language: Evidence from Williams syndrome. *Journal of Memory and Language, 53,* 163–185.

Lenneberg, E. H. (1967). *Biological foundations of language.* New York: Wiley.

Liberman, A. M., Cooper, F. S., Shankweiler, D. P., & Studdert-Kennedy, M. (1967). Perception of the speech code. *Psychological Review, 74,* 431–461.

Liberman, A. M., Harris, K. S., Hoffman, H. S., & Griffith, B. C. (1957). The discrimination of speech sounds within and across phoneme boundaries. *Journal of Experimental Psychology, 53,* 358–368.

Luria, A. (1979). *The making of mind.* Cambridge, MA: Harvard University Press.

Maess, B., Koelsch, S., Gunter, T. C., & Friederici, A. D. (2001). Musical syntax is processed in Broca's area: An MEG study. *Nature Neuroscience, 4,* 540–545.

Marcus, G. F. (1999). Rule learning by seven-month-old infants and neural networks: Response to Altmann and Dienes. *Science, 284,* 875a.

Marcus, G. F., Vijayan, S., Bandi Rao, S., & Vishton, P. M. (1999). Rule learning in 7-month-old infants. *Science, 283,* 77–80.

Marcus, G. F. (2001). *The algebraic mind: Integrating connectionism and cognitive science.* Cambridge, MA: MIT Press.

Marcus, G. F. (2006). Cognitive architecture and descent with modification. *Cognition, 101,* 443–465.

Marcus, G. F., Fernandes, K. J., & Johnson, S. J. (2007). Infant rule learning facilitated by speech. *Psychological Science, 18,* 387–391.

Markson, L. & Bloom, P. (1997). Evidence against a dedicated system for word learning in children. *Nature, 385,* 813–815.

Mervis, C. B., Morris, C. A., Bertrand, J., & Robinson, B. F. (1999). Williams syndrome: Findings from an integrated program of research. In H. Tager-Flusberg (Ed.), *Neurodevelopmental disorders* (pp. 65–110). Cambridge, MA: MIT Press.

Morris, C. A. & Mervis, C. B. (2000). Williams syndrome and related disorders. *Annual Review of Genomics and Human Genetics, 1,* 461–484.

Nadel, L. (1999). Down syndrome in cognitive neuroscience perspective. In H. Tager-Flusberg (Ed.), *Neurodevelopmental disorders* (pp. 197–222). Cambridge, MA: MIT Press.

Newport, E. L. (1990). Maturational constraints on language learning. *Cognitive Science, 14,* 11–28.

Nishikawa, K. C. (1997). Emergence of novel functions during brain evolution. *BioScience, 47,* 341–354.

Nishikawa, K. C. (2002). Evolutionary convergence in nervous systems: Insights from comparative phylogenetic studies. *Brain Behavior and Evolution, 59,* 240–249.

Oakes, L. M. & Ribar, R. J. (2005). A comparison of infants' categorization in paired and successive presentation familiarization tasks. *Infancy, 7,* 85–98.

Pica, P., Lemer, C., Izard, V., & Dehaene, S. (2004). Exact and approximate arithmetic in an Amazonian indigene group. *Science, 306,* 499–503.

Pinker, S. (1994). *The language instinct.* New York: Morrow.

Pinker, S. (1997). *How the mind works.* New York: Norton.

Pinker, S. (1999). *Words and rules: The ingredients of language.* New York: Basic Books.

Pinker, S. (2002). *The blank slate.* Viking Penguin.

Plomin, R. & Kovas, Y. (2005). Generalist genes and learning disabilities. *Psychological Bulletin, 131,* 592–617.

Saffran, J., Aslin, R., & Newport, E. (1996a). Statistical learning by 8-month old infants. *Science, 274,* 1926–1928.

Saffran, J., Aslin, R., & Newport, E. (1996b). Word segmentation: The role of distributional cues. *Journal of Memory and Language, 35,* 606–621.

Saffran, J. R., Johnson, E. K., Aslin, R. N., & Newport, E. L. (1999). Statistical learning of tone sequences by human infants and adults. *Cognition, 70,* 27–52.

Saffran, J. R., Pollak, S. D., Seibel, R. L., & Shkolnik, A. (2006). Dog is a dog is a dog: Infant rule learning is not specific to language. Unpublished manuscript.

Schlaug, G. (2001). The brain of musicians. A model for functional and structural adaptation. *Annals of the New York Academy of Sciences, 930,* 281–299.

Senghas, A. & Coppola, M. (2001). Children creating language: How Nicaraguan sign language acquired a spatial grammar. *Psychological Science, 12,* 323–328.

The SLI Consortium (2002). A genomewide scan identifies two novel loci involved in specific language impairment. *American Journal of Human Genetics, 70,* 384–398.

Toro, J. M. & Trobalón, J. B. (2005). Statistical computations over a speech stream in a rodent. *Perception & Psychophysics, 67*, 867–875.

Trainor, L. J., Wu, L., & Tsang, C. D. (2004). Long-term memory for music: infants remember tempo and timbre. *Developmental Science, 7*, 289–296.

Tyrell, D. J., Stauffer, L. B., & Snowman, L. G. (1991). Perception of abstract identity/difference relationships by infants. *Infant Behavior & Development, 14*, 125–129.

Tyrrell, D. J., Zingaro, M. C., & Minard, K. L. (1993). Learning and transfer of identity-difference relationships by infants. *Infant Behavior and Development, 16*, 43–52.

van der Lely, H. K. (2005). Domain-specific cognitive systems: Insight from Grammatical-SLI. *Trends in Cognitive Science, 9*, 53–59.

van der Lely, H. K., Rosen, S., & McClelland, A. (1998). Evidence for a grammar-specific deficit in children. *Current Biology, 8*, 1253–1258.

Vouloumanos, A. & Werker, J. F. (2004). Tuned to the signal: the privileged status of speech for young infants. *Developmental Science, 7*, 270–276.

Vouloumanos, A. & Werker, J. F. (2007). Listening to language at birth: Evidence for a bias for speech in neonates *Developmental Science, 10*, 159–164.

Younger, B. A. & Cohen, L. B. (1983). Infant perception of correlations among attributes. *Child Development, 54*, 858–867.

15

Neuroimaging Tools for Language Study

LISA FREUND*

There can be no doubt that there is a tremendous amount of language learning during infancy, as clearly shown in the chapters in this volume. The behavioral methods that have predominated in the infancy research addressing early language learning have been fruitful and will continue to be so. With current neuroimaging technology, we also have the opportunity to investigate the early neural structures and processes supporting language learning, even prior to behavioral demonstrations of that learning. Developmental neurobehavioral and language development researchers are now well poised for increasing significantly our understanding of how typical and atypical developing neural structures and brain function affect infant interactions with the linguistic environment and how variance in early linguistic learning environments can influence developing brain function and structure.

Anatomic magnetic resonance imaging (MRI) has become a leading tool for the quantitative, noninvasive study of brain development primarily associated with developmental disruptions or disorders such as cerebral palsy, premature birth, autism, developmental language delay, attention deficit hyperactivity disorder, neurogenetic disorders, and reading and other learning disabilities. Yet there remains a crucial need for developmentally accurate MRI data to determine the actual ranges of variation in brain structure that can be expected for healthy infants and young children. Without a valid, representative standard of normal brain growth, researchers cannot determine accurately abnormalities

* The opinions and assertions herein are those of the authors and should not be construed as representing the policies of the National Institute of Child Health and Human Development (NICHD), the National Institutes of Health (NIH), or the U.S. Department of Health and Human Services.

during brain development or answer confidently questions about brain–behavior–environment interactions during typical development.

It is true that studies characterizing normal, anatomical brain development during school and adolescent ages have increased rapidly over the last decade (e.g., Blanton et al., 2001; Courchesne et al., 2000; Giedd et al., 1996; Gogtay et al., 2004; Kanemura, Aihara, Aoki, Araki, & Nakazawa, 2003; Lange, Giedd, Castellanos, Vaituzis, & Rapoport, 1997; Mukherjee et al., 2001; Paus et al., 1999; Schmithorst, Willke, Dardzinski, & Holland, 2002; Sowell & Jernigan, 1998). It is also true that MRI studies of brain development from newborn through preschool ages are particularly scarce. Those that are available have advanced our understanding of early brain development but are limited by very low numbers of subjects and lack of longitudinal data (e.g., Ashikaga, Araki, Ono, Nishimura, & Ishida, 1999; Barkovich, 1998; Martin, Krassnitzer, Kaeline, & Boesch, 1991; McGraw, Liang, & Provenzale, 2002; Mukherjee et al., 2001; Neil et al., 1998). Furthermore, many of these studies have used clinical populations of sedated infants and young children, thus compromising generalization to typically developing children (Almli, Rivkin, McKinstry, & Brain Development Cooperative Group, 2007).

Much of the limitation in past studies has been the result of the inherent difficulty of scanning very young children, nonchild friendly physical attributes of MRI scanners such as imaging coils designed only for adults, and overly loud and long scanning sessions. More recent technological developments include dedicated neonatal and child-sized imaging coils with dramatically increased resolution, scanners that are not as loud when capturing images, and faster scanning times. These improvements have made high-quality anatomic imaging of the infant brain, as well as diffusion tensor imaging (DTI; imaging of white-fiber tracts in brain) and proton MR spectroscopy (a means of measuring brain chemistry) feasible within a reasonable imaging time (Barkovich, 2006).

The National Institutes of Health (NIH) has long recognized the major gap in the field of pediatric neuroimaging of a comprehensive assessment of normal anatomic brain development across each of the key phases of child development, including infancy and preschool, school age, and adolescence. As a result of recommendations from scientists participating in NIH-sponsored scientific workshops, conferences, and specific NIH requests for information from the scientific community, the NIH is funding a multicenter project to provide research and clinical communities with a large, representative database of anatomical MRI data for typically developing children from newborn (10 days old) to over 21 years old. The database includes longitudinal anatomical MRI data and correlated medical history, family history, and developmental cognitive, language, neurological, and behavioral assessments (Evans & Brain Development Cooperative Group, 2006). The database sample is large (more than 500 across all age groups), is demographically diverse, and is generally representative of gender, race, ethnicity, and income level established by the U.S. Census Bureau (2000) and the U.S. Department of Housing and Urban Development's Office of Policy Development and Research (2003). Six pediatric study centers (PSCs) serve as principal recruitment and data-acquisition sites and are located at Children's Hospital Boston, Children's Hospital Medical Center of Cincinnati, University of Texas Health Science Center at Houston, University of California–Los Angeles, Children's Hospital of Philadelphia, and Washington University Medical Center in Saint Louis. A data coordinating center (DCC; Montreal Neurological Institute, McGill University) manages the imaging and database aspects of the project. DTI and spectroscopy data are collected on a subset of the study participants. The project overall is titled the NIH Pediatric MRI Study of Normal Brain Development (referred to herein as the Pediatric MRI Study). The first public release of the database was in May 2007, and it can be downloaded at http://www.bic.mni.mcgill.ca/nihpd/info/.

The Pediatric MRI Study was designed to include both cross-sectional and longitudinal components. Perhaps the most unique aspect of the Pediatric MRI database is the relatively large sample of participants with ages from the neonatal period through four years. The sample totals 106 typically developing children and is made up of 11 cohorts of children that enter the study at predetermined ages, (i.e., the cross-sectional component). Each of the 11 cohorts is re-evaluated at least two additional times at specified ages, for a minimum of three scans (the longitudinal component). The very youngest children (infants) are scanned more frequently with shorter intervals than older children in order to capture the rapid changes in brain development during the first year of life.

All participants recruited for the NIH Pediatric MRI study are born full term (> 37 weeks, 3 days), with equal representation of males and females. Race, ethnicity, and income are distributed in a demographically balanced sample to mirror proportions defined by the U.S. Census Bureau. Table 15.1 shows the race and ethnic distribution of the sample of infants and preschoolers to date (from Almli et al., 2007). Measures of family income level, parental education level, and parental occupations serve as indices of socioeconomic status. For the youngest group of participants, recruitment is conducted using a community-based strategy that includes hospital venues (e.g., maternity wards and nurseries, satellite physician offices, and well-child clinics), community organizations (e.g., day-care centers, schools, churches, and other types of community centers), and siblings of children participating in other studies.

Once signed informed consent is obtained, a comprehensive screening process is conducted with the parents to ensure that the candidate child and family do not possess medical or family histories that exclude them from participating in the project (see http://www.bic.mni/mcgill.ca/nihpd_info Evans & Brain Development Cooperative Group, 2006 for a complete inclusion/exclusion listing).

Table 15.1 Race/Ethnicity Distribution for U.S. Census 2000 and Objective 2 Sampling Plan

Race/Ethnicity	% Census	% Sampling plan
White/Caucasian	69.1	69
Black/African American	12.1	12
Asian	3.6	4
American Indian/Alaska Native	0.7	1
Native Hawaiian/Other Pacific Islander	0.1	1
Hispanic or Latino (of any race)	12.5	13
Some other race + two or more races	1.9	
	100%	100%

Source: From Almli et al., in press (with permission).

In addition, questionable brain-scan findings are reviewed by two board-certified neuroradiologists plus the neuroradiologist at the specific site of the brain scan; agreement that the finding is abnormal or pathological leads to child exclusion. Other questionable conditions and situations that have the potential to be exclusionary are reviewed by a group of physician investigators to determine inclusion or exclusion by simple majority.

Each successfully enrolled child receives full evaluation at a series of preselected ages (i.e., time points) that are defined by the child's age cohort. Evaluation at each time point includes the following:

1. A rescreening evaluation of the child and family
2. Developmental, behavioral, and neurological evaluation of the child
3. Evaluation of the child and family via parental questionnaire
4. MR evaluation of the child's brain

A final study sample representative of normal, healthy brain and behavioral development is ensured by the comprehensive and strict nature of the screening-exclusion criteria adopted by this study.

At each evaluation time point, a child receives a comprehensive, age-appropriate neurobehavioral test battery (including neurological examination). The behavioral testing battery used with the infancy-through-4.5-year group can be found in Almli et al. (2007). All behavioral tests in the battery have standardized administration and scoring procedures. The testing battery is completed in less than 3 hours for the oldest children, less than 90 minutes for children 1 year and younger, and in approximately 20 minutes or less for newborn infants. The selected tests also have a strong history of widespread use in both clinical assessment and research on child behavioral development and are generally readily available for future studies. Specific assessments that also serve as exclusionary behavioral assessments include the Bayley Scales of Infant Development-Second Edition (BSID-II; Bayley, 1993), the Preschool Language Scale-Third Edition (PLS-3; Zimmerman, Steiner, & Pond, 1992), and the Differential Abilities Scale (DAS; Elliott, 1990), which are all standardized and normed assessments. Scores greater than two standard deviations below the mean of 100 (i.e., scores < 70) are exclusionary for those assessments (see http://www.bic.mni/mcgill.ca/nihpd_info). Preliminary analyses of the infant assessment data reported by Almli et al. (2007) show that the mean BSID-II score (normed mean of 100 + 15) is 100.2 for the current sample and that the mean PLS-3 (normed with a mean of 100 + 15) is 112.0.

A well-practiced protocol is used for scanning unsedated young infants and children (see Almli et al., 2007). Newborn infants (i.e., 0:0 [10–14 days post-EDC]) and infants at 0:3 are scanned during daytime or nighttime sleep. Infants are fed, swaddled, and fitted with ear plugs and monitoring equipment (pulse oximetry), and then the supine infant's head is positioned within the magnet coil. The infant is visually monitored by staff throughout the scan process (e.g., McKinstry et al., 2002; Neil et al., 1998). Older infants (e.g., 0:6) and children through 4:5 are less likely to fall asleep in the strange environment of the scanner room during the day or night than are neonates. As a result, infants and children ranging in age from 0:6 through 4:5 generally receive adaptation protocols that prepare them for the scan, and the scans are conducted at the child's normal night bedtime. The adaptation protocols were designed so that the child would be able to fall asleep in the scanner room, tolerate application of sound protective materials and head positioning into the quadrature coil, and not awaken in response to the sudden onset and volume of scanner noises (Almli et al., 2007). The protocols involve parent education, mock scanner practice, earplugs to get used to at home, and a CD or audiotape of MRI sounds to play at home when child is awake and sleeping.

MRI scanning relies on stimulation of atomic nuclei components and detection of resulting relaxation times of nuclei making up brain tissue to return to equilibrium. MR relaxation rates fall dramatically over the first 12 to 18 months, necessitating modifications to an MR protocol that would be suitable for older children and adults (Evans & Brain Develement Cooperative Group, 2006; Jones, Palasis, & Grattan-Smith, 2004; Nowell et al., 1987). The MRI protocol for infants and young children in the NIH Pediatric MRI study can be found in Almli et al. (2007) and is designed to gather structural MRI data for segmentation and parcellation studies using T1 and T2 relaxometry. The project uses MR General Electric and Siemens scanners at different sites, but all are 1.5 Tesla (T) field strength. Both living and inanimate phantom data are regularly collected to ensure that the different scanners are appropriately calibrated. The MR pulse sequences, timing parameters, and image resolution are selected so that comparable image contrast and quality are achieved across both imaging centers (Evans & Brain Development Cooperative Group, 2006). The imaging protocols employed in the current research were optimized to produce maximum contrast among constituent brain tissues scanned at 1.5 T field strength.

More than 225 scans of infants and preschool aged children have been completed as part of this study without a single adverse event involving the child or parents. Given that the scans in this project have been safely performed on nonsedated, sleeping infants and young children, it is likely that similar nonsedation studies could be performed on naturally sleeping children with underlying neurologic and psychiatric deficits. As discussed in Almli et al. (2007), the key for successful, nonsedated scanning is to have both the child and the parent comfortable enough for the child to sleep in the scanner room.

An example of the quality of longitudinal scans obtained through this project is shown in Figure 15.1 (from Almli et al., 2007). We anticipate that brain atlases,

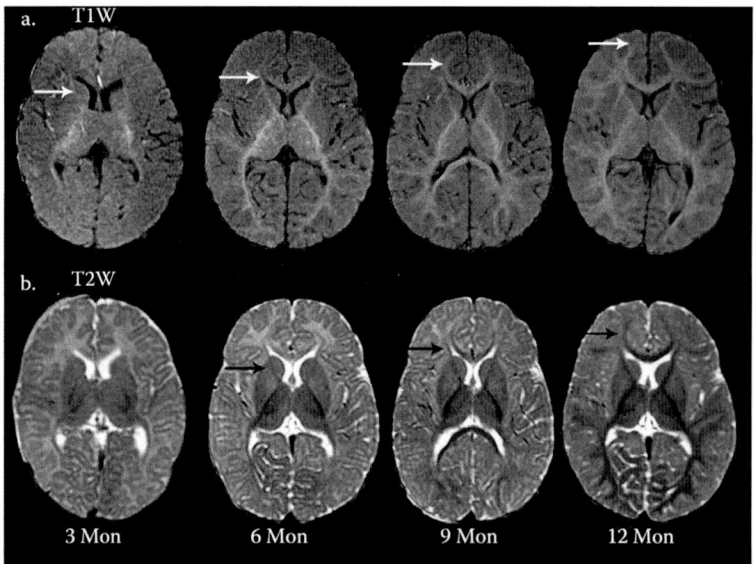

Figure 15.1 Brain maturation illustrated in images from a single participant at 3, 6, 9, and 12 months of age. Row a images show maturational trends of increasing myelination from occipital to frontal lobes (caudal-to-rostral), and from central to subcortical white matter (medial-to-lateral) as the subject ages. Note the progression of myelination into the frontal lobe as indicated by the white arrows. Row b images show a similar but delayed trend with age. T2 shortens as myelin matures (black arrows), which manifests as signal reduction in mature white matter. (From Almli, C. R., Rivkin, M. J., McKinstry, R. C., & Brain Development Cooperative Group, 2007, *Neuroimage, 35,* 308–325. With permission.)

templates, and growth curves for normal, healthy brain development for infants, preschoolers, and older children based on the data collected for the NIH Pediatric MRI Study will establish understanding of the normal, healthy "variability" range of whole-brain and regional brain structures during development and will further the ability to identify relationships among measures of brain and behavioral development. It is also anticipated that researchers investigating atypical brain development in clinical and special populations will draw upon the NIH database for comparison or control neuroanatomical data and correlated medical, demographic, cognitive, language, and behavioral assessments.

Additional information about the NIH MRI Study of Normal Brain Development can be obtained at the project public website (http://www.brain-child. org), via the project protocol document (register for protocol document release via rozie@bic.mni.mcgill.ca) or from project procedure documents available at http://www.bic.mni/mcgill.ca/nihpd_info.

The scientific study of infant language and cognition is well poised to incorporate links to the underlying neurobiology of these domains of child development. Some have already begun to use neuroimaging techniques. For studies that have not already done so but have an interest in using these techniques, not only can the Pediatric MRI Study data serve as typical comparison data, but the procedures that have been so carefully worked out can also serve as a model or guide

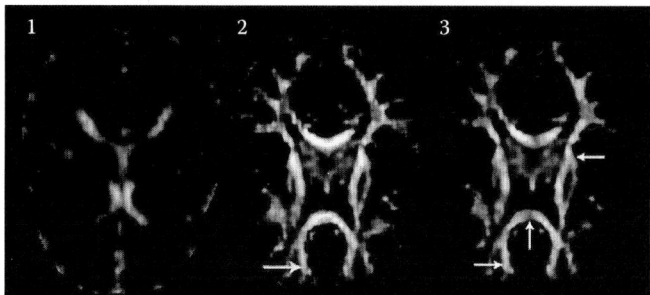

Figure 15.2   DTI scalar parameter maps (same 18-month-old toddler as shown in Figure 15.2). After computation of the diffusion tensor, scalar parameter maps were derived to characterize average diffusion and diffusion anisotropy: (1) Mean diffusivity is a measure of average (total) diffusion. (2) Fractional anisotropy is greatest in highly ordered, tightly packed white-matter tracts. The center arrow highlights that fractional anisotropy contrast precedes the contrast changes on T1-weighted (Figure 15.1, black arrow) and T2-weighted images (Figure 15.1, black arrow). (3) Fiber maps indicate the orientation of white-matter tracts: fibers oriented anterior to posterior (upper arrow), fibers passing through the image plane (lower arrow), fibers oriented left to right (middle arrow).

for collaboration across sites and across projects. As we continue to investigate the infant pathways to language, surely the neurobiology of infant language development is one such pathway that will increasingly be integrated with behavioral data. Doing so in ways that can enable data sharing and collaborative analyses will enhance what is learned from studies and can potentially enable investigators to answer both the specific questions of interest and larger, overarching questions with the same data.

REFERENCES

Almli, C. R., Rivkin, M. J., McKinstry, R. C., & Brain Development Cooperative Group (2007). The NIH MRI study of normal brain development (objective-2): Newborns, infants, toddlers, and preschoolers. *Neuroimage, 35*, 308–325.

Ashikaga, R., Araki, Y., Ono, Y., Nishimura, Y., & Ishida, O. (1999). Appearance of normal brain maturation on fluid-attenuated inversion-recovery (FLAIR) MR images. *American Journal of Neuroradiology, 20*, 427–431.

Barkovich, A. J. (1998). MR of the normal neonatal brain: Assessment of deep structures. *American Journal of Neuroradiology, 19*, 1397–1403.

Barkovich, A. J. (2006). MR imaging of the neonatal brain. *Neuroimaging Clinics of North America, 16*, 117–35, viii–ix.

Bayley, N. (1993). *Bayley Scales of Infant Development* (2d ed.). San Antonio: Psychological Corporation, Harcourt Brace and Company.

Blanton, R. E., Levitt, J. G., Thompson, P. M., Narr, K. L., Capetillo-Cunliffe, L., Nobel, A., et al. (2001). Mapping cortical asymmetry and complexity patterns in normal children. *Psychiatry Research, 107*, 29–43.

Courchesne, E., Chisum, H. J., Townsend, J., Cowles, A., Covington, J., Egaas, B., et al. (2000). Normal brain development and aging: Quantitative analysis at in vivo MR imaging in healthy volunteers. *Radiology, 216*, 672–682.

Elliott, C. D. (1990). *Differential Ability Scales*. San Antonio: Psychological Corporation, Harcourt Brace and Company.

Evans, A. C. & Brain Development Cooperative Group (2006). The NIH MRI study of normal brain development. *Neuroimage, 30*, 184–202.

Giedd, J. N., Snell, J. W., Lange, N., Rajapakse, J. C., Casey, B. J., Kozuch, P. L., et al. (1996). Quantitative magnetic resonance imaging of human brain development: Ages 4–18. *Cerebral Cortex, 6*, 551–560.

Gogtay, N., Giedd, J. N., Lusk, L., Hayashi, K. M., Greenstein, D., Vaituzis, A. C., et al. (2004). Dynamic mapping of human cortical development during childhood through early adulthood. *Proceedings of the National Academy of Sciences of the United States of America, 101*, 8174–8179.

Jones, R. A., Palasis, S., & Grattan-Smith, J. D. (2004). MRI of the neonatal brain: Optimization of spin-echo parameters. *American Journal of Roentgenololgy, 182*, 367–372.

Kanemura, H., Aihara, M., Aoki, S., Araki, T., & Nakazawa, S. (2003). Development of the prefrontal lobe in infants and children: A three-dimensional magnetic resonance volumetric study. *Brain Development, 25*, 195–199.

Lange, N., Giedd, J. N., Castellanos, F. X., Vaituzis, A. C., & Rapoport, J. L. (1997). Variability of human brain structure size: Ages 4-20 years. *Psychiatry Research, 74*, 1–12.

Martin, E., Krassnitzer, S., Kaelin, P., & Boesch, C. (1991). MR imaging of the brainstem: Normal postnatal development. *Neuroradiology, 33*, 391–395.

McGraw, P., Liang, L., & Provenzale, J. M. (2002). Evaluation of normal age-related changes in 41 anisotropy during infancy and childhood as shown by diffusion tensor imaging. *American Journal of Roentgenology, 179*, 1515–1522.

McKinstry, R. C., Mathur, A., Miller, J. H., Ozcan, A., Snyder, A.Z., Schefft, G.L., et al. (2002). Radial organization of developing preterm human cerebral cortex revealed by non-invasive water diffusion anisotropy MRI. *Cerebral Cortex, 12*, 1237-43.

Mukherjee, P., Miller, J. H., Shimony, J. S., Conturo, T. E., Lee, B. C. P., Almli, C. R., et al. (2001). Normal brain maturation during childhood: Developmental trends characterized with diffusion-tensor MR imaging. *Radiology, 221*, 349–358.

Neil, J. J., Shiran, S. I., McKinstry, R. C., Schefft, G. L., Snyder, A. Z., Almli, C. R., et al., (1998). Normal brain in human newborns: Apparent diffusion coefficient and diffusion anisotropy measured by using diffusion in tensor MR imaging. *Radiology, 209*, 57–66.

Nowell, M. A., Hackney, D. B., Zimmerman, R. A., Bilaniuk, L. T., Grossman, R. I., & Goldberg, H. I. (1987). Immature brain: Spin-echo pulse sequence parameters for high-contrast MR imaging. *Radiology, 162*, 272–273.

Paus, T., Zijdenbos, A., Worsley, K., Collins, D. L., Blumenthal, J., Giedd, J. N., et al. (1999). Structural maturation of neural pathways in children and adolescents: In vivo study. *Science, 283*, 1908–1911.

Schmithorst, V. J., Wilke, M., Dardzinski, B. J., & Holland, S. K. (2002). Correlation of white matter diffusivity and anisotropy with age during childhood and adolescence: A cross-sectional diffusion-tensor MR imaging study. *Radiology, 222*, 212–218.

Sowell, E. R. & Jernigan, T. L. (1998). Further MRI evidence of late brain maturation: Limbic volume increase and changing asymmetries during childhood and adolescence. *Developmental Neuropsychology, 14*, 599–917.

U.S. Census Bureau (2000). *SF1 and SF4*. Retrieved from http://factfinder.census.gov

U.S. Department of Housing and Urban Development's Office of Policy Development and Research (2003). *FY 2003 Income Limits*. Retrieved from http://www.huduser.org/datasets/il/fmr03/index.html.

Zimmerman, I. L., Steiner, V. G., & Pond, R. E. (1992). *Preschool language scales—3*. San Antonio: Psychological Corporation, Harcourt Brace Jovanovich, Inc.

16

Pathways to Infant Language Research
Commentary and Future Directions

Peggy McCardle, Lisa Freund,
and Gary Marcus*

The study of human language development is notoriously diverse, divided both theoretically (in terms of questions such as innateness and domain specificity) and practically (with methods ranging from habituation to diary studies and foci from syntax to discourse). A key goal of the 2006 conference sponsored by the Merrill Advanced Studies Center and the Eunice Kennedy Shriver National Institute of Child Health and Human Development was to bring together scholars representing a broad range of research approaches, to discuss what they have in common, how they differ, and what could be learned across them, such that we might generate new ideas and move the field forward.

As the content and organization of this book makes clear, the conference had three main foci:

1. How infants manage to recognize patterns and generalize from them
2. How infants connect early word forms with meaning
3. The role of social interaction in infant language and learning

The papers articulate well the current state of investigation in each of those areas. Nonetheless, and in a sense by design, they also raise many questions that remain to be answered. In this final chapter, we provide a brief commentary on certain aspects of what has been brought together in this volume and highlight what

---

* The opinions and assertions herein are those of the authors and should not be construed as representing the policies of the National Institute of Child Health and Human Development, the National Institutes of Health, or the U.S. Department of Health and Human Services.

we feel to be the key questions and research directions that emerged from the conference discussions and from this edited volume of work, which was informed by those discussions.

GENERALIZATION

Generalization is clearly at the heart of language acquisition; children don't merely parrot their parents but go well beyond the specific sentences that they've heard. The contributions in this volume by Richard Aslin and Elissa Newport (Chapter 2), LouAnn Gerken (Chapter 4), Gary Marcus and Hugh Rabagliatti (Chapter 14), and Jenny Saffran (Chapter 3) collectively raise the question of the relation between the shape of language and the nature of human capacities for pattern recognition. Presumably no language would last long if it were not learnable; language must thus co-evolve (at least in the cultural sense) with the capacities of humans to acquire it.

Studies of artificial languages represent a potentially powerful route for understanding what it is infants *can* learn, but they must be taken with caution for several reasons. In the first instance, the materials and modes of presentation used in most artificial languages are relatively impoverished with respect to the structures and environments of real languages. Most artificial language studies present children with comparatively simple grammars, disembodied from any genuine meaning or social context. Inasmuch as current studies focus on *how* children learn, rather than merely what they know and when they know it, current studies provide a major advance over prior work and a real opportunity to obtain firsthand evidence into the very mechanisms of language acquisition. But the ecological limitations of artificial language tasks must be recognized. The failure of a child on a task (e.g., in disembodied contexts) might not map onto failure in more interactive contexts. Language cannot be learned from television alone, and the input in many current studies—which generally lacks any referential meaning—is even more impoverished than a TV broadcast. Current studies have largely focused on word segmentation and rudimentary syntactic learning; what has yet to be addressed is whether those aspects of natural language could be learned from pure streams of meaningless words. There is much work yet to be done in translating from the lab to the real world.

A second question that has received more attention is the relation between rule learning and statistical learning. Clearly, this debate is in part a function of terminology. While any information that can be counted is arguably statistical, the claim that infants are statistical learners could simply reduce to the trivial claim that infants acquire language from information. Likewise, the debate about rules—and whether they are, say, co-extensive with statistics—necessarily depends on how they are defined. (One of us has proposed that the vital property of a rule is that it serves as an operation defined over variables rather than specific instances, presumably disjoint from the notion of tracking transitional probabilities between specific instances but perhaps overlapping with some broader notion of statistics as the simple accumulation of evidence). Clearly, for debates like this to be meaningful and convincing to those not immersed in them, parties will need to agree on terms.

Regardless of the terminology used, the notion of constraint looms large. Where any database is compatible with multiple characterizations, it is incumbent on the child to choose some hypotheses as more plausible than others; there simply is no such thing as a truly "equivalent learner," equally open to all possibilities. Each of the chapters here offers the beginnings of a character- ization of the kinds of regularities that children are most attuned to; this clearly represents progress for the field. Nonetheless, as is generally acknowledged by the chapters in this volume, the current attempts at identifying constraints are still somewhat arbitrary and are not fully systematic. A useful next step might be a serious, field-wide discussion on how to collectively and systematically gain a better understanding of what constraints are and how they bear on language development.

HOW CHILDREN CONNECT EARLY WORD FORMS WITH MEANING

Before a child can connect a full-blown sentence with a meaning, that child must learn how to connect the form of (at least some) individual words with the meanings of those individual words. Gerken (Chapter 4), Janet Werker and Christopher Fennell (Chapter 6), and Sandra Waxman (Chapter 7) take steps in this direction, investigating how it is that children begin to relate sound and meaning. Werker and Fennell focus on the contribution of sound—how do chil- dren take what they know about the sounds of their language and relate that to candidate meanings? The crux of the problem is that neither sound nor mean- ing are stable; different speakers utter a given word in different ways, and most words convey different meanings in different contexts. When a child hears, for example, a similar notion expressed by two similar-sounding words, how does she or he know whether those two similar-sounding words are actually differ- ing instantiations of a common word or genuinely different words? Waxman asks how much children know about the privileges accorded to words belonging to different grammatical categories. At what point does a child know that an adjective picks out a different sort of thing than a noun, and how does a child come to know that?

From yet another perspective, Patricia Kuhl (Chapter 12) provides intriguing evidence that children who master the phonetics of their native language early tend to move ahead of their peers, acquiring larger vocabularies (as measured at 18 months) and moving more rapidly toward complex grammar (as measured at 24 months). Still, some of these early gains dissipate (e.g., vocabulary curves seem to come together around 24 months).

Judy Deloache, Patricia Ganea, and Vikram Jaswal (Chapter 8) add an important, ecological perspective, emphasizing the importance of human interaction as not only a tool for gathering information on how young children learn but also as a contributor to that learning. They also focus on the importance of context in the building of children's mental representations and in changing them. Mabel Rice (Chapter 5) reminds us of the importance of examining individual differences, emphasizing the robustness of language acquisition even in the face of language impairments. These chapters together highlight the importance of communication across researchers and across paradigms and approaches, if we are to gain a true picture of how infants and young children learn language, which changes over time and which varies based on multiple input and contextual factors.

THE ROLE OF SOCIAL INTERACTION

Andrew Meltzoff and Rechele Brooks (Chapter 10), Leslie Cohen and Jason Brunt (Chapter 13), and Deloache and colleagues (Chapter 8) address social factors relevant to infant language development. Meltzoff and Brooks emphasize gaze following and if and to what extent infants are sensitive to whether an adult's eyes were open or closed. They have demonstrated that gaze-following behavior is significantly associated with later vocabulary growth. A key question is, as it so often is in infant language, whether the effects are causal: Are the children who look longer simply brighter or more curious? Or is there a direct mechanism by which longer looks lead to larger vocabularies? Or are there neurodevelopmental factors that mediate between gaze behavior and vocabulary growth? Cohen and Brunt report the beginnings of a study designed to address these sorts of questions. Deloache and colleagues raise the crucial issues of the role of social interaction in facilitating learning and in supporting the development and revision of mental representations through that learning. Also in the realm of social interaction is the work of Susan Goldin-Meadow (Chapter 11), where she demonstrates a developmental progression in which the combining of gesture and single-word production precedes production of word combinations. In terms of causality, it will also be important to investigate whether social interaction is essential or predominantly facilitative.

METHODOLOGY

Looming across all these content questions—the nature of generalization, mechanisms for acquiring word meaning, and the role of social interaction—are deep and as yet unanswered questions. One widely used methodology involves measuring infant looking times, and there is much yet to be understood about what precisely governs a child's choice to look—or to look away. Issues of novelty preferences versus familiarity preferences remain not fully answered. It may be that comparing work across laboratories and attempting some replications across laboratories can shed light on this issue, as has begun to happen in the forum that this volume represents. In the long run, one hopes either for a more direct methodology, a viable and informative combination of methods, or a more explicit understanding of what mental processes drive the methods that we currently use.

Cohen and Brunt (Chapter 13) provide an excellent analysis of two techniques commonly used to assess word learning (the switch paradigm and intermodal preferential looking), while John Colombo, Jill Shaddy, Otilia Blaga, Christa Anderson, Kathleen Kannass, and Allen Richman (Chapter 9), Lisa Freund (Chapter 15), and Rice (Chapter 5) all emphasize the importance of other measures and approaches, including longitudinal assessments of attention (Colombo et al.), studies of individual differences and of impaired populations (Rice), and neuroimaging studies of the neural underpinnings (Freund). A key challenge will be to integrate such techniques with the more "representational" concerns of those interested in characterizing the constraints and learning mechanisms that guide the acquisition of language. Such work, while complex and challenging, is crucial to sustaining and increasing the current momentum of the field of infant language and cognition.

MOVING FORWARD

As was noted in the introductory chapter to this volume, the new millennium holds many challenges for the behavioral and brain sciences. The importance of what have been often seen as heavily biological areas, such as genetics and neuroscience, now embraces the combining of behavioral and more biological investigations so that the separation between behavioral genetics and quantitative genetics is less and so that the two aspects are increasingly being integrated in ways that are mutually beneficial to what used to be viewed as almost separate domains. The study of early cognitive and language development are clearly benefiting from and taking advantage of the constantly emerging new developments in neuroscience tools and methods. And these tools are being used to move us toward an understanding of the neural processes implicated in rate and patterns of development, enabling us to learn much about both typical development and developmental delays and disabilities. Researchers from fields as diverse as education, early child development, clinical psychology, linguistics, genetics, and developmental neuroscience all recognize the importance of linking our knowledge of early experience, heredity, and brain development and function. Brain–behavior relationships are both epigenetic and transactional: Brain structure can be seen as both a cause and an effect of experience. Thus, the stage was set for a conference such as the one held in September 2005—and the chapters in this volume have fortunately raised many questions that call for innovative, creative methods, measures, and approaches and that offer some research challenges that the field can embrace as potentially fruitful future directions.

The authors in this volume raise a number of questions for the field to consider:

- Is social cognition necessary for language or mainly facilitative?
- Do children possess a mechanism for adding or reifying new representations (e.g., phonemes, words, syntactic constructions), or do they accumulate memory traces of specific utterances?
- Is statistical learning the universal learning mechanism, or is it one among many (e.g., rule learning)? To the extent that there is a multiplicity of mechanisms, what happens when they are in conflict?
- Do children acquire aspects of language (e.g., syntax) from analysis of purely structural regularities or from links between language components (e.g., syntax and semantics)? And what is the role of social interaction in the acquisition of these aspects of language?
- What is the initial state—that is, what mechanisms or knowledge are unlearned and available for use, even prior to experience?
- What aspects of language are heritable, and what aspects are most significantly impacted by context and experience? Given correlations between parental input and child performance, how can we disentangle contributions of genetics from contributions of linguistic input?
- How can we best move beyond or enhance the use of the preferential looking paradigm? For example, within looking time, are there ways to assess degree of preference as opposed to simple binary choice?
- How can we tease apart developing competence from progressively increasing performance?
- How can we distinguish between contributions of input (i.e., what children hear) and intake (i.e., what children actually process)?

Clearly, this list of questions is only a part of what the field needs to and no doubt will be addressing in future years. As several of the chapters indicate, we need to seek convergent evidence before we can make strong, causal statements about infant language learning. The use of multiple indicators of infant attention and change over time will move us far. In addition, the integration of new physiological and neuroscience measures can contribute much. Not only focusing on how infants learn and generalize as part of typical development but also taking into the account the range of both normal variation and individual differences and the full range of ability and disability will enhance our knowledge of language learning. And the integration of behavioral and quantitative genetics will further enhance that information. When seeking to "generalize," we should consider that there really may be two senses of "generalizability" in the study of infant language: one addressed previously, which is the issue of generalization from specific input to underlying abstract representations; and the other being generalization of the findings across children or the extent to which laboratory findings translate to the real world of children, not just the world of linguistic input.

It is of course a cliché to state for any field in any time that more research needs to be done. It is nonetheless also true for infant language and cognition. As noted at the beginning of this volume, we need new paradigms, and we need to explore new ways of using old paradigms. We need new measures and new approaches to measurement. We need to continuously refine and improve our theories and to embrace opposing theories as opportunities to creatively engage in the best demonstration of our science with an open mind. We need to cross disciplines and enter the laboratories of others and to learn and share. The field needs studies that will incorporate both behavioral and quantitative genetics and that will examine the full continuum of infants and children, both typically developing and impaired, across the full range of diversity that we see in this nation. Laboratory studies should be only a starting point, not an end in themselves. Our investigations of infant language learning must also move out of the laboratories where possible and into the communities, and we must examine the role of a variety of contexts and the experiences they provide or do not provide—that is, we must study not only advantaged infants and children but also those living in disadvantage.

It is our hope that this commentary and the many excellent chapters contained in this volume will yield important insight not only into what is known but also into what remains to be discovered. We see this volume as only a beginning; the researchers who contributed the chapters have in many cases already begun to collaborate or at least to sustain communications where they did not exist before the conference from which this volume arose. The book was planned as an attempt to expand collaborative endeavors to the field more broadly. The challenges raised will, we hope, stimulate the field to address them. It is also our hope that this volume will provide some motivation to find innovative and useful ways to proceed with new discoveries. If researchers build new collaborations and dialogues across laboratories and disciplines, studying the full range of infants and their abilities, then our evidence can truly converge, and we can learn much more than we now know about how the magic of language development occurs. And when that "magic" does not happen, we will have more information about how and why. We will know more about how we can enhance the language and cognitive capabilities of all children.

Index

A

Absent reference
  age differences in use of, 128–129
  comprehension of, 125–126
Abstract linguistic structures, 277
Abstract rule learning, 277, 279–280
Acceleration of vocabulary growth, 182, 184
Acoustically fragile contrasts, 227
Action-test trials, 110–112
Action words, 246
Adaptive behavior, 49
Adjacent item conditional probabilities, 51
Adjectives
  extended to object properties, 101
  identification of, 109
  level of understanding of, 106
Adult interaction value, 6–7
Adult labeling, 121–125
Adult-to-child knowledge transfer, 121, 123–125
Agreement marking correctness, 75
Agreement/tense omission model (ATOM), 72–73
Ambient language, see Native language
Articulation and perceptual assimilation model, 86
Articulatory phonology and perceptual assimilation model, 86
Artificial categories for experiments, 250–251
Artificial grammar learning by adults, 37
Artificial language studies
  extension to real, 20
  relationship to natural language, 298
Artificial lexicon studies, 20
ASD (Autism spectrum disorders), 66, 230
Associative learning, 87
AT (Attention termination phase), 150
ATOM (Agreement/tense omission model), 72–73

Attention

Attention
  development and later language development, 160–161
  development of, 145–146
  disengagement, 148, 149
  and later vocabulary size, 175
  longitudinal assessments of, 301
  overt, 22
  and short looking, 161
Attentional control, 229
Attentional predictors of vocabulary, 143ff
Attention termination (AT) phase, definition, 149
Attractors in acoustic space, 86
Auditory interference, 254, 257–258
Auditory perceptual constraints, 227
Auditory processing
  interference with categorization, 253–254
  interference with visual processing, 247
Auditory resolution, 228–229
Auditory streaming, 21
Autism markers, 230
Autism spectrum disorders (ASD) as exclusion criterion for SLI, 66
Automated tasks, 100, 102
Automated task testing, 106–113
  control of variables, 106–107
Auxiliary *be*, 72
Auxiliary *do*, 72

B

Baby Label and Object Category Knowledge (BLOCK) inventory, 9, 251, 254–255, 261
  potential for use, 263
Bayesian approach to generalization, 54
Bayley Scales of Infant Development-Second Edition (BSID-II), 146–147, 291
Behavioral and Brain Sciences, 11

M

Macaques' neural responses to language-related stimuli, 35
MacArthur-Bates Communicative Development Inventory (MBCDI), 146–147, 175–176, 215
  assessment with, 155–159
  Finnish, 225
  forms of, 155
  use of, 182
Magnetic resonance imaging (MRI), 287–288
Magnetoencephalography (MEG), 231
  brain-behavior link study, 2–3
Maintenance patterns, 86
Mandarin affricate-fricative contrast, 216–217, 236
Mandarin nonnative contrast, 220
Manipulative books, 131–132
Marking, see Double marking; Single marking
Maternal behavior and language development, 171–172
Maternal education level and vocabulary growth, 184
Mathematical reasoning acquisition, 269
Maturation
  vs. experience, 235
  and word associations, 263
Maturational mechanisms and LLE, 78
Maturation of auditory cortex, 228
Mature function prediction, ix
MBCDI, see MacArthur-Bates communicative Development Inventory (MBCDI)
Meaning and word learning, 299–300
Mean length of utterance (MLU), 67
  delays in, 70
  in gesture translation by parents, 204–205
  growth synchronized with vocabulary, 72
  language delay and, 74
  predictors of growth, 71
  SLI status and, 70–71
Measures of perception, 7
MEG, see Magnetoencephalography (MEG)
Mental representations
  age differences in use of, 128–129
  updating, 127–129
Mental retardation, 268
  as exclusion criterion for SLI, 66–67
  language impairments and, 67–68
Methodologies, 300–301; see also Automated task testing; Live interactive tasks; Switch task methodology

infant speech perception, 85ff
  for speech perception and word learning, 85
  word learning and categorization, 9
  word-object associations, 245–246
Miniature languages, 32
Mismatch negativity (MMN), 219–222, 223–224
Mispronunciation recognition, 89
MLU, see Mean length of utterance (MLU)
MMN, see Mismatch negativity (MMN)
Models of linguistics, 16
Modularity and learning, 39
Morphemes, 72
  errors of use, 75
Morphologic cues, 101
Morphosyntactic skills and vocabulary growth, 162
Morphosyntax, 72
  errors and clause structure, 74
  extended optional infinitive hypothesis, 77–78
Motherese, 169–170
Mother's education and language delay, 74
Motor control disorders correlation with language disorders, 270
Motoric imitation and brain area, 270
Motor skill development as predictor of LLE status, 69
Movement following, 180–181
  not gaze following, 176
MRI, see Magnetic resonance imaging (MRI)
Multidimensional acoustic space attractors, 86
Multi-disciplinary investigative approaches, 301–303
Multilevel modeling, 222; see also Growth-curve modeling
Multiple cues, 43
Multiple labels as cues to multiple objects, 122
Multiple language streams, 25
Multi-tasking reduces performance, 22
Music perception in the brain, 270

N

Naming and category formation, 102–103
Naming phrases, 91
Native language
  discrimination and language development, 220
  infant perception and language acquisition, 215
  infant sensitivity to, 85–86